We Rise to Resist

ALSO BY PAULA VW. DÁIL
AND FROM McFARLAND

Mother Nature's Daughters:
21st Century Women Farmers (2017)

Hard Living in America's Heartland:
Rural Poverty in the 21st Century Midwest (2015)

Women and Poverty in 21st Century America (2012)

We Rise to Resist

*Voices from a New Era
in Women's Political Action*

Edited by Paula vW. Dáil
and Betty L. Wells

McFarland & Company, Inc., Publishers
Jefferson, North Carolina

LIBRARY OF CONGRESS CATALOGUING-IN-PUBLICATION DATA

Names: Dáil, Paula vW., editor. | Wells, Betty Lynn, 1950– editor.
Title: We rise to resist : voices from a new era in women's political action /
edited by Paula vW. Dáil and Betty L. Wells.
Description: Jefferson, North Carolina : McFarland & Company, Inc.,
Publishers, 2018 | Includes bibliographical references and index.
Identifiers: LCCN 2018001698 | ISBN 9781476671642
(softcover : acid free paper) ∞
Subjects: LCSH: Women—Political activity—United States. |
Feminism—United States. | Political participation—United States. |
United States—Politics and government—2017–
Classification: LCC HQ1236.5.U6 W4185 2018 | DDC 305.420973—dc23
LC record available at https://lccn.loc.gov/2018001698

ISBN (print) 978-1-4766-7164-2
ISBN (ebook) 978-1-4766-3295-7

BRITISH LIBRARY CATALOGUING DATA ARE AVAILABLE

Front cover image of Women's March on Washington © 2018 katiebordner/Flickr

Printed in the United States of America

*McFarland & Company, Inc., Publishers
Box 611, Jefferson, North Carolina 28640
www.mcfarlandpub.com*

This book is dedicated to every woman who is protesting,
in some way, the political climate in 2017 America,
and to her sisters and brothers in this battle,
around the nation and around the world,
who are supporting her efforts.

Table of Contents

Acknowledgments

Editing a book of collected essays is not the same as writing a book. To be successful, the task requires a high level of harmonious cooperation among a lot of people. Bearing this in mind, the essays in this book would not have been possible without the committed, collegial efforts of a lot of people, including the essayists themselves. Each essayist has been deeply dedicated to the herculean task of making women's voices heard during what is, for many women, a frightening political era in American history. Each has been truly great to work with and deeply committed to doing whatever needed doing to help women speak out, loud and clear, even when it involved several revisions. These women (and men) are perfect role models for how people of differing backgrounds and perspectives can work together toward an outcome that benefits everyone. Members of the United States Congress should heed their example.

The essayists who were not included in the book helped us out by allowing portions of their essays to be quoted. You are all brave, articulate women and it has been our great pleasure to get to know you and work with you.

Several ad-hoc reviewers assisted in making decisions regarding specific topics we didn't have the expertise to judge on our own. Other colleagues listened as we hashed out ideas and tried to thread our way through topics during times when events were changing faster than we could possibly keep up with. Others read drafts, offered comments, read again, and then again maybe a third or a fourth time.

Katilyn Peck put in many hours as a reviewer, and then as a line editor for every essay that we accepted. Professors Chuck Park, Alice A. Thieman and Edna Park were faithful followers of the project from the beginning. They read, thrashed out ideas, and sent valuable information, contacts, and ideas our way on a regular basis as we progressed. If there was an idea in there somewhere, these folks helped us find it.

The project never would've happened without Bill Ladewig's heartfelt, serious commitment to "help out." In many respects, this book was his idea to begin with, and he stepped up to the challenge by reading, suggesting revisions, re-reading, and discussing every essay we received. This amounted to more than 400 hours of concentrated time spent making sure the essayists' voices were clear, and twice that much time discussing the essays with Paula to be sure the essayists' messages were powerful and to the point. The book was always on his mind, just like it was on ours.

As the lead editor, I (Paula) also want to acknowledge Betty Wells. She is the other person without whom this book would never have happened. She recruited essayists, reviewed essays, and pursued ideas I never could have possibly followed up on. Her efforts made the book much richer and more complete.

This book belongs to all of you!

Introduction

November 8, 2017: Another Day
That Will Live in Infamy

Paula vW. Dáil

The world will never be the same.—Cher

January 1, 2016

"How serious are Americans about electing Donald Trump their president?" the young German tourist sitting across from me asked. "We've been worried about that too," the middle-aged woman sitting next to the German, whose name tag indicated she was from Nova Scotia, echoed. "As America's neighbors, we have more than just a casual interest in American foreign policy," she said. "Europe is very concerned about the Trump possibility," the German said, looking directly into our eyes.

We were having this conversation over lunch on New Year's Day, 2016, during a day trip on a ship passing through the Panama Canal. Both my husband and I reassured our tablemates that Donald Trump was a flash in the pan. "Once Americans start voting he'll be knocked out of the race pretty quickly. I don't see anyone taking him very seriously, and I don't think he's that serious either," my husband said. "Unless Vice President Biden decides to enter the race, and it doesn't look like he will, it's fairly certain Hillary Clinton will be our next president," I added, with a broad smile and a thumbs-up.

"Well, anyone would be better than Donald Trump," the German remarked, adding, "he [Trump] would be a disaster." We all agreed, and turned our attention back to our canal guide.

November 8, 2016, at 9:15 p.m. central standard time.

Whenever I feel anxious about something, I head straight for a Mexican restaurant, and election night was no exception. My husband and I had decided to eat Mexican food with friends, who had invited us back to their house for dessert afterwards, and to watch the election returns. Our plan was to celebrate the election of the first woman president of the United States and I'd brought a bottle of champagne to mark the occasion.

We walked into the living room and Joe flipped on the TV. Wolf Blitzer, looking as stunned as a deer caught in headlights, was saying that all projections indicated Donald Trump would be the next president of the United States. All four of us stood in the middle of the living room with our coats on, saying nothing.

An hour later, each of us was standing in the same place. We still had our coats on, had never taken our eyes off the television screen, and were too dumbstruck to say anything.

Finally, Joe broke the silence. "Jesus Christ," he said. "I didn't serve in the United States Marines and fight through two tours in Vietnam to end up on military disability and then have my country wind up in the hands of this [descriptive expletives deleted]." Joe had been a proud Marine, and I saw his bottom lip quiver as he swiped his hand down his face. My husband, an Army officer during the same era, echoed similar sentiments, only louder, then hung his head.

Julie told Joe that if he died while Donald Trump was president hell would freeze over before she'd accept a flag "from the president of the United States on behalf of a grateful nation" during the military rites at his funeral. "Me either," I whispered, faintly nauseous at the thought of Donald Trump's fingerprints on anything affecting my personal life.

What we all knew, but wouldn't say out loud, was that we'd just lost our country— that this land was no longer our land, that the values we held dear had just been assigned to the trash heap of history, and that we were on a backward slide into the unknown with no apparent stopping point. A political earthquake had destroyed the homeland we knew and loved, rendering it unrecognizable, and perhaps irreparable, during our lifetimes. Deep in our hearts, we knew that America the beautiful wasn't going to be beautiful anymore and that feeling "proud to be an American" would, all too soon, become a distant memory. The sky had fallen.

My husband and I left about an hour later, never having taken off our coats or eaten our favorite dessert that only Julie makes. The champagne sat sweating and unopened on the dining room table. I don't think we said goodbye; we just walked out the back door, got in our car, and drove home.

Like the over 71,000,000 other Americans who did not vote for Donald Trump, we knew that we would remember this night for the rest of our lives. We would never forget where we were and what we were doing when we first learned that a man who had promised to "drain the swamp" and "make America great again," then proceeded to break every rule of political civility and ignore minimally acceptable behavior towards women, minorities, the poor, the disabled, the socially disadvantaged, and immigrants became president. A man who had a loose relationship with proven facts and was a "mentally out-of-control, Twitter-addicted, narcissistic maniac"[1] was now the new leader of the free world.

I couldn't help wondering what the nice German tourist and lovely woman from Nova Scotia we'd met in Panama must be thinking. Even though my husband and I appeared confident that we knew what we were talking about, they would realize we didn't have a clue about the realities of American politics. Sadly, they were right—and we weren't the only ones who had been taken by surprise.

Even stalwart leaders of Trump's own political party had failed to support him. Several Republican senators and members of Congress, including Senator John McCain (R-AZ), the 2008 Republican presidential nominee, said they wouldn't vote for Trump. Senator Lindsey Graham (R-SC) called Trump "a nut job" and warned that the Republican Party had gone "batshit crazy."[2] Many Republicans refused to campaign on his behalf, but, unwilling to abandon their party entirely, split hairs by saying they would "support, but not endorse" him, whatever that meant. Members of both political parties were indicating, mostly privately, that it was obvious Republicans would lose another presidential election. Republicans worried that they were going to lose both houses of Congress, too.

In the end, none of this mattered, because Donald Trump won the U.S. presidency anyway. As a bonus, voters served up a Republican Congress. It was a watershed moment in American political history.

How Did This Happen?

> We have just elected an openly sexist, racist, self-interested megalomaniac
> to the highest office in our country. It's a dark day.—Rashida Jones

In many respects, one person's guess is as good as another's when it comes to trying to explain how it came about that Donald Trump, who wasn't a particularly committed Republican and had never run for political office of any kind before, defeated former U.S. Senator and Secretary of State Hillary Clinton, a mainstream Democrat and the far more qualified frontrunner candidate throughout the election season. Clinton believes several factors interacted to cause her defeat.[3] Among these are endemic misogyny, then FBI Director James Comey re-opening the investigation into her emails in a letter to Congress 11 days before the election, deliberate Russian interference in the election process, and voter suppression.

Political theorists around the world have speculated about how the outcome no one saw coming actually arrived. These are the statistics they have used to develop their own, unique theories regarding the 2016 election results[4]: there are 218,959,000 registered American voters. Prior to the 2016 election, 69 percent of these registered Americans indicated they would vote, as compared to 76 percent of voters who cast a ballot in the 2012 presidential election, when incumbent Democratic President Barack Obama defeated Republican candidate Mitt Romney. This suggests that, for whatever reason, there was significantly less overall interest in the 2016 presidential election during the approach to November 8.

Actual voter turnout in 2016 was 132,899,453 (55 percent). Besides less overall interest in the election outcome, reasons for this level of voter apathy included difficulties with the voting process itself, indecision about which candidate to support and disliking them both, or presuming that Secretary Clinton, the hands-down statistical favorite in every poll, was going to win, so there was no point in making the effort to vote. What was not clear, and impossible to ascertain, was how many of the 61,898,584 votes Donald Trump ultimately received were votes in actual support of his agenda, and how many were votes against Hillary Clinton.

Secretary Clinton is a controversial, deeply polarizing political figure who is not generally well-liked. She brought considerable political baggage with her into the 2016 presidential race, dating back to her husband's 1992–2000 presidency. Despite these inherent disadvantages, she was a pro-choice candidate with stellar political credentials, widespread domestic and foreign policy experience, and a political philosophy that supports government stepping up to help the disadvantaged. She won Democratic primary after Democratic primary, eventually outrunning Senator Bernie Sanders (I–VT) whose surprising popularity created a competitive democratic primary season and stopped

Secretary Clinton from a default, unchallenged nomination. Ultimately, she prevailed to become the first woman nominated by a major party for president of the United States.

This was Hillary Clinton's second try at the highest office in the land. This time she managed to push past her ongoing stumbling block, which was that many people, including women, deeply distrusted her, and resented what they perceived to be her sense of entitlement toward the presidency. Nevertheless, she received nearly three million more popular votes than Donald Trump, and lost the presidency only because these votes did not come from states with enough electoral votes to guarantee her win in the Electoral College, where the final decision on the election outcome is made.

Donald Trump, on the other hand, used his reality television experience to run a highly entertaining, play to the lowest common denominator, campaign. He tapped into the frustrations of the lower middle-class and, in campaign rally after campaign rally, relentlessly stoked their anger and resentment.

Other than Hillary Clinton, no one was more surprised by his victory than Donald Trump himself, who became the sixth president of the United States to serve without winning the popular vote.[5] More importantly, his win occurred in spite of the fact that he was widely labeled a pussy-grabbing misogynist with abundant evidence to back up this claim, and that 73 percent of all registered voters, and 52 percent of the American population, are women.

Clearly, this outcome could not have occurred without support from women voters, which begs the question of why a woman would vote for Donald Trump? The easy answer is that some individuals (both men and women) are single-issue voters, and there were a lot of hot-button issues to grapple with in the 2016 election.

Reproductive healthcare, repealing and replacing the Affordable Care Act (ObamaCare), and immigration were headliners in the 2016 election. Following close behind was support for the middle class, in the form of bringing back manufacturing jobs that had been lost as a result of NAFTA (North American Free Trade Agreement), which is a hold-over trade policy of the Clinton administration, and TPP (Trans-Pacific Partnership), negotiated during the Obama Administration. Some Americans were outraged by laws allowing same-sex marriage, thought climate change was hoax, and generally felt the country had swung too far to the left under President Obama, who they viewed as a liberal, tax and spend Democrat.

A woman in a rust belt state like Ohio, whose husband lost his $28 per hour manufacturing job during the Clinton administration and has never again earned that much money, would find the promise of bringing jobs back to America very seductive. A Christian conservative, pro-life woman would not support a pro-choice candidate. A woman who lives in a southern border state and believes that undocumented immigrants present a threat to her or her family's personal safety would support stricter immigration policies and erecting a wall along the Mexico border to keep Hispanics out. A woman whose son or husband served in the military in Iraq and Afghanistan fighting radical Islamic terrorism would support a U.S. travel ban on Muslim nations. And anyone who has difficulty meeting their own or their family's healthcare costs would favor repealing current healthcare law on the promise that the replacement would lower healthcare insurance premium costs. Trump stood for all of these.

For likely Trump voters, the Cold War ended a long time ago, and the possibility that Trump colluded with Russia, or that Russia interfered in the American election outcome, which were ongoing campaign themes, was too far removed from their daily struggles to matter very much. And while they're curious about Trump's tax returns and his refusal to release them, and reveal to the American people the extent of his business dealings with certain countries, these were not sufficient reasons to vote for Hillary Clinton because, in their minds, her email security failure was worse.

Another possible explanation for Trump's success was that the women, and men, who supported the Trump candidacy understand the realities of American life and underlying culture much better than the idealistic "bleeding heart" liberals who continually cried foul throughout the campaign. Maybe Trump supporters, who are mostly middle-aged men, saw aspects of themselves in Trump and didn't view his behavior toward women as reason enough to abandon him as a candidate.

Voters know that politicians lie and that the world is full of bullies and apparently did not see these as reasons to dismiss Donald Trump either. And, they might have felt so jealous of, threatened by, or simply afraid of a strong, successful, clever and opinionated woman that they just couldn't bring themselves to vote for one, even if she was the far more qualified candidate whose policies and political philosophy would make their lives better.

At its core, this was a race between a well-qualified career politician and the ubiquitous Trump brand, which blended seamlessly with Trump the candidate and provided him with unpaid advertising and other resources that it is impossible to place a value upon or match dollar for dollar. Trump had the financial ability to self-fund his campaign, to use his own airplane, hotels and golf courses, and to access the services of limitless staff and other resources on a daily basis. He did not have to spend his time fundraising. Because of his fondness for outrageous tweets, Trump was headline news nearly every day. He could not have asked for more in terms of continual public exposure.

In monetary terms, Trump spent about 75 percent less than Secretary Clinton, had one-tenth the number of paid staff and one-third the number of campaign offices. He used existing office space he already owned and staff he already employed, and reimbursed himself as donations came in. By the time the nominating conventions were over, Trump had spent about $8 million on advertising; Secretary Clinton spent $37 million during the same time period.[6]

While concerns about Trump's ties to Wall Street billionaires were raised often, many notable billionaires did not back Trump's candidacy, including Microsoft's Bill Gates, financier Warren Buffett, and the conservative Koch Brothers who have frequently funded candidates for state and national office. However, none of this mattered because Trump had enough disposable cash on hand to back himself.

Finally, the impact of Donald Trump's entertainment value upon potential voters should not be underestimated. For eleven years he starred in the reality television show "Celebrity Apprentice" where viewers saw him as a strong and decisive leader willing to fire anyone who didn't "measure up." Although the show's viewership declined from 21 million to just over 4 million under Trump's leadership,[7] many voters could easily have associated him with this show and failed to realize that he was an entertainer playing to viewer ratings, and that his show was not a glimpse into his true leadership ability.

And this is where the rubber meets the road in terms of trying to explain how Donald Trump defeated Hillary Clinton to become president of the United States. Most voting pattern analyses suggest that the same individuals (i.e., poor, low-wage workers, less-educated) who would benefit most from the strong government programs Hillary Clinton favored supported Donald Trump. Other than to say that these were disenfranchised, emotional rather than rational voters, no political pundit or analyst has been able to satisfactorily explain this outcome.[8] Regardless, Trump's victory profoundly upset women around the world, but none more than American women, who shuddered at the thought of life under his political leadership.

For several weeks after the election I spent extra time volunteering on the soup line in a nearby rural community. I like talking with the people who come for this free meal and to use the food pantry, the free medical clinic, and the free shopping opportunity in the community closet each week. These are folks who exist hand-to-mouth and heavily depend upon multiple government-sponsored programs and were perhaps, I believed, the right people to lend insight into the election outcome.

To a person, everyone I approached said they were glad Donald Trump won. When I asked why, the most common response was "because I hate Hillary Clinton." When I asked whether they had voted, most said no, but claimed they would've voted for Trump if they had cast a ballot. Others said they didn't like either candidate or didn't see how the election outcome would affect them one way or another and sat it out. No one said they would have voted for Clinton. Several cited practical reasons for not voting, including health problems and transportation issues.

Nevertheless, the reality of the 2016 presidential election, despite his claims otherwise, is that Donald Trump began his term in office with only 28 percent of eligible American voters supporting him. This is not a mandate; it is a small minority of total voters and indicates that 155 million voters (72 percent) either did not care enough to vote or did not support his candidacy. What is not known is how many of the 45 percent (86 million) voters who didn't bother to vote favored Trump's agenda.

Regardless, either consciously or unconsciously, it's reasonable to assume non-voters decided they could live with either outcome. The real danger in this minority rule political scenario is that Trump has the benefit of a Republican majority in both houses of Congress that can put into law the things he wants changed, and he can change a lot in the two years before the 2018 midterm elections.

Women recognized this possibility even before the election results were finalized, and weren't about to let a pussy-grabbing bully gain political traction. As a result, what began as a Facebook posting in the early hours of November 9th by a grandmother in Hawaii quickly grew into a worldwide protest against Donald Trump's presidency, led by women.

"He's not my president," women proclaimed, as they organized a march on Washington for the day following his inauguration. On January 21, 2017, women around the world marched in solidarity with millions of American women, in cities all across the country.

Seven million women, on every continent across the globe, had decided they were not going to accept a woman-groping hatemonger as a world leader. They had no intention of staying silent and allowing Donald Trump to set the course for women's lives going forward.

This Book

> This hurts and it's going to hurt for a very long time, but I'm not giving
> up, and neither should you.—Hillary Clinton

Like the essayists who contributed to this book, I underwent a lengthy period of profound grieving following November 8. I felt like a displaced person without an anchor, and I didn't want to talk to anyone or do anything. My thoughts were riveted on a moment several years previously when I was walking down the international arrivals corridor at O'Hare International Airport in Chicago. I had been on an extended trip through Asia and the Middle East and had flown back to the U.S. through the South Pacific. It had been an exhausting, grueling 30 hours spent sitting in airports in 6 foreign countries and on airplanes that ranged from 12 passenger puddle-jumpers to jumbo jets that actually had bathrooms. As I rounded the corner in the side transit corridor, I was greeted by a rotund, ruddy-faced, red-haired Chicago policeman standing beside a huge American flag, hands in his pockets and hat tipped onto the back on his head. "Those of you holding passports issued by the United States of America, bear to the right," he barked, "and welcome home."

Every time I thought of this in the days following the election I teared up. I couldn't stop wondering whether I would ever again feel like America is home.

Finally, after refusing to go to the local bar on a Saturday afternoon to watch the University of Wisconsin football game on a big screen TV—something that, in previous years, would only have occurred if I were dead—my husband said we had to talk.

"You have to do something about this," he said.

"About what?" I asked

"Your reaction to the election … you're not yourself. Not even the dog wants to be around you," he groused. Normally we don't communicate through the dog, so I knew he was serious.

"There's nothing I can do about how I feel," I muttered. "I'm sorry it upsets the dog."

"You can't go on this way. You have to do something," he repeated. We sat in silence for several minutes, hugging our coffee cups and staring at the floor.

"Look, I feel as badly about this as you do," he finally added. What he was gracious enough not to say was that he was getting tired of listening to me carrying on about what a disaster Trump would be for women, and then not saying anything at all for days at a time. I kept repeating what my friend Alicia, a devout Catholic, said the morning after the election. "If this is what God bless America means, then I don't believe in God anymore." She hadn't returned to church since the election.

"You obviously care about this, and you need to find an outlet for that energy or you'll drive us both into the happy academy," he said, without smiling. "Maybe you ought to write a book about the election."

"I'm already in the middle of writing a book and I'm not looking for more work," I reminded him. He pointed out that I'd been spending all my time watching *Say Yes to the Dress* on television and reading trashy novels and hadn't touched the book project since the election.

"I'm pretty sure you're not the only woman in America who's upset right now. Why don't you contact some of them and ask them to write about how they feel about what happened? Collect some stories…. I'll even help you out," he offered. As an award-winning writer himself, my husband was making me an offer that was very hard to turn down. But I wasn't sure I wanted to, or even could, muster the energy needed to accept it.

"It's not like I'm wildly patriotic and would be strongly motivated by an unquestioning love of country," I said. While I consider myself a good citizen in that I vote in every election, and try to stay abreast of current political concerns, I was also a serious anti-war protestor and never, ever considered serving in the military. You won't see me waving the flag at a 4th of July parade.

"Think about it," my husband urged, "because I think you care a lot more about your country and what's just happened to it than you're willing to admit."

A few weeks later, in a last-minute decision to forgo a funeral I should attend, I opted instead to participate in the January 21, 2017, Women's March in Madison, WI. The event hadn't received much press and I didn't know what to expect, but it wasn't the first time I'd taken to the streets in Madison, so it was, in some respects, just another protest march I felt compelled to show up for.

What was anticipated to be a crowd of 20–25,000 turned out to be 130,000 women, and the men who love them, packing the isthmus between the statue of Abraham Lincoln at the entrance to the University of Wisconsin–Madison campus and the state capitol, less than a mile away. For me it was 1967 all over again when, as a graduate student, I was a Vietnam War protestor on the UW campus—and both a lonely and profoundly energizing experience.

Lonely because Jessie, my one surviving friend from that time, didn't feel up to coming with me. "I'm not going to live long enough to see the damage he does turn around," she said. "There are no words for how depressing that is…. I just don't want to deal with it," she told me. It was one of the saddest conversations we'd ever had.

Energizing because, in addition to my generation, I saw many mothers with their daughters, and young women who understood that, for women, the political has become deeply personal and the personal had never before been so political, and that every right they enjoy today was the result of a hard-fought battle finally won by women activists before them. It was heartwarming to see that not only did they understand their foremothers' sacrifice, but also they were willing to step up and do their part now.

As I stood on the capitol steps on that chilly January afternoon, grateful that it hadn't begun snowing yet, and looked back all the way down State Street to the university, all I could see was a sea of pink pussy hats. "I sure don't see how any politician thinks getting millions of women pissed off is a good idea," the man standing next to me, looking back in the same direction, muttered to no one in particular. Good point, I thought.

After the speeches were over and the crowd was breaking up, I sat in a local bar waiting for my husband, who had gone to the funeral, to pick me up. I offered to split a beer with the woman sitting next to me, her white hair springing forth from her Green Bay Packer hoodie, over which she'd placed a bright pink hat. Her feet were swinging from the bar stool and she'd folded her walker under the counter. I asked her how it went? "Fine," she said. "Just fine…. I can't walk up the stairs anymore, but I'll be god-dammed if I'll just sit back while some pussy-grabber steals my country. I'll defend it with my own bare hands, if that's what I have to do," she said with conviction, and then took a long draw off her beer. She said her name was Florence, adding that she was a 96-year-old retired Navy nurse who had served in Korea, and whose mother had been a Navy nurse until she married her father, who had died in the Japanese attack on Pearl Harbor. "I learned what serving my country means pretty young," she said, "and I'm sure as hell not going to quit now … not as long as I'm still breathing." I asked her if she needed a ride home, and she said no, the van from her assisted living facility was picking her up. If a 96-year-old woman with a walker has the energy to protest Donald Trump, I thought, I can certainly step up and do my part.

On our way home after the march, over a pizza and another beer, I told my husband

More than 125,000 people, representing 45 percent of the total population of the city, jammed the one-mile isthmus in Madison, WI, on January 21, 2017. This march was one of more than 700 marches worldwide that supported the Women's March on Washington in D.C. held on the same day.

that if he was serious about helping me with an essay project giving women an opportunity to voice their frustrations over the Trump election, I was in. "Then let's get going, because we've got a lot of work to do," he smiled.

This is how a collection of essays from women, using their voices to speak truth to power, was born. The rest was amazingly easy, with one caveat: working on this project was like trying to drink water from a fire hose—information poured in much faster than we could process it and we had great difficulty staying on top of the political chaos surrounding the Trump administration. This was particularly true during the summer of 2017, the sixth through ninth months of Trump's presidency.

Getting Organized

> Do not sit still. Do not weep. MOVE. We are not a nation that will let
> HATE lead us.—Katy Perry

Once I made up my mind I was going forward with the book, the means for this seemed to find me, beginning when Betty Wells, an active faculty member at the same university I had left a few years previously, put out a request for essays from women who were upset about the election outcome on a list-serve to which we both subscribe. I contacted her about collaborating on a book project to collect protest statements from women. She thought it would work and had the time to help me. After McFarland agreed to publish a book of essays on the 2017 women's movement, we proceeded to breathe life into the idea with two goals in mind.

First, in the wake of the deeply upsetting Trump victory, we wanted to create an opportunity for women's voices to be heard. We knew that, unlike previous women-led uprisings, this one was not centered on a single issue. Instead, the 2017 political effort included a myriad of concerns women had about the future of our nation and our planet. With this in mind, we wanted women to tell us what they were upset, fearful and angry about, how they saw the future under a Trump administration, and how they were pushing back.

Second, using the words of the women themselves, we wanted to document the birth of what had exploded, with historically unprecedented speed, into a new and well-organized women's movement. As academics, we envisioned hundreds of master's theses and doctoral dissertations in sociology, political science, psychology, and other social science and related disciplines attempting to dissect this unique era in American political history, and we wanted women's voices to be a primary data source for these researchers. In other words, we wanted women to be first-person writers of the evolving historical record of a new political era they were defining, on their terms.

With the above in mind, we knew it was important to include women of all ages from all backgrounds, so we began by both recruiting essayists individually and posting a general call for submissions on relevant, issue-oriented websites and social media. The result was essay submissions from across the country authored by young women protesting for the first time in their lives and by retired warhorse activists who were appalled by Donald Trump's election and what it means for their grandchildren's futures that they, sometimes truly heroically and with great personal effort, showed up to protest once again.

We quickly realized that there are many groups of women, including immigrants, non–English speakers, native tribal women, and others we wanted to include, but were unable to reach. For various reasons, including fear of retaliation or being "found out" while they are living under the radar, these women were not comfortable committing their thoughts and feelings to paper. While they would tell us what they were thinking, they didn't want their words published in a book, and so wouldn't sign a publication release form. However, this does not mean these women don't have something very important to say. Their voices are just as important as the women who are comfortable expressing themselves publicly through the written word.

We wanted the book to write itself, so other than deciding to focus on only domestic issues, we imposed as little structure as possible. We wanted essayists to tell us what was bothering them rather than trying to shape the book according to what we thought women might be thinking, and saw our role as being the instrument through which their thoughts and concerns came to life.

We received many more essays than we could include in one book and engaged the assistance of several colleagues to help us determine which essays fit best. The essays sorted themselves into the categories that ultimately became the book sections. "United We Stand, and Together We March," "Indivisible, We March On: A New Women's Political Movement Arises" and "The Right to Protest: Warhorse Activists Report for Duty—Again," comprise a total of 8 essays detailing the evolution of the 2017 women's movement. "Alternative Facts: Donald Trump off the Rails," "Not My President: America Goes Dark" and "Climate Reigns Over All: Fighting Pipelines, Seeking Justice, Saving the Planet" contain a total of 10 essays addressing the effects of Mr. Trump's personality, leadership style, and view of, for example, climate-change science. "Sick in the USA: When the Personal Becomes Political," "The Lamp Beside the Golden Door Grows Dim: Immigration in 2017 America," "Somewhere Over the Rainbow: America's Gender Anxiety" and "When Blind Justice Isn't Blind: Women Face the Criminal Justice System" contain 11 essays combined outlining concerns about healthcare, immigration, gender, and criminal justice. Finally, "Saving Public Education One Teacher and One School at a Time," "When They Go Low, We Go High: Swimming in the Deep Rivers of Racism" and "When We Fight, We Win: United, We Move Forward" includes a total of 8 essays on public education, racism, and the next generation of women activists.

The book's lead essayist is award-winning feminist theologian Mary Hunt, cofounder and co-director of the Women's Alliance for Theology, Ethics, and Ritual (WATER), a non-profit education center committed to theological, ethical, and ritual development by and for women. Founded in 1983, WATER's mission is to use feminist religious values to create social change and endeavors to support and create a place for all disenfranchised people, including women and individuals across the LGBTQIA (Lesbian, Gay, Bisexual, Transgender, Queer, Intersexual and Asexual) spectrum in a community of faith. Mary casts protest actions in the spiritual terms women often seek and are naturally drawn toward as they engage in social justice efforts.

Unitarian minister the Rev. Sandra Ingham, who has been active in the "Beyond the War" movement, speaks to the perpetual American gender wars and misogyny embedded in the wider culture that aren't going away. As she asks in the concluding essay, what does this mean for women going forward into the dark abyss of a Donald Trump administration?

From the first essay through to the last, essayists explain why they feel compelled to speak out against the Trump administration. For example, social activist Pam Kidd shows us, in pictures, why she rode a bus with her daughter and granddaughter from Nashville, TN, to Washington, D.C., to attend the women's march. Writer Kathy Steffen speaks to the fear she had to overcome in order to "not let her fraidy-cat show" as she traveled from rural Wisconsin to Washington, D.C., wearing a pink hat one of her friends knit for her. For the first time in her life she would commit an act of protest by standing in solidarity with other women against Trump.

Midwestern inner-city high school teacher Darlynne L. Campbell and award-winning writers Danielle James and Erica Gerald Mason, living in Indiana, Brooklyn, NY, and Georgia respectively, offer a Black women's perspective on living in what they thought was a post-racial America until Donald Trump was elected. Rachel Eliason writes about being transgender in a Trump political environment. Daughter-mother essayists Rebecca Gorman and Michelle Bowdler write about LGBTQIA concerns in a family setting where two mothers are raising children.

Climate change warrior Miriam Kashia (IA) speaks to the threats embedded in the Trump administration's view of climate change. Traumatic brain injury survivor Alexandria A. Cunningham explains how healthcare turned into hellcare, and how healthcare reform proposals fail to ensure she will have healthcare coverage.

Retired Wisconsin Supreme Court Justice and award winning, worldwide advocate for restorative justice Janine Geske reflects on why women are not always treated fairly by the criminal justice system. Rabah Omer speaks to the fears and concerns she feels as a Sudanese Muslim-American citizen, and exiled poet Ari Belathar, currently living in the U.S., writes about the concerns immigrants have regarding proposed immigration policies.

Union organizer Ruth Burgess Thompson takes a deep dive into how conservative politics, having turned so far to the right, are making the personal extremely political for women of childbearing age, particularly in Iowa. Scott Thompson explains why the men who love the women who are protesting feel compelled to support them, and why he traveled with his wife from Iowa to Washington, D.C., to do it.

Each section includes an introduction that places the essays in context so that 5 or 50 years from now readers will understand why, in 2017, women are so upset, and so willing to step up and speak out to reclaim their country. These are powerful essays of hope and resolve to never give up flowing from the hearts of women with deeply held convictions about the dangers they face in the Trump era. They are very clear about what they believe "making America great again" really means, which is not, in their view, what Donald Trump claims it means.

Finally, because this is a book about the birth of a new political movement, it is about beginnings. There is no conclusion, because it hasn't been written yet.

One of the biggest challenges we faced was that, from the outset, the Trump administration has been buried in controversy and political upheaval, causing the ground to shift under the country's feet daily. Frequently, issues particularly concerning immigration and health care changed on an hourly basis, and what was true yesterday is no longer true today. Partly this was a result of Trump's erratic pattern of non-stop, 24–hour tweets in which he was prone to making outrageous and frequently false statements. The media felt compelled to pursue these comments on the off-chance there was a news story buried in there somewhere. However, in this political environment, trying to analyze and explain Trump administration policies was like trying to nail Jell-O to a wall—nothing stuck.

What this scenario verified beyond a reasonable doubt is that the Trump administration has been, from the beginning, a rudderless ship reacting to whatever came its way. There never was a carefully thought-through agenda for the country or a solid plan for carrying one out if it had existed. This is not too surprising, considering Mr. Trump assumed the presidency having no prior political or other public leadership experience whatsoever. He had no way of knowing that you can't govern a democratic nation in the same way you run a real estate development company. Women intuitively recognized this, and immediately reacted to the danger his presidency presented.

Politicians everywhere would be wise to listen very carefully to these voices because not only are most members of the 52 percent female majority of the American population, they also have something important to say about America's future. They are active participants in American society and will not return to the days of barefoot and pregnant being their primary career option—ever.

Anyone who thinks otherwise could not possibly be more wrong.

Notes

1. Jake Tapper, State of the Nation, CNN, November 13, 2016.
2. Donna Cassata, The Big Story, www.ap.org, February 26, 2016.
3. Hillary Rodham Clinton, *What Happened?* (New York: Simon & Schuster, 2017).
4. www.electproject.org.
5. Others were John Quincy Adams, Rutherford B. Hayes, Benjamin Harrison, and George W. Bush. Andrew Jackson, lacking a clear majority, became president by vote of the House of Representatives. Historians generally agree that none of these men distinguished themselves as President of the United States.
6. Allan Smith, "$52 Million to $0: That's How Much Hillary Clinton's Campaign Is Outspending Donald Trump's on TV Ads," *Business Insider* (August 26, 2016).

7. www.nbc.com.

8. For a broader discussion of why Donald Trump won, see Arlie Russell Hochschild, *Strangers in Their Own Land: Anger and Mourning on the American Right* (New York: The New Press, 2016). Also see Katherine Cramer, *The Politics of Resentment: Rural Consciousness and the Rise of Scott Walker* (Chicago: University of Chicago Press, 2016). Cramer analyzes how conservative Scott Walker became governor of Wisconsin and contends that the national election results mirrored Wisconsin's political mood, writ large.

Section 1. United We Stand, and Together We March

Paula vW. Dáil

> Congress shall make no law respecting an establishment of religion or pro-
> hibiting the free exercise thereof; or abridging the freedom of speech, or
> of the press, or the right of the people peaceably to assemble, and to petition
> the government for a redress of grievances.
> —The First Amendment to the United States Constitution
> and Article One of the Bill of Rights, passed in 1791.

Once upon a time in ancient Greece, Lysistrata, a strong Athenian woman with a great sense of leadership and individual responsibility, decided it was time to end the seemingly endless Peloponnesian War between Athens and Sparta. She invited women from the various Greek city-states to a meeting to hatch a plan. They decided to withhold sexual privileges from their menfolk as a means of forcing them to stop fighting and end the war. Not surprisingly, the plan worked.

This play, written by Aristophanes and originally performed in 411 BCE, is one of the earliest known statements about women and social protests. It speaks to two universal truths about effective social action: there is power in numbers, and women can bring about the change they desire if they are willing to work together to achieve their goal.

The ability to speak truth to power in the halls of government is central to any democracy. Without this sacred right, a representative government, and the republic for which it stands, would not be of, by and for all the people. It would be a dictatorship.

Across history, much of what has occurred in America has been the result of large social protests. Dr. Martin Luther King, Jr., who led the 1960s civil rights movement, believed protesting was a moral responsibility. Albert Einstein saw protest as a necessary choice one must make in order to avoid complacency. Ella Wheeler Wilcox said that the failure to protest in the face of wrongdoing is cowardly. And Holocaust survivor Eli Wiesel pointed out that there may be times when we are powerless to prevent injustice, but we must never fail to protest it.

None of this is news to women, who have been protesting what they have perceived as moral and social wrongdoing, in various forms, since the beginning of human history. Women have marched for suffrage, demolished taverns in the name of the Women's Christian Temperance Union and led the workers' strikes that ultimately led to the Russian Revolution. Mother Jones led the effort to form a coal miner's union, one of the

15

earliest efforts to protect labor rights. Simply by refusing to move to the back of the bus, Rosa Parks ignited the Civil Rights Movement. Gloria Steinem, Betty Friedan and Bella Abzug spearheaded the new feminist movement. Marsha P. Johnson, a Black transgender woman, and Stormè DeLarverie, a butch Black lesbian, incited the Stonewall Riots in New York City in 1969, which became a turning point in gay liberation and the Lesbian, Gay, Bisexual, Transgender, Queer, Intersex and Asexual rights movement.

Every one of these efforts has been fueled by brave women stepping up to speak truth to power, holding onto the courage of their convictions through the inevitable storm that follows, and not backing down. With this much success to build upon, it's no surprise that Donald Trump's ascension to the U.S. presidency has sparked another women's movement. It's also not surprising that a chilling turn in the history of protest movements occurred when candidate Donald Trump ordered his security detail to remove three protesters from his March 16 campaign rally in Louisville, Kentucky. "Get 'em outta here!" Trump shouted.

The protesters sued the Trump campaign, claiming their First Amendment right to protest had been violated. In his defense, Trump's lawyers argued that he had every right to call for the removal of the protesters since they "obviously interfered with the Trump campaign's First Amendment rights by vigorously expressing their disdain for Mr. Trump…." Lawyers also argued that protesters have no right to express dissenting views as part of a campaign rally of the political candidates they oppose."[1] A federal judge disagreed with the defense argument, and the case proceeded to trial. Trump's legal team decided to appeal the ruling to a higher court "before subjecting the President to 'unique' and extraordinary burdens of litigation."

Meanwhile, in an alarming, but not surprising, trend under President Trump, the right to protest has come under siege. Twenty states have introduced bills to impede this fundamental right and in doing so are using their legislative power to configure one of the greatest threats to American democracy in in the nation's history. For example[2]:

- North Dakota Republicans proposed legislation to legalize running over protestors if they are blocking roadways.
- The Arizona State Senate expanded the state's racketeering laws to allow police to arrest anyone involved in a protest and seize their assets, thus treating demonstrators like organized criminals.
- In Portland, Oregon, activists that organized against police killings of black men, were grouped with white nationalists, and the countless systems of racism throughout local, state, and federal governments that the Department of Homeland Security has identified.
- In Minnesota, following the police shooting death of African American Philando Castile, protests shut down part of a highway. In response, Minnesota legislators drafted bills that would punish highway protestors with heavy fines and prison time and would make protesters liable for the policing costs of an entire protest if any were convicted of unlawful assembly or public nuisance.
- Republicans in Washington State are attempting to reclassify disobedience protests that are deemed "economic terrorism" as civil felonies.
- Lawmakers in North Carolina want to make heckling lawmakers a crime.
- In Indiana, conservatives want to allow police to use "any means necessary" to remove activists from a roadway.

- Colorado lawmakers are considering a substantial increase in penalties for environmental protesters. Under the measure, protesters face felony charges and can be sentenced to up to 18 months behind bars and fined up to $100,000.
- The Virginia state legislature is considering a bill that would dramatically increase punishment for people who "unlawfully" assemble after "having been lawfully warned to disperse." Those who fail to do so could face a year in jail and a $2,500 fine.
- The Wisconsin legislature is considering a bill that will force the state universities to expel students arrested for protesting on campus.

How successful any of these efforts will be remains to be seen, but the possibility that they might be is extremely frightening.

The entire history of American women is one of struggle and facing down danger—leaving homelands, crossing oceans in the hulls of ships, having babies in covered wagons as they traveled across the Great Plains to settle the American West, raising families on the sod house frontier, getting jobs, and figuring out how to support themselves. The examples are endless. From this perspective, Donald Trump and his conservative political movement is just another challenge to overcome, which, across their history, women have done many times before, know how to do, and have no problem rising to the occasion to do once again.

United We March

> Never underestimate the power of a woman to change something. It's the only thing that ever has.—Margaret Mead

Hawaii grandmother and retired Indiana lawyer Teresa Shook's reaction to Donald Trump's election as the next president of the United States was a mixture of profound shock and deep sadness. The difference between Teresa and the millions of others who felt the same way was that she decided she had to do something about it immediately. The night of the election, right before going to bed, she created a Facebook event page calling for a march on Washington the day after the Trump inauguration. Initially, she received 40 responses; by the time she got up the next morning she had 10,000. Just 24 hours later, 300,000 women thought this was a great idea.

Meanwhile, several time zones away, New York fashion designer Bob Bland had a similar idea. She'd already created the "Nasty Women Vote" and "Bad Hombre" t-shirt designs in response to Trump having called Hillary Clinton a "nasty woman" and referred to Hispanics as "bad hombres." Bland suggested a "Million Pussy March" named for Trump's Access Hollywood "grab 'em by the pussy" remarks. "I think we should build a coalition of ALL marginalized allies + do this," Bland wrote on Facebook on November 10th. "We will need folks from every state + city to organize their communities locally, who wants to join me?!?" A lot of people wanted to join.

Three New York–based activists agreed to co-chair the national march: Tamika Mallory, a gun control advocate; Carmen Perez, head of Gathering for Justice, a criminal-justice reform group; and Linda Sarsour, who recently led a successful campaign to close New York City public schools on two Muslim holidays. Together, these women brought critically needed organizational skills and diversity to the effort, and then rolled up their sleeves and got to work.

Only 10 weeks later, 600,000 women marched on Washington, D.C., and another 4,500,000 American women joined in sister marches in 408 American cities and towns. An additional 2,000,000 women in 168 cities worldwide marched in solidarity with their American sisters. Millions of women worldwide were, indeed, very angry that a misogynist had just been elected as the leader of the free world, and any politician who didn't recognize the implications of this was badly out of touch with the people they had been elected to serve.

Award-winning feminist theologian, lecturer and writer Mary Hunt, the lead essayist for this collection, understands the power of women coming together and views the 2017 Women's March as the spiritual awakening many women were seeking as they struggled to find their way to resist a Trump presidency. In "Moving Forward Together: Women's Marches as Spiritual Practices," Mary stresses the importance and the power of inclusivity as we move toward the future.

Political activist and writer Pam Kidd, who oversees the children's advocacy organization Children of Zimbabwe, explains why she traveled from north Nashville, TN, to Washington, D.C., to protest Donald Trump's election. Through her photo essay, "Good Morning, America," Pam illustrates what she found when she arrived and how the experience has sustained her going forward toward the future.

NOTES

1. Kenneth P. Vogel, "Trump Lawyer: No Right to Protest," www.politico.com, April 20, 2016.
2. U.S. Protesters in Grave Danger Under Trump. www.commondreams.org, April 2, 2017.

Moving Forward Together
Women's Marches as Spiritual Practices

MARY E. HUNT

The roaring success of the January 2017 Women's March on Washington and the many related marches around the world signals a new spiritual vibrancy that supports action for social justice. This spirituality is not a pious acquiescence to the inevitable, but a lively, feminist presence in a world whose survival is contingent on both resistance and creativity.

Few pundits predicted a Trump victory in November 2016. Even fewer foresaw the wave of reaction, especially feminist, that accompanied the new administration's stunningly unsettling and unjust policies. Large numbers of people took to the streets in a heartfelt effort to reject in public and wholesale terms the values of greed and "America first" that were articulated in sexist, white supremacist, xenophobic statements and policies. Marchers (and those who supported from home) were intent on expressing our embrace of Earth, our welcome to the newly arrived on our shores, and our firm conviction that each life matters, especially the lives of Black people and women so cruelly and crudely treated by members of the new administration.

The marches on January 21, 2017, the day after the inauguration of the 45th president of the United States, were a welcome global phenomenon. The election was a referendum, serious push back on the many achievements of the last forty years—particularly in health care, civil rights, women's rights, LGBTIQA (Lesbian, Gay, Bi-sexual, Transgender, Intersexual, Queer, Asexual) rights, deeper awareness of the needs of immigrants and people living with disabilities. But it was an Electoral College win in which 3 million more people voted for the loser than the winner. Russian intrusion into the electoral process, and the possibility that the winning campaign may have colluded in such a breach of democracy, remain to be clarified.

For many people, the sense of disbelief following the election gave way to despair. A bitterly disappointing win for a candidate who distinguished himself by his crass behavior toward women, on top of an unfolding policy agenda that is destroying global progress by boasting torture, walls, and aggression issued in spiritual malaise for many progressive people. That a wildly unpopular man bested the most viable woman candidate in American history, although he lost the popular vote, only increased the spiritual dissonance. The organizers' genius insight to invite and ignite people for action touched a nerve.

We needed a major push, and marches led in the direction of stronger than ever resistance to injustice. It was gratifying to be part of the enormous wave of women of color–led energy, actions worldwide that reflected not a lockstep agenda but the willingness of many people to express their outrage and commitment to an inclusive, just future. This did not happen overnight, and one march was not the end of the action. Like all spiritual practices, this one needs to be repeated, changed, and shared. But it made for a common new start and for that the organizers deserve kudos.

Millions of people participated in the first marches, from the huge crowd that gridlocked Washington, D.C., for hours to the handful of women scientists and their penguin friends who protested in Antarctica against threatened cuts to federal research funding. Sociologist Dana Fisher, in a careful look at this and subsequent marches, finds that the resistance is not slowing down. So-called "protest fatigue" has not set in as many who marched for women also marched later for science, the environment, and then for immigrant and LGBTIQA rights. This does not surprise spiritual feminists who have long insisted on an intersectional analysis and interstructured solutions to myriad social problems. The marches were a case of putting that approach to the service of social change.

As footsore marchers debriefed, most people in many places were singing the same song: huge numbers of diverse folks; overwhelming good will in sometimes crowded conditions; creative, constructive manifestations of progressive opinions; a deep sense of not being the only ones who opposes the policies and practices of a presidential administration hell bent on American hegemony; and new resolve to bring about justice. The role of religion and spirituality in all of this is telling, though not in the measurable ways of how many people belong to religious group X, or the percentage of those who practice faith Y. Rather, religion and spirituality in the broadest sense of what connects (religare in Latin) were on the march in post-modernity

The coming together is all. It happens in women's living rooms, virtually online, and in many third spaces around the world. So many people gathered in Washington, D.C., in January 2017 that the Metro was overwhelmed; large parts of the city were closed to vehicular traffic. In towns and cities on every continent folks of all gender identities and sexual orientations, young and old responded with their bodies to ideologies of hate and exclusion that characterized the Trump presidential campaign.

The very act of gathering is a spiritual statement. These marches and rallies are not feel-good fests, but serious, if at times light-hearted (a popular chant is "We want a leader, not a creepy tweeter.") manifestations of people who are working to create a just world. Nary an arrest was reported during the January D.C. march.

However, as resistance has grown in the six months that followed, coalitions are more fragile, and insistence on multi-dimensional agendas has led to arrests at some demonstrations. For example, the 2017 Capital Pride Parade was disrupted by progressives who wanted to see an agenda more inclusive of racial/ethnic minorities and less dependent on corporate sponsors. "No justice, no pride" was their claim. The Equality March for Unity and Pride the next day in D.C. featured a more inclusive agenda, more explicit connections between/among issues, less emphasis on sexual (mostly masculine) freedom, more emphasis on justice. Note that it was the newly crafted, more grassroots event, not the decades old, now largely underwritten pride parade that was a fulsome expression of a complex agenda that feminists endorse.

Speeches and music add content to these marches. Pink hats, now both winter and summer versions, make a statement against sexual violence. But the heart of the matter is being there, showing up, embodying something that puts the brakes on the dismantling of affordable health care, bans on immigrants, violence against people of color, and lower tax rates for wealthy people that are hallmarks of the new administration.

At first blush, the role of religion is relatively minor in these actions. Unlike their predecessors during the Civil Rights and anti–Vietnam War protests, clergy and religious leaders are not generally in the vanguard of the marches though some religious people speak at rallies. The lead groups of the mother march in D.C. were Planned Parenthood (women's health), the Natural Resources Defense Council (climate change and fossil fuels), Emily's List (electing pro-choice Democratic women candidates), and NARAL Pro-Choice America (choosing abortion, birth control, sex education, and healthy pregnancies).

The so-called religious left is enjoying a bit of a renaissance. But in its institutional expressions like the National Council of Churches, Sojourners, even the Moral Monday groups, it remains largely patriarchal in substance. That means mainly male leadership without primary attention to issues of women's well being, especially reproductive justice including legal abortion. It implies a silo approach to issues rather than intersectionality. And, it means a preponderance of language, imagery, hymns, and preaching that are replete with "Lord," "Father," "Ruler," and "King" as if decades of feminist work to diversify religions had never happened.

There are partner groups of many stripes in current organizing including those working against gun violence, in favor of girls' education, on peace and environmental issues. Religious groups are among them, but as often as not they come from the margins of the traditions rather than from their institutional hearts. For the Women's March, several Jewish organizations, Unitarians both at the national and local level, the Federation of Protestant Welfare Agencies, Catholics for Choice, and Faith in New York were among the official partners.

Most on the partner list were secular groups ranging from the well-known Human Rights Campaign to the lower profile Rachel's Network which brings environmental concerns, philanthropy, and women's leadership together. One group called VERVE focuses on human rights and women's friendships, a niche market, but an important and potentially world-saving one. Who knew about it and what category does it fit?

Feminist spirituality is one of the most useful explanatory constructs for talking about what is happening. What brings people together is not a particular dogma or doctrine. To the contrary, participation in organized religions is on the wane in the U.S. with "nones" far outpacing "nuns" for new members. Vision and hope are lived out in multiple ways, which need not be competing or mutually exclusive. But that way of thinking about the world, as if there is no one right answer, no single correct route from birth to death, no unified worldview is not what most people hear from their religious traditions. Instead, they are taught to follow The Way, The Path, or some other unitary approach that smacks more of concern about market share than helping people find ways to live out their commitments in solidarity with others.

The challenge of twenty-first century religion is to find ways to live with many different, sometimes overlapping, ways of being in community. It is not easy, but the marches prove that many people are willing to try. That is what feminist spirituality incarnate looks like walking down the street.

These marches are not simply the unleashed energy of disappointed voters, nor were the January ones a counter inaugural. They were expressions of values and commitments that are shared more broadly, held more deeply, and manifest more diversely than many people, including the organizers, realized. That surprise says something about the need to vocalize, amplify, and publicize feminist spiritual values in all of their complexity.

Some local religious institutions played a helpful, if supporting, role for the marches. Selected churches and synagogues opened their doors (especially their bathrooms) and plugged in their coffee makers to provide for the physical and spiritual needs of those marching. Some hosted non-violence training sessions in advance of the events. People availed themselves of their hospitality without necessarily being affiliated with the group.

Traditional religious services were connected to some of the marches. In Washington, D.C., for example, the National Council of Jewish Women co-sponsored a Shabbat service, and the First Congregational Church of Christ offered a prayer service before the march. Catholic nuns and their friends planned to meet following prayer in a Catholic church on Capitol Hill. In the end, many communities, including the Women's Alliance for Theology, Ethics, and Ritual (WATER) with whom I gathered, discovered that there were simply too many people at the march to meet up with a large group. So everyone just fell in and marched together. It was appropriate to the day and remains a useful metaphor for what lies ahead since so much more unites us than divides us.

Progressive religious groups were out in force as banners and signs revealed. But the real story, in my view, is the more generalized spiritual sense of the marches that reflects a more diffuse, but no less effective, source of motivation. Some of it is reactive—against the threats to Obamacare, in opposition to discrimination against immigrants, in horror at the greed and profit taking, and struck by the fact that Trump's environmental policies will almost certainly exacerbate climate change.

But most of the spiritually rooted values are affirmative—wanting health care, quality schools, safe drinking water, equal opportunity in housing and employment—for everyone without exception. There is a groundswell against war and torture. Climate change is taken seriously and racism is abhorred. Women, LGBTIQA people, and immigrants are outsiders no more.

Such spiritually based commitments are by their nature general and visionary. Think: "love your neighbor." But they translate into policies and actions that the current administration is ignoring, overturning, and otherwise reshaping into a xenophobic, solipsistic social fabric that is as dangerous as it is repugnant. No wonder the groundswell was so enormous and spirits to high.

The arts play a major role in social change. So, it was not surprising that on the day of the Women's March in D.C., the National Museum of Women and the Arts opened its doors without charge. Hundreds of people, many of them new to the thirty-year old museum had their first glimpse of a collection that is almost exclusively made up of work by women. "Nasty Women" tours were popular that day as docents showed off the extraordinary riches of the permanent collection. Now "Fierce Women" tours are a regular offering at NMWA, which is a beautiful space dedicated to showcasing the best of women's artistic offerings. The building was originally a Masonic Temple. Now it is a temple of a feminist sort.

The intentionally broad agenda that attracted millions to march requires that no one is completely satisfied but that everyone is willing to give a little. Such is a functional definition of democracy. As the great singer and cultural worker Bernice Johnson Reagon of Sweet Honey in the Rock put it years ago, "If you are in a coalition and you're comfortable, you know it is not broad enough." Feminist spirituality is like that—at once coalitional and at the same time lived out in very particular local expressions whether liturgical, ritual, artistic, athletic, culinary, or some other creative form.

There was discomfort at the marches just as there is in society and spirituality. White supremacy remains a signal problem that organizers have to confront and participants cannot forget. All is not sweetness and light in as fractured a society as ours, where antiracism, Black Lives Matter, and inclusion demand serious attention. So, too, in feminist spiritual circles problems like Christian hegemony and the right not to be religious need to be focused on and confronted.

Social ethical issues are sources of conflict as well as change. Abortion emerged as a potential wedge issue in the marches, but this time it did not finally divide. Happily, people who are uncomfortable with legal reproductive options, including some Catholics, embraced the larger justice agenda without focusing narrowly on one issue. After all, Planned Parenthood does a great deal to help women bring healthy pregnancies to term, as well as provide legal abortions. There is no litmus test for participation but organizers of such events can determine their sponsors and partners according to their own criteria. Those who disagree are welcome to organize their own gatherings. That is why under the umbrella of feminist spirituality there are people who hold differing and sometimes contradictory views on matters like abortion, access to guns, and the death penalty.

Living with the discomfort of diversity in order to move forward is not a sign of cheap relativism, but a hallmark of feminist spirituality. Without abandoning one's beliefs, it is possible to pass over the rigid, narrow foci that have kept patriarchal ecumenical and interfaith efforts from succeeding. It is not a sign of rampant secularization, but evidence of reasonable and responsible religiosity and better forms of spirituality, which are expressed by embracing a shared vision of human flourishing and cosmic harmony.

These marches are about far more than individual choices. They are about structural barriers to full participation like racism, sexism, ableism, and the like that must be eradicated. They are about the world adults want to bequeath to their children and grandchildren, and the world those children will pass on to theirs. Quite simply, no one issue determines the future, but all condition what it will look like and who will survive to live it.

Calling this spirituality does not relegate it to a mystical realm or get one off the hook for critical analysis. Instead, this kind of feminist spirituality is a way of seeing social change for the common good as at the heart and soul of the human project in which all are invited to participate.

The proof of the marches' power will unfold as issue after issue demands attention. In the first few days of the new administration, executive orders flew fast and furious to keep immigrants out, to gag federal agencies working on environmental issues, to build walls and pipelines, to roll back health care for millions, and otherwise impose a despotic rule on a democracy. As the first year of the Trump presidency unfolds, the depth and depravity of the project comes into clear view: fake news, a Supreme Court justice who is very conservative, bans on immigrants, insults to leaders of other countries, withdrawal from the Paris Climate Agreement, not to mention countless blatant lies, personal attacks all of which add up to an even grimmer reality especially for people who are marginalized and at risk. No wonder we march.

Resistance is crucial, but so too is the creativity to build the scaffolding of a just and sustainable society. Feminist spiritualities, in all of their diversity of expression and priorities, in all of their performative power are a great source to spark and sustain this work. The visceral memories of the marches, both for those who participated in person and for those who observed, are motivating factors. We know what democracy looks like, and we know how it feels to be moving in the same direction, however slowly and deliberately, sometimes gridlocked and stymied, but in time and with cooperation, making our way together.

Good Morning, America
A Photo Essay

PAM KIDD

The message remains, nestled deep in my laptop notes. I doubt that I shall ever delete it. I had written it on the cusp of November 8, 2016, ready for an early Facebook post on November 9. It reads: "We have elected a fine woman, a knowledgeable woman, an intelligent woman who is fully equipped and ready to serve our country and its people. We have elected a grandmother as president of the United States of America. GRAND-MOTHER! Good morning America!"

Like so many others, I was sure of the outcome of the 2016 presidential election. I had immersed myself in the process, worked hard, campaigned diligently, registered voters, gave more money than I could afford and ended my efforts by working the polls from 7 a.m. till 7 p.m. on election day.

And then, the impossible happened. The candidate who won the popular vote had not won the presidency. Instead, a career flim-flam man whose narcissism glowed like a neon light throughout the campaign was declared the 45th president of the United States. There didn't seem to be single flash of peace in his orbit. A long trail of rancor, hatred, prejudice, selfish-

A participant in the January 21, 2017, Washington, D.C., women's march carries a sign referencing Hillary Clinton's college graduation photograph and the caption "Voted Most Popular 2016."

ness, lies and nepotism followed his campaign as he found dark, sinister ways to say, "make America white again."

Like my family and most of my friends, I floated in a haze of disbelief. As a life-long optimist, I vacillated between thinking, "he will never be inaugurated," and "something unexpected with save us from this unimaginable predicament."

Next, I sunk into a strange hibernation from reality. I decorated every corner of our house for Christmas. Two weeks before Thanksgiving. I threw myself into organizing a massive toy drive for the needy children in our community. My husband and I watched British mysteries every night.

Sensing the rising fear among our Muslim friends, our Hispanic friends, our LGBTQIA friends, our Jewish friends, and our African American friends, we started our own "safety pin campaign" urging others to join us as we tried to transform ourselves into safe places for those threatened by our newly elected president's hate-filled rhetoric.

I am safe.

If you are
Muslim,
a woman,
LGBQ*,
a person of
color,
Latinx,
trans*,
an immigrant,
disabled,
afraid...

I am here.

Speak...

I'll listen.
I'll hold you.
Stand up for you.
Sit down for you.
Shut up for you.
Do what I can
to let you know

I love you.

This sign is how
you'll know me.

#safetypin

A poster advertises a safety pin campaign conceived by women in Nashville, TN, to reach out to Muslim, Hispanic, African American, Jewish and LGBTQ communities. The project's goal was to create safe places for marginalized people to be comforted in the wake of Donald Trump's election as president of the United States.

I created my own personal la-la land. I needed a hideout from truth where I could wait for the miracle that would erase this nightmare and leave us all laughing with relief.

Then one day my daughter, Keri Cannon, posted a rather unexpected message on Facebook about an organic group called Pantsuit Nation. "If you are as bummed out as I am," the message read, "and if you need someone to talk to, I'm having a gathering at my house on Saturday. It doesn't matter that we don't know each other. If this speaks to you, you are welcome to come."

Sixty women, mostly strangers, walked into her house that Saturday and found each other. Soon there was talk of a women's march on Washington, D.C., the day following the inauguration, and my daughter and her friends were looking into chartering a bus from Nashville. Still living in that stupor of confusion, all I knew to say was, "I'm in."

The mood in the Nashville parking lot where our bus was waiting in the early morning hours of January 20 was surreal.

My daughter Keri, her daughter Abby and I dragged our suitcases toward the bus, just like other women who were floating in with the fog from every direction.

The media was there and several camera-flanked reporters were offering microphones for interviews. If one of them had shoved a microphone in my face and asked why I was going to the march, I would have talked in circles, working my way through a variety of life experiences, trying to find the answer. But, at this point, I had no answer.

Earlier that morning my favorite news source had hit me hard with the new administration's plans to eliminate the National Endowment for the Arts and the National Endowment for the Humanities. There were plans to privatize the Corporation for Public Broadcasting, and agencies such as the Minority Business Development Agency. The Legal Services Corporation, the Paris Climate Change Agreement and Grants for Violence Against Women were also destined for the chopping block. Added to this were the threats being made to immigrants, the talk of Muslim registries, the vulgar disrespect for women, the disregard for the wellness of the world ... the list seemed endless.

I was walking toward the big bus in a blue haze realizing that a civilized culture, climate concerns and simple human kindness were no longer going to be part of the fabric of our country. Boarding the bus, I looked around and found a sea of faces, mostly women. Few were familiar.

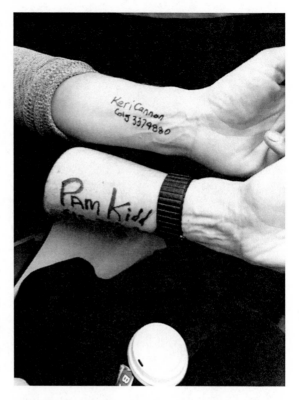

Pam Kidd and her daughter wrote their names and phone numbers on their arms to identify themselves in case they were separated or injured during the march.

Keri and I found a seat near the back and Abby connected with some of her friends. There were nine kids on the bus.

The mood was subdued. We were all suddenly overwhelmed with the weight of inauguration day and what we were about to do. Much of the speculation about what might happen next was turning into ugly reality. As we rolled out of Nashville and time ticked on, the unbelievable became more and more real. Decency was vacating the White House, and indecency was moving in.

Ahead, in our nation's capital, bedlam was tarnishing Trump's inauguration day. The city was, at times, like a war zone with rioting, tear gas, stun guns and over 200 arrests. With the threat of violence upon us, we were instructed to prepare ourselves for the worst. We were required to write our names and contact numbers in bold black across our inner arms. It was a disquieting moment, realizing that the unknown waited and we really had no idea what to expect.

"Have bail money ready," I half-jokingly texted my husband. I felt a shiver of fear. My daughter. My granddaughter. What were we stepping into? The mood on the bus grew solemn.

We settled in for a long ride—twelve hours, maybe more, we speculated. As we became acquainted with our fellow travelers, the rows of faces turned into a group of

Pam Kidd (left), with her granddaughter, Abby Cannon (center), and her daughter, Keri Cannon (right), prepare to travel from Nashville, TN, to Washington, D.C., on January 21, 2017, to participate in the Women's March on Washington in solidarity with women worldwide.

This "I MATTER—YOU MATTER" sign carried by a protestor at the Washington, D.C., women's march, pleads for unity and equality, rather than division, among all ethnicities in America.

hopeful human beings from Nashville, and nearby towns like Franklin, Lebanon and Hendersonville. One young couple drove over from Florence, Alabama. Another came from Lake Guntersville. They were, to a person, the kind of people Keri, Abby, and I call friends. Hopeful. Caring. Well-informed. Ready to step out and engage themselves in whatever they feel called to do. These were people ready to stand, to march, for something bigger than themselves. Yet, I don't think any of us completely understood why we were there.

I was beginning to sense that something was rising up from deep inside our better selves. It was that primal knowledge, so perfectly stated by the young boy in Mark Childress' book, *Crazy in Alabama*, who, when he saw a line of black people being turned away from a voter registration event, said simply, "this ain't right."

Each of us, in one way or another had received that simple message, and it was powerful enough to cause us to change our schedules, make our reservations, show up and board the bus.

We rode for hours, arrived too late for dinner, crashed in our hotel rooms, then missed our chance for breakfast in our rush to get to the train station by 7 a.m.

Then, unexplained … unexpected … the magic broke through, right there in the metro station. It came in waves … it followed us onto the train…. It was electric and alive. It was everywhere: in the chants, in the words written across the signs, and on the faces of the people who held them.

The throngs of people were growing. Their energy was flowing out. It was as though everything I had dreamed humanity might be was coming together, moving forward, fixed on the destination ahead. When we exited the train station and stepped out into the street, we saw thousands of women in pink hats. Pink hats everywhere, as far as I could see.

Left: Marchers crowd into the Washington, D.C., metro trains to travel to the women's march at the capital. *Right:* A man holding a pink hat sits next to an African American woman also riding into Washington, D.C., for the women's march, carrying a sign declaring that America's doors will stay open to all immigrants.

Left: Marchers in pink hats carrying signs exit Washington, D.C., mass transit trains and walk toward the capital. *Right:* Women crowd the streets of Washington, D.C., for as far as the eye can see, marching for their cause.

A father wearing a pink hat in solidarity with women marchers in Washington, D.C., hoists his daughter on his shoulders so that she, too, can see how many people believe in women's rights.

Suddenly we were swept up into an ever-widening expanse of hope. Men, women and children of every race, religion, and culture had come together as one. We came simply, believing. And in this sea of faces, peace descended. There was no pushing, rudeness or complaining. We were there together, moving in sync—slowly moving toward something I couldn't yet understand.

The crowds were unprecedented. The rally stretched out in every direction. We had no contact with the media, but back in Nashville, my husband David got a text through to us: "Breaking News! Hundreds of thousands rally in D.C.!"

The "march" eventually poured out over 14 blocks, covering every side street in downtown D.C. The city was virtually shut down.

Still, no problems. No rioting. No negativity. The policemen were friendly. Many smiled, some laughed out loud with the pure wonder that comes from seeing people come together for a higher cause.

It would later be called the largest event of its kind in our nation's history. It was reported that not a single arrest was made

The media kept referring to the march as a protest. The word "gathering" would have been a better fit, because once you found a spot, you pretty much had to stay there. Keri, Abby and I huddled close, listening to speakers, musicians, and poets. We smiled, we laughed, and we greeted "our" people. We feasted on the thousands of signs, from artsy to professional to handmade.

We stayed on for hours. Over and over, I reminded myself that this was perhaps one of the best days of my life because I was

Women march across the Washington, D.C., Mall carrying hundreds of signs supporting causes important to them that they believe a Trump administration will negatively impact.

there at a precise moment in history, and I was sharing it with my daughter and grand-daughter. But there was more…

For ten hours, we stood in the midst of all this with no food, no snacks, nothing to drink, no bathroom breaks. Yet I wanted to hold on to the day. I wanted to float there forever.

The day after the election we had fallen on the sword. We believed that our America had disappeared, and that our beloved Hillary who we had taken the time to get to know, had been destroyed.

How easy it had been to fall for the big lie and believe that vulgarity and dishonesty, gaucheness, greed and a profound lack of caring had taken over and would prevail. Disparity and helplessness had shrouded our days.

We had failed to notice that only 26 percent of eligible voters had cast their vote for Trump. A minority of our population had elected someone who will claim his hour in the limelight of the "world stage" and then be gone forever.

For a time, we had allowed this small minority who had lapped up a campaign filled with lies to steal our country and steal our power—and now we were here to take our country, and our power, back.

Now we were here, filling our nation's capital to overflowing. And all across the country, and all around the world, people like us were doing the same.

We came to protest something evil. We were greeted with a rising swell of something good.

Here, on the streets of our Nation's capital, we rediscovered America.

The groundswell of the women's march sent a message loud and clear, from "sea to shinning sea":

Women and men march along the street in front of the Washington, D.C., National Archives on their way to the protest on the steps of the nation's capital.

With the United States capital in the background, marchers carry their causes forward.

Donald Trump, you cannot take our dream.
Our spirit is soaring.
Our people are strong.
We the people, will prevail.

Toward the end of the day a man carrying a sign with a picture of a woman from the 40s pasted on the front caught my eye and captured my heart. Underneath the photo, he had written her name in full, followed by the words: "She wanted to be a civil engineer."

I stopped. I couldn't gather myself enough to pull out my phone and record the moment.

Silently, I stood, thinking of my own mother. I longed to have her intelligent face, the one my granddaughter and I had clipped to a Clinton—Kaine campaign poster, fixed on a big poster board. It would have read: "Arlene Cochran Dunn Hester.... She should have been an English professor."

Right then, right there, the moment wrapped around me. All the "whys" were crystal clear.

The people, the races, the religions, the places or origin, the skin colors, the sexual preferences, the stand for civil rights, human rights, LGBTQIA rights, Mother Earth rights, the right to be treated with dignity, the right to be respected for exactly who we are … the right for every woman to have equal rights along with every man … the People … as Sandburg said … *The People, Yes.*

Each in our own way, we were all there for the same reason. We were looking up. We were visioning a higher plane for humankind than had just been thrust upon us.

He who has temporarily taken over the oval office is not my president… and everything he destroys, "We the People," will rebuild.

This wasn't the good morning in America I'd originally envisioned early on Election Day. In some ways it was better, because now I knew, with every beat of my sad and discouraged heart, that no matter how dark the dawn, there was still hope. I'd seen it with my own eyes, heard it with my own ears, and felt it in my own soul. I know that we, the people, will reclaim and rebuild OUR nation. Donald Trump is temporary, and he is NOT MY PRESIDENT.

Top: **Pam Kidd (L) and her granddaughter, Abby Cannon (R) hold up a poster from the Clinton-Kaine election campaign with Pam's mother's photograph attached. The gesture signifies the hope Hillary Clinton's campaign brought to the cause of successfully advancing women's rights.** *Bottom:* **The bumper sticker on the back of this woman's coat sums up women's reactions to Donald Trump's election. "Not my Voice; Not my Values; Not my Beliefs; NOT MY PRESIDENT."**

SECTION 2. INDIVISIBLE, WE MARCH ON

A New Women's Political Movement Is Born

PAULA vW. DÁIL

… one nation, under God, indivisible, with liberty and justice for all.
—Pledge of Allegiance

The 2017 women's march organizers knew that if the protest was to have any lasting impact, they had to find some way to capture and sustain the energy it was sure to inspire. This was the framework around which Indivisible, a progressive political initiative that has its roots in the women's march, was created.[1]

The effort began with online publication of "Indivisible: A Practical Guide for Resisting the Trump Agenda." The 23-page instruction manual, authored by former Congressional staffers, identified ways to peacefully and effectively resist the anticipated swing toward conservative, right wing politics in the executive branch of government that was expected to occur as the Trump administration developed its policy agenda.

The handbook was the brainchild of Ezra Levin, Jeremy Haile, Leah Greenberg, and Angel Padilla. Levin worked as an aide to Congressman Lloyd Doggett (D–TX) and Greenberg, his wife, worked as an aide to Congressman Tom Perriello of (D–VA). In an attempt to deal with their grief following the Trump election, Levin and Greenburg began creating a Google document explaining how constituents could connect with congressional aides and express their political concerns. Soon, Padilla, Jeremy Haile, and dozens of other staffers for Democratic members of Congress joined in creating the Internet document. Within hours of its online publication, Google servers were crashing under the load.

By mid–February 2017 the Indivisible website had received 10 million visitors and 6 thousand Indivisible groups had sprung up around the country. Utilizing a 70–member team of volunteers Indivisible began offering joint public information calls with other activist groups, such as MoveOn.org. and Organizing for Action. Mushrooming rapidly, the group formed a 501(c)3 and began raising money.

"After the election of Donald Trump, we saw an uptick in the number of Facebook groups and online activists who were very well-meaning but were giving very bad advice," said Sarah Dohl, another of Doggett's staffers and a co-author of the Indivisible Guide.

"People were being urged to do things like call House Speaker Paul Ryan (R–WI) or to sign an online petition. Unless you live in the 1st District of Wisconsin, Paul Ryan doesn't work for you, and he does not care what you have to say," she stressed, adding that knowing how to protest effectively is very important to eventual success.

The guide explains that calling one's own Members of Congress (MoC) is one of the key strategies moving forward. It reminds concerned voters that their representatives' primary concern is getting re-elected, which gives voters control over the conversation. "MoCs want their constituents to think well of them and they want good local press. They hate surprises, wasted time and most of all, bad press that makes them look weak, unlikable and vulnerable."

Indivisible is modeled after the Tea Party Movement, which focused on local activism as a means for obstructing the Democratic Party agenda following Barack Obama's election. The authors believed the same strategies used by the conservative Tea Party could be adopted by progressives to target Republicans members of Congress and stonewall what they viewed as Trump's "bigoted and anti-democratic agenda." Their plan called for resisters to attend Republican town hall meetings, call and visit congressional offices and show up at their public events.

Republican MoC's, particularly those who had been shouted down at town hall meetings in their districts, accused Indivisible members of being "paid protesters" working for Hungarian-American investor, business magnate, philanthropist, author and billionaire George Soros. While Soros has been known to meddle in American politics, there was never any solid evidence that he was funding protestors—but the Republicans had to blame somebody.

Since its original publication, Indivisible's authors have expanded the website to include further resources and ideas for organizing local movements. The guide, which is updated regularly, and is available in English and Spanish, has become the bible for the women's political action movement. "We don't think that we're the leaders in this movement," Dohl says. "We really think it's the folks on the ground who are meeting in living rooms and auditoriums and libraries across the country, and really getting out and hitting the pavement to visit their members of Congress' office."

In August 2017, plans for another women's march were announced. The details were to be worked out through conference calls and a meeting in October 2017, in Detroit. Meanwhile, Indivisible has grown to include two or more groups in every congressional district in the country. The organization uses social media to communicate with members.

The birth of a new women's political movement, born out of women's heartfelt desire to "do something" to resist the Trump presidency, wasn't at the forefront of most women's thinking when they decided to join the January 21, 2017, Women's March immediately following the inauguration. That an organized, purposeful movement has emerged, and included both men and women, has been an unanticipated, very positive result.

In her essay "The Resonance of Resistance," University of Maine student Ashley Goff describes her decision to travel 600 miles to Washington, D.C., in the dead of a northeastern winter, to engage in a political protest for the first time in her life. Encouraged by her soon-to-be mother-in-law, who agreed to attend the march with her, she encountered a crowd larger than half the entire population of her home state, all gathered in one place. The experience changed her in ways she never anticipated.

Alexandria Cunningham, a traumatic brain injury survivor, explains why participating in the January women's march was so important to her, and what the effort took from her in both physical and emotional terms. Her essay, "January 21, 2017: Marching in a Wheelchair," bears testimony to the commitment women have to defending their rights against the assaults the Trump administration promises to deliver.

Living in a remote rural area, essayist Patti Herman describes how she decided to push back against the Trump administration. "When the Whole World Is Silent, Even One Voice Becomes Powerful" is a statement of systematic resistance in circumstances where huge crowd support is unavailable yet individual commitment is strong.

NOTE

1. www.indivisible.org

The Resonance of Resistance

Ashley Goff

Knees locked up. Sore and stiff in all the wrong places. Nervous anticipation fooling my mind into believing I am any sort of well rested. I am ready for this. I cannot control the experience I am about to have, but I will embrace all of the elements I feel. Letting go, I step off the bus onto the cold, wet pavement at Robert F. Kennedy Memorial Stadium in Washington, D.C. *You ready?*

Do not be fooled by reading this. I am not a special snowflake, committed to building a better nation for all and becoming that one female who breaks that glass ceiling. I wish I did more for my community. I wish that I had more time to contribute to the resistance and to lift my fellow peers up. Still, I try to make time. I take opportunities to tell my story and to inspire others who may have never gone to a protest. I want to give them the confidence to march that I didn't have when I did it.

I did not know who I would be by the end of that weekend in January. I will tell you however, that at the end of this story, I felt my soul on fire. I felt a confidence no 5'1" white girl from Maine has ever felt before. *Spoiler alert.*

Have you ever been in an *almost* head-on collision? You somehow swerve in time and you don't get totally obliterated by that douche bag in the big black truck. Your heart, stomach, and one kidney jump into your throat and you lose your breath. Then you breathe it all out. Maybe pull over, collect yourself, and give a little thanks to fate. That is not how I felt November 9 at 1:00 a.m. I got hit by that douchebag in the big black truck, with a "Make America Great Again" sticker on the back. The glass smashed in my protected little world and landed in my hair, clothes, and lap, lacerating my heart. I received the worst whiplash imaginable, and all of the air went out of my lungs. I was horrified and honestly bruised in my soul. *Wait, no, this isn't really happening? Is it...?*

I tried to sleep the morning after the election, but I couldn't. I slept for maybe 30–45 minutes at a time and then woke up again. Constantly checking Facebook, news websites, CNN, *The New York Times*, and they all read that same dreaded name. And no, his name is not worthy of my fingers on my keyboard. The comments said things like: *How do I tell my child that the bad guy won? How is this possible? She had more votes! He is a sexist, racist, horrifying person....* "An American Tragedy" is what *The New Yorker* penned the morning after. *Where's the pill to make this go away?*

By November 9 I had been awake for so many hours, I decided to sweat out the poison. The morning after I went to Fityoga, which is run by Ramona, at 6 a.m. I hadn't gone in a few weeks, I was not sleeping well and getting up so early on the days I could sleep in was a rough choice. That morning, I was furious. I was heartbroken. I felt like I was just dumped by the same asshole that I went running back to three times before. I was hurt and wanted to push out that feeling of negativity somehow. We always end the quick 50-minute workout with bowing our third eye and thanking ourselves for giving ourselves love and thanking ourselves for working hard so early in the morning. I was not ready for what came next—the realization that no matter how hard I sweat, no matter how hard I cry, the future is still the same. Ramona said that we must look for the light in this darkness, look for the joy, seek it, and embrace it. *That morning we felt nothing but sorrow. But we were together.*

I did not have to go to work until 11:30, but this Wednesday morning was one of the longest mornings of my life. I read too much on the Internet. I wallowed. I cried. I was full of hatred still. I closed the laptop and thought about how the kids were going to be that day at work.

I am a preschool teacher, and the kids I am lucky enough to work with are incredibly smart individuals with inspirational, amazing parents. I knew that, for the children, the world would not be changing in the same way it was for some others. I knew that I could take the time to be angry, to feel the emotions that I felt at that moment, because that is what I try to bestow on my own students. Accept your emotions, but don't let them run who you are. You can feel angry, but don't let anger feed your actions. I had to find the joy. Push away the worries and fears for now. I wrote that morning, "Today I grieve, but today I will also work tirelessly to show the importance of acceptance, empathy, and lifting up those who may be powerless and disenfranchised. Love trumps hate, always." *Time to rise above.*

Loving your job is not a common feeling among people; a lot of people can't stand their jobs. Just waiting to go home, hope that you earned enough money to feed yourself and the others in your care. I know that my job is hard at times, but I am lucky enough to feel joy everyday working with these preschoolers and my fellow teachers. When I pulled into the driveway that Wednesday morning the first thing I saw, hanging on the gate to the school, was a sign. *This Is an Election-free Zone, Peopleplace = Joy.*

Parents seemed to want to pick up their kids a little earlier on that day. Just wanting to protect them that much more the day after the election. What future can we guarantee for them? Is there anything within our grasp anymore? As an educator, I fear my students accepting anything other than what their wildest dreams are. However, the new man in charge in Washington is a raving lunatic, quick to make hurtful decisions and to judge others. Is this who my students are supposed to look up to? Is this the America we are raising our children in?

It's only four years; chances are he is going to be impeached soon after election. In the meantime, what will happen to our education system? What will happen to our immigrant friends and families, the ones that deserve to be here just as much as anyone else? Take it day by day I tell myself. I ask the parents how they are doing? Their answers are some version of, *doing the best we can be. That's all we can do.*

Weeks later, I'm still wondering, what I can do? It's a dreary December, not a lot of snow so far. Then I start to see it everywhere online. January 21, 2017, the Women's March on Washington. Like an actual protest? The day after the inauguration? Is this the beacon? Is this what I need to do? I've never done anything like this before. It is not long before people start to set up bus locations to go down to D.C. Is this a safe choice? What about all the rioting that is going on around the country? I begin to think this is time to not be scared anymore, the worst has already happened. *Time to rise-up.*

"So, I heard about this protest that's going to happen. I'm wondering if you would want to go with me?" Sarah, my soon-to-be mother-in-law, looks at me. *Well, that could be fun!* I thought. I knew that I would want someone to be there with me, to help if something were to go wrong. I also really wanted to have this experience with her, because she, too, was saddened and furious by the outcome. She was looking for a way to speak up and rise-up too. Only later did I realize that she would be such an incredible piece to this trip, not only for me, but for everyone on the bus. Handing out Kind pins, wanting to create a quilt to represent the journey we would be going on, and being so supportive of everyone's journey.

And then the day of the march finally arrived. I double checked the belongings, put another layer on, jeans over leggings, and took a group photo in front of the bus. Blaze orange was the color to represent Maine. We broke off into little groups, knowing that there were going to be at least 200,000 people there. It was important to stay together. As we started walking from the bus, I felt this sensation that the credits were about to roll. That I was about to wake up and not get to know what happened to the group of travelers. I have this same feeling as soon as the lights go dark right before the band comes on stage or right before we go on a long car ride. I worry about missing the story. This time I was part of that story. I just didn't know what story I was walking into.

I knew that there were going to be thousands of people here, absolutely hundreds of thousands. There could probably be more than Obama's inauguration. How prepared would I be to be surrounded by so many people? I have been to concerts, stuck in the middle of a punk-rock show like a sardine, but this was political.

Be careful, call me when you get there, and take lots of photos. My fiancé, who wanted to come with me, knew that this was a movement for me to experience, plus I was going with his mother. Instead, he was home, watching the news stories flood the television.

Before leaving for this march, I participated in de-escalation training offered by the two women who organized our group to leave from Rockport, Maine, Ramona and Alix. We learned how to defend ourselves and de-escalate with words and a strong stance, not physical violence or swearing. "I do not need to engage with you. And I will not apologize." There is that fear of people trying to hurt others trembling inside. *Please don't riot. Please march peacefully.* I get a text from my fiancé: "dude, there's a shit ton of people there. Be Careful! Love you!"

Isn't it funny how people tend to roam together? Following where crowds go like sheep, joining a random long line just to see what everyone is waiting for. I walk beside my dear mother-in-law, Sarah, who used to live and work in D.C. I am so happy to follow her like the little Bambi that I am in the big confusing city. She is happily explaining to anybody who asks which way to go or how the streets were lined up. To her it all makes sense. The further we walk along, the more people seem to flow right along with us. As we walk along the cobblestone houses and walkways, people stand in their yards waving hello with their little kids, waving people in to use their bathroom. Such kindness. They treat us like we are all on a special mission, offering food and love. We continue to walk up the historic streets, soon there isn't even room for cars to go through. The people driving are not even furious; they let masses of people go by, waving and smiling. *Wait ... everyone really seems happy that we are here. And they are all wearing pink pussy hats.*

That feeling, when your purpose shifts, when you become inspired to keep going, and any feeling of failure escapes your mind took over. All I see is the capitol building straight ahead; we walk down the visitor path. Every person I see is smiling ear to ear, people are taking photos of everyone's signs, we join together and take a group photo knowing that this is a triumphant feeling, marching on the capitol. One sign reads, "Why are you so obsessed with my uterus?"

The flow of people felt like a busy supermarket an hour before dinner time, when we all plan to eat, but might not have an exact idea of what we need to get to eat. I hear someone talking on a P.A. system somewhere off in the distance, but I can't make it out. Are we close to the presenters? I feel so excited to be here, that worry of violence or angry protestors is fading quickly. I can see from the people I am surrounded by that we all just want to send a message. We walk around the other side of the capitol, headed down towards the National Mall. Try and imagine that feeling you get when you see the love of your life, your child smile and say they love you, or your favorite Ben and Jerry's is on sale. Coming around that corner was true euphoria. I thought there were a lot of people before, but now I gasp because I can only see a flood of people and signs up ahead, wrapping their way around buildings like a cozy blanket. I hear the start of a chant along to a beat: "show me what democracy looks like! This is what democracy looks like!"

Our footsteps resonate throughout all the beautiful streets and I know that that this is one of those days that I will remember forever. My body is feeling better, the 13–hour bus ride stiffness is fading away. We walk behind a bigger group of people; I take a photo of their pussy hats, so amazed that this is our symbol. We walk down a beautiful alleyway to check out my mother-in-law's old house that she lived in more than 20 years ago. We stop and take pictures, in such tourist style. We walk out of the alley, and can't believe my eyes. The flowing river of people coming from every direction is awesome. I try to read their signs as we start to walk along with the mass of various pink-hatted people. Such incredible artistry. Powerful messages. I hear people playing drums off in the distance. We come closer and closer, and then I see it. The capitol, and the largest group of people I have ever seen. *We are here.*

When walking turns into marching a powerful feeling overtakes you. I highly recommend it. How quickly the group of people around you becomes so much closer, we all instantly take each other's hands to stick together. We are walking towards the National Mall, where we believe the presentations are and where we are supposed to start marching. The drumming becomes louder. The pace of movement slows down. I feel like a child just following the leader, I want to open my eyes even wider than they are, just trying to read all of the different messages. I am trying to look at all of the different faces of the people around me. *He has tiny hands! Act justly, love mercy, walk humbly.*

One young man climbed onto a street pole, 3rd Street SW, holding up a sign, "Women's rights are under attack. What do we do? Stand up! Fight Back!" It was really inspiring to see men standing up for women. They want to take away our reproductive rights; I then see a sign that says, "We will never go back" with coat hangers attached underneath. So powerful. I look to my right as a young group of teens marches by. They are furious that they did not get a say in the outcome of this election, but will be adults living in the outcome. My eyes start to well up because I am furious for them as well. They are intelligent young women and are fearful for their future as well. They chant, "We did not get a vote, but you will hear us roar!"

Because we all have been awake since 4 a.m., it feels much later than it is. One of the members of our group is in a wheelchair and we aren't sure which way the flow of the crowd is going, but we are in the thick of it and there is no way out now. The kindness people showed, letting us by without hesitation is incredible. People shouting to us, "Hey, Mainers! We are from Maine too!"

It was like being part of the biggest block party. Everyone was so happy to be there. I felt so safe; everyone gives each other their own little space bubble on the National Mall. We are all hearing different chants coming by in waves through the crowd, like we are breaking some sort of sound barrier with our voices. "We want a leader, not a creepy tweeter!" was one that makes me laugh. The cold starts to sink in more since we are not moving as much. Trying to shake it away, knowing that we haven't even started marching yet. I can hear the speakers pushing the sound of justice and support of the movement come over the crowd. The most incredible feeling is hearing the sound of cheers start far away and then naturally make it's way over to us. We start cheering, not entirely sure for what, but we want to keep the excitement alive. It is close to 2 p.m. now; we begin walking down the national mall towards the National Monument. Tired yet still buzzing, I feel engulfed by the beauty around me. I can see the peak of the monument proudly standing through the fog. *She's a beautiful beacon of hope.*

Even though I do not hear any of the presenters speak, I hear the voices of the people around me. The chants, the power in the people joining together was truly enlightening. The power of lifting each other up is immeasurable. I am afraid to speak up and join them, but I surprise myself and burst out, "This is what democracy looks like!" The girl with the loud speaker, her voice breaking, pushes through, and it sounds like an uprising of warriors. The strongest women defending the rights of every woman because that is what we need to do.

We marched for each other. I marched for all my fellow women, my students, and their futures. I marched for my future children and the world I want them to live in. I marched for the women who face more oppression, racism, and sexism than I face because their issues are important to me as well. I marched for myself. I marched to show that I can support my own rights. And I will do it again. We walked on towards the White House.... *Oh no I won't keep quiet ... no more.*

January 21, 2017

Marching in a Wheelchair

Alexandria A. Cunningham

During the last semester of my undergraduate studies, an accident occurred that altered the trajectory of my life. A constant and intractable migraine secondary to a traumatic brain injury (TBI) invaded my body. Left with a host of debilitating neurological symptoms, my condition forced me to adapt. On the infrequent occasions when I am physically capable of bathing, a shower chair keeps me upright. Heavy shades drape over every window in my home to block out intrusive and painful sunlight. The crinkling sound emanating from a bag of chips and the click clacks of a keyboard rapidly drive my pain levels to astronomical levels. Unsteady on my feet, I use a walker or a wheelchair to compensate for my issues with balance and stamina. Scraps of paper with notes to myself that I cannot recall writing litter my home. Physically and emotionally, my sense of self continues to evolve each day.

Prior to sustaining my first TBI, my heart overflowed with passion. Philosophy was my subject of choice, and every day I experienced a new and enamoring text. To single out just one subset of Philosophy and deem it my favorite proves nearly impossible. The wonder of Philosophy is that it intersects with so many other disciplines, allowing me to explore areas of thought I would not have otherwise encountered. Perhaps my broad set of interests is what attracted me to a more inclusive and intersectional style of feminism. A feminist standpoint provides a lens through which I evaluate many texts, decisions, and actions; I even planned to pursue a PhD in Philosophy specializing in social theory and feminist thought. While that dream currently exists in a state of suspension, life as a disabled individual enables me to reconsider my views regarding social justice and the intricacies of my feminist identity enlightened by a new set of lived experiences.

Pre-injury, I loved marching in the streets. My first major encounter with the "in the streets" world of social justice was a protest I helped organize during my senior year of high school. Because I grew up in a tiny town housing merely 800 people and located in southern Illinois, a sense of adventure and novelty accompanied this organized resistance. Incidentally, I also skipped class for the very first time to attend the demonstration. The Westboro Baptist Church (WBC) invaded Troy, a town within my school district, to protest the funeral of Senior Airman Bradley Smith. While I did not personally know Senior Airman Smith, I was quite aware that the WBC had earned a nasty reputation. No family deserves to endure the hatred that the WBC preached, so we organized. I spoke with friends and other students about the events happening in our community, and I found another group of students determined to counteract the efforts of the WBC. We joined together, secured our permits, and hosted a counter protest in Senior Airman Smith's honor. A few friends and I continued following the WBC for the rest of the day as they made their regional rounds, and I think this could be described as the day I fell in love with activism.

My love of activism flourished further during my years in college where I was both surrounded by and marching beside lovely people with different life experiences than my own. Individuals who were well versed in social and feminist theory befriended me, and at every opportunity afforded to them, they kindly blew my mind. My world glowed brighter because of the academic and life experiences these people shared with me. The most generous gift any of them ever bequeathed to me, though, was gently calling me out when it was necessary. Informing a friend that behind one of her statements some incredibly problematic ideas lie lurking comes as no easy feat. No one bore the obligation to educate me about my own privilege, flaws, and ruptured thinking, yet at the risk of rejection or ridicule, they corrected me. No word possesses the capability to express how grateful I am for their bravery and benevolence.

Without constructive criticism from people housing a different set of experiences than my own, my views of myself and activism would be too narrow to truly assist anyone but myself or individuals with nearly identical intersections to my own. This type of activism fails to represent the inclusive and just activism we should all be striving toward. At a time when the civil rights of all people are jeopardized, activists have an obligation to defend all rights, not their rights alone. We must give credence to marginalized communities and amplify their lived experiences rather than simply magnifying our own; failing to do so results in marginalized experiences being drowned out by the very people proclaiming to help. Just as our privilege lies within the questions we are never required to ask ourselves, exclusion occurs when we fail to consider the questions others must ask themselves. Simone de Beauvoir argued that one cannot be free while others are oppressed. In order to access this genuine freedom we must be attentive, and we must tweak the lens through which we view activism at a fundamental level. By failing to consider the struggles that marginalized groups face, some current notions of how one qualifies as a "true activist" can work to exclude rather than include individuals who are already oppressed. One of my worst fears is that activism will continue failing to serve marginalized communities. As a disabled woman, I now realize that even the manner in which we tend to conceptualize activism as an abstract concept works to exclude rather than include many disabled people.

When people explain what activists do, they often depict an individual with a sign and a megaphone out in the streets with other like-minded people fighting for a cause. It is easy to conjure up images of or describe young people handing roses to police officers, activists being dragged away by authority figures while passively resisting, and people using riot shields as a mirror to perfect their pout. Many passionate young people present with a tendency to romanticize the "out in the streets" work that activists perform. When most look over the course of history, they cling to iconic figures and gravitate toward moments that are retroactively deemed to define a movement. While this approach certainly has appeal and the ability to inspire others to become politically autonomous and motivated beings, it can also be egregiously and erroneously exclusive.

When we focus on the big moments, we miss all the small details that allowed that moment to occur. We assign the success of a movement to only those and those alone who are capable of swarming into the streets. We think not of all the phone calls people make to their representatives or the heart-felt letters that rouse deeply emotional responses from those with power. We ignore the thousands of small actions of everyday people that quietly chip away at the culture we live in and silently pave the way for real change to occur. The true problem is found in the fact that we have a distinction between the actions of activists and everyday people in the first place.

I used to be an in the streets activist. I lived for the moments that I could spend in service to good causes. I thought that the most effective way to usher in change was rooted in dramatic and romantic gestures. Surely a large group of people gathering together and demanding that their view be considered is the pinnacle of any movement, right? How many people we can gather in the streets is definitely the best way to gauge our success, yes?

The answer to the former question is a hard no. In The Streets Activist Alex was not only incorrect, but she was unintentionally excluding and hurting people with that line of thinking. Today, at the ripe old age of 25, I identify as more of an In the Sheets Activist Alex. I promise, this is far less sexy than one might initially assume. Because of my disability, I now pass more time in bed or on the couch than ever before. Intense and unrelenting pain, nausea, vomiting, photophobia, phonophobia, depression, anxiety, and balance issues comprise only a portion of the symptoms I deal with on constant or daily basis. Composing this essay is something I am required to accomplish in short bursts with many breaks, and even given those accommodations the process is increasingly painful and aggravating to my body.

However, this serves as precisely the reason that I write. I need my "in the streets" activist friends to know that I am happily enduring a great burden even when I am incapable of being physically present with them. More importantly, I need my fellow "in the sheets" activists to know that their actions and efforts are not only enough but are imperative if we desire our movement to flourish and succeed. "In the streets" and "in the sheets" activists might be engaging the movement in vastly different ways, but neither is more crucial than the other. The difference is that the "in the sheets" activists remain invisible while the spotlight shines brightly in the streets. "In the sheets" activists are accomplishing those thousands of small actions like phone calls, letters, engaging in political discussions online, or creating and sharing politically themed art, that we tend to forget.

Since the onset of my first injury, I have struggled immensely with this idea that purports that the "in the streets" model represents the highest form of activism. Rather than passion, my heart often overflows with grief and guilt. A kind of emotional paralysis has all too frequently washed over me, leading me to think that my purpose in life remains not only unfulfilled, but is impossible to fulfill because of my disability. I have often convinced myself that because I am unable to engage politically the way I once could my efforts remain futile. I imagine myself as trapped inside a statue, unable to move. Unable to effectively communicate my concerns. Surrounded by stone, immobilized. My only choice is to watch silently as acid rain erodes my very being.

One day I realized that disability should never force anyone emotionally into this statue-like state. The guilt that overwhelmed me stemmed not from a personal failing on my part, but rather represented the result of adherence to an ableist view of activism. Much of the "in the streets" activism remains inaccessible to disabled individuals. Activists taking the lead on large rallies are often incapable of providing an answer as to whether an event will be wheel-chair accessible, and without an answer in the affirmative to this question, as a roller I am unable to consider attending. Marches require a certain amount of physical stamina, the ability to comfortably find oneself surrounded by a large crowd, and a high tolerance for noise. Sit-ins require a person to be physically capable of standing, sitting, or lying down in the designated environment. While enduring the fumes of tear gas or being placed under arrest is not healthy or convenient for anyone, the experience is quite different for someone who is disabled (or undocumented or beyond the gender binary or a person of color or any other marginalized demographic, for that matter). As a TBI survivor, a small knock to the head that would fail to register for most could have quite devastating consequences concerning my current and future health. Behind bars, a refusal to provide me with my appropriate medications would come as no surprise. If teargas was to be unleashed and panic ensued, I could easily be knocked down, fall out of my wheel chair, and find myself trampled.

These concerns and more clawed at the forefront of my partner/caregiver's mind when I expressed an interest in attending the Women's March in our city. Ultimately, we decided to attend. While we prepared to the best of our ability to account for every variable and the march occurred without incident, I was physically wrecked following the dissipation of the post-protest elation. My neurological symptoms, including outrageous pain and nausea, spiked rapidly. Because of my disability, I am unable to perform many simple self-care tasks even on a good day. Welcoming newly elected President Trump to the Oval Office with resistance meant the world to me, but attending was beyond reckless. My physical condition was not gravely affected for a few hours, but rather for the entire week following the event, and this denotes the best-case scenario for someone in my situation. An event that is a literal walk in the park to you would likely consume my physical and mental well being for days or even weeks.

If we desire our movement to be successful, we need to start valuing the work of the "in the sheets" activists and the activists who are not able, for any reason, to put their boots or wheels on the ground. When individuals are discouraged and sure that their contributions constitute nothing more than a minor boost to the cause, they terminate their participation. "In the streets" activists cannot be effective without "in the sheets" activists, so a failure to recognize the efforts of all activists, not just our romanticized version, is certain to be detrimental to the movement as a whole. Disabled people like myself often think that since we are unable to attend big rallies, we are not needed. We do not matter. We are not as good or as pure or as deserving or as essential. We actually embody each of those traits, and the effects that political decisions can have upon disabled individuals tower over us, causing us to feel helpless and accept a lack of political efficacy as our norm. To all my wonderful in the streets activist counterparts, please remember that beside each one of you exists someone in the sheets who cares just as much as you do and is, in all ways possible for them, working as bravely as and passionately as you are.

When the Whole World
Is Silent, Even One Voice
Becomes Powerful

Patti Herman

The early hours of November 9, 2016, found me wrapped in a blanket on my couch, listening in disbelief as the election results were confirmed. I remember shaking uncontrollably, feeling physically and emotionally overwhelmed by the news. For weeks afterwards I created a scenario in my mind in which the election results were overturned and the world worked its way back to some semblance of normalcy. It was the only thing I could do at that point to retain some sense of hope for the future.

As weeks turned into months and it appeared that the changed scenario I was envisioning was not going to happen, I had to figure out how I was going to go forward. How would I resist the situation that our country was in while maintaining my physical, emotional and spiritual equilibrium? How would I live my life in a way that was positive and not let myself get pulled down by the divisiveness that our country was experiencing? One thing I knew for sure: I was not going to allow Trump and the Republican administration to live in my head and dictate my wellbeing. I had to develop a resistance strategy that did not consume my every waking hour while also making me believe that my actions were making a difference.

Some of my friends made the decision to disconnect from the news altogether and disengage from any resistance. While that wasn't the right approach for me, I understood that they were overwhelmed and needed to retreat in order to maintain their overall health. Others made the decision to vilify anyone who supported the Republican administration, which often led to fractured friendships and contributed to further divisions. That didn't seem the route for me because I saw it as allowing the current administration to insert themselves into my relationships with others and I was not going to give them that power.

I chose to take a stand for resistance through two main actions. First, I found opportunities to be with others who were engaged in peaceful resistance through such events as the Women's March and the Science March. Participating in these gatherings reminded me that I was part of something bigger than myself and restored my hope for a different future. As I looked at the masses of people that surrounded me I was flooded with emotion, thinking about the connection we all had with one another. With so many people united to restore our country to its better self we had to be able to make a difference. These gatherings were the shot in the arm that I needed to keep up my resistance. I'll continue to look for more opportunities to gather with other like-minded people as we go forward.

The second action I decided on was to commit one morning a week to communicating with my elected representatives through phone calls and emails and, when possible, face-to-face meetings. I wasn't new to this strategy, having communicated with elected officials in the past on issues that were important to me. However, I find that this action is similar to my writing practice: I need to discipline myself to do it on a regular basis in order to make it part of who I am. I knew that only by embracing it in this way—as something that defines who I am—would I continue this particular resistance strategy over time. And, despite my earlier fantasies of a cataclysmic happening that would reverse the outcome of the November election, I realized that this current mockery of a democratic government is not going to be short-lived and I have to commit to resistance for the long-term.

I've been intentional in telling other people about my two resistance action strategies, even though at times it feels uncomfortably like self-promotion. I tell others about my actions because I want to help people see that these are strategies that anybody can use if they so choose and there are resources out there to help them. People who have never contacted their elected officials may feel like they don't know how to do this and need to know that there are research-based websites that provide tools for this purpose. They also need to keep their expectations for their own involvement at a level that is manageable for them; if they expect too much of themselves they will be overwhelmed and give up. Likewise, people who have never joined a resistance march need to know that they can be part of these events in whatever way they are comfortable, whether it's walking quietly as part of the group or carrying a sign and shouting slogans. They need to understand that it's the act of showing up that matters.

And that leads me to the question that I often get from people when I tell them about my resistance actions: do you think the things you're doing really make a difference? My answer is that I do believe it's making a difference, both on a public and on a personal level.

Sometimes it's difficult to think that my phone calls or emails are having any influence at a public level when I see some of my elected officials consistently voting on legislation in lock step with their party line. This seems to happen despite what I believe are many, many contacts from constituents who are urging legislators to take a thoughtful look at what is being proposed and make a decision that serves the people they are supposed to represent, rather than serving the party. However, even though it may not appear that my communications are influencing the votes by some of the Republican legislators from my state, I am encouraged when I see legislators in other states who are taking a stand against legislation that they see as not being in the public interest, even though their party supports that legislation. Maybe the voices of resisters helped them come to this belief and maybe it was something else, but it gives me hope when I see any elected officials casting a vote that goes against what their party has dictated. And it inspires me to continue to contact my legislators and share my thoughts in the belief that my voice, combined with all the other voices of resistance, will get through to them and make them think about the effect of their actions on the people.

I also believe that legislators can't help but be impacted by seeing thousands (and hundreds of thousands) of people coming together peacefully to send a message, whether that message is related to respect for women, respect for science, or any other issue. Some elected officials have issued public statements that accuse people engaged in peaceful demonstrations of being radicals. However, I'm willing to bet that, if they're honest with themselves, those elected officials know at least one person who they would define as being a person deserving of their respect who has taken part in peaceful resistance gatherings. Dismissing the actions of an entire group of people becomes more difficult when you have a personal connection to even one of those people.

I know without a doubt that my resistance actions are making a difference on a personal level. We are living in a time when there are new revelations every day about things that the Republican administration is doing to diminish our quality of life—assaults on basic human rights, health care, the environment, the arts, education, and on and on. It would be easy to feel powerless and succumb to despair. But I believe that I am a person who has value, no less and no more than any other person, and that my value brings with it a degree of power that gives me the right and the responsibility to make my voice heard. Malala Yousafzai, a Pakistani woman and an activist, put it this way: "When the whole world is silent, even one voice becomes powerful."[1] I believe that if we stay silent we give over our power to voices that are not speaking in the best interests of large numbers of people in our country…. And I am not willing to be complicit in allowing that to happen. By engaging in resistance actions and being one voice among many, I stoke my own internal fire that keeps me involved in this important work.

I started this essay by describing my feelings of being physically and emotionally overwhelmed on election eve. There are times when I still feel that way, nights when I lie awake and fear for our country's future. I do what I can to get through those times and then I look for the next opportunity to engage in resistance. I truly believe that we can—we must—do this in order to take back our country.

NOTE

1. Malala Yousafzai (with Christina Lamb), *I Am Malala: The Girl Who Stood Up for Education and Was Shot by the Taliban* (New York: Little, Brown, 2013).

SECTION 3. THE RIGHT TO PROTEST
Warhorse Activists Report for Duty—Again

PAULA VW. DÁIL

I am no longer accepting the things I cannot change. I am changing the things I cannot accept.—Angela Davis

America in the 1960s, particularly after the assassination of President John F. Kennedy, was a deeply divided nation. When Vice President Lyndon B. Johnson assumed the presidency following Kennedy's death, he inherited growing political unrest on several fronts—civil rights, Vietnam, and an emerging new feminist movement, among others. It was a "pick your protest" era, and the choices were as varied as the population itself.

The 1960s second-wave feminist movement, under Betty Friedan and Bella Abzug's capable leadership, was relentless in its efforts to free women from the dominant patriarchy and move them forward into the public sphere. Women activists fought long, and they fought hard for what they believed was their due. Ultimately, they won some major victories.

The U.S. Supreme Court had upheld *Roe v. Wade*, legalizing abortion and awarding women control over their reproductive rights, and therefore their lives. They gained some ground on equal pay for equal work, and legal protections in divorce and abuse situations, but not enough.

In terms of legal protections for women, they made the most headway with the landmark civil rights legislation, which included women in its definition of "minority." Both white and non-women viewed this a mixed blessing: it provided them with new opportunities and opened previously closed doors, but did not afford them truly equal status with white males, which was their goal.

Meanwhile, the Civil Rights Movement set out to claim the rights African American citizens were entitled to, and which, despite emancipation nearly 100 years previously, had remained politically and socially inaccessible. The sweeping 1965 Civil Rights legislation crafted by the Johnson administration declared discrimination on the basis of both race and gender illegal. This guaranteed equal opportunity for women and blacks in employment, education, sports and any other enterprise that accepted federal dollars.

The African American community was no longer automatically sentenced to a lifetime in the back of the bus, biology was no longer automatically a woman's destiny and pregnant housewife was not her only career choice. This was a landmark victory for minorities all across America.

The second-wave feminist movement faded out with the failure to pass the Equal Rights Amendment to the U.S. Constitution. Nevertheless, the 1960s changed women's lives in some important, deeply personal ways. They took Simone de Beauvior's words, "one is not born a woman, one becomes one," to heart, and began to realize that they could define their lives for themselves. This was the last well-organized political movement focused on women's rights, until Donald Trump showed up on the national political stage.

The idea of Donald Trump as America's next president horrified millions of women, particularly those who had been active in the 1960s social protests. These were the women who didn't think Trump could possibly succeed because they believed America had moved beyond the misogynistic rhetoric and insults toward women that Trump so freely expressed. Most were deeply discouraged to discover how wrong they were.

The women who had helped win the earlier battles over women's rights, civil rights, and against an unpopular war were tired and didn't really want to take on Donald Trump or another political cause. Most had happily retired from social activism and moved on to other pursuits and weren't interested in signing up for the hard, difficult, energy-draining and frustrating work of political protest. They'd already done their part and had earned a quiet, leisurely retirement from public activism.

Admittedly, they worried that the next generation would take for granted all that they had inherited as a result of their grandmother's efforts, but knowing how hard and time-consuming political action is, the warhorse activists were willing to step aside and let the next generation fight their own battles, just as they'd fought theirs. Then, Donald Trump was elected president of the United States—and this was unacceptable.

The generation that had previously fought so hard for women's rights had daughters, granddaughters, and great-granddaughters whose futures were in jeopardy, and, suddenly, there was too much at stake to just sit this one out. From somewhere deep in their hearts, these women mustered the energy to come out of retirement and, once again, as they had done before, they took to the streets in an effort to prevent a backslide in women's rights that they had fought so strenuously to win earlier in their lives.

In her essay "I Can't Believe I Have to Protest This Shit Again," Milwaukee native Sandra J. Callaghan explains what her lifetime of social activism has cost her, and why she carries on anyway. For her, activism is a moral calling. Plainly, and simply, it is the right thing to do.

Rebecca Roth writes about why activism was important to her earlier in her life, why she answered the call in 2017 by "Putting on My Marching Shoes" albeit reluctantly, once again. While keenly aware of her limits today, more than fifty years after she first became involved in the 1960's protest movement, she stepped up anyway, because she believes her granddaughters' futures depend upon it.

In "Grandma, We Were Never the Mess," granddaughter Ahna Kruzic maps the intersection where generations of family and social expectations for women collide. She explains why the social battles women have had to fight over and over again are not their fault, not of their own making, and not easily fixed.

I Can't Believe I Have
to Protest This Shit Again

Sandra J. Callaghan

The morning after the November 2016 presidential election, my daughter Alicia warned me not to turn on the television news or read Facebook postings. She knew how upset I was that Donald Trump won the election. We were in shock. Both of us were filled with a foreboding sense of dread of what the next four to eight years of not just a Republican presidency, but a presidency held by a man already known to be a disrespectful womanizer, might mean for every marginalized citizen in our country. It was clear to me that our country's sociopolitical pendulum was going to swing to the far right. Again.

I've witnessed these swings several times nationally and locally. In my lifetime, the incremental gains of social justice, once enacted, had held. Until now. Almost every day when I read about a new assault on individual freedom coming out of Washington, I hear my daughter's voice saying to me in the late 1980s, when *Roe v. Wade* was being challenged, "Mom, you have to do something." Alicia is 44 years old now. She is a lesbian. I am afraid of how the attack on human rights might affect my daughter after I am gone. So, I am resisting, because:

- I am a divorced, almost 65-year-old white woman collecting Social Security and will soon be on Medicare. (Obviously it is extremely important to me that those programs are not cut.) In 2014, I was diagnosed with breast cancer and completed my treatments in 2015. I am a cancer survivor. My employer's health insurance program enabled me to get great care. That insurance also meant that I didn't lose my home. When my job was eliminated in January 2016, I was able to continue my health insurance coverage through COBRA—at a cost of $728/month that will carry me through to Medicare coverage. So, I've been keenly aware of the importance of affordable health care.
- I began working full-time immediately after graduating from high school in 1970. In 1971, I married for the first time. My family doctor wouldn't prescribe birth control because of his religious beliefs. Two weeks after I got married I became pregnant. My daughter, Alicia, was born when I was 20 and I divorced in 1973. I decided to have my child even though I wasn't prepared to be a mother at such a young age. But, I also knew that if I had decided not to have a child the laws prohibiting abortion wouldn't have stopped me.

- I continued to work full-time until my job was eliminated at the end of 2015. While working full-time I also raised my daughter Alicia and put myself through college and graduate school (attaining dissertator status in Urban Studies). I took advantage of student loans, which I paid back, and student loans are important to me.
- My three sisters and I (two older and one younger than me) grew up in a working-class household. Both my parents were strong union supporters and Democrats. My dad was a union factory worker who also worked a part-time night job as a union grocery store stocker for 25 years to provide for his family. My mother often worked part-time as a union grocery store clerk to help support the family. I have vivid memories of them discussing political candidates during presidential elections.

  I often wonder how Karen and Sherrie can hold such strong Republican beliefs having grown up in the same home I did. I can only attribute my sister's archaic beliefs to some lasting vestiges of our Catholic upbringing, having grown up in Milwaukee, a city known for its residential hyper-segregation, and the fact that my parents, like so many people of their generation, were bigots.

- I took different messages from my religious and bigoted upbringing than two of my sisters. I chose to stand up for the rights of others. Sometimes that meant standing toe-to-toe with a bully, like the time in grade school when I stopped some boys from picking on a young girl on the school playground. In high school, I shamed some kids on our school bus who were calling a foreign exchange student from Madagascar racist names and I sat beside him on the bus. A few years later I stopped a former brother-in-law from physically abusing my oldest sister, Kathy, when the entire family was out at a bar.
- Although my parents were prejudiced, both of them also told me that I could become anything I wanted. So, the message I got from them was that women deserve to be as independent as they want. Without knowing it at the time, I was on my way to becoming a feminist. In high school, I was elected to our student council, learning how to represent others.
- When I was the first one from our nuclear family to graduate from college my dad, who was in a hospital bed recovering from open-heart surgery, said, "I knew you could do it. I'm proud of you." My mom was thrilled. She was the one who encouraged me to enroll in our area's first full-time weekend college program when I was a full-time 25-year old working single mother.

  When I walked across the stage to get my diploma, the president of Alverno College, Sister Joel Read, said, "Wear your cap and gown and go see your father in the hospital." I did.

- During the late 1980s and early 1990s, while working, I was in a union and became a steward and then a unit vice chairwoman. I was simultaneously an elected member of a local school board and its president for three years. I experienced both sides of union negotiations. So, I learned how important unions are and how important and valuable quality public education is to our communities. I also learned a valuable lesson about how important it is to face your electors when something goes wrong and take responsibility for your decisions because I experienced firsthand the power of the collective voices of an angry electorate.
- Over the past 40-some years I have witnessed the loss of power of America's union workers as sector after sector has whittled away at union rights with an initial

strategy of offering older union workers the opportunity to keep their higher wages and benefits while offering younger/newer workers lower wages and benefits. Eventually, as workers aged out, the younger workers didn't enjoy the benefits of unions, often supporting right to work laws in their states.

In the late 1980s, when Alicia came home from school and told me that I had to do something to stop the potential threat to a woman's right to choose I was honestly honored to feel that she thought I was capable of doing something.

- In 1989, I flew to Washington, D.C., with my best friend and neighbor Karel to participate in the National Organization of Women's "March for Women's Lives." Before leaving for the march, I visited my mother to tell her what I was about to do. I wasn't sure how she would react. To my surprise, she teared up and thanked me, saying that she lost several friends to coat hanger abortions when she was younger.

Almost immediately after the presidential election I saw a Facebook posting that announced a women's march would be held in Washington, D.C., on January 21, 2017. I knew I would participate in the march in some way. A few days later another posting announced a supporting march was scheduled for the same day in my state's capital of Madison, Wisconsin. I accepted the invitation and joined two friends, Karel and Colleen, in the Madison Women's March. Other friends wanted to march too but their health issues prevented them from joining us.

All three of us are in our 60s, and volunteered to be marshals. When we arrived at 9:30 a.m. for the volunteer training, the organizers said they were expecting 5,000 to 10,000 people to join the march. That evening the Madison marchers were estimated at 100,000–125,000. I was proud to participate in an event that I hoped would send a message to all our elected officials that millions of us will oppose limiting the rights of all human beings.

During the event, I posted a few photos on Facebook of us participating in the march. Many of my friends and a few family members congratulated us and thanked us for our efforts. My oldest sister, Kathy, said she was really proud of me. Kathy is not political.

The following day, my other two sisters, Karen and Sherrie, posted a photo on Facebook of female soldiers with the caption, "Here are the real women who march and fight for our rights." I was shocked and deeply hurt because I perceived their shared postings as a personal insult. The photo insulted the millions of people, including myself, who joined in women's marches around the world.

As I thought about it, I wasn't surprised that Karen and Sherrie disagreed with my political views. Throughout the 2016 election process the two of them often posted information in support of Republican ideals. Out of respect for, and at the request of, a few Republican friends who asked that political postings be kept to a minimum during the election process I restrained myself and kept my political postings to a minimum. So, whenever Karen or Sherrie posted their political views, sometimes infuriating me, I ignored their postings. When Trump won the election, I decided I wouldn't keep quiet any longer. It has taken several months for us to begin talking to each other again.

My recent political activism is not the first time I've felt compelled to take action. In 1980, I ran for public office and was elected to a local board of education. (I was elected the board's president in 1985 and served on the board until 1991.) During my six-year service as a school board member I became much more acutely aware of, and knowledgeable about, the differences between Republicans and Democrats at the state and local level. It was during this time that Wisconsin voters elected Tommy Thompson, a conservative Republican who led the country in establishing the School Choice program. Our state's sociopolitical pendulum had swung once again to the far right.

Wisconsin's sociopolitical history is one of contrasts. Historically we elected several progressive governors and U.S. senators, the country's first lesbian U.S. senator Tammy Baldwin, and three socialist mayors in Milwaukee. We also elected Senator Joseph McCarthy, the Red Scare leader of the 1950s. (I was vaguely aware of the impact of the Red Scare—the belief that there was a communist growing under every rock—growing up when I was continually warned by my parents not to join political groups.) We also recently elected union-buster conservative Republican Governor Scott Walker and ultra conservative U.S. Senator Ron Johnson. The headquarters of the John Birch Society, a conservative advocacy group, is also located in Appleton, Wisconsin.

While in D.C. for the 1989 march, Karel and I visited the offices of our senators and our congresspersons to voice our support for women's rights. We still chuckle about the fact that our elected representatives assumed that because we were from Waukesha County, and because we dressed in business suits, that we were conservative Republicans. They were surprised when we let them know we supported abortion rights.

When we got home I wrote to all the state representatives of my school district and Governor Thompson telling them I supported a woman's right to choose and expected each of them to respond with their positions. Meanwhile, in conservative Waukesha County, one of the state senators embarrassed me at a Waukesha County Chamber of Commerce meeting by saying loudly, in the building's hallway where others were present, "Sandi, I got your letter about supporting abortion. I disagree with your pro-choice view."

I also received a letter at my place of employment, which was opened by a co-worker, from the Republican U.S. senator, thanking me for my visit to Washington and letting him know of my position on abortion. These two incidents made it clear to me that politicians can be quite underhanded when they are in positions of power and want to embarrass opponents.

My experiences with my Republican elected officials after the 1989 March for Women's Lives did not stop me from supporting women's rights. During the summer of 1993 another friend, Colleen, and I were Planned Parenthood clinic defenders, getting up every morning at 5:00 a.m. to join others in surrounding area clinics, endeavoring to keep them open to anyone wanting to get services at the clinics. Colleen and I were pro-choice organization captains, often standing between supporters and protesters to ensure violence didn't erupt.

Since the 2017 Women's March, I have continued to be active in political messaging by attending Affordable Health Care rallies, the March for Science, sending emails, letters, postcards and calling my elected officials—at the federal, state, and local levels. I've also sent donations to the Democratic Party (which I've never done before) and to Tammy Baldwin, the Democratic senator from Wisconsin. I also joined the American Civil Liberties Union and the Human Rights Campaign.

Over the course of my lifetime I've learned to value and appreciate the challenges so many of us face and to realize that people who are different from me—especially those of color—face dissimilar challenges and don't benefit from "white privilege" as I do. Part of my learning process was through formal education, while I was attaining my master's degree in Urban Affairs from the University of Wisconsin–Milwaukee. As a result of that higher education process my eyes were opened to the systematic enforcement of social structures keeping so many people, particularly people of color and women, in lower income levels. But I was also living in Waukesha County, Wisconsin's seat of the Republican Party, so I often faced opposition to my liberal views.

I was proud when we elected Barack Obama as our first African American president. I was happy when our country passed laws that punish perpetrators of hate crimes and gave same sex couples the right to marry. Because my daughter is a lesbian I am always worried that she might become a victim of someone else's ignorance and hate.

I am deeply concerned about the climate of anger that now seems to pervade our society. It is certainly troubling to me and I don't understand what is going on. I think my white privilege may be clouding my ability to understand. I only know that since the 2016 presidential election, for the first time in my life, I am generally afraid. It seems as if every day some new, bizarre announcement is coming out of D.C. that is an attempt to tighten the reigns of freedom.

I wish that at this point in my life I didn't have to take part in these marches. But, I am reminded of one of the signs I saw at the Women's March. It said, "I Can't Believe I Have to Protest This Shit Again." When someone does ask me why I'm participating in the resistance marches and activities I say, "It is my duty." I am resisting for my daughter, for myself, and for my friends.

I have no suggestions about how those of a socially liberal persuasion can reach across the seemingly strong divides to convince more individuals that the principles of our democracy must be protected so they can belong to everyone. I only know that *continued resistance* is essential to make sure our elected officials know that we are holding them accountable.

For me, it's no longer about Hillary. Nor is it the fact that a Republican was elected president. The reason I am so motivated to get involved in current political/social movements is because President Trump appears to me to promote social division and social oppression. I am doing my little bit in my corner of the country to show my support for the issues of importance to me. I feel like the efforts of social/political protestors who have been active since January 21, 2017, are having an impact. I hope we'll be able to hold the line.

Putting on My Marching Shoes

Rebecca Roth

"I'm putting on my marching shoes," I said to my granddaughter when I met up with her at a Dakota Access Pipeline protest. It was mid–November 2016 and still warm in Albuquerque as we gathered outside the Army Corps of Engineers headquarters. My granddaughter had made a sign I eventually co-opted because she had to get on with her life, school and kids and, as a retired person, I could stay. I had a feeling marching shoes would be needed eventually, but at that time I had no idea how much.

It seems I have been marching or standing on street corners with a sign for most of my life. The first time must've been around 1965, when I stood with a few other women holding a Ban the Bomb sign. That may have been my first protest against the Vietnam War, but it certainly was not the last.

Perhaps my largest anti-war demonstration was in June 1967 when, with my two young sons in a stroller, thousands of us gathered to march to the Century Plaza Hotel in New York City, where President Johnson was hosting a dinner. That one became violent when police on horseback descended upon us waving batons and hitting those who could not run away fast enough.

Many more times I put on my marching shoes and protested. "Hey, hey Pinochet, how many kids did you kill today?" Not long after, I joined the Sandinista Marching Band. By that time, I'd moved to Baltimore and could easily get to demonstrations in Washington, D.C. It seems like there was never a time without a cause, and I faithfully marched for them all.

So, it was with a familiar feeling that, in November 2016, I told my granddaughter that I was on my way. Did I feel rejuvenated or tired? Probably a little bit of both. I'm 77 years old and don't have as much energy or enthusiasm for political causes as in past years. But Donald Trump's election as president of the United States was a hard blow. For weeks afterwards, I would wake every morning and struggle to believe it all over again. Did this really happen? How can this be the reality I'm living in?

The days went by, and word went out about a women's march in Washington, D.C. Since I am now living in New Mexico, getting to the march would require a lot of effort. Nevertheless, as I realized that this movement began as the reality of the election results rolled over us, somehow it became important to me. Perhaps it was the lifeline needed to keep me busy, and somewhat sane, between November 8 and January 21. So, I joined an estimated half million or more women and went to Washington, D.C., energized by the marches all over the country and around the world.

I returned to Albuquerque to find a new movement had started. Indivisible, it is called, and it is fueled by a guide several former congressional staffers wrote. They had looked at the methods the Tea Party had used to do political action and worked with those to ideas to develop a guidebook for resisting the Trump administration. I learned that many Indivisible groups were forming all around the country. A good friend told me about Indivisible Duke City (Albuquerque's nickname) forming near my house.

Meetings began. Questions arose. We explored what we were most interested in among several categories of concern. I chose climate change and immigration. In just two weeks the immigration group was up and running!

By this time more demonstrations were happening. My friend and I went to a pro-immigration march at the Albuquerque Civic Plaza. We found many other enthusiastic, committed people carrying all kinds of signs. We decided signs were a great addition to our voices, and when the next demonstration took place at the University of New Mexico (UNM) and included a march, we were sign-ready!

The main idea for that march was health care, and I decided to focus on abortion rights. This is something I've been advocating for a long time. Even after the U.S. Supreme Court upheld Roe v. Wade in 1973, I found I was needed at abortion clinics to protect women who, in order to enter the clinics, had to pass through crowds of so-called religious people holding up large signs showing bloody body parts and screaming "Don't kill your baby." My sign for the UNM demonstration and march said "I Can't Believe I'm Protesting This Shit Again! Support Reproductive Freedom."

It has turned out that my marching days are far from over. I was unable to march on Tax Day due to surgery, but recovered quickly and attended the March for Science. Over 4000 people showed up in Albuquerque alone, and I was happy to join them. Next is the climate march, and I'm already busy making my sign.

I find that I'm not doing the things I vowed to do following the 2017 Women's March. I have stopped making phone calls to legislators, but remain involved with the people in my group focused on immigration issues.

Sadly, I have come face to face with my weaknesses. I am more of a dilettante than a worker. When cocktails parties were in vogue, I could discuss books and politics because of having read the reviews in the Village Voice. I was more hands-on with movies because I loved them and did not find it difficult to drive into Los Angeles to stand in line for an Andy Warhol film. Now, I keep up with politics by skimming newspapers and opinion pieces. I have always used my voice in support of progressive politics, but now am faced with a different situation—one that requires me to dig deeper. I know I need to get to work, but the work seems harder than ever before.

My Indivisible group has done a lot of work on immigration. We met with an immigration attorney and some of the group worked hard to put together an impressive Town Hall meeting. Not only did I not do any work on it, I couldn't attend. Nevertheless, I became informed on the issue.

Leaving no resistance stone unturned, I have joined a small group of women who get together once a month, at the start of the new moon, to perform a binding ceremony. "A what?" you ask. Well, we are bringing together the forces of the earth and sky to stop politicians from doing harm to people and the planet. The purpose is to "bind" them from harmful acts.

We bring photos of those we wish to bind and after calling on the spirits of the four directions (north, south east and west) to protect us, we burn the photos while calling upon the spirits to bind the person or person whose photo we are burning. We say words like "Bind these persons so that they can do no harm to any human soul, or tree, animal, rock, stream or sea."

We are not the only people doing these ceremonies. There are binding groups all over the country, and maybe in other parts of the world. I have never before participated in anything like this but I love the people involved and am hoping to widen my belief systems.

Some days I think we may be doing some good, as the politicians seem to be either in trouble or stymied when trying to pass terrible health care reform and tax reform. After all, magic happens.

Many of us took a welcomed break from politics and protests during the Obama administration. Personally, I did not like some of the things he did, but I always trusted him to veto the worst bills Republican legislators sent to him. As a result, my resistance muscles had grown weak and lacked exercise when Trump took office. It's been hard to build those muscles back up once again, particularly at my age. Sometimes it's two steps forward followed by one step back. Regardless, I'm still working at it, and can still tie the shoelaces on my marching shoes.

How long will the efforts so many are putting forth be needed? Looks like the answer to this question is "a very long time."

Meanwhile, the crazy Right calls us snowflakes, meaning we're weak and don't have staying power. They seem not to understand that we are strong, and getting stronger. Even if our marching shoes have been packed away in a closet for a very long time, they are out now, and everyone knows that when you come out of the closet you are very, very awake!

Grandma, We Were Never the Mess

Ahna Kruzic

I work with women, and we're changing the world. We're organizing to transform our realities. And we're building the future today. There are some men who exist in these spaces, too.

My grandmother left my grandfather at the age of 79. I saw her bruises. He pushed her down the stairs once. No one but Grandpa knows whether he was trying to kill Grandma. Intent doesn't mean a lot when you're at the bottom of the stairs. She told everyone else she fell.

My family stopped talking to Mom when she helped Grandma leave.

Later, Grandpa was diagnosed with lung cancer. Grandma said she'd go see him in case his time was short, but that she couldn't bear the thought. She died of a stroke not long before she was supposed to see Grandpa. On Christmas Eve. Not even a year after she left him. Before she died, Grandma looked at me and said, "Ahna, women knowingly make such a mess of their lives. I'm not sure how, but it's so sad."

What if we didn't have to exist in such messes?

But Grandma didn't realize we weren't making the messes. I'm so sorry she didn't know. My family buried Grandpa next to Grandma. For eternity. That's not what she wanted.

When we were little, my brother's best friend was a kid named Jake. He was four years older than me. I grew up with him, and looked up to him. When I was about 12, Jake started watching me while I slept. Then one night, I couldn't pretend I didn't notice anymore as he touched the inside of me. What if, at 12 years old, and last night, we could sleep instead of worrying about who would come into our rooms to touch us?

Not long after, my friend's middle school boyfriend threw rocks at her face after we left his baseball game to get an ice cream cone. Kile was his name. I was there, so I told Kile to fuck off. I was scared. My friend's mom told me not to get involved. That he'd just get angrier, and my friend didn't need that.

I imagined things weren't like this elsewhere.

I went to college early. When I was 16, I went to my first academic research conference. I thought... "I'm finally out of the mess of southern Iowa!" Look at all these smart, leftist people. No bruises on these grandmas' arms, I thought. On the first day of the conference, my faculty mentors introduced me to the chair of a program I was interested in for graduate school. He looked me up and down and said, "I know you. You're the young pretty one with the long legs."

And then I got angry. I haven't stopped being angry. Sometimes, when I'm tired, I think of that moment. For fuel. Later, I got a job as a community organizer. Most of the staff were women. Thank god, I thought. Some relief, finally. Hopefully.

The meetings were often a few men talking to each other. Many women nodding. Or speaking. But our ideas were only acknowledged when stolen. So, we nodded instead. When we pointed this out to the men, I was told I was crazy. It's in my head, he said. How dare I bring down the movement with my imagination? With my crazy?

So, I left. I tried, anyways.

I left to work on farms. I left really far away this time. I knew I couldn't leave the mess. But I could pull so many weeds and empty so many buckets of rabbit urine and take so many hallucinogens my arms and my brain would be too tired. It was good fun for a while.

But then I woke up to a man touching me one night. I broke. But I pretended I didn't because Mom was visiting the next morning, and maybe she'd believe I was okay if I couldn't. Mom makes everything okay again, and she did this time, too. What if we weren't contemplating what's worse—the shame of not speaking our lived experiences, or the shame of not being heard when we do?

I came back to Iowa. And I went to grad school. I wanted to learn where I had grown up. Leaving didn't work. Maybe staying would?

Not long after, the Dakota Access pipeline was slated to cross Iowa. At the same time, our state's ongoing farm crisis resulted in farmers losing their land, workers losing their livelihoods, and our water gaining a whole lot of pollutants.

I was in school, sure, but mostly I organized. I organized with my community for a just reality, against the corporate takeover of our homes and our loves. But mostly I organized against the mess. No, it was through the mess, not against it. We just plowed right through it, made our own space. We organized through the men who asked us to take notes while they yelled on bullhorns, the men who got in our faces when they didn't like the consensus that had been reached, the men who took credit for the events we planned, the men who told us to stop, to step aside, and to relax.

It was then that I knew then that I couldn't leave the mess. Instead, I had to organize through it. I haven't stopped being angry, but I haven't stopped organizing, either.

I found home. In Iowa. In the mess. Through the mess.

I had to leave, for a job. When I came back for a visit a few months later, I stayed at my friends' house. They made me cheese sandwiches, chip dip, and love. I also stayed at my mom's house. She made me laugh, cry, and love. I still worried about who would come into my room, about the mess, but I felt safer than ever before. At home. In Iowa.

Grandma, we were never the mess.

SECTION 4. ALTERNATIVE FACTS
Donald Trump Off the Rails

PAULA vW. DÁIL

He's no ordinary con man. He's way above average—and the American political system is his [Trump's] easiest mark ever.—*Rolling Stone* magazine

On September 27, 2017, nationwide polling results revealed that the majority (64 percent) of Americans consider President Donald Trump unfit for office.[1] In other words, even though he claims otherwise, most Americans don't believe President Trump is doing a good job. Trump's response to his critics is to claim that his has been "the most successful first nine months of any presidency in American history" during which, on his first European trip as president, he gave "the greatest speech ever given by a president on foreign soil."[2]

Throughout history political leaders have been vilified—sometimes justifiably, and sometimes not. As a general rule, however, it is unusual to poll the "fit to serve" question. However, when Donald Trump entered the American political arena, he brought about a dramatic shift in the rules of political gamesmanship that has led to a lot of questions about his ability to lead.

Some wrote Donald Trump's political behavior off to rookie mistakes being made by a candidate who had never held political office. Others, having observed candidate Trump's behavior throughout the presidential campaign, were more alarmed and expressed much greater concern.

Yet somehow Donald Trump has, so far, managed to weather every political storm that blew his way. Words and actions that had, in the past, derailed other politicians, didn't faze him. Senator Lindsey Graham (R–SC) called Trump a "nut job" and "batshit crazy." "I think he's crazy, and I don't say that lightly," Senator Jack Reed (D–RI) said following Trump firestorm regarding health care legislation. Others were even less accepting of his behavior, but in the end, it didn't matter. Trump was, it seemed, politically indestructible, and he prevailed because, during his years in the entertainment industry, he had mastered the art of manipulating an audience.

Trump had also revealed a disturbing Machiavellian character trait: if he doesn't like the question, he attacks the questioner; if he doesn't like the message, he attacks the messenger; if he doesn't like the story, it's fake news. It was against this backdrop that, on November 29, 2016, three weeks after Trump's election, three distinguished women physicians specializing in psychiatry wrote the following letter to President Barack Obama[3]:

President Barack Obama
The White House
1600 Pennsylvania Avenue NW
Washington, DC 20500

November 29, 2016

Dear President Obama,

We are writing to express our grave concern regarding the mental stability of our President-Elect. Professional standards do not permit us to venture a diagnosis for a public figure whom we have not evaluated personally. Nevertheless, his widely reported symptoms of mental instability—including grandiosity, impulsivity, hypersensitivity to slights or criticism, and an apparent inability to distinguish between fantasy and reality—lead us to question his fitness for the immense responsibilities of the office.

   We strongly recommend that, in preparation for assuming these responsibilities, he receive a full medical and neuropsychiatric evaluation by an impartial team of investigators.

Sincerely,
Judith Herman, M.D. Professor of Psychiatry
   Harvard Medical School
Nanette Gartrell, M.D.
Dee Mosbacher, M.D.

It would have been extremely difficult for President Obama, in his capacity as the outgoing, opposition-party president, to act on this recommendation. Nevertheless, it is noteworthy that three eminently qualified women were the first to officially recommend that, based upon his observable behavior, Donald Trump be psychiatrically evaluated, and then took the unprecedented step of documenting their concerns to the sitting president of the United States. Unquestionably they weren't the only medical professionals who had observed Donald Trump and drawn similar conclusions, but these three women were the ones brave enough to act.

   A few months into Trump's presidency, the American Psychoanalytic Association (APsaA) a professional organization of mental health professionals, told its 3,500 members that, contrary to previous practice, they don't have to abide by the Goldwater Rule[4] as concerns President Trump.

   The decision was made "amid growing concern about Donald Trump's mental health," explained APsaA past president, Dr. Prudence Gourguechon, adding that it has occurred because "Trump's behavior is so different from anything we've seen before." Gourgeuchon went on to say that the organization "does not want to prohibit our members from using their knowledge responsibly." She stressed that the APsaA "does not consider political commentary by its individual members an ethical matter."[5]

   In the wake of the Trump election many mental health experts have called for greater flexibility regarding the Goldwater Rule. An online petition calling Trump "mentally ill," started by psychiatrist John Gartner, has received more than 55,000 signatures since April. Nevertheless, the American Psychiatric Association, has, so far, continued to endorse the Goldwater Rule.

   Since assuming the presidency, Trump's chief means for engaging an audience is through his Twitter account, @realDonaldTrump, that he claims has 31 million followers.

Together with the unscripted, off-the-cuff remarks that erupt at nearly every public appearance he makes, these 140-character messages, typically delivered while most Americans are sleeping, have provided the public with their best insights into his thinking. For example, he has promoted conspiracy theories (Barack Obama wiretapped Trump Tower) having no basis in fact and continually bullies members of Congress who do not agree with him or support his agenda.

Within the span of 24 hours, Trump hailed Senator John McCain as "a great American Hero" for returning to Washington to cast a vote on the pending health care legislation, and labeled McCain "a traitor to his party" when he voted against the Republican sponsored bill. Earlier Trump had denied hero status to McCain, a Vietnam prisoner of war, by remarking, "He's not a war hero. He's a war hero because he was captured. I like people who weren't captured."[6]

As the "real Donald Trump" has continued to emerge, the picture of four years under his leadership has grown even more frightening. "The messages of racism, the lies, the fraud, the sexism—he's sending a lot of really horrible messages to our children," said sociologist DeShanne Stokes.[7]

Meanwhile, storm clouds began enveloping the Trump administration almost immediately, centering on the president's mysterious relationship with Russia. It is generally believed he has had, and continues to have, extensive business dealings with Russia, but his refusal to release his tax returns makes this difficult to prove.

It is also widely believed that Russia substantially interfered with the 2016 presidential election and was instrumental in Hillary Clinton's unexpected defeat.[8] Trump himself claims not to believe this, despite email evidence of communications between the Russian ambassador to the U.S. and his former campaign chairman, Paul Manafort, his son-in-law, Jared Kushner, and his son, Donald Trump, Jr. All three were summoned to testify before both Senate and House Intelligence Committees investigating the Russian connection to the election outcome, and if it is proven that the Trump campaign colluded with Russia to manipulate the election outcome, it will be a treasonous offense.

According to the *Washington Post*, President Trump "personally dictated a statement in which Trump Jr. said he and the Russian lawyer had "primarily discussed a program about the adoption of Russian children" when they met in June 2016. The statement, issued to *The New York Times* as it prepared a story, emphasized that the subject of the meeting was "not a campaign issue at the time."[9] The claims were later determined to be misleading, primarily because Trump has never been known to express any interest whatever in Russia's child adoption policy.

Eventually Donald Trump, Jr., acknowledged he attended the meeting after receiving an email indicating that damaging information would be provided about "crooked Hillary Clinton," as Trump often referred to her, as part of a Russian government effort to help his father's campaign.[10] The extent of the president's personal intervention in his son's response, and later in the public statement about the meeting, adds to suspicions that Trump's direct intervention leaves him vulnerable to accusations of a cover-up and/or obstruction of justice, which are grounds for impeachment.

As a result of the legal jeopardy he finds himself in, Trump hired a team of private lawyers to publicly represent him on these issues. Meanwhile, Attorney General Jeff Sessions, who was closely involved with the Trump campaign, recused himself from the Russia investigation, allowing an assistant to appoint a Special Counsel, former FBI director Robert Mueller, to officially investigate the matter.

Throughout this time, Trump has relentlessly criticized Sessions for recusing himself from overseeing the FBI's Russian investigation. "If I would have known he was going to recuse himself, I would've hired someone else," Trump tweeted, implying that he chose Sessions for the position because he thought Sessions, in his position as attorney general, could protect him. However, Sessions' recusal was a factor leading to the appointment of Mueller, which then prompted Trump to inquire about the limits of his power to issue pardons, including for himself, and explore potential avenues for undercutting Mueller's work.

On August 4, 2017, Mueller impaneled a federal grand jury in Washington, D.C., to further advance the Russia probe. The grand jury has the power to subpoena witnesses, who must testify under oath (or invoke Fifth Amendment protections against self-incrimination) and documents, including the president's tax returns. It is the grand jury's responsibility, based upon a review of the evidence it obtains, to issue indictments.

Leaders, both at home and abroad, find Trump's unpredictable leadership style deeply troubling, and no president in recent memory has begun his term of office by generating the level of controversy Trump has created. Additionally, the president's increasingly serious legal concerns, particularly this early in his presidency, are major distractions for his administration.

Six months into Trump's term of office (which, he claims, has been the "most effective six months in presidential history," despite having made no progress on his campaign promises or passed significant legislation) chaos reigns in the West Wing. During a 10-day period in July, as a direct result of President Trump's leadership style, the following occurred:

- Senator Charles Grassley (R–IA) Chairman of the Senate Judiciary Committee, rebuked President Trump for his repeated tweets and statements brutalizing Attorney General Jeff Sessions. Senator Lindsey Graham (R–SC) said "there will be hell to pay" if Trump attempts to fire Sessions in an effort to stonewall the Russia investigation.
- General Joseph Dunford, Chairman of the Military Joint Chiefs of Staff, was blind-sided with a tweet from the president announcing that transgender individuals would be banned from military service. Dunford responded by saying that there will be "no change" to any military policy, including personnel, until Defense Secretary James Mattis evaluates it and decides how to proceed. In other words, the Pentagon will not allow the president to use his Twitter account to make military policy. Soon after, the Secretary of the Navy Admiral Ray Mabus said that any patriot who wants to serve the country should be allowed to do so.[11]
- The Boy Scouts of America (BSA) were appalled and embarrassed by the president's speech at the 20th annual National Boy Scout Jamboree, which is a traditional invitation extended to sitting presidents. Trump decided to forgo the opportunity to speak to the young men about public service, civic virtue and patriotism and, instead, treated the event as a political rally in which he blasted Hillary Clinton and Barack Obama and then talked about the "hottest" parties in New York and referred to a rich friend who "did things I can't reveal to a young audience."

  A few days later, the president claimed, falsely as it turned out, that Michael B. Surbaugh, BSA Chief Scout Executive, called to tell him that he did "a great job."

In reality, Surbaugh never contacted the president; instead he posted an apology to anyone who was offended by the president's speech on the BSA website.[12]

- Trump hired Anthony Scaramucci, a Wall Street insider, as White House Communications Director. White House Press Secretary Sean Spicer resigned in protest. Scaramucci, insisting that he answers only to Donald Trump, proceeded to unleash an unprofessional and vulgar rant against White House Chief of Staff Reince Priebus, calling him a "fucking paranoid schizophrenic" and promising to "take him down."[13] Priebus resigned the following day. Within hours Trump hired General James Kelly, formerly Secretary of Homeland Security, as the new White House Chief of Staff. Kelly took office the following Monday morning and immediately fired Scaramucci.
- Repeated attempts to repeal and replace ObamaCare efforts failed and the program remains the law of the land.[14]

President Trump's poll numbers, which have never been good, and have continued to decline since he took office. He began his presidency with a 43 percent approval rating, and six months later only 33 percent of Americans approved of his job performance, a ten-point drop, according to major presidential pollster Quinnipiac University.[15] Particularly troubling for Trump is that 50 percent of non-college educated white voters, a key voting block in his base, disapprove of his job performance.

Overall, respondents indicate that they believe Trump is abusing the office of president and believe he views himself as above the law. Pollsters note that six months into his presidency, Trump's approval ratings are the lowest of any president in modern history, adding that a staggering 71 percent of those polled don't believe the president is "level-headed" and express ongoing fears over his ability to pull the nuclear trigger.[16]

Observing the Trump administration in action is akin to watching a production in the theater of the absurd. The story line changes hourly, sometimes quite dramatically. While this is captivating entertainment, it is deeply alarming when these occurrences reflect the functioning, or lack thereof, of the government of the United States of America and the leader of the free world.

While president Trump continues to deny the chaos surrounding him and to claim that, "everything is fine," many others, at all levels of government and among the general public feel the country is out of control, and finds this deeply unsettling. Nevertheless, White House staffers continue to insist the best response to anything Trump does is "to let President Trump be himself."[17]

In an attempt to explain Trump's unusual leadership style, former house speaker Newt Gingrich (R–GA), an informal adviser to Trump said, "You have to start with the idea that Trump won a hostile takeover of the Republican Party by beating 16 other candidates. Then he won a hostile takeover of government by beating Hillary Clinton, and on both fronts there are people who have not accepted the outcome. He'll spend all eight years of his administration dealing with that kind of hostility."[18]

Meanwhile, examples of Trump's unsettling leadership style continue to accumulate. Sociologically, the deeply disturbing concern is that, if this goes on long enough, there is real danger Trump's behavior will begin to feel normal, and the general public will grow used to, and become more accepting of it. If this occurs, the damage to the American political culture will take generations to recover from, if it ever does. Nevertheless, then White House Assistant Press Secretary Sara Huckabee Sanders defended Trump, saying,

"If he gets attacked, he fights back," and expresses little concern that, as president of the United States, he should be held to a higher standard of public behavior.

With this in mind, cognitive psychologist and retired university professor Alice A. Thieman, echoing Drs. Herman, Gartrell and Mosbacher's concerns, as well as those of others in the mental health field, offers further insights into Donald Trump's personality in her essay "The Emperor Has No Clothes."

Attorney Jennie Lusk, formerly director of the New Mexico American Civil Liberties Union, an assistant New Mexico state attorney general, addresses the bullying aspect of Donald Trump's behavior, in her essay "The Bully in the Bully Pulpit."

Award-winning writer and 9–11 widow Nikki Stern, who was recognized by Search for Common Ground, an international conflict resolution NGO, takes a different approach to examining Donald Trump's leadership. She questions his authoritarian approach to governing and advocates for resistance in the form of civic engagement, and standing up to political bullying in whatever form it takes.

Together, these essayists argue that resisting the Trump agenda is vital to preserving our democracy. It is a patriotic act, because we love our country, and it is the right thing to do because we love our children.

NOTES

1. Quinnipiac University presidential poll, www.thehill.com, September 27, 2017.
2. www.cnn.com, September 20, 2017.
3. www.huffingtonpost.com, December 16, 2016.
4. The Goldwater rule was adopted after the mental health of presidential candidate Barry Goldwater's' mental health was questioned, and it was decided that it was unethical for mental health professionals to comment upon the mental status of an individual they had not personally evaluated.
5. Mahita Gajanan, "Psychiatrists Disagree Over Whether They Should Discuss Trump's Mental Health," *Time,* July 25, 2017.
6. www.cbsnews.com, July 15, 2015.
7. www.dushannestokes.com.
8. These reports appeared in every major news source worldwide. The can be verified through www.washingtonpost.com, www.thenewyorktimes.com, www.reuters.com, www.associatedpress.com., to name a few.
9. www.washingtonpost.com, July 31, 2017.
10. *Ibid.* Also verifiable through all major news sources, as noted.
11. www.cnn.com, August 11, 2017.
12. www.scouting.org.
13. www.washingtonpost.com, August 12, 2017.
14. See the section titled "Sick in the USA: When the Personal Becomes Political."
15. Andrew Rafferty, "Poll: Trump Approval Hits New Low," www.msnbc.com, August 3, 2017.
16. *Ibid.*
17. "Trump Insists There Is No Chaos in White House," www.losangelesdailynews.com, July 31, 2017.
18. "Trump Faces More Threats to His Authority. www.washingtonpost.com, August 5, 2017.

The Emperor Has No Clothes

Alice A. Thieman

Only three times in my life has the president of the United States brought me to tears. I cried the day John F. Kennedy was assassinated, the day we elected Barack Obama as our first Black president, and the moment I learned Donald Trump had won the 2016 presidential election.

I don't wear my patriotism on my sleeve for all to see, but I truly love my country. I get teary when hearing the "Star-Spangled Banner," or singing "America the Beautiful," or watching a military band march in a July 4th parade.

The election of an egotistical, misogynistic, pathological liar to the highest office in our land has broken my heart. Donald Trump is the worst elected president in my lifetime—yes, worse than Nixon, Reagan, and Bush (43). I truly believe his presidency will have overwhelmingly negative consequences that will reach far beyond what we are able to comprehend today.

In my youth, I protested against the Vietnam War, marched for Civil Rights and actively supported the Equal Rights Amendment. These memories reveal that I am no longer young or vigorous, and not nearly as energetic as I once was. It's been a long time since I have been motivated to speak up about a political issue.

But now I am worried and frightened about the country in which my grandchildren and great grandchildren are growing up. What will be the quality of their lives? Will they have affordable health care? Will they be able to retire someday? Will there still be protected National Parks? Will they be able to afford to travel to them? Will they continue living in the United States? These are all issues I care deeply about.

In the 1800s, Alexis de Tocqueville, a French diplomat and political scientist, visited and wrote about the United States, calling it "The American Experiment."[1] Many consider him to be one of the most astute early observers of American Democracy. After spending several months traveling across the United States, he wrote, "The surface of American society is covered with a layer of democratic paint, but from time to time one can see the old aristocratic colours breaking through."[2]

Another quote from Tocqueville provides a startlingly accurate portrayal of current life in America: "I know of no country, indeed, where the love of money has taken a stronger hold on the affections of men."[3] Tocqueville was observing our country during the onset of the Gilded Age, an era that eventually gave rise to the robber barons (e.g., Carnegie, Duke, Rockefeller, owners of steel plants, tobacco companies, Standard Oil, etc.) who used abusive practices to harvest their riches off the backs of poor working people. Human rights abuses during this time ultimately led to formation of labor unions, fair trade laws, child labor laws, and other restraints on the ultra-rich.

Now, a new generation of robber barons has emerged, and they are stealing our liberty, our security, our safety, and our democracy. This movement had been developing gradually, until Donald Trump's election threw our democracy into free fall. For the first time in my life, I feel as if I'm living in a third world country or a banana republic.

With this in mind, I want to say aloud what I believe the 73 million people who did not vote for Donald Trump have been thinking all along: our emperor president has no clothes. He is a robber baron the likes of which we've not seen in modern times and, in my carefully considered opinion as a cognitive psychologist, he is emotionally, and perhaps, mentally ill.[4] My reasons for this conclusion, the facts of which are already widely known, follow.[5]

Trump has a very loose relationship with the truth. He extols his success as a superb businessman who has built a great fortune. While he does possess a great fortune, he inherited much of it from his father, Fred, who was a very successful real estate developer. And, Fred got a financial start from his father who left him the equivalent of $500,000 in today's dollars.[6]

During their business partnership, father and son were both fined for discriminating in their rental properties against African American renters. The Trumps fought the fine, and eventually settled, still claiming no wrongdoing. This experience, as one of his early lessons in how to do business, taught Donald how to be a ruthless businessman who will "adjust the facts" to suit himself.

After the death of his father, Donald continued in the real estate development business, alongside a cadre of lawyers whose sole job is to protect him from the legal consequences of his actions. This is important when considering that Donald's greatest talent is as a con man who sees no need to play fair. There are numerous lawsuits pending (and many more have been settled in the past) that involve his refusal to pay workers, contractors, and others. His strategy is to exhaust lawsuits, often by filing counter suits, until the plaintiffs either run out of money or accept a settlement of cents on the dollar. His business dealings in Atlantic City are a prime example of this business model.

Trump has survived several ups and downs in his development business, admitting that his corporations filed for bankruptcy four times. Eventually he moved into television, producing and starring in *The Apprentice*, a show where contestants competed for a chance to work in the Trump organization.

His birther movement attempting to deny Barack Obama's citizenship, claiming that he was not born in the United States, gained him further notoriety during a time when he was toying with the idea of entering politics. Never mind that the entire effort was based on a proven falsehood—it worked anyway.

Since the 2015 announcement of his candidacy for the U.S. presidency, Trump has continued to make unsubstantiated claims against his rivals, minorities, the disabled, women, and anyone he, rightly or wrongly, determines is against him. These outbursts change depending upon the circumstances and upon what Trump perceives to be his best advantage in the argument.

Since his election, Trump continues to bully and denigrate anyone who is the focus of his anger on any particular day or week. For example, after praising FBI Director James Comey, he began a campaign against him and eventually had him fired, probably because of the ongoing Russian collusion investigation. Similarly, he goaded Sessions, the attorney general, into more aggressive actions against immigrants, and into reintroducing the harshest possible sentences even for non-violent crimes. At the time of this writing, he has focused his ire on Mitch McConnell, the Senate Majority Leader, because repeal and replace of the Affordable Care Act (ACA) did not pass in the 2017 summer session. The general consensus was that the quickly thrown together bill, without bipartisan hearings, reduced the Medicaid subsidies by a staggering amount, and lacked presidential leadership.

During the presidential campaign, Trump made numerous grandiose promises such as we will have "the greatest health care plan, everyone will be covered," "revisions to simplify the tax code," "save all the jobs for the U.S.," etc. He promised everything would be done in the first 100 days, and that his presidency would be the greatest presidency in American history! Such grandiose behavior is extreme, particularly when saturated with illusions of grandeur; it is also irrational and the fantasy of someone with a relaxed connection to reality.

Most recently, Trump claimed that no president in history has ever been treated so unfairly. How can this be when compared to President Nixon, who was forced to resign or face impeachment, and President Lincoln, who was uniformly condemned as he led the country into the Civil War? To date, Trump has suffered no consequences for anything he has said, or done, either as a candidate or as president.

After mental health professionals speculated about the mental health of Barry Goldwater in the 1964 presidential campaign, the American Psychiatric Association added an article to their code of ethics stating that mental health professionals should not attempt to diagnose an individual whom they had not personally evaluated. Despite this long held professional restraint, many mental health professionals have stepped up to question Donald Trump's mental health. In fact, recently the American Psychoanalytic Association emailed their members informing them that they are free to speak responsibly about the mental health of politicians. I believe that questioning his mental health is not only reasonable, it is obligatory on the part of those qualified to know the difference between a normal and an abnormal personality.

To this end, I feel compelled to examine our president's behavior in light of mental and emotional disorders described in the Diagnostic and Statistical Manual (DSM) compiled by the American Psychiatric Association.[7]

The behaviors previously described, as well as other observations of Trump's behaviors, lead me to conclude that he fits perfectly within the criteria of a Narcissistic Personality Disorder. This is a mental condition in which the individual has a distorted self-image, is unstable and prone to experiencing intense emotions, is overly preoccupied with vanity, prestige, power and personal adequacy, lacks empathy, and has an exaggerated sense of superiority.[8]

Since Trump's election, he has been preoccupied with how overwhelming his victory was and repeatedly states, "I would have won the popular vote if the illegal votes were thrown out." Not only is this obsessive, it is contrary to fact. There is no evidence of illegal voting anywhere. Another of the numerous examples of his narcissism is that, contrary to the photographic documentation, he insists his inaugural crowd was greater than Obama's inaugural crowd, and was the largest in modern times.

Trump exaggerates his achievements, claiming tremendous wealth but refusing to release tax returns that would verify his statements. Many suggest that his secrecy is hiding the fact that he is not as wealthy as he claims. And, suspicions abound that, despite his lavish lifestyle, he may be deeply in debt, particularly to Russia.

Despite their arrogant and boisterous behavior, individuals with personality disorders suffer low self-esteem. Thus, envy of his predecessor is the most likely source of Trump's campaign rhetoric promising to reverse everything the Obama administration achieved. In reality, so far, other than executive orders aiming to reverse every achievement attributed to his predecessor that legally can be changed by executive order, Trump has done nothing entirely on his own. In fact, several of his executive orders are tied up in the federal courts into the foreseeable future. In addition, he is badgering Congress to repeal and replace the Affordable Care Act (ACA), but offers nothing to replace it. It doesn't appear to bother him that repealing the ACA will take health care access away from 23 million Americans.[9]

Another of Donald Trump's characteristics is a lack of impulse control. Impulse Control Disorder is characterized by impulsivity, an inability to resist a temptation, urge or impulse that may harm self or others. Trump's addiction to Twitter reveals a strong problem with impulse control. Despite his family, his staff, and numerous others telling him to stop his compulsive remarks on Twitter, he cannot seem to restrain himself, even to the detriment of his public image, which is certainly of high importance to him.

Another recent example of lack of impulse control occurred when Trump revealed classified information to two Russian visitors. His need to brag about how important he is by being in possession of "great intel" resulted in very inappropriate, perhaps illegal, information sharing to representatives of an adversarial government. And, who can forget his claims of being able to "do anything" to women when you are a star!

Not having access to his personal habits outside of media coverage, I can't offer, but nevertheless strongly suspect, that there are many, many other examples of issues involving a lack of impulse control. Lack of impulse control coupled with his narcissistic tendencies make for an extremely dangerous president who could start a nuclear war on impulse, without thinking through the consequences of this action.

The DSM-5 does not specifically list misogynist behavior as part of Narcissistic Personality Disorder, but similar characteristics such as having a sense of entitlement, taking advantage of others to get what you want, requiring constant admiration, behaving in an arrogant manner, and expecting special favors and unquestioning compliance with your expectations are. These characteristics are consistent with those displayed by a misogynist, who attacks and intimidates women with the intent to control. Trump has repeatedly exhibited these traits as reported in the public press.

After *New York Times* columnist Gail Collins wrote a less than flattering column about Trump, he sent her a copy of the column with her photo circled and "The Face of a Dog" scrawled across it. During his presidential campaign, Trump didn't like a question from Megyn Kelly of Fox News (at that time), and said, "She had blood coming out of her whatever." He characterized Hillary Clinton's bathroom break during the debates as "disgusting." And, everyone remembers Trump encouraging the chanting at his rallies of "Lock her up," directed at Hillary Clinton. Viewers of the debates were well aware of Trump's body language designed to intimidate Clinton; he repeatedly walked in front of her, and interrupted her three times as often as she interrupted him, as reported by the moderators.

Psychologist Dan McAdams published an article in the *Atlantic* in which he drew from psychological research to create a profile of Donald Trump.[10] As he reported, psychologists have found five personality characteristics to be very descriptive and stable: Extroversion; Neuroticism; Conscientiousness; Agreeableness; Openness. Most people score near the middle on each dimension, but there are characteristics associated with very high or low scores. McAdams wrote that "Across his lifetime, Donald Trump has exhibited a trait profile that you would not expect of a U.S. President: sky-high extroversion combined with off-the-chart low agreeableness." McAdams did not directly examine Trump, but, as he states, Trump's behaviors are very public. A main characteristic of high extroversion is relentless reward seeking, which Trump clearly exhibits. But, the most worrisome characteristic is his lack of agreeableness. During the campaign, as well as after, Trump calls journalists, the press in general, political opponents, and at times members of his own party "losers," "weak," "disgusting." His behavior is generally rude, arrogant, and lacking in empathy. Many sources have indicated that while he has many associates, business and political, he has almost no friends. The only people he trusts are his family, and that has led to his unqualified daughter and son-in-law pretty much running the administration! This is clearly nepotism and a tragedy.

In interviews, long-time associates of Trump have said that he used to be a more complex thinker. He certainly is not a complex thinker now. Unless he is reading from a script, he rambles, often losing his train of thought. His general conversational style is one of confusing partial sentences and obscure references, with an occasional non-word thrown in! When not scripted, his language is simplistic and not reflective of analytic or complex thought. Rather than being detailed, his intelligence briefings are broken down into a few bullet points or, better yet, pictures.

These characteristics suggest the possibility of mild cognitive impairment, a disorder that would not be surprising in someone his age who finds himself in extremely stressful circumstances on an ongoing basis. This disorder may never get worse, but it can sometimes be a predictor of eventual dementia.

In my view, President Trump is also a classic pathological liar, which is another symptom of a personality disorder. While many people, including politicians, exaggerate the truth, omit information, and sometimes lie outright, as a general rule normal people are deceptive in order to cover up a behavior they are trying to hide. This doesn't make it right, but it is what normal people may do.

Conversely, pathological liars lie when there is no need and have nothing to hide except their weak ego. And, the lies of a pathological liar can easily be disproven. Thus, when Trump claimed that his inaugural crowd was larger than his predecessor's the fallacy was in plain view. Yet, to protect his low self-esteem, he had to fantasize that his crowd was bigger. In other words, no way could anyone else have a bigger, more adoring crowd than he did.

Numerous other examples of Trump's pathological lying include his claim that illegals are "pouring" over the U.S.-Mexican border, thus we need a big, impenetrable wall. Scores of well-documented reports show this not to be true. Immigration from Mexico has declined in recent years, and the criminality of immigrants, both legal and illegal, is significantly lower than the native born.[11]

In the face of these facts, it's fair to wonder what those who voted for Trump, and continue to support him, are thinking? Apparently, they believe his braggadocio and lies, and using his well-developed con man skills, he plays them like a fiddle! Because no one likes to be wrong, his loyalists don't want to publicly admit that their chosen emperor has no clothes.

Reviewing the characteristics of unstable personalities in comparison to Donald Trump's lifelong behavior leads me to conclude that he is emotionally and, perhaps, mentally ill. He does not behave like a normal person in society. That he is not ill enough to require hospitalization is not unusual. There are scores of similar individuals who function well enough to manage in society but, nevertheless, are not mentally healthy. However, in all of United States history, there has never been a president whose behavior gives as much pause as Donald Trump's does.

So how do I account for his success? While his wealth and election to the presidency attest to his ability to soar to great heights, my theory is that Donald Trump has been a shill for most of his professional life. He is the front man, the decoy who others prop up to get what they want. Long before he jumped into politics, he paid many media, image, legal and other professionals to do the work of his organization, to protect him, to promote him as a great developer, and on and on. These professionals, together with his family, have become extremely rich by working behind the scenes to make Donald Trump look like an extremely smart, highly successful businessman. However, I contend that he is a straw man, the emperor whose flaws no one wants to admit, and left to his own devices he would collapse.

However, what may prove to be the real tragedy of Trump's presidency are not his own quirks, although they are bad enough. The real tragedy is that he has allowed a boatload of charlatans into the highest echelon of our government. He has made no attempt to "drain the swamp"; instead, he has hired the nastiest, most vicious swamp dwellers he could find! Speaker of the House Paul Ryan, Senate Majority Leader Mitch McConnell, and others, are our elected leaders, yet they pander to Trump and put their own ambitions ahead of what is good for the country. There is also evidence that Trump's aggressive and tough-talk behavior is inciting white supremacist groups and provoking rival nations, like North Korea. Trump spews angry, hateful, and irrational comments daily with no consultation with his cabinet or other policy makers. And, he has yet to put forth any coherent policy agenda for any area. Such rogue behavior is incredibly dangerous.

The Trump administration will undoubtedly go into the history books as the most corrupt in history, worse than the Teapot Dome scandal of the 1920s and the Watergate scandal of the 1970s. But even this historical fact wasn't enough to motivate me, now a 76-year-old great grandmother, to become politically active again. What did motivate me to start spending less time on the golf course enjoying my retirement and more time actively engaged in resisting the Trump administration is the thought that my grandchildren, great grandchildren, and the future generations of Americans will have to live with the effects of the Trump administration policies.

What can I, as one person, possibly do to push back against the world Trump is creating? I only know that I won't remain silent. Instead, I will speak up in letters to the editor and in marches in the streets. I will say publicly what others know, but won't say—that Donald Trump is a dangerous, unstable leader. I will pay attention, I will pray, I will vote, I will show up at town hall meetings, and from the bottom of my heart I will resist in all the ways a 76-year-old great grandmother can resist. I love my country too much to be silent, and I cannot abandon my grandchildren's future by standing by and doing nothing while a mad man rules my nation. Our freedom of speech, assembly, equality, and all the other rights we enjoy must be preserved if the American Experiment is to succeed.

NOTES

1. Alexis de Tocqueville. Democracy in America: Volumes I and II. (1835). Translation by Henry Reeve (Kindle Edition).

2. *Ibid.*

3. *Ibid.*

4. While I have no formal training in the mental health field, I hold a Ph.D. in cognitive psychology and have considerable knowledge of the professional literature addressing various aspects of mental illness and personality disorders.

5. Michelle Dean. "Making the Man: To Understand Trump, Look at His Relationship with His Dad," *The Guardian*, March 2016.

6. Diagnostic and Statistical Manual of Mental Disorders, 5th Edition: DSM-5 (Philadelphia: American Psychiatric Association, 2013).

7. *Ibid.*

8. *Ibid.*

9. Currently the Congressional Budget Office, which scores the impact of federal legislation, estimates that both the House and Senate versions of health care reform will cause at least 23 million people to lose health care coverage over the next 10 years.

10. Dan P. McAdams, "The Mind of Donald Trump," *The Atlantic*, June, 2017.

11. The Criminalization of Immigration in the United States: Special Report, *Ibid.*

The Bully in the Bully Pulpit

Jennie Lusk

I was just as devastated by the outcome of the 2016 presidential election as the other 73.5 million people who didn't vote for Donald Trump. I felt the election as a personal tragedy, as if I had lost something or someone dear, and indeed I had.

The problem with the outcome wasn't just a matter of likely policy shifts to come, terrible though I expected them to be. It was something much more personal: a disappointment in our country and its tolerance of shallow, careless, disengaged, selfish leaders. Somehow the administration of Barack Obama had led me to forget the recent regimes in both parties where the president seemed more concerned with image than with substance, and I got spoiled.

Although I disagreed with many of Obama's most significant foreign policy decisions, I lived for eight years with a sense that he was a real human being. Apparently, he thought about what he said, as he was saying it. He worried, thank goodness. He learned and was eager to apply new information. He was intelligent and cultivated and funny. Altogether, he was a fully dimensional human being, imperfect and flawed, but animated by his own thoughts rather than those scripted through focus groups. I believed I could count on his honesty and genuineness even when I disagreed with his actions. I didn't worry that he was up to no good and I didn't know it.

During the 2016 presidential campaign, it was clear the man now in office intended to pit us against each other and, while we were fighting each other, rob us blind. His campaign's opening salvo about Mexicans as criminals took my breath away, assuming as it did that true Americans hated, resented, distrusted and looked down on the people over the border who are our relatives and ancestors. The founders of my home state of New Mexico delayed joining the United States until our state constitution institutionalized bilingualism. The man now empowered to serve as commander-in-chief spread hatred as the presidential campaign expanded, insulting a Hispanic judge, Gold Star parents, and every woman with the audacity to believe she might be more than a sex object. He played to the fears of a slice of the country with some residual power and distilled his peculiar brand of hatemongering to one set of opposites: us and them.

Us and them. Black and white. Him and her. Right and wrong. The extremes were at the core of this president's purpose in running and of the reactionary impulses of those who voted for him.

Now, five months into what already seems an interminable four years, the president has shown his true colors. Several times he described the Manchester bomber[1] as a "loser," apparently using the worst epithet he could devise. Wow. Was the worst fault of a suicide bomber who killed scores of children being a "loser"? Only if the person evaluating the faults is a person whose moral compass is broken.

A person who fails to recognize that safety is a privilege of power is more likely to risk the lives of others. A person who measures life and death on the axis of wins and losses cannot possibly know, as do those unprotected by a phalanx of security, the vulnerability humans tend to feel when confronted by the possibility of a random bomb. The world for us is certainly not merely a stage or all of us merely players. We are, instead, breathing, heaving, loving masses of human beings trying to survive and contribute something to our children regardless of whether this president believes we win or lose by doing so. This is not a game unless, of course, you are a game-player who considers yourself above it all.

Whether the young man who blew himself up in Manchester, in another case of world-wide terrorism that includes the U.S. won or lost at some abstract "game" of life is irrelevant. Relegating his and his victims' deaths to a score on a playing field masks the hugely troublesome fact to everyone but the new president: someone was willing to blow himself up, using a suicide bomb, to make a political statement. No matter how horrible the result, someone was willing to give up his life in a single act of protest, and while this happened in England, it also happens in the U.S.

The willingness to sacrifice one's whole body is undeniably impressive to anyone who has a shred of humanity left, whether or not the bomber's world view is accepted. Unless we have our biological humanity drilled, drained or trained out of us, we can feel the agony of another person's death just as we feel our children's pain. Ignoring this and pretending that living and dying human beings are only part of a game observed from remote universes is playing at being God. And, of course, that hubris is the most troubling aspect of this administration: the man most Americans did not vote for considers himself above it all, imposes no limits on himself, exhibits no interest in introspection and is bored with his own conscience.

The only people I have known who believed they were safe from the consequences of their own actions were bullies. They knew they could behave as badly as they wished, without paying any personal price. I've known plenty of guys like our current president—bullies of one brand or another—and I would wager that most voters have known them too.

My experiences with bullies have taught me to prepare for a sudden sucker punch when patriotic bullies tear up at the strains of anthems reminding them of the nobility of courage and freedom. I know that, in their next breath, they inevitably hammer anyone and anything different into submission to their will.

I know to anticipate outrage and physical violence shortly after a bully is made to feel uncomfortable because of being unable to deal with human emotion. I know this because I grew up watching bullies:

- I watched silently as my best friend's father, who had several inches and at least 30 pounds on his son, belted her big brother for teasing us and pulling our hair. Even though her brother was undeniably a bully intent on making us cry, her father's unobstructed blows made me cry harder, even after I went home.
- I was spared the humiliation of being sprayed with deodorant by my fellow students as I trailed behind the daughter of the local NAACP leader on the first day

Vicksburg public schools were integrated. The white public school kids whose parents hadn't bought them a private school diploma still had social status on the girl I joined at school that day. Witnessing the crazy eyes of my peers jeering at her, unrestrained by adults who could have, and should have, put a stop to it changed me forever.

- I already knew whom to blame for the events that led to a photograph emblazoned on the front page of our local newspaper over the cutline, "Longhairs shorn." The guy smirking on the sidelines of the photo was a guy who flunked out of high school but managed to claw his way into the powerful position of local jail guard. He had the power to lock people up even for vagrancy and, while they attempted to sleep, beat them. He used the staff coffee pot to break the jaw of another of my hippie friends.
- I remained silent as my own sister lost fight after fight with our determined parents who forced her screaming into charm school and ballroom dance lessons that required white gloves and formals. My parents had each other and all of uptight society behind them, while my sister had no one but me to stick up for her, and I remained silent despite knowing that her valor spared me the same confrontations with power that I, too, would have lost.
- I grew up navigating the terrain between hurt and hatred of the young military school cadets in my hometown who, like the current president, were simultaneously the cream of the crop and their families' outcasts. Purged from families who did not know what else to do with them, they suffered hazing and ranking of their military training and then turned that violence against the community, particularly girls like me, whose pussy they grabbed as casually, as brutally and as often as possible.

Because of these experiences, and my acquaintance with other bullies of the president's stripe, I joined others of my weary generation gathering the day after the 2017 inauguration. We were determined to withstand whatever was necessary, prepared to be beaten down but nevertheless be counted among those unwilling to accept that our imperfect system gave the worst man imaginable the power to smash the system utterly.

Protests have always seemed solemn and risky business. My mom and her middle-aged buddies in People for Peace, protesting burial of radioactive waste in the unstable ground of southern New Mexico, risked being hauled into jail just like war and civil rights protesters did. As former suffragettes told it decades later at ACLU volunteer events, they were very aware, if not terrified, of the risks required to gain the right to vote for themselves, their mothers, their daughters, their granddaughters, my daughter and my granddaughters. They knew the link between voting and using the vote to preserve a woman's holy right to determine how her body will and won't be used.

The suffragettes did not expect to be accepted any more than their mothers and sisters marching down New York City streets were as they joined in silent protest with gags over their mouths, as the U.S. entered the First World War. Even in this century, you could be all but trampled by a horse standing 17 hands (68″ at the withers) high, in armor provided by the federal government to the local police. This is what happened to my dear daughter when she led her buddies out of high school pounding on trashcans to decry Dubya's [President George W. Bush] invasion of Afghanistan.

Undoubtedly, there were risks in taking to the streets, so I was prepared for the worst at the Albuquerque, NM, Women's March was wholly unprepared for what I actually encountered: a party thrown by a new generation of jubilant women ready and willing to put their lives on the line with confidence they would win.

What a pleasure, and a surprise, it was to see that sea of pink pussy hats! Bold pink! Not this pastel sugar-and-spice-and-everything-nice disempowerment pink of waiting our turns, making nice, holding our tongues and never dirtying our hands. These were bold pink hats, on young women who had knit them for their daughters as well as their friends. Imagine!

Those millennial pussy women were unified with their celebratory families. Their husbands joined them, carrying their sons and daughters on their broad shoulders. Their partners laughed and carried their little dogs in their purses. These women knew each other from work AND from play dates and did not seem awkward and isolated, as my generation was, with a jaw set to do it all and have it all in our so-called liberated households. These younger women performed high kicks in a silly chorus line celebrating Title IX,[2] unlike the girls of my generation who entered relay races with an air of apology as well as a hope for victory. They had fabulous signs, much cleverer than ours, that protested "I'm sick and tired of carrying this same old sign for the past thirty years."

The millennials amassed in Albuquerque's civic plaza that wonderful day were having none of the solemnity of protest—and perhaps that is a change worth marking and celebrating, as evidence that there is a majority united against the dark turn of events that led to the current cast of characters inhabiting the White House. The most effective expression of First Amendment rights, at least as demonstrated that day, included humor and song against a thin-skinned bully.

I went to the protests resigned to the day's events but returned delighted and invigorated by the realization that, despite the outcome of the election, for the first time in my life I'm part of a majority—the majority that did not vote for Donald Trump. Now it's time to celebrate that fact and move forward with a sense of pride rather than a sense of dread, fear, loathing or trembling unto death.

Because this president is depressingly familiar, just another incarnation of the same old bloated bully we've faced down in countless other places and other times, we have some insight into what will be effective in getting him and his cronies out of office. But I could begin to get down to business in earnest only when I dropped the fantasy of escaping the U.S. to be embraced with open arms by the rest of the world.

It's possible that my focus on this president's potential for destroying our nation is in proportion to denial of the national sins I have done little to correct over years since the new century began. The more I focused on him, the more I was able to close my eyes to the possibility that the world cratered by our drones will have little pity for me, an American who never took to the street to protest the war crimes of the first 15 years of the 21st century, who remained silent until an embarrassingly brutish new president was put in place by the Electoral College. Regardless, I know that, as the anti–Trump majority coalesces through protests, this president, and the current administration, will eventually be driven from the halls of power.

Earlier, as a protester in the minority, I learned the sad lesson that a darkness in the human spirit accompanies dominance, as those with power seek more power and forget the joy of pumping their own blood through their own bodies rather than sucking it out of the bodies of their soldiers, children and servants. Most of us have lived in some sort of minority, isolated by race, gender, orientation, age, abilities, religious persuasion, regional background or economics, so we also know that dominance can be transitional and that temporary weakness has strategic benefits. The assessment of wins and losses flips, depending on the day, and the battle.

Now, as part of a majority spurred into action by the 2016 election, I hope to find myself among people who recognize how important it is to overcome the temptation to abuse power and to find ways to institutionalize inclusion. I hope that the majority in which I participate will reject the notion the United States is all powerful. I believe this new majority can find a way to solve the tricky problem of unleashing the unearned assets hoarded by the one percent if we bear in mind the necessity of nourishing the bodies and the minds of the next generations who will inherit our problems. We can remember to demand and spend the peace dividend that should be paid back for decades of building war at the expense of negotiating a way to live together on the planet. While we're at it, we can stop generating toxic waste by funding more nuclear plants, quit lying about being able to handle half-lives of poisons safely and instead handle the nuclear arsenal we've already built. We can dismiss the notion that we can cause global warming without suffering its ill effects. All of these are connected to human rights issues, and women's rights are human rights, just as human rights are always women's rights too.

More practically speaking, I intend to work with others to put our local, state and national legislators on notice that we care, we're watching and we will work against them if they favor the richest few against those in our voting majority. I am finding time to help others in concrete ways rather than worrying only about whether my social security will be adequate. Just as important, some of us are running for office and no doubt will discover how hard it is to make good policy, as opposed to sitting on the sidelines critiquing it. Although I expect we will find less unity, unanimity and bon ami within our majority as we set our own shoulders to the wheel, I know that learning how to disagree on strategy while sharing in purpose is the stuff that builds democracy.

Above all, I will use my experiences to focus on the rich territory found between extremes, knowing that artificial divisions between us and them, haves and have-nots not only trigger my worst tendencies to bully, but also tend to divide me from the secrets of my own heart. I know I have traded on the power and wealth I have as an American to live on the labor and resources of others across the globe, and I have an inkling my consumer demands differ in degree rather than in kind from that of the current president.

My hope is that as I prepare to dance in the streets on the day this insufferable lot is replaced with people of conscience, I will have developed a solid habit of inclusion, accepting everyone I possibly can as family and working to recognize humans as humans rather than as only allies or opponents. I hope I will have established some personal limits on exploitation of others in the world. I hope I can set a course and keep to it in working to create a world where America's sons and daughters are protected because they are known to be global citizens morally engaged with the rest of the world.

If I'm ever going to have the luxury of sleeping through the night again, I need to quit focusing on our country's most obvious bully and do what I can to fix long-standing problems that result in large part from reacting to bullies and exclusion. I know that as Americans we have too much blood on our hands and too much wealth on our backs to play innocent and we may have waited too long to make amends to those—including future generations— we've already shortchanged. Of course, I hope it's not too late to establish a better course, but whether it is or not, I know in these times that it's necessary for me to take whatever next steps I can to try to invest in the political territory between false dichotomies posed by the man in the bully pulpit.

Notes

1. A May 22, 2017, shrapnel bomb detonated at the exit of an Ariana Grande concert in Manchester, England, reportedly injured 199 and killed 23 people including the bomber.

2. Since enactment of Title IX of the Education Amendments Act of 1972, 20 U.S.C.A.§§ 1681, et seq., a majority of girls participate in high school sports.

On Whose Authority?

Nikki Stern

Long ago, which is to say at the beginning of this century, terrorists commandeered planes and sent them into buildings. It was the first such attack by a foreign power on American soil and it rendered us vulnerable and angry. We responded with a show of unity and resilience that helped even the most grief-stricken among us keep going.

Then came the outrage. Political leaders and pundits alike clamored for retaliation. They made sweeping generalizations about particular religions and ethnicities. Never mind that large numbers of Americans didn't know or didn't bother to learn who was on the plane that killed my husband along with thousands of others. We were engaged in a war of good versus evil. Our moral authority endowed us with the right to avenge our dead and defend our way of life. You were either with us or against us.

My impulse was to push back against the excessive self-righteousness. I resented those who politicized the deaths of our loved ones. I hated listening to lectures about the ethical justifications for waging war against Iraq, a non-participant in the original attack. I was furious with a president who insisted he was on a mission from the Almighty Himself to fight terrorists and end tyranny. I never believed family members like me might wield our own limited version of moral authority, as if our suffering made us virtuous and our virtue made us experts on a variety of subjects.

It's human to want strong leadership and decisive action in uncertain times. Yet moral authority was always going to be an imperfect response. The idea has for centuries provided cover for charlatans and other bad actors, from presidents to parents to priests. Moral authority suggests exclusivity. It presumes the rest of us aren't privy to the special brand of goodness bestowed upon the chosen few.

Sixteen years ago feels like an eon. You'd be hard pressed to find a single institution, organization, or individual that commands the degree of respect or reverence moral authority requires. Almost no one claims or pretends to be driven by a higher purpose anymore. There may be one exception: the current pope, Francis. The 266th leader of the Roman Catholic Church is a man so humble and so inclusive he seems to have appeared on planet Earth from another time and place altogether.

Otherwise, moral authority, claimed or unclaimed, is dead or dying. In place of unquestioned influence that at least pretends to be rooted in a desire to do good, we have allowed another version to rise, a bellicose authority that brooks no opposition.

Authority is as old as time and people who abuse power are as familiar as the air we breathe. Writers like Charles Dickens had plenty of material to draw upon, thanks to an oppressive London class system in which gains were measured by how many people the oppressor could control. The cruel boss, the wicked stepmother, and the sadistic nurse are the staples of melodrama. The power to intimidate lends to the marginally better off a sense of superiority.

Authority works best when people are afraid. Something else I observed immediately after 9/11: my small-town police officers—and those in other communities—began affecting shaved heads, jackboots, and an attitude that read like a warning. Not all of them by any means but too many to make me comfortable. I get it; we were all scared. But these men and a few women as well projected not resilience but a kind of self-aggrandizing aggression. Take that, exaggerated or imagined threat. I'm more badass than you.

Not reassuring or inspiring.

Years later, despite an effort to promote a culture of hope, we are once again seized with a full-time siege mentality, thanks to never-ending narratives about terror and dystopia. Our fear has generated a paramilitary mindset that permeates every part of our culture. Many ordinary men and women in ordinary positions of moderate responsibility now believe they're members of an elite army dedicated to preserving order at all cost.

Treating people badly has fewer consequences than you might imagine. Insurance companies can drop you, employers can fire you and owners can refuse to serve you. Meanwhile stores can kick you out for shopping while minority. As for recourse, you can get online and register your dissatisfaction. You can also restore your sense of control by carrying your sidearm into post offices, coffee shops, churches, and restaurants where families now eat with their heads down and their eyes averted so as not to irritate the aggrieved person with the gun.

In 2016 we elected a president with a tenuous relationship to the truth, a love of insult and provocation, and a hearty disinterest in the welfare of those around him. He does what he does and he says what he says and if it's wrong, he shrugs. In private, if reports are to be believed, he is furious and incredulous that he can't run the government like he ran his business, which is to say, like a kingdom where his word is absolute.

Which is why, when presidential aid Stephen Miller declared the president's authority is not to be questioned,[1] I shuddered. So did plenty of others, including a respectable number of journalists, after which Donald Trump labeled the media an "enemy of the American people."[2]

One does not question the king.

The Oxford English Dictionary defines authoritarianism as "the enforcement or advocacy of [a form of government that demands] strict obedience to authority at the expense of personal liberty."[3] You may believe Americans' attraction to the notion of personal liberty would prevent us from permitting any acts by our government that abridge the rights of others. At which point I might point out that Americans have become disturbingly selective about whose personal freedoms concern them. The 2016 election and beyond uncovered the appeal to a particular segment of a get-tough ethos, accompanied by harsh talk and punitive measures when directed against "outsiders" or "opponents." Lock them up. Knock them down. Throw them out. Send them back. Do whatever you need to. We'll help.

The affection for authoritarian behavior is spreading. Self-styled soldiers who maintain order (at least in their minds) are present in every facet of our lives. They patrol our borders and highways. They issue or revoke our passports, grant or deny our loans, oversee our schools, review our medical records, make our laws, and let us on or off a train or a plane. They are members of the school board, the garden club, and the neighborhood watch. They are anyone with the power to say "stop" or "no" or "not while I'm in charge."

It takes a village.

Congress embraced opposition politics years before the current administration came to power. We have a class of representatives who were elected to say "no." Now that they have a leader who is on their team, they can't move any significant legislation forward. Maybe that's why they give the impression that they dislike both their jobs and their constituents. At town hall meetings, many show their utter contempt for the people they purport to represent. They have no interest in anyone who is not a member of their base. Free of what they snidely refer to as "political correctness," they are comfortable with openly opposing any support for food for the poorest and care for the oldest, never mind clean water, clean air, or safe roads.

The paucity of empathy is nowhere as apparent as in discussions about healthcare. It makes sense to explore how government can spend more effectively and efficiently. However, several congressmen easily crossed from frugal to heartless with their public statements about extending or preserving coverage. One argued that poor and homeless people were morally, spiritually, and socially opposed to obtaining healthcare. Another let slip that he didn't believe the sick deserved healthcare because they probably weren't living good lives. Still another admitted he begrudged a healthcare system that would have him paying for pre and post-natal care.

Maybe these guys don't know how democracy works. More likely they subscribe to a version of democracy that doesn't involve helping those less fortunate. I can't come up with another explanation for their surly, resentful, exclusionary positions.

We brought this on, this low point in our history. We saw it coming and did nothing about it. Instead of paying attention, we grew careless. We measured our small gains and relaxed while a clear minority begged a bully to make the country "great" (read, "like it used to be"). Some of them feared terrorism and some were terrified by change. Some felt left behind and some felt misunderstood. Some confused anger with power. Then there were those who, egged on by unseen forces, thought it would be fun to shake things up, as if representative democracy were a Magic 8 Ball or a funhouse ride rather than a complex system that needed careful treatment.

Perhaps that's why I start each day wondering what has become of our shared belief in a common set of values that celebrate equality and opportunity for all. Didn't there used to be at least a nod to the idea of a social contract that protects our weakest? What happened to respect for the institutions, the individuals, and the history that have made our country a place where people want to live, raise their children, and, yes, vote? Were we ever at a point where civic engagement was a virtue? Will we ever be again?

I can offer a qualified "yes." If there's a silver lining in all this naked ambition, it's that we can see more of what's going on. Absent the pretense of responding to the will of the American people or helping one's fellow man, the actions of those who would game the system have become more transparent. Americans are responding. In the weeks after Donald J. Trump was sworn in as president, several independent monitors began to catalogue the unprecedented number of untruths emanating from the White House. George Orwell's *1984* and Sinclair Lewis' *It Can't Happen Here* have been selling briskly and have reappeared on school reading lists. So have pocket copies of the Constitution, one of which was memorably brandished by Khriz Khan, the Muslim-American father of a slain decorated soldier when he spoke at the Democratic Convention. Opposition groups have formed and subscriptions to the top digital/print news services have soared. Beyond the marches, which are symbolic but short-lived shows of support, hundreds of organizations and movements have taken root.

The resistance risks missing two developments. First, the United States could return to an exceptionally regressive version of moral authority. It might take a horrific event or it might simply involve a new president with a rigid set of beliefs. Margaret Atwood's once-again popular book *The Handmaid's Tale* posits a near future in which "making the country great" means accepting a controlled society underpinned by a selectively literal interpretation of the Old Testament. The brutal hierarchy that emerges subjugates women and murders so-called "deviants." Whether or not you believe the possibility is imminent or remote, consider this: legislators in Texas and elsewhere keep trying to attach discriminatory amendments to legislation under the guise of protecting religious freedom. In one such instance, the result might be a nurse who views homosexuality as a sin refusing treatment to a gay patient. And bear in mind that in 2017, women still earn 80 percent of what their male counterparts do.

Second, we will win the battle and lose the war if we ignore the level of manipulation that lies beneath and extends beyond a single election cycle. It's no secret there are forces at work whose primary goal is to maximize revenue and accrue power no matter the cost to the rest of us. We all know elections can be rigged and disinformation can be spread easily on social media. Outrage can be exacerbated or manufactured. The sad truth is that keeping the masses distracted works to advance certain agendas currently kept out of sight.

For now, though, the curtain may be lifting just a little. If we stay strong, we can stand up to bullies. If we stay focused, we can hold officials at every level accountable. If we stay informed, we can separate truth from fiction. And if we stay attentive, we can challenge authority whenever and wherever we see it used to punish, oppress or tyrannize.

NOTES

1. Jack Holmes, "Stephen Miller Is Ready for His Authoritarian Close-Up," *Esquire Magazine*, February, 2017.

2. Michael Grynbaum, "Trump Calls the News Media The Enemy of The People," www.newyorktimes.com, February, 17, 2017.

3. "Authoritarian," *The Oxford Dictionary*, www.oxforddictionaries.com.

Section 5. Not My President
America Goes Dark

Paula vW. Dáil

My child is dead, and I heard what Donald Trump said about why she died, so no, I won't meet with Donald Trump.—Susan Bro

The reasons those women who opposed Donald Trump's candidacy were upset when he won varied widely, and it wasn't just about his bullying and misogyny. Women were worried about their health care, their reproductive rights, immigration, the environment, education, and everything else that, woven together, comprises the fabric underpinning American women's lives. Many consoled themselves with the thought that, just maybe, Trump would surround himself with advisors who were broader minded and more politically knowledgeable than he was. They hoped the White House would be staffed by individuals who had the best interests of the entire country at the forefront of their minds, and were not merely concerned about pleasing Trump's political base. In the end, they were deeply disappointed, but should not have been surprised, considering the man Donald Trump selected as his running mate.

Mike Pence came onto the Republican presidential ticket after having been a six-term Republican Congressman representing Indiana. He was Indiana's sitting governor at the time Trump named him as his vice presidential choice. Pence brought considerable political acumen, deeply held Evangelical Christian beliefs, and very conservative social and personal values to the ticket, and Trump needed all of those.

Pence says his approach to politics is governed foremost by being a born-again Christian. "I'm a Christian, a conservative, and a Republican, in that order," he is often quoted as saying.[1] In keeping with this philosophy, he is so staunchly anti-abortion that, while in Congress, he brought the federal government to the brink of a shutdown in an ultimately failed attempt to de-fund Planned Parenthood, one of the primary providers of low-cost reproductive and preventive health care for women.

Pence strongly supports religious freedom, and believes the only valid marriage is between a man and a woman. He is strongly influenced by American political theorist Russell Kirk, a moralist, historian, and social and literary critic who wrote *The Conservative Mind.*[2]

"The true conservative," Pence explains, "is animated by the principle of driving toward the ideal solutions that are grounded in economic freedom and individual liberty, but also understanding that compromise is part of the conservative approach to governance. I don't believe in compromising principles, but I do believe in finding a way forward on the basis of authentic common ground."[3] A Trump loyalist, Pence is a masterful political dodger who stays on message, regardless of what the message is.

Several of Trump's appointees to White House advisory positions also caused alarm. Many are extraordinarily wealthy (net worth greater than $10 million) Goldman Sachs alumni with little direct political experience or grasp of ordinary people's daily lives. This group includes Steve Mnuchin, who became Secretary of Treasury, Gary Cohn, who was appointed director of the White House Economic Council, and Steve Bannon, who moved from CEO of the Trump election campaign to chief strategist for the Trump White House. A hard-core "America first" immigration hawk who is tough on trade policy, Bannon struck fear in the hearts of many, and for good reason.[4]

Originally an investment banker, Bannon entered politics through his connection with Breitbart News, a no holds barred, ultra-right-wing media organization that got behind Trump's campaign early and pushed hard to get him elected. Often characterized as the Grim Reaper, he represents the "alt-right" thinking prevalent among the 45 percent of Trump's political base who are not college educated, are low-income, and comprise a significant voting block.[5] While ultra-conservatives loved him and hate groups were thrilled when he became a White House insider, his assent to power deeply upset moderates and liberals.

"I like Steve [Bannon] and I respect him. He's a good man," Trump has said often. Because he is a combative and unorthodox Republican who fostered a puppet-master image, with Trump being the puppet, it is widely believed that Bannon's fingerprints have been on most policy decisions coming out of the Trump White House in the early months of his administration.

Another Trump appointee that caused grave concern was Alabama Senator Jeff Sessions, who became Trump's Attorney General. Sessions mirrors Pence in terms of ideology and is not known to be sympathetic to LGBTQIA issues, immigration concerns, racial tensions or any easing of criminal sentencing guidelines. "Sessions is Trump's Good Housekeeping seal of approval, in a policy sense," said Mark Krikorian, executive director of the Washington-based Center for Immigration Studies, a group that advocates for stronger restrictions on both legal and illegal immigration.[6]

Other appointees included conservatives Sebastian Gorka as deputy assistant to the president, and Stephen Miller as senior policy analyst. Peter Navarro was named director of the National Trade Council, Dina Powell as deputy national security advisor, Don McGahn was appointed White House legal counsel, former Republican National Committee (RNC) Chairman Reince Priebus was made chief of staff, and Sean Spicer, also coming from the RNC, was selected as press secretary. Billionaire former Exxon Oil CEO Rex Tillerson was chosen as secretary of state.

On the military side, Generals James Mattis, John Kelly, and H.R. McMaster were appointed Secretary of Defense, Secretary of Homeland Security (until he was appointed White House Chief of Staff), and National Security Advisor, respectively. General Joseph Dunford was named chairman of the Joint Chiefs of Staff. Hope Hicks was named Director of Strategic Communications and, in a position created just for her, as chief spokesperson during the Trump campaign, Kellyanne Conway became Counselor to the President. Her chief responsibility has been to book herself on television talk shows and continue promoting Donald Trump.

Eyebrows shot up when Trump appointed his son-in-law, Jared Kushner, as his senior advisor and his daughter, Ivanka Trump, who is also Jared's wife, as his special assistant. The chief concerns, besides nepotism, are that both come from the wealthy business sector, neither has any political or public policy experience whatsoever, and their only qualification for entering the White House grounds as anything other than as tourists are that they are Trump family members.

In total, 17 of the 21 top positions in the White House were filled by white men. The remaining four were filled by white women. There were no African American, Native American, Asian, Muslim, Hispanic, Latino or other minority representation among senior staff. Almost immediately upon taking up residence, Trump fired the White House chief usher, Angella Reid, the first woman and second African American to hold the position, for reasons that were never made clear.

With so many rookies at the helm, it was not surprising that, from the outset, the White House has been in constant disarray, even if Trump, who appears to thrive on chaos, didn't think so.[7] The Executive Branch of government has been continuously plagued by infighting, tension (particularly between Bannon and Kushner) and disorganization. Bannon, who had received clearance to sit on the National Security Council, was openly contemptuous of the president's son-in-law and didn't trust his political instincts. "Jared's a dope," Bannon said on more than one occasion.[8]

With these individuals as his closest advisors, and chaos as the prevailing work environment, Donald Trump met his Waterloo in the 72 hours between August 11 and August 14, 2017. Several thousand neo–Nazis, Klu Klux Klan members, white nationalists and other home-grown hate groups carrying high-powered assault rifles and lit torches reminiscent of Klan activities in prior decades, marched into Charlottesville, Virginia. They came from around the country to protest the removal of Confederate General Robert E. Lee's statue from a city park. Violence broke out, and hours went by without so much as a tweet from President Trump. It was surprising that the normally loquacious, verbally abusive Trump, who has never been known to refrain from expressing an opinion on anything, remained silent on Saturday morning, even after Virginia governor Terry McAuliff declared a state of emergency and activated the national guard.

Meanwhile, in a clear act of domestic terrorism, a neo–Nazi sympathizer from Ohio drove his speeding car into the crowd of counter-protestors at a high rate of speed, killing one woman and injuring several others. Soon afterwards, a police surveillance helicopter carrying two Virginia State Police crashed, killing both. Three were killed, including Susan Bro's daughter, Heather Heyer. Countless were seriously injured. Silence.

Finally, on Saturday afternoon, Trump tweeted a response: "We ALL must be united & condemn all that hate stands for. There is no place for this kind of violence in America. Lets come together as one!"

About two hours later Trump issued a statement that began, "We condemn in the strongest possible terms this egregious display of hatred, bigotry and violence on many sides—on many sides." The statement was vague and left plenty of room for interpretation. The president had failed to call out the hate-group perpetrators by name. Instead, he blamed both the perpetrators and defenders, and did not call the deadly speeding car incident domestic terrorism. Later that evening, Trump sent "best regards to all of those injured."

When asked what the president meant by "on many sides," a White House spokesperson responded: "The President was condemning hatred, bigotry and violence from all sources and all sides. There was violence between protesters and counter-protesters today." When pressed for examples of what exactly the president saw or heard from the counter-protesters that was bigoted or hateful, the spokesperson failed to respond.

It wasn't until Monday, August 14, 2017, more than 48 hours after the hate groups invaded Charlottesville that the president called out the white nationalists who started this conflict by name. What should have been a swift, clear and simple statement condemning what occurred in Charlottesville took Donald Trump three days to utter. As a result, he found himself standing alone among Republicans and Democrats, both of whom viewed his handling of the situation as days too late, and much too weak. Many felt the nation was in moral fight for its soul, and Trump diplomacy not only failed to acknowledge the gravity of the situation, he showed no contempt for the perpetrators.

Then, on Tuesday, August 15, 2017, President Trump, furious at the criticism leveled at him for his lukewarm remarks on Saturday and Monday, abandoned his previous remarks and again blamed both sides for the Charlottesville violence. "I think there is blame on both sides," the president said in a combative exchange with reporters at Trump Tower in Manhattan. "You had a group on one side that was bad. You had a group on the other side [the "alt-left"] that was also very violent. Nobody wants to say that. I'll say it right now.... I've condemned neo–Nazis. I've condemned many different groups. Not all of those people were neo–Nazis, believe me. Not all of those people were white supremacists by any stretch.... Some were very good people."[9] The push back was immediate, from all spheres of the political spectrum, and from both the public and private sectors.

In addition to the political firestorm from both Republicans and Democrats, religious and civil rights leaders called for firing Bannon and Gorka, who had both been associated with the white supremacist "alt-right" movement and have ties to anti–Semitic, right-wing groups in Hungary. "Supporters of white supremacists, violent extremism, racial bigotry, and new–Nazis should not serve in the White House or in any level of government," said Vanita Gupta, president and CEO of the Leadership Conference on Civil and Human Rights.[10]

Resignations flooded into the White House. One after another, high-profile business leaders who were members of several economic advisory and manufacturing councils resigned in protest over Trump's remarks. Included were Alex Gorsky (Johnson & Johnson), Andrew Liveris (Dow), Bill Brown (Harris Corp), Brian Kranich (Intel), Denise Morrison (Campbell Soup), Dennis Muilenburg (Boeing), Doug Oberhelman (Caterpillar), Elon Musk (Tesla), Greg Hayes (United Technologies), Inge Thulin (3M), Jeff Fettig (Whirlpool), Jeff Immelt (G.E.), Jim Kamsickas (Dana), John Ferriola (Nucor), Kenneth Frazier (Merck), Kevin Plank (Under Armour), Klaus Kleinfeld (Arconic), Marillyn Hewson (Lockheed), Mario Longhi (U.S. Steel), Mark Sutton (Ford), Mark Fields (International Paper), Michael Dell (Dell), Michael Polk (Newell Brands), Richard Kyle (Timken), Richard Trumka (A.F.L.-C.I.O.), Scott Paul (Alliance for American Manufacturing), Thea Lee (A.F.L.-C.I.O.), and Wendell Weeks (Corning).

The Strategic and Policy Forum, chaired by Stephen Schwartzman, who heads Blackstone, one of the nation's largest investment firms, and which is intended to advise the president on economic policy also collapsed. Included among those members who left were Adebayo Ogunlesi (Goldman Sachs), Bob Iger (Disney), Daniel Yergin (HIS Markit), Doug McMillon (Walmart), Elon Musk (Tesla), Ginni Rometty (IBM), Indra Nooyi

(PepsiCo), Jack Welch (G.E.), Jamie Dimon (JP Morgan), Jim McNerney (Boeing), Kevin Warsh (Hoover Institute), Larry Fink (Blackrock), Mark Weinberger (EY), Mary Barra (G.M.) Paul Atkins (Patomak), Rich Lesser (BCG), Toby Cosgrove (Cleveland Clinic), and Travis Kalanick (Uber).

Both groups had already received several resignations because of Trump's decision to pull out of the Paris Climate Accord. However, the mass resignations following Charlottesville forced Trump to disband both councils.

New York City megachurch pastor A.R. Bernard stepped down from Trump's unofficial Board of Evangelical Advisors. Bernard's Brooklyn-based Christian Cultural Center claims a membership of 37,000 and is considered the largest evangelical church in New York City.

Liberty University President Jerry Falwell, Jr., who has been a staunch supporter of Donald Trump, tweeted that he was "so proud" of Trump for his "bold truthful" statement on the Charlottesville tragedy. Students responded that Falwell's alignment with Trump was a source of "shame and anger" and called on alumni to return their diplomas to Falwell's office by September 5th. By publicly severing their ties with the Lynchburg, Virginia, school, including present and future support, the graduates hoped that through their action the school would realize that Falwell's political position could jeopardize future enrollment.

The Susan G. Komen Breast Cancer Research Foundation was the first organization to respond to the president's Charlottesville remarks by redirecting its largest annual fundraiser away from Trump's Mar-a-Lago resort in Florida. The American Red Cross, The Cleveland Clinic, The American Cancer Society, and The Salvation Army quickly followed by rescheduling their annual events at other sites. By mid–August, more than 20 groups who had engaged the services of the Mara-Lago resort in the past decided not to use the facility again.

Kennedy Center 2018 honorees Norman Lear, Lionel Ritchie and Carmen de Lavallade all announced they would not attend the traditional White House reception prior to the Kennedy Center ceremony. "In light of the socially divisive and morally caustic narrative that our existing leadership is choosing to engage in, and in keeping with the principles that I and so many others have fought for," de Lavallade wrote on her website.[11] Trump responded by announcing that neither he nor Melania Trump would be attending the Kennedy Center Honors this year. Except for extenuating circumstances, sitting presidents traditionally have attended the ceremony.

The president's Committee on the Arts and the Humanities took their response one step further, and not only resigned en-masse, they called for the president to resign too. The resignation letter, signed by all 16 council members, called out Trump's "hateful rhetoric and support of hate groups and terrorists."[12] The first letter of each paragraph, read vertically, spelled "RESIST."

On Friday, August 18, 2017, Bannon left his position in the White House. The following Friday, Gorka also left. It was reported that Bannon had been fired, although by whom, and for what reason, was not clear. It was never determined whether Gorka was fired or resigned.

Bannon immediately returned to Breitbart News as executive chairman, leading to widespread speculation that he was wasn't really fired, but was being sent back to the media world, where he would be able to shore up Trump's political base without the political restraints imposed upon White House staffers. Others posited that Bannon was taking too much attention away from Trump. Either way, Bannon never missed a beat in his continuing assault on the left.

"The Trump presidency that we fought for, and won, is over," Bannon told The Weekly Standard the afternoon he left the White House. "We still have a huge movement, and we will make something of this Trump presidency. But that presidency is over. It'll be something else. And there'll be all kinds of fights, and there'll be good days and bad days, but that presidency is over," he said.[13] "His [Trump's] natural tendency—and I think you saw it this week on Charlottesville—his actual default position is the position of his base, the position that got him elected… "I feel jacked up. I am definitely going to crush the opposition. There's no doubt," Bannon said, referring to himself as "Bannon the Barbarian."

The fallout from Charlottesville continued. As days went on, the White House remained mostly silent on Charlottesville, and Trump's only allies appeared to be Pence and former Klu Klux Klan Imperial Wizard David Duke, who had tweeted his thanks to Trump for his handling of the Charlottesville protest.

Calls for Congress to censure Trump, which Speaker of the House Paul Ryan (R–WI) did not support because he felt it would be "distracting" increased, along with calls for impeachment. Senate Majority Leader Mitch McConnell (R–KY) stated privately that he "doubts Trump can salvage his presidency."[14] For several weeks, Trump and McConnell, who has been in Washington for a long time and is very politically astute, had been locked in a political cold war that threatens to cripple the Republican majority in Congress.

Trump's next public appearance was on August 20, 2017, in a campaign speech. Although Phoenix Mayor Greg Stanton had asked Trump not to come to his city, in order to allow more time for healing following Charlottesville, Trump showed up anyway. In a boisterous, unrestrained rant he re-litigated the coverage of the Charlottesville incident, blasting the media for dishonest and biased reporting, and claiming he did everything right. He concluded by saying that he will build a border wall, even if he has to "shut down the government to do it," referring to upcoming budget negotiations. Neither of Arizona's Republican senators appeared with him, and several hundred protesters gathered outside.

Similar to the Charlottesville incident, reaction to Trump's remarks was fast, unflattering, and engendered serious concerns regarding his mental stability. "There was no sanity there. He was like a child blaming a sibling on something else," CNN's Don Lemon said immediately after the rally. David Chalian, CNN's political director, added that Trump was "totally unhinged" during the speech.[15]

Rick Wilson, a conservative pundit, went even further: "It was an astounding chain of lies tied together by lunatic asides by a man who obviously is mentally unstable. I mean, I'm not joking about it or being a smartass; this is a man who is not well," Wilson said.[16] "This is a man who is not qualified or mentally or morally fit to be the president of the United States and tonight was one more proof of it." Calling the speech "downright scary and disturbing," James Clapper, the former director of national intelligence, indicated he was worried about Trump exercising the powers of the presidency. "I worry about frankly the access to nuclear codes. In a fit of pique, if he decides to do something about Kim Jong Un [North Korea] there's actually very little to stop him."[17]

On August 24, Washington Post editorial writer Eugene Robinson called for a serious conversation about Trump's mental health and proposed the possibility of invoking the

25th Amendment, which allows the vice president and the Cabinet to relieve the president of his "powers and duties" if he is unable to discharge them.[18] "It is uncomfortable to talk about the president's mental health. But at this point it is irresponsible not to," Robinson wrote.[19]

Trump's failed moral and domestic diplomacy has raised many very serious questions about race and politics in 2017 America. Although many women, and men, would like to claim that Donald Trump is "not my president," he is, and concerns about the damage he may do during his presidency have increased dramatically during the first months of his presidency.

In "Dancing with the Devil: Donald Trump's Moral Failure," I describe the events in Charlottesville during August 10–12, 2017, that proved to be a turning point in the Trump presidency. Both the president's response and the bi-partisan political and public backlash to his response are documented in the exact words of the speakers. Many view the Charlottesville incident as revealing "the real Donald Trump"[20] and have come to regard him as a morally impotent leader aligned with the wrong side of history.

In her essay "Diversity En Masse," Danielle James points out that all of us have multiple identities we need to honor and explains her concerns about American pluralism going forward. She argues that just surviving is not enough and that developing good interracial communication that reflects the diversity in America is an absolute necessity. Although her essay was written before the Charlottesville incident, she identifies many of the issues that are at its core.

Ruth Burgess Thompson's essay, "The Administration of Running with Scissors Strikes Fear in the Hearts of Everyone but Fetuses and the NRA," brings politics down to the state level. Written from Iowa, which is dead center in America's heartland, she reveals how conservative politics have changed women's lives in some deeply upsetting ways.

NOTES

1. www.indystar.com, July, 21, 2016.
2. Russell Kirk, *The Conservative Mind* (Washington, D.C.: Regnery Publishing,1953, 2001).
3. www.indistar.com, *Ibid.*
4. For an additional discussion of Bannon's influence, see the section titled "When Blind Justice Isn't Blind: Women Face the Criminal Justice System."
5. The alt-right, or alternative right is a term applied to a loosely defined group of people having far-right ideologies and reject mainstream conservatism in favor of white nationalism, white supremacy, and other, similar beliefs.
6. www.cis.org
7. See the section titled "Alternative Facts: Donald Trump Off the Rails" for further discussion.
8. https://twitter.com/#!/ClaraJeffery, editor of Mother Jones Magazine.
9. Michael Shear and Maggie Haberman, "Trump Defends Initial Remarks on Charlottesville; Blames Both Sides," *The New York Times*, August 15, 2017.
10. www.msn.com, August 15, 2017.
11. www.carmendelavallade.com
12. www.businessinsider.com August 17, 2017.
13. www.weeklystandard.com, August 17, 2017.
14. Alexander Burns and Jonathan Martin, "McConnell Doubts Trump Can Save Presidency," *The New York Times,* August 15, 2017.
15. www.cnn.com, August 23, 2017.
16. *Ibid.*
17. www.huffingtonpost.com, August 23, 2017.
18. Eugene Robinson, "It's Time to Talk About Trump's Mental Health," www.washingtonpost.com, August 24, 2017.
19. For more on this issue, see the section titled "Alternative Facts: Donald Trump Off the Rails."
20. Wolf Blitzer, www.cnn.com, August 13, 2107.

Dancing with the Devil
Donald Trump's Moral Failure

Paula vW. Dáil

"No one is born hating another person because of the color of his skin or his background or his religion...."—Barack Obama

On Friday, August 11, 2017, a crowd of more than 1,000 people comprised of mostly young, white men carried lit torches and outsized Nazi and Confederate flags while chanting the "Blood and Soil" Nazi slogan,[1] and marched into Charlottesville, Virginia. They had come to Charlottesville from across the country to protest the city's decision to remove a statue of confederate General Robert E. Lee from Emancipation Park. "We're here to fulfill the promises of the Trump administration to make America great again," David Duke, former imperial wizard of the Klu Klux Klan proclaimed. "This is why we voted for him, and today marks a turning point in our efforts to take back the country."[2] Standing behind Duke were hundreds of men armed with chains, shields, helmets, and guns, ready to "take back our country" by force, if necessary.

The white supremacist militia, consisting of neo–Nazis, members of the alt-right[3] and white nationalists that had invaded Charlottesville were met by counter-protestors, mostly Charlottesville residents, who believed they had a right to determine the racial climate of their city and that, moving forward, obvious reminders of the Civil War and the Confederacy were best assigned to the archives of distant memory.

During the next 24 hours, protesters clashed, violence erupted, the governor of Virginia declared a state of emergency and activated the National Guard, and three people died. One was a young woman counter-protester killed in a clear act of domestic terrorism by a neo–Nazi sympathizer from Ohio who drove his speeding car into the crowd of counter-protestors. The other two lives lost belonged to members of the Virginia State Police who had been sent to the scene to restore order. Throughout, the president of the United States and supposed moral leader of the nation was silent. Thirty hours went by without so much as a tweet.

Finally, early Saturday afternoon, the president tweeted a tepid, barely audible response: "We ALL must be united & condemn all that hate stands for. There is no place for this kind of violence in America. Lets come together as one!"[4]

About two hours later Trump issued a statement that began, "We condemn in the strongest possible terms this egregious display of hatred, bigotry and violence on many sides—on many sides." The statement was vague and left plenty of room for interpretation, failed to call out the hate-group perpetrators by name, and did not call the deadly speeding car incident domestic terrorism. Again, barely audible.

When asked what the president meant by "on many sides," a White House spokesperson responded: "The President was condemning hatred, bigotry and violence from all sources and all sides. There was violence between protesters and counter-protesters today." When pressed for examples of what exactly the president saw or heard from the counter-protesters that was bigoted or hateful, the spokesman failed to respond. Later that evening, Trump sent "best regards to all of those injured."

On Monday, August 14, 2017, three days after they had invaded Charlottesville, the president, in a stronger condemnation, finally called out the white nationalists who started this conflict by name. The next day he walked himself back and once again, in a jaw-dropping attempt to claim moral equivalency between the hate groups and those defending themselves against the hate groups, reiterated his position that "there was blame on both sides—both sides." Duke tweeted his thanks to the president for holding steadfast to his position that both sides in the Charlottesville were to blame. The response was bipartisan, swift and furious[5]:

"There is only one side in this," tweeted former vice president Joe Biden.

"The President's talk of violence 'on many sides' ignores the shameful reality of white supremacy in our country today, and continues a disturbing pattern of complacency around such acts of hate," House Minority Leader Nancy Pelosi said. Former Democratic presidential candidate Hillary Clinton, who had described a worrisome "emerging racist ideology" in her campaign, tweeted that her "heart is in Charlottesville today." Later, she added, "the incitement of hatred that got us here is as real and condemnable as the white supremacists in our streets."

Former Arkansas governor Mike Huckabee (R) tweeted: "'White supremacy' crap is worst kind of racism—it's EVIL and perversion of God's truth to ever think our Creator values some above others." Senator Marco Rubio (R–Fla.) and Sen. Cory Gardner (R–CO) both urged the president to use the words "white supremacists" and to label this as a terrorist attack. Rubio then went on a tweetstorm: "The organizers of events which inspired & led to #charlottesvilleterroristattack are 100% to blame for a number of reasons," he tweeted. Later, Rubio added, "Mr. President, you can't allow #WhiteSupremacists to share only part of blame. They support idea which cost nation & world so much pain," he wrote. "When entire movement built on anger & hatred towards people different than you, it justifies & ultimately leads to violence against them."

Former Republican presidential candidate Mitt Romney stated, "No, not the same. One side is racist, bigoted, Nazi. The other opposes racism and bigotry. Morally different universes." Romney later called for Trump to "Apologize to America and the world." Senator John McCain (R–AZ) released a strongly worded statement that said, in part: "White supremacists and neo–Nazis are, by definition, opposed to American patriotism and the ideals that define us as a people and make our nation special." Senator Orrin G. Hatch (R–Utah) tweeted: "We should call evil by its name. My brother didn't give his life fighting Hitler for Nazi ideas to go unchallenged here at home."

Speaker of the United States House of Representatives Paul Ryan (R–WI) tweeted: "We must be clear. White supremacy is repulsive. This bigotry is counter to all this country stands for. There can be no moral ambiguity." House Republican leader Kevin McCarthy (R–CA) said in a statement that the violence was "a direct consequence of the vile and hateful rhetoric and action from white supremacists." House Republican Whip Steve Scalise (R–LA) who was shot earlier in the summer, during baseball practice for the annual congressional Republicans vs. Democrats baseball game, tweeted: "We must defeat white supremacy." Sen. Jeff Flake (R–AZ) tweeted: "We cannot accept excuses for white supremacy and acts of domestic terrorism. We must condemn them. Period."

Members of the conservative Republican House Freedom Caucus, were more direct in criticizing the president for his remarks: Rep. Justin Amash (R–MI) mocked Trump for calling the white supremacists "very fine people," noting that they chanted "racist and anti–Semitic slogans." Rep. Charlie Dent (R–PA) tweeted that the president "must stop the moral equivalency! AGAIN, white supremacists were to blame for the violence." Rep. Ileana Ros-Lehtinen (R–FL) tweeted, "Blaming 'both sides' for #Charlottesville?! No. Back to relativism when dealing with KKK, Nazi sympathizers, white supremacists? Just no." "No words," Sen. Mark Warner (D–VA) tweeted, along with a video from the president's unscripted Tuesday news conference. Former Attorney General Eric Holder tweeted: "This is a time to choose sides—simple as that. There is a right side and an immoral one." "If you are showing up to a Klan rally, you are probably a racist or a bigot," Rep. Will Hurd (R–TX) told CNN.[6] "Apologize…. Racism, bigotry, anti–Semitism of any form is unacceptable." "As a Jew, as an American, as a human, words cannot express my disgust and disappointment.

Democratic representatives were equally critical of the president's remarks: "This is not my President," Sen. Brian Schatz (D–HI) tweeted. "Great and good American presidents seek to unite not divide. Donald Trump's remarks clearly show he is not one of them," Senate Democratic leader Chuck Schumer (D–NY) said on Twitter. Rep. Mark Takano (D–CA) tweeted: "I did not attend the inauguration because I felt President Trump lacked 'moral legitimacy.' This is exactly what I was talking about." House Democratic leader Nancy Pelosi (CA) said, "The president's continued talk of blame 'on many sides' ignores the abhorrent evil of white supremacy, and continues a disturbing pattern of complacency around acts of hate from this president, his administration and his campaign for the presidency," adding that, "From the beginning, President Trump has sheltered and encouraged the forces of bigotry and discrimination."

Virginia Gov. Terry McAuliffe blasted the president's remarks. "Neo-Nazis, Klansmen and white supremacists came to Charlottesville heavily armed, spewing hatred and looking for a fight. One of them murdered a young woman in an act of domestic terrorism…. This was not 'both sides,'" he said. "We need real leadership, starting with our president."

Senator Bob Corker (R–TN), who chairs the Senate Foreign Relations Committee, told reporters, "The president has not yet been able to demonstrate the stability nor some of the competence that he needs to demonstrate in order to be successful. And we need for him to be successful. He also recently has not demonstrated that he understands the character of this nation. He has not demonstrated that he understands what has made this nation great. Without the things that I just mentioned happening, our nation is going to go through great peril."[7]

Senator Tim Scott (R–SC) the only African American Republican senator, in a strongly worded statement, said, "I am not going to defend the indefensible. I'm not here to do that. I'm here to be clear, and to be concise and succinct. His [Trump's] comments on Monday were strong. His [Trump's] comments on Tuesday started erasing the comments that were strong. **What we want to see from our president is clarity and moral**

authority. And that moral authority was compromised when Tuesday happened. There's no question about that. We should all call that on the carpet. I certainly have."[8]

There are at least 700 other monuments to the Civil War and the Confederacy in 31 states across America, which suggests that Charlottesville could happen over and over again. The president's reaction to Charlottesville was no different than claiming both sides were responsible when Hitler's Nazis exterminated six million Jews, because the Jews resisted the Gestapo brown shirts when they invaded the Warsaw ghetto. The Nazis were wrong. There was no moral equivalency in that situation and there is no moral equivalency in this one.

The 917 currently active extremist hate groups in America[9] view Trump's tepid reaction to Charlottesville as empowering and a positive reinforcement of their cause.[10] Everyone else sees his reaction as a catastrophic failure of moral leadership.

This emerging extremist hate movement cannot go unchallenged. It is clearly up to we, the people to face down this threat, because our president is morally unable to step up and lead us through this crisis. The soul of our nation rests upon our individual and collective ability to resist. There is no other choice, because to fail to step up to this challenge is to dance with Donald Trump's devil and be complicit in the moral teardown of America.

NOTES

1. "Blood and soil" was a key slogan of Nazi ideology and German nationalism. The phrase has been adopted as a rallying cry by twenty-first-century American neo–Nazi and white supremacist groups.

2. www.cnn.com August 12, 2017

3. The alt-right is an ultra-conservative movement that mixes racism with white nationalism and populism.

4. @realdonaldtrump

5. Unless noted otherwise, all tweets are from a report by Dartenorro Clark, www.nbcnews.com.

6. www.cnn.com, August 15, 2017.

7. www.bloombergnews.com, August 17, 2017.

8. www.politico.com, August 17, 2017.

9. www.splcenter.org, 2017. It is impossible to count the number of individuals belonging to these groups because their activities are internet-based. The Southern Poverty Law Center also documents a 17 percent increase in hate groups since Donald Trump formally entered national politics.

10. The Daily Stormer, a major hate group website, moved to the dark web the day following their post endorsing the president's remarks on Charlottesville.

Diversity En Masse

Danielle James

Pussies lined the horizon. They touched the clouds and scraped against Manhattan's office buildings. Tampons clotted with blood were tucked into envelopes and dropped into mailboxes. Donations to Planned Parenthood were made under Mike Pence's name. Mailboxes swelled with post cards stamped with colorful uteri. Some contained words of support and were aimed at fellow women, many were laden with sharpness and flung at the conservative white men who are in the position to make decisions that affect all of us. In a nation divided by the election of a government that led with hubris rather than thought, women collectively worked together to reclaim their rights after being disregarded.

As a woman, I was proud to see the turnout of women, children, and men at the Women's March in New York City. As a Black woman, I wondered what it meant that this march was so well attended by protesters yet, compared to the other marches I'd participated in, was sparsely guarded by police officers. The marches where we protested the poisoning of clean drinking water. Police brutality. The killing of innocent Black women, children, and men. The attempts to justify their murders. Was I to feel excited that the multiple groups I belong to, due to my multifaceted identity, had a common opponent to battle against? Or was I justified in being bothered that "Black Lives Matter" was the only chant that got stuck in marchers' throats and refused to spread out?

In sociology, it is asserted that members of oppressed groups are required to obtain a dual consciousness.[1] They must know and understand their social environment from their own disadvantaged point of view *and* from the point of view of their oppressor. W.E.B. Du Bois describes this concept in *The Souls of Black Folk*, "It is a peculiar sensation, this double-consciousness, this sense of always looking at one's self through the eyes of others, of measuring one's soul by the tape of a world that looks on in amused contempt and pity. One ever feels his two-ness."[2]

As I marched, friends and allies by my side, I felt both a sense of collectivism and it's opposite. Yes, the people around me were my allies, but were they my allies in every sense of the word? Or did they only serve as allies to me (and I to them) when it came to the mutual causes we cared about? Many of the people walking along New York City's streets had only recently felt the jolt of attack on their identities. They had just begun to discover the pain and frustration of being discriminated against because of their essence, something they could not possibly ever change, even if they wished to do so.

I thought of my grandmother, an Ashkenazi Jewish girl from Poland who grew up in Belgium. She was only 16 years old when World War II broke out and was separated from her family and forced to go into hiding. As a teenager, she had to view herself through her point of view *and* that of her oppressor in order to understand her position in society as a Jewish girl in a Nazi-occupied country. Eventually, she had to take it drastically further and mimic her oppressor in order to survive. In doing so, she was forced to suppress her own identity and adapt the look, naming conventions, and manner of speech of the same people who were out to exterminate her. The culture she had grown up with was to be eradicated, as was her name, and all connection to her family. In an abhorrent way, the stifling of her own identity in order to take on that of her oppressor resulted in her surviving the war; however, along with it came a lifetime of depression and survivor's guilt. All but two of her family members died in concentration camps. Those who did survive the war often spoke of a combination of luck and help from others.

It's well known that many underground resistance networks sprung up during the Nazi invasion. Allies who didn't agree with the government's policies collaborated for and with those who were targeted. In Belgium, the Comité de Défense des Juifs worked to place Jewish children underground and in non–Jewish households. They forged false identification papers, and had a network of volunteers who carried out tasks that could cost them their lives if caught. It is this organization that placed my grandmother to live and work as a maid with the family she stayed with until the war was over. In the documentary, "The Righteous Among the Nations," Andrée Geulen, a Comité de Défense des Juifs member shared she decided to help Jewish people after learning they were being taken captive and murdered by Germans. She stated, "Suddenly you start seeing everything neat and clear. It is like if someone opens a curtain in front of you."[3]

This is the insight I craved from my fellow marchers. The realization that just because something may not affect you directly, it is still worth fighting for, advocating for, or protesting against. As my friend and I pasted glitter slogans on colorful cardboard, we felt energized. Throughout the day, we noticed how few other signs matched the sentiments ours shared: the value of Black lives and that of sex workers. Yet, I remained hopeful that the feelings that propelled our fellow marchers to come out and publicly protest could be the starting point of their curtains being opened. While some white women may never fully understand what it's like to live as a Black man in America, perhaps experiencing the discomfort and outrage at statements made during the 2016 election cycle, is enough to start generating more empathy. It is this emotion that caused members of groups who were not being persecuted to band together with those who were. It is this emotion that was the catalyst to maintain the organization that contributed to saving my grandmother's life.

Still, survival can be considered a victory; but what happens once the war is over and you're forced to start a new life in a society that violated your rights? Are you able to fight back? Or is your sense of self so merged with that of the oppressor that their projection of you becomes part of your identity?

Today, racism, anti–Semitism, sexism, and other prejudices are still prevalent, and preconceived notions taint many opportunities for different cultures to come together. Our government is made up of men who believe women should be forced to have children they do not want. Who believe that people brought to the United States as children should be sent back to countries they were born in but cannot remember. Who believe women shouldn't marry other women, and men shouldn't marry other men. Who refuse to consider sex and gender as anything but binary. Who believe whichever religion they practice should be taken into account when making laws that apply to people with vastly different beliefs. Who believe refugees from war-torn countries are not entitled to a safe place to live. Who believe the color of one's skin determines the value of one's life.

Because of all these beliefs, I'm concerned. I'm concerned about my friends who've lived in the United States longer than I have but are considered less American than me, only because I happened to be born in a hospital in Manhattan. I'm a first-generation American who grew up abroad; they're first-generation Americans who are forcefully excluded from becoming citizens. I'm concerned about my brothers, who can at any time, for any reason, by any police officer, get shot and killed. I'm concerned about my sisters, who, much too frequently, are victims of sexual violence and denied the care they seek. I'm concerned. And angry. Angry with the people in government who do not care about the full breadth of the population of this country, and only choose to serve those who are most like them. Angry at lawmakers who think women are responsible for bearing and raising the child of the man who raped them. Angry at the juries who continue to accept the overused discourses of guns that were mistaken for tasers, children being labeled as thugs, and the constant justification for killing Black women, children, and men who "appeared to be a threat," yet turned out to be harmless, a fact uncovered only after their bodies had been punctured by multiple rounds of bullets. Angry at marchers who were appalled by statements of molestation due to one's perceived gender but felt comfortable with murder due to one's perceived race.

It is here that dialogue as a form of activism comes into place. In *Interracial Communication: Theory into Practice*, Mark P. Orbe and Tina M. Harris discuss how engaging in dialogue helps people understand one another's experiences and bridge the gap.[4] Resolution is not always possible, and thus not a required outcome. Instead, the goal is to continue to communicate and engage in dialogue with each other.

In addition to being a woman, I'm also a sister, girlfriend, worker, student, writer, feminist, activist, and more. I'm Black. I'm Jewish. I'm Jamaican. I'm Belgian. I'm American. I don't believe in any god. All of these personas contribute to the way I see and experience the world from a particular standpoint that is very different from a white male's perspective. Similarly, I'm viewed through a different lens by coworkers, friends, family members, and strangers, and each interaction is influenced by the relationship, position, and point of view of both myself *and* the other party.

As an individual and a member of multiple cultural and gender groups that continue to be systemically oppressed, one way that I assert authorship of my identity is through my writing. People may look at me and read me one way, perhaps even through a stereotypical lens, but through my writing, the same people get to understand my relationship with the world and explore the dissimilarities that exist due to the respective places in society we inhabit. When I write, I tend to debunk the traditional narrative and create a relationship between form and content, which, in turn, allows me to explore the space that exists between my different cultural and personal identities. The space that causes me to simultaneously march in solidarity *and* in protest.

Perhaps my desire in preserving these multiple view points, rather than merging them together, is gained from my mother, who took me to the Synagogue on holidays but never taught me to believe in god, and considers herself Jewish and not Belgian. Or perhaps it was my father, a Jamaican man who was raised in America, and identifies as a true New Yorker, who cultivated this idea.

Ultimately, the plural perspectives that shaped my experience in the Women's March in New York City, and are represented in my work, reflect my point of view, which was fostered in my childhood household. A place where there were no white men making decisions for the rest of us without taking into consideration how that affected us. A place where multiple generations, cultures, and personas effortlessly co-existed.

As I trekked through New York City's avenues, wearing my Black Lives Matter shirt and waving my double-sided pussy-slogan signage, I thought of the historic moment that was unfolding. The warning this occasion signaled to the conservative white men in power who decided to ignore, ridicule, and force their decisions on us. I thought of a quote from Carole Maso's essay "Break Every Rule" that I'd read years ago in my first creative writing course, that still applied on this particular day, "If through language, through literature, through what we make we refuse to accept our limitations, if we are wild and unruly and unswerving in our conviction and irreverence, will those who try to contain us get it finally?"[5] They might not get us, the fragmented groups in society whose oppression sometimes does and sometimes doesn't intersect, but together, we'll make sure they cannot ignore us.

NOTES

1. Julia T. Wood, *Gendered Lives: Communication, Gender, and Culture* (Belmont, CA: Wadsworth Publishing, 2012).

2. W.E.B. DuBois, *The Souls of Black Folk* (New Haven, CT: Yale University Press, 2015).

3. Lemathematique31. "The Righteous Among the Nations." YouTube video, 23:11. Posted April 2013. https://www.youtube.com/watch?v=p9HRn7P3-FU.

4. Mark P. Orbe and Tina M. Orbe, *Interracial Communication: Theory into Practice* (Thousand Oaks, CA: SAGE, 2013).

5. Carole Maso, "Break Every Rule," *Break Every Rule: Essays on Language, Longing, and Moments of Desire* (Berkeley, CA: Counterpoint Press, 2000).

The Administration
of Running with Scissors
Strikes Fear in the Hearts
of Everyone but Fetuses
and the NRA

RUTH BURGESS THOMPSON

I am a political junkie living in America's Heartland, home of the Iowa caucuses and lots of corn—13.7 million acres of corn, growing in big fields that stretch east to west between the Mississippi and Missouri Rivers, and north to south between politically progressive Minnesota and acutely conservative Kansas. Brutally hot in the summer and brutally cold in the winter, Iowa boasts a population of 3.13 million people and 15 million hogs. Seven times more pigs than people inhabit some of the richest farmland in the world.

I live and work in Des Moines, the state capital, located just about dead center in the state. I'm fortunate to work close enough to the place where Iowa laws are made to make a quick run across the street to attend legislative hearings during my lunch hour. As a left-leaning liberal, I do this not only to resist, but also to bear witness to the carnage.

Iowa occupies a special place in American politics, because, beginning in 1972, every four years it hosts the "first in the nation" race for president of the United States. Most recently, on February 1, 2016, hearty Iowans braved sub-zero temperatures to caucus in 1681 precincts across the state and cast their vote for president. The process is a lengthy, convoluted one that results in a straw poll to select the favored candidate. Some people believe that the winner of the Iowa Caucuses will go on to win the presidency, but this isn't true. In 2016, Ted Cruz and Hillary Clinton won the Iowa Caucuses. That night Donald Trump told us he "loved Iowa" anyway and might buy a farm here. He only came back to Iowa twice after that, each time promising to "make America great again," and then went on to win Iowa's six electoral votes, and the presidency. No matter the final outcome, every presidential election year begins with all eyes on Iowa.

Until May 24, 2017, Terry Branstad was our 39th and 42nd governor, holding the distinction of being the longest serving governor in American history. He resigned to accept President Trump's offer to become the U.S. Ambassador to China. No one is quite sure how a governor who was born, raised, and has never lived anywhere other than Iowa, which is smack in the middle of the United States of America, ended up as America's chief diplomat in the largest, most influential country in the entire Pacific Rim and all of Asia. Republican Lt. Governor Kim Reynolds succeeded Branstad and became Iowa's first female governor.

Iowa's General Assembly is comprised of 88 Republicans and 61 Democrats, with 27 percent of the Iowa House of Representatives and 7 percent of the Senate being women. All but seven of the women are Democrats. Both U.S. senators and three of the four U.S. representatives from Iowa are Republican. Senator Charles Grassley is an elder statesman in Washington and still actively farms back home. Our other senator is a freshman who castrates hogs on her day off.

This is the political world I live in on a daily basis. While I've witnessed the very best, and the very worst in Iowa's political leaders, we are currently suffering through what I call "The Administration of Running with Scissors" because they remind me of out-of-control kindergartners with something sharp and potentially dangerous in their hands. Also, because their tendency is to cut out everything and anything that represents change, progress, or hope for better lives, especially for women. In my view, Iowa lawmakers, nearly all of whom are men, lack the good judgment to avoid pissing on their own shoes when they visit the strictly gender-enforced restroom.

For example, three stunningly hateful and contradictory pieces of legislation dropped on the same day:

- SF2 would allow a woman who sought and received an abortion to sue the physician who performed the abortion for emotional distress, with no statute of limitations. This means that five, 10, or 50 years after an abortion a woman, for whatever reason, later comes to regret, she can sue the physician she asked to, and consented to, perform the procedure. This is to save imaginary taxpayer money.
- SSB1008 would force people who file suit and lose to pay the legal fees of the party they filed suit against. While this may discourage frivolous lawsuits, because no one can predict the outcome ahead of time, it also discourages valid ones, and encourages shady practices to continue, on the assumption that the violator isn't likely to get sued or be otherwise held accountable.
- SF2 would end the Family Planning Waiver, causing the state to lose 2.7 million federal dollars which would then be pulled from other underfunded social service programs. This is real taxpayer money.

This year we've seen bills that declare fertilized eggs are persons and can sue their doctors, and using contraception, other than condoms, was declared murderous behavior toward potentially viable fertilized eggs. I get that the legislators love zygotes, but can't help wondering why they don't seem equally predisposed toward educating living, breathing children.

The saddest and most offensive thing I saw was on March 14, 2017, when I watched 38 male senators, and one female senator, pass a twenty-week ban on abortions. Forget that most non-viable pregnancies are not diagnosed until after 20 weeks gestation, and that this bill hurts women during what is possibly the most heartbreaking time she'll ever face—when she discovers her wanted pregnancy is doomed but she will, nevertheless, be forced to carry the fetus to term, knowing that it will either die at birth or live only a few, agonizing hours or days.

Iowa is not a good place to be pregnant. Further, someone better tell State Senator Mark Chelgren that his degree from Sizzler U doesn't qualify him to practice gynecology. Someone also needs to tell State Senator Ken Rozenboom that the tired old fetus in a jar story he keeps trying to tell on the floor of the senate is an urban legend that's been around at least since I was in puberty.

Someone needs to tell Senator Brad Zaun that he can't show up drunk at his girl-friend's house, pound on her window and call her a slut at the top of his lungs and still claim to respect and want to protect women. And, someone needs to take Senator Amy Sinclair aside and tell her to stop passing legislation that hurts women and start remembering that she is one of us. Personally, I'm torn between giving her a hug, just to show her what one feels like, and moving to her district to run against her.

I've watched the GOP majority attack voting rights, Planned Parenthood, public sector workers, minimum wage workers, Des Moines Waterworks, LGBTQIA protections, education, and yes, even paper bags. Apparently, the only thing they don't hate this session (besides cold hard cash from the Koch brothers) are guns.

They love guns so much that they want us to be able not only stand our ground with them, but carry them on school campuses, in libraries, and even in the Capital building. Considering how much harm Republicans have done in the few short weeks they've had the majority, they should probably rethink that one.

Here's my quick 2017 Iowa Legislature recap:

- Lawsuits bad, except if you're a zygote, then lawsuits good.
- A non-viable pregnancy: bad for the fetus, forget about the mother.
- Death for prison inmates, who cares?
- Saving imaginary taxpayer money: Good
- Wasting real taxpayer money to punish Planned Parenthood: Good
- Stand your ground, regardless of what the ground is: Good
- Local control: Good except when it's not
- Women controlling their own bodies: Bad
- Government controlling women's bodies: Good
- Protections for people who are LGBTQIA: Bad
- Collective bargaining: Bad
- Fair wages and worker protections: Bad
- Asking paper or plastic: Bad
- Clean water: Bad
- Public education: Bad
- Voting Rights: Bad
- Guns: Great
- Zygotes: Good, Good, Good—zygotes are always Good

Some of these proposals eventually passed, and some didn't. Regardless, these are the issues the Iowa legislature spent its time debating during the 2017 legislative session. Unpredictable political shenanigans, hatefulness, and nonsense prevailed. It was a comedy show where no-one was taking their job seriously.

Another election cycle will begin in a year. In the meantime, right now, we need to be holding every member of the general assembly accountable, giving credit to those who deserve it and heaping shame on those who deserve it and holding on to the energy and anger we feel right now all the way through the 2018 midterm elections.

The other thing that we absolutely must do is everything possible to minimize the harm to people who absolutely will be harmed by these sanctimonious douche-bag legislators. We must RESIST in every lawful way possible. Democrats, Independents, Progressives, Pink Pussies, Bernie bros and Betties, Clintonistas, Resistors, Indivisibles and just level-headed decent folks who care about social and economic justice must all band together, show up, and push back. Women must vote like our uteruses depend upon it, because they do. We must #DoTheMostGood while they're doing the most harm—then we'll be able to say to them, "Buckle up, buttercups—or you're going down."

SECTION 6.
CLIMATE REIGNS OVER ALL
Fighting Pipelines, Seeking Justice, Saving the Planet

BETTY L. WELLS

> We do not give up on our beautiful planet. We do not give up on a future for every species. We will never give up on our campaign for climate justice.—Women's Environment and Development Organization's Global Call for Climate Justice

On April 22, 2017, people marched for science. One week later, they marched for the Earth, as fears about the damage the Trump administration would do to the environment were being realized. A July 2017 report, Sidelining Science, from the Union of Concerned Scientists,[1] has documented assaults on science, climate change science in particular, through the appointment of hostile agency administrators, rollback of regulations, suppression of data, and silencing of scientists.

Both Oklahoma's Scott Pruitt, named to head the Environmental Protection Agency (EPA), and former Texas governor Rick Perry, named to head the Department of Energy, have ties to the oil and gas industry, as does Secretary of State Rex Tillerson, former Exxon Mobile CEO. These and other Trump appointees favor profits over public protection.[2] In addition, Pruitt, Perry, Tillerson, Interior Secretary Zinke, and U.S. Department of Agriculture Secretary Sonny Perdue are all on record denying longstanding scientific consensus on climate change. Trump's USDA science advisor nominee, Sam Clovis, has raised eyebrows given his climate change denial and lack of scientific credentials, among other reasons.[3]

On June 2, 2017, Trump directed the U.S. out of the Paris Climate Accord, fulfilling a campaign promise while snubbing global efforts to curb global warming[4] and demonstrating "blatant disregard for the threat of climate change—and the impacts that Americans are already experiencing"[5] Withdrawal is not final until the day after the next presidential election, November 4, 2020, but the Trump administration has been busy undermining the agreement with regulatory rollbacks. On March 8, Trump signed a Presidential Executive Order on Promoting Energy Independence and Economic Growth targeting Obama-era regulations to reduce the U.S. carbon footprint and prepare the country for climate change. The order demands review of all regulations deemed to threaten domestic energy production to ensure that the costs to industry do not outweigh the benefits to the public, and removes the obligations of energy producers and automakers to consider the consequences of their actions on climate change. Included in this order is the disbanding of and withdrawal of documents from the Interagency Working Group on the Social Cost of Greenhouse Gases.[6]

Efforts to suppress, eliminate and distort data were noted as early as January, with the disappearance of webpages.[7] In early March, EPA's Pruitt withdrew a November 2016 request for information collection on methane emissions at the request of attorneys general from seven states with strong oil and gas industry interests. This stopped data collection on the emissions of methane, an explosive gas released in large quantities during oil and gas drilling and from gas pipeline leaks, with 30 times the heat-trapping effect of carbon dioxide.[8] Data suppression is also enacted by pressuring scientists, for example, by instructing them not to use the word climate change. The USDA Natural Resources Conservation Service (NRCS) field staff were among those ordered to not use the term "climate change" in working with agency clientele.[9] Such measures produce a chilly, even hostile, work climate, and affect the morale of government scientists and dampen the willingness of others to pursue public service. Scientific advice has been circumvented and scientific grants are subject to review by political appointees.[10]

Climate change and climate activism is the focus of essayists in this section. In his first week in office, Trump issued an executive order reviving the Dakota Access and Keystone XL pipelines, both halted by Barack Obama. He directed the Army Corps of Engineers to expedite the further environmental review for the Dakota Access pipeline announced by the Corps in December 2016.[11] The Corps completed this expedited review and gave the go ahead on February 7.[12] Trump announced the approval of a permit to build the Keystone XL pipeline on March 24, clearing the way for the $8 billion project.[13]

Climate marches and protests are not new. Scores of pipelines crisscross the continent, and the globe for that matter, and in recent years many projects have become the focus of activists and landowners. Pipeline fighters around the world understand that the continued extraction of oil and growth powered by extracted carbon is destabilizing our climate and jeopardizing our future.

But not even the controversial Keystone XL project generated as much worldwide attention and scrutiny as the Dakota Access pipeline.[14] At a historic news conference halfway around the planet in September 2016, President Barack Obama was fielding questions as the first sitting U.S. president to ever visit the Southeast Asian nation of Laos. He wasn't prepared when a Malaysian woman turned the topic to an oil pipeline being built 8,000 miles away in the Midwest U.S. This exchange marked the Dakota Access Pipeline as a global cause for climate protesters and indigenous rights activists, while the new administration joined the fossil fuel industry to sow doubt on the validity of climate science and promulgate alternative facts to feed climate change denial and skepticism.

The U.S. leads the world in climate change denial. The enormity of economic interests served by climate change skepticism influences how people think about the climate. In an August 2017 interview, Al Gore noted how fossil fuel company public relations firms resemble those hired by tobacco companies a few decades ago.

> The large carbon polluters have spent between one and two billion dollars taking the playbook from the tobacco industry, which [in response] to the scientific consensus linking cigarettes to lung cancer

and other diseases … hired actors and dressed them up as doctors and put them on camera to falsely reassure people that there were no health risks to smoking cigarettes. And 100 million people died during the interim before policies were finally changed. They've hired the same PR firms, and it's deeply unethical.[15]

Gore puts climate denial, often attributed to culture war, in the larger context of people's lives and the huge economic changes wrought by globalization—stagnating wages for middle income families, and jobs lost to automation or exported for lower wages. People began to question the experts who charted the globalization path and its failure to improve their lives. And so says Gore: "a demagogue comes in and says, we're going to return to the past. Everything's going to be fine. That has an understandable appeal. It's not working, because it was never based on reality." Regarding globalization, elites were caught unaware; increasing inequality kept their incomes going up.[16]

Expert opinions often advance the interests of experts or the political and financial establishment. Some will cede democratic control to corporations without thought for consequences.[17] Science can function without democracy, but democracy needs science— but not just any old science. Democracy needs science for the public good, not just private profit. Democracy needs scientists—imbued with humility, transparency and respect— to enter the fray; not to talk down to citizens, or claim to have an unbiased corner on objective truth. Democracy needs citizens to hold government, public institutions and scientists to account, and to fight for publicly funded research. Democracy needs citizens and scientists to contest alt-facts, expose efforts to mislead, call out disinformation, and ask who benefits from publicly funded research.

Feminists caution against confusing experts' abstractions with empirical reality. Climate change and resource extraction is no abstraction for those surviving day-to-day, seeking food, water, safety and shelter. The human impacts are not, will not be distributed evenly. The poor, disproportionately women, and those most reliant on natural resources for their livelihoods or with the least capacity to respond to natural hazards—droughts, landslides, floods and hurricanes—will bear the brunt,[18,19] whereas the wealthy have buffers against climate excesses. Climate change is thus both an environmental justice and a feminist issue.

A reflexive self-aware activism will attend to differing interpretations of situations. This is not capitulation into a post-truth[20] world, but rather a wariness of claims to a singular truth. We all have different bodies, origins, histories and standpoints, as well as unique perspectives shaped by culture and ideology. Differences will affect what we determine is true and what is false. Truths are multiple, fractured, partial, and contingent because we accept different things as true.[21] We will gain a fuller picture of a situation with more eyes on it, when we consult the perspectives of others—the more the better.

In "Fighting for Climate Science," Gabrielle Roesch-McNally draws from her talk at the climate march in Corvallis, Oregon. She both defends and challenges science. She asks science to hold up democratic ideals of equity, environmental justice and sustainability, and expresses concern for the most vulnerable and marginalized among us. She calls for a new science paradigm and calls out scientific political agnosticism.

Miriam Kashia, Angie Carter and Danielle Wirth resist by fighting pipelines in places undercut by the Bakken pipeline (another name for the Dakota Access pipeline). They do what they can to radically amend our relationship to fossil fuels and challenge powerful economic interests.

It has taken Miriam a march across the nation, two arrests (thus far) and more. In

"The Making of a Climate Action Warrior" she tells the story of her transformation from concerned citizen to climate warrior, and asks, "How could I not?" For Miriam, direct actions speak louder than words. She seeks to inform and inspire and will talk to anyone. She sagely advises us not to reproach, because guilt doesn't get us anywhere.

Angie Carter's essay, "Homecoming," describes her Bakken Pipeline Resistance Coalition work in her home state of Iowa. Tracing lines that cross geographically and generationally, she connects Iowa's heavily fossil-fuel and export dependent agriculture, built on cheap oil and exceptional prairie soils, to climate change.[22] Iowa is a conduit for oil now flowing underground. Surplus corn is transformed into ethanol, which is blended into the gasoline that fuels the nation's cars.

Love of the Planet is Danielle Wirth's touchstone as she witnesses on behalf of "all our relations." In "Road Talk: Conversations That Keep us Going" she shares her long experience as a citizen scientist and activist in both direct and indirect resistance. Walking on shifting sand is her metaphor for staying the course and not succumbing to despair. In a sentiment similar to Miriam's, she explains that quitting is not an option: "I can do no less."

NOTES

1. Jacob Carter, Gretchen Goldman, Genna Reed, Peter Hansel, Michael Halpern and Andrew Rosenberg. Sidelining Science Since Day One: How the Trump Administration has Harmed Public Health and Safety in Its First Six Months. Center for Science and Democracy at the Union of Concerned Scientists. Cambridge, MA. July 2017. Retrieved August 28, 2017 from http://www.ucsusa.org/sites/default/files/attach/2017/07/sidelining-science-es-ucs-7-20-2017.pdf.

2. *Ibid.*, pp. 13, 14.

3. The names of Tillerson and nominee Clovis have surfaced in the context of the Trump Russia investigation, with speculation that Tillerson's connections to the oil and gas industry and Exxon's oil leases in Russia may have factored into the Trump administration position in favor of removal of Russian sanctions. Clovis was a Trump Campaign operative who vetted Carter Page, who is currently under investigation by Special Counsel Robert Mueller.

4. http://www.cnn.com/2017/06/01/politics/trump-paris-climate-decision/index.html Ret. Aug 14, 2017.

5. Carter et al., p. 17.

6. *Ibid.*, p. 18.

7. *Ibid.*, p. 26.

8. *Ibid.*, p. 19.

9. Jenna Amatulli, USDA, says they never told staff to use "weather extremes" instead of "climate change" but email correspondence just after the inauguration indicates otherwise. www.huffingtonpost.com, August 30, 2017.

10. Carter et al., *Ibid.*, pp. 10, 29.

11. www.motherjones.com/environment/2017/02/dakota-access-pipeline-standing-rock-trump, August 14, 2017.

12. www.pbs.org/newshour/rundown/army-corps-grants-final-permit-finish-construction-dakota-access-pipeline, August 14, 2017.

13. www.voanews.com/a/keystone-pipeline-permit/3780178.html, August 14, 2017.

14. John Holt. November Dec 2016 http://www.argusleader.com/story/news/2016/11/19/how-did-dakota-access-become-worlds-largest-pipeline-protest/94036392, August 14, 2017.

15. Chris Hayes interview with Al Gore, www.msnbc.com, August 14, 2017.

16. In the Hayes interview, Gore owns up to being one of the experts, but says they did a better job in the 1990s respecting the social contract and the obligation to create new opportunities in job training and education for those hurt and damaged by the changes driven by technology and the economy.

17. Colin Macilwain, "The Elephant in the Room We Can't Ignore" *Nature Magazine*, www.nature.com, March 2016.

18. www.un.org/womenwatch/feature/climate_change/factsheet.html, August 14, 2017.

19. www.unfccc.int/gender_and_climate_change/items/7516.php, August 14, 2017.

20. "Post-truth" was Oxford Dictionary's 2016 Word of the Year, https://en.oxforddictionaries.com, 2016.

21. Kathleen Higgins, "Post-Truth Pluralism," www./thebreakthrough.org, 2013.

22. Estimates vary widely (15% to over 30%) depending on geographic area, type of fuel in question (oil, natural gas, or biofuels), and kind of emission (methane, carbon dioxide or nitrous oxide). Whatever the source, they mix in the atmosphere. www.epa.gov.

Fighting for Climate Science

Gabrielle E. Roesch-McNally

In the spring of 2017, in Corvallis, Oregon, I marched for science. I spoke to a small but mighty crowd of people, wearing my "Union of ~~Concerned~~ Pissed-off Scientists" t-shirt and made noise in the streets with fellow neighbors, colleagues, and friends. I spoke that day about why we need to defend scientific research, especially research that is focused on understanding climate change and applying tenets of environmental justice. In this essay, I share some of my musings from that day and other connected thoughts on why I am so pissed off.

Our ability to do relevant, needed, publicly funded science is under threat and so too is our democracy. In the United States, the recent threats to maintaining a vibrant and publicly funded scientific enterprise are unprecedented. A scientifically grounded and evidence-based public policy is fundamentally tied to a democratic society. That is why I cannot remain silent, particularly as the work of many in the scientific community, especially those doing climate change and environmental work, is threatened or dismissed by politicians who find it politically expedient to ignore the ample evidence of our fossil fuel addiction with attendant environmental degradation and documented patterns of environmental injustices. Those with political and economic power want to ignore the truth that climate change, as Naomi Klein claims, "is a civilizational wake-up call. A powerful message—spoken in the language of fires, floods, droughts, and extinctions—telling us that we need an entirely new economic model and a new way of sharing this planet."[1] We need to be spending more time, not less, on solving this economic and eco-logical crisis, yet those in power are seeking to dismantle, ignore, and obfuscate the sci-entific evidence pointing towards the need to radically transform our profligate relationship to fossil fuels and the economic system that underpins their supremacy.

I am moved to act largely because of my experiences growing up in Utah, spending much of my childhood in the mountains and desert and learning to love the natural world. I have always sought, and found refuge in nature. I began to understand, as Terry Tempest Williams[2] asserts, "that the world is meant to be celebrated" yet through this love comes many opportunities to confront loss. My sadness over hearing the many cre-ative ways that humans inflict destruction on other humans and non-human communities has ebbed and flowed in my life as I struggle to find ways to wrestle with what it means to celebrate the natural world and reconcile our social-ecological relationships.

In my own work, I have sought to better understand what motivates human behavior in the face of global climate change; I want to know, in the face of so much evidence suggesting environmental decline with very real consequences to the health of social and ecological systems, why it is so difficult to create individual and collective change? So I explore what motivates behavior—in short, what individual and structural influences constrain and enable pro- environmental action. I am endeavoring to do work on behalf of the public good as so many others are and I am so deeply upset that we must fight so hard *just* to maintain the status quo that we are less able to fight for more relevant and actionable science that will enable us to tackle complex and wicked problems like climate change and environmental injustice.

As I find myself increasingly fired up about defending "science" and scientific research, I also face an interesting dilemma regarding my relationship with what science is. Science is not a monolith and it is not always conducted with democracy, justice, and sustainability at its forefront. Of course, many who "do science" are fighting hard to conduct the most rigorous work they can and much of the social and biophysical research on climate change is a great example of scientists endeavoring to do good work in the name of the public good. It is worth noting, however, that human beings are the ones doing scientific research and therefore the questions we ask, the ways we conduct experiments, the results we uncover, are filtered through our unique individual, as well as cultural, biases and can, intentionally or not, perpetuate oppressive tendencies that are embodied in our social and economic systems.

When using standpoint feminist epistemology, we embrace this knowledge and situate ourselves in our work by clarifying our own unique perspective and intersecting identities that influence how we see the world and why and for whom we do our research. There are, of course, many examples of scientific research being conducted in ways that clearly seek to oppress and subjugate the "other" (for some egregious examples, read up on the Tuskegee Syphilis Trials or the life of Sarah Baartman as the "Hottentot Venus"); suffice to say that the scientific endeavor is not purely objective and will always be influenced by those who have power, wealth and a desire to control, which also includes my own privileged experience as a social scientist who is also a white, middle-class woman living in the Northwestern United States. As a scientist, I must consistently reflect upon and confront how my own intersecting identities influences how I do research, including examining the types of research questions that I pose and assessing who and what are the potential beneficiaries of my work.

Yet in these times, I find myself defending scientists in this post truth world and advocating for fellow scientists, many who are conducting rigorous scientific research on climate change and environmental injustice, many of whom have to defend themselves and their work in an increasingly hostile context. Yet I agree with visionaries like Jane Lubchenco that we cannot do science the same ways we have done in the past, as "today's challenges demand an all-hands-on-deck approach wherein scientists serve society in a fashion that responds to societal needs and is embedded in everyday lives. Humility, transparency, and respect must characterize our interactions."[3] To conduct science in such a way ensures that scientific endeavors more closely embody democratic ideals.

It isn't *just* about fighting for more research dollars or to preserve publicly funded research programs. It is also necessary to confront systems of power and those actors that aim to maintain the status quo because they profit from inaction and are served by an ongoing campaign to delegitimize and rollback the work done to progress, albeit far too slowly, climate and environmental justice efforts. In the spirit of offering up solutions as a way to work through my anger, I want to suggest some action items for protecting and enabling a research paradigm that will get us closer to building a scientific paradigm that embodies democratic ideals.

First, we need to fight efforts to dismantle publicly funded research programs. We should be fighting to maintain and increase this work but we should also hold government accountable for doing science in pursuit of the public good, including protecting and understanding the natural world that sustains us, and further elevating the voices and concerns of the most vulnerable and marginalized. The Environmental Protection Agency's environmental justice program is a good example of a much-needed program that is critically endangered given the current hostility towards this kind of work done in the public realm.

Second, we need to challenge notions about what it means to be a scientist who is publicly engaged, particularly for those of us who do applied work that has a potential to inform public policy and solve real world problems. Many scientists view themselves and their work as politically agnostic yet these times, including the massive March for Science (April 22, 2017) and the People's Climate March (April 29, 2017), suggest that this view is shifting. Organizations such as Union of Concerned Scientists are dedicated to science-based action in an effort to bring about a healthier and more sustainable world by linking both science and policy. 500 Women Scientists[4] is an example of women in STEM (Science, Technology, Engineering, and Mathematics fields) who are trying to train a more diverse group of scientific leaders while using the language of science to build bridges and enhance global diplomacy. More scientists need to learn and, I would argue, push the boundaries of what it means to be an engaged citizen as well as finding ways to use their scientific expertise to highlight social and ecological catastrophe and help illuminate and, in many cases, advocate for solutions.

Finally, we need to fight back against alternative facts that abound in this post truth world, a world where those in power are trying to sow seeds of doubt on the validity and necessity of much scientific work. Yes, scientists can learn to communicate their work to broader audiences to dismantle some of the layers of public mistrust—leaders like Katherine Hayhoe, atmospheric scientist from Texas Tech University, is a great example of scientists making communication and community engagement, specifically with climate skeptics and evangelical Christians, their mission. However, it is critical that we continue to shine the light on the ways that disinformation campaigns have shaped the acceptance of climate science in America and what the consequences of that have been. Well-documented efforts by sociologists Aaron McCright and Riley Dunlap[5] and many others, have helped to shine the light on the very intentional effort on behalf of the fossil fuel industry to shape climate beliefs in the public sector. It is time to be honest about these efforts and contest them when and wherever we can.

I want to end with a quote from one of my heroes, Nobel Peace Prize winner and awe inspiring woman, Wangari Maathai, who started the Green Belt Movement[6] where food security, women's empowerment and ecological restoration were linked to improve the lives of rural communities in Kenya and beyond. Maathai said, in her autobiography written in 2006[7]: "Those of us who witness the degraded state of the environment and the suffering that comes with it cannot afford to be complacent. We continue to be restless. If we really carry the burden, we are driven to action. We cannot tire or give up. We owe it to the present and future generations of all species to rise up and walk." I offer this essay as a way to honor her and the many others who continue to fight for a more just and livable future, where scientific endeavors uphold democratic ideals of equity, justice and sustainability. I continue to explore ways to develop knowledge that is shared and utilized in ways that solve real-world problems and elevate the voices and concerns of those who don't have societal and political power and privilege. I am still finding my way but I am on the path and I continue to walk.

NOTES

1. Naomi Klein, *This Changes Everything: Capitalism vs. the Climate* (New York: Simon and Schuster, 2015).

2. Terry Tempest Williams, *When Women Were Birds: Fifty-Four Variations on Voice* (Basingstoke, UK: Macmillan Publishers, 2013).

3. Jane Lubchenco, "Environmental Science in a Post-Truth World," *Frontiers in Ecology and the Environment* 15, 1, p. 3, 2017. http://onlinelibrary.wiley.com/doi/10.1002/fee.1454/full.

4. Women Scientists: https://500womenscientists.org/.

5. Riley E. Dunlap, and Aaron M. McCright, "Organized Climate Change Denial." *The Oxford Handbook of Climate Change and Society* (New York: Oxford University Press) 2007, pp. 144–160.

6. Greenbelt Movement: http://www.greenbeltmovement.org/.

7. Maathai Wangari, *Unbowed: A Memoir* (New York: Anchor Books, 2008).

The Making of a
Climate Action Warrior

Miriam R. Kashia

The scene is deafening, chaotic and confusing. I can't hear anything but the thunderous sound of the drill boring under the Mighty Mississippi. Behind me on a dirt ridge are some water protectors, and 100 more spread completely around the fence perimeter. I watch as a few people begin tackling the eight-foot fence. They are immediately apprehended as they drop to the ground.

More than 20 law enforcement officers—police, sheriff deputies, and state troopers—are scattered inside the fence watching us. I see some pipeline security guards wearing yellow reflective vests among them. My adrenalin is pumping and I'm trying to focus. We don't really have a plan except to stop that drill, to halt this threat to the Mississippi River, to end the lies and corruption and greed, to terminate the flow of fossil fuels that are killing our planet.

I'm *not* here to get arrested today. I recently paid a hefty fine for a prior arrest while attempting to protect the Des Moines River from this same pipeline. Today I'm only a support person.

Now I see my 80-year-old friend Ann, who is recovering from knee replacement surgery, scrabbling under the chain-link fence someone is holding up for her. She struggles to her feet with the aid of her cane and looks around to get her bearings. I watch as a uniformed officer takes her by the arm and slowly leads her off to a waiting van.

"Oh hell," I yell to no one in particular. I turn around to the screaming crowd behind me on the hill. "Come on! We have to go together. Let's do this! They can't arrest all of us! Let's go! We can stop the drill if we go together! Follow me! Come on!"

I doubt they hear me, and I know they don't follow me. I head by myself over a portion of the fence that has just been flattened to the ground by several protesters. On the other side I creep behind some large objects—I'm not sure what they are but they provide a modicum of cover. I'm stealthily making my way toward the humongous drill. If I can get to it, they will have to shut it down—if only for an hour or a day. I want to cost the pipeline company a lot of money, because I know they are on the verge of going broke. I desperately want to do whatever I can to prevent this menace to the Mississippi. I know in my heart of hearts that *they* are the offenders, not me.

Now one of the officers turns his head and spots me. The jig is up. I'm caught before I can get to the drill. I'm cuffed with plastic zip ties and led to a van. I wait as others are loaded in vans, 30 of us in all. We are hauled off to the Lee County Jail. Three hours later, the paperwork complete, we are released. We've been charged with "misdemeanor trespass," given a hearing date, and sent on our way. The shadow of a $500+ fine hangs over us.

The drill didn't stop—not for a single minute. I am frustrated and disheartened. We have made this effort for nothing.

I am 74. I did not plan to spend my retirement fighting huge drilling machinery along the Mississippi River. I certainly did not expect to be giving dozens of presentations, leading workshops and retreats, attending endless meetings, and traveling far and wide to demonstrate, rally and protest. And I definitely never intended to get myself arrested. But somewhere along the way, I was transformed from a "concerned citizen" to a "climate action warrior."[1]

I was a sympathetic observer on the sidelines during civil rights and Vietnam War protests in the 60s when I was in college and then raising two children and working full time. It never occurred to me that I was capable of doing what they were doing. I joined a National Organization for Women (NOW) consciousness raising group in the 70s, but apart from awakening my own inner feminist and sympathizing with the struggle for gender equality, I didn't see a role for myself. I was trying to keep food on the table and manage life as a single parent.

With hindsight, I realize now that people don't just wake up one morning and decide to be an activist. We don't get up, drink our coffee, and go out to join the ranks of those who are willing to put everything on hold to be a part of some chaotic movement for the greater good. Somewhere deep inside I can see that I have been preparing to play my role in this global climate crisis my entire life.

Growing up the daughter of a Methodist minister, I absorbed values of justice, kinship and compassion for all life. We learned to love our neighbors (which included everyone, everywhere—no exceptions). We had powerful and loving models for speaking out against tyranny and greed. On family camping trips, I learned to love nature. As an adult, I took up almost any activity I could that took me outdoors: bicycling, cross-country skiing, hiking, camping and backpacking, canoeing and kayaking. Nature, the rocks and trees, the animals and birds, the sky and mountains, the forests, plains, rivers and lakes, have always felt like a part of me, or more aptly, I am a part of them.

In college, I read Paul Ehrlich's *The Population Bomb*[2] with great concern. Rachel Carson's *Silent Spring*[3] was a wake-up call. I was learning that we had become a danger to ourselves and to our Earth-home. In recent years when I encountered James Hanson's *Storms of My Grandchildren*[4] and Bill McKibbon's *Eaarth*,[5] something new awakened in me. I began paying attention to the growing climate crisis, its science and causes. The pressure to step outside my comfort zone was starting to feel explosive. I needed to do something. And I needed to do it now. And I didn't have a clue as to what or how. Then one day while browsing the Internet, I clicked a link that brought up this:

THE GREAT MARCH FOR CLIMATE ACTION
L.A. to D.C from 3/1/14 to 11/1/14
3,000 miles—7 million steps

It was recruiting volunteers for a cross-country march of modern day "Paul Reveres." They would sound the alarm, educating and motivating people all across America about the looming climate crisis. I was ripe, eager and ready. At 71, I was still in good health and good physical condition, and I thought to myself, "I can do this." In about a minute, I was in. And, as they say, the rest is history.

The Great March for Climate Action turned out to average a basic group of about 35 people, sometimes more, sometimes fewer, who traversed the USA for 8 months, primarily camping, sometimes sleeping in gymnasiums or church basements, meeting with local folks for potlucks and conversation, speaking in schools, churches, community centers, holding rallies in towns and cities all along the way.

We created a community of support among ourselves named One Earth Village, and dealt as constructively as we could with the inevitable conflicts and difficulties. It was grueling living outdoors and walking an average of 17 miles a day. It was also one of the two greatest adventures I've ever undertaken—the other being my two years in Africa with the Peace Corps when I was 62. Through desert heat, blizzards, tornado warnings, rainstorms, blisters, aching knees, the flu and constant fatigue we persevered. We can never measure any effects of what we did. What we do know for certain is that it transformed and radicalized us, the marchers. My life was changed forever.

We saw with our own eyes and hearts rapidly emerging impacts of our changing climate on communities and families. We witnessed the "sacrifice zones" created by toxic fossil fuel infrastructure constructed in the poorest of communities. We noticed with great sorrow the absence of songbirds, monarch butterflies, and clean flowing streams. We listened to tragic stories of people affected. Everywhere we walked there was stark evidence of the damage our unbridled capitalist economy and materialistic culture are creating. I began as a concerned citizen; by the end I was a "climate action warrior."

Here is what I've learned:

1: Direct Actions speak louder than words.

We're learning that traditionally "following the rules" doesn't work. Agencies such as the EPA set rules dictated by the industries that are being regulated. The very act of "regulating" toxins makes their use legal. It also makes it impossible to protect our communities and ourselves.

For example, we are told that there are limits on Big Ag's pollution of rivers. But because no effective watchdogs are put in place, polluters go ahead and create sewers out of our waterways.

To demonstrate the futility of following the rules, here is an excerpt from an opinion piece I wrote that was published in an Iowa newspaper.[6] All the following was done in attempting to legally block the DAPL/Bakken pipeline:

Thousands of Iowa citizens—just ordinary people like me and the 100Grannies—have made phone calls, written letters, sent emails, signed petitions, filed electronic comments on the Iowa Utilities Board (IUB) website, marched in parades, sent letters to editors and opinion editorials to our local newspapers, held rallies and marches, attended Dakota Access information meetings, testified at the one-and-only public IUB hearing, contacted our legislators and the governor, dropped banners from bridges, participated in flotillas down Iowa rivers, created a satirical street theatre event called "In Bed with the Bakken" in front of the IUB, held news conferences, filed lawsuits, and made as much noise in as many ways as we could think of to demonstrate how serious we are about protecting Iowa's soil and water from the terrible threat this pipeline poses to Iowa and the Earth.

We have also stood in solidarity with landowners who have been forced to sacrifice their precious Iowa farmland through the illegitimate use of eminent domain solely for the private profit of an out-of-state corporation.

I finally concluded that risking arrest through non-violent direct action (civil disobedience) is the only avenue left to me to fight this ultimate injustice. We have tried everything else. Our government, which is charged with the protection and well-being of its citizens, is instead, protecting and benefiting the fossil fuel corporations.

The only way to win against any form of injustice is by refusing to play by their rules.

2: You cannot do this alone. We need one another. Find your people.

After the climate march, it was my great fortune to be part of a number of local environmental activist groups. With them I find community, support, and opportunities. The members have become my beloved friends and fellow travelers.

3: If your heart isn't in an action, don't do it.

Find your unique niche and don't try to be anybody else. Everyone has a role in co-creating a livable future with economic, social and environmental justice for all. Obligation, fear and guilt are not appropriate motivators for activism.

4: Take regular breaks.

Even with good planning, built in fun, and a community of support, the life of a dedicated activist is financially, physically and emotionally draining. If we try to do too much and don't maintain a measure of balance in our lives, we can fall into despair and give up. Burnout is a constant threat. Find your most effective R&R and use it. Then return to the fray refreshed and ready.

5: Trust that every failure on the journey leads one step closer to success.

We cannot know the impact of our ripples. When I returned home after walking over seven million steps across America with the Great March for Climate Action in 2014, the local paper interviewed me for a front-page article. "I'll talk with anyone who will listen to me," I said, "anywhere, anytime about what we did and why we did it."[7]

Be careful what you say. In the past three years, I have given some 50 presentations and the requests aren't stopping. I've spoken to small groups of a half-dozen people and to gatherings of 150 or more. At first, I focused on the amazing story of our march across the country and why we did it. Later my growing activism became the focus of my talks. My goal has always been to inform and inspire, never to blame or reproach anyone.

6: Everything and everyone is connected.

I have learned a new word—"intersectionality." It's not in the dictionary, but it is a valuable and growing concept whose time has come. It means, simply, that all injustice is connected.

I used to say that the climate crisis is so critical that working on any of the other myriad important issues was like rearranging the deck chairs on the Titanic. I quit saying that when I began to understand that all injustice is interconnected. We are all interconnected. Everything is interconnected.

Here's one of my favorite quotes from the legendary naturalist John Muir: "When we try to pick out anything by itself, we find it hitched to everything else in the universe."[8]

7: Remember that we are standing for love and truth and justice. Be the change.

We cannot solve any injustice if we hold the same energy of anger, alienation or hatred that is at its root. We cannot break down barriers and create solutions if we demonize and hate the oppressors.

That lesson was dramatically apparent at Standing Rock. The culture of the movement was prayerful; the intent was to peacefully and persistently stand for truth and justice. I loved being an ally and witnessing the phenomenal cultural renaissance and the courageous stand for their rights over their land and water.

The morning after the 2016 election I climbed out of my tent at Standing Rock, unaware of the outcome. I headed for "media hill," the highpoint of camp where people gathered to use their phones. The minute I saw my friend's face—I knew.

I fell into her arms sobbing, feeling inconsolable and hopeless. She took me down to a circle of people gathered around the sacred fire. As I took my place in the circle, a woman next to me with whom I'd volunteered in the mental health first aid teepee saw my distress. She told me she'd just come from talking with one of the elders and wanted me to know what he said to her. "Today we will dance and drum and sing. We will not give in to fear, because fear is what feeds the darkness." The relief and resolve I felt was immediate and lasting.

Many Iowans have been fighting the DAPL/Bakken pipeline for nearly three years. As I write this, toxic crude oil has begun flowing from the fracking fields of North Dakota across North and South Dakota and Iowa to Illinois for distribution on the global market. "If you drill, it will spill." We know this will happen. We just don't know where or when.

I've been arrested at peaceful, non-violent actions twice in Iowa, first in an attempt to stop the drilling under the Des Moines River in central Iowa and then along the Mississippi River in southeast Iowa. About thirty people were arrested with me in each action. For the Des Moines River action, I paid my fine, gave a speech at our news conference after our hearing, and went home to fight another day.

For the Mississippi River arrest described at the start of this essay, I and four other members of 100Grannies.org, pled not guilty. We demanded a trial. We spent several months in preparation, only to have the case dismissed. It was a disappointment, to say the least. I believe they simply did not want us to have our say in court about the necessity of what we did and they did not want to see the headlines: " '100 Grannies 5' on Trial for Protecting Mississippi River."

My arrest for a peaceful attempt to prevent an oil spill disaster on the Mississippi River was a travesty. Boring under our farmland and our rivers in order to pump oil for private profit on the world market when the nations of the world agree that we must focus now on transitioning to sustainable energy is unconscionable.

Because I cannot be complicit by ignoring this reality, I broke a law. I walked onto property that had been taken by eminent domain from a farmwoman against her will. This for a pipeline owned by an out-of-state for-profit corporation. I was trying to halt a dire threat not only to the Mississippi but also to life on Earth. How could I not?

From a moral standpoint, on October 1, 2016, at the Mississippi Stand in Lee County, Iowa, the law protected the evildoers and arrested those who stood in harm's way for the greater good. In my view, this is a crime against nature and humanity.

> Do not be daunted
> by the enormity of the world's grief.
> Do justice, now.
> Love, now.
> Walk humbly, now.
> You are not obligated to complete the work,
> but neither are you free to abandon it.
> —Rabbi Tarfon—1st century

NOTES

1. "Warrior," I have learned, means "protector" to the Lakota people.
2. Paul Ehrlich, *Population Bomb* (New York: Ballantine Books, 1968).
3. Rachel Carson, *Silent Spring* (Boston: Houghton Mifflin, 1962).

4. James Hanson, *The Storms of My Grandchildren: The Truth about the Coming Climate Catastrophe and Our Last Chance to Save Humanity* (New York: Bloomsbury, 2009).

5. Bill McKibben, *Eaarth: Making a life on a Tough New Planet* (New York: Times Books, 2010).

6. Iowa City Press Citizen, 11/27/14.

7. *Ibid.*

8. John Muir, *My First Summer in the Sierra* (Boston: Houghton Mifflin, 1911), p. 110 of Sierra Club Books 1988 edition.

Homecoming

ANGIE CARTER

My friend, Sylvia, and I stand on an old farmstead overlooking the South Skunk River valley in Mahaska County, Iowa. There's not much up here but an old corncrib, a root cellar, and a small barn. Sylvia points to the remains of an old coal mine in the distance to the northwest. To the northeast, she points to a power line crossing the river along the edge of her family's property. The Dakota Access pipeline now crosses beneath that power line, beneath the river.

Sylvia and I first connected in the winter of 2014. She lives and works in Hawaii, but was back in Iowa, as she occasionally is throughout the year, managing her family's land near Oskaloosa. Her family had received a letter stating that their farmland was in the proposed path of the pipeline and so Sylvia returned that winter to attend informational meetings the Iowa Utilities Board held in each county along the proposed Dakota Access pipeline route. At the time, I was a graduate student at Iowa State University and part of a growing coalition formed in resistance to the pipeline. Sylvia and I have more in common than our shared opposition to the pipeline; we are both the 7th generation of our families to call Iowa home, and we are both descendants of white settlers whose race entitled them to farmland claims along the South Skunk River.

Today, we're walking her family's land and are accompanied by Sylvia's daughter, Sarah, Sarah's boyfriend, Daniel, and Willa, my dog. We apply generous coatings of sunscreen and mosquito repellent before descending the hill to the wooded floodplain.

In July 2014, the *Des Moines Register* published a front-page story about a pipeline proposed by the Texas-based Energy Transfer Partners. The project would require both condemning tracts of Iowa's farmland and obtaining permits from the U.S. Army Corps of Engineers to cross Iowa's rivers. The process by which natural gas pipelines and utility projects are approved and constructed is familiar in Iowa, if not always welcome. Iowans are also familiar with debates about environmental policy—agribusiness has a heavy hand in framing statewide discussions about soil erosion, water pollution, and climate change. An oil pipeline, though, was an entirely different thing.

Iowa has never been an "oil state," yet it is thanks to oil that Iowa's landscape is now a monoculture of corn, hogs, and soybeans. In a time when wind turbines tower across the horizon and the state is deeply invested in the production of corn-based ethanol fuel, it can be easy to forget that Iowa's agriculture is powered by oil; crops require an increasingly toxic cocktail of petroleum-based herbicides and pesticides, and their planting, harvest, and transport requires gasoline-powered vehicles.

Big Oil may be a new player on Iowa's political landscape, but, as Sylvia pointed out while standing on the hill, Iowa is no stranger to extraction. First, the land was colonized and commodified by white settlers. Then, it was made "productive" through the plow and coal mines. Now we continue to mine Iowa's fertile soil for ever-ubiquitous cheap corn. The prairie's deep roots created the soil, but it was thanks to cheap oil that farm size increased, machinery grew ever larger, and petroleum-based chemical inputs were made possible.

This is the first time I've stood above a crude oil pipeline. Dakota Access bored under this hill and beneath the river in the fall of 2016, so the pipeline is 50 feet or so under my feet. Downhill I watch the South Skunk flow by where a small yellow sign on a yellow pole states, "WARNING PETROLEUM LINE" with a number to call in case of emergency. Uphill is where some brave activists from the Mississippi Stand camp crawled into the pipeline last fall, delaying the completion of this river crossing for a while. Weeds grow tall around me. Above me stretches a big blue sky. Does anything feel different? I wait.

I grew up in rural Iowa during the 1980s Farm Crisis. My generation has been pretty good at leaving the farm, leaving town, and leaving the state. Seven years ago, I moved back to Iowa to pursue graduate study in sociology and sustainable agriculture. I returned to the town where my great-great grandparents' graves rest in the city cemetery, where I'd graduated high school, and where my parents still live. My plan was to study sustainable agriculture and sociology at Iowa State University, where four generations of my family had studied before me. Iowa was "home," but I did not know yet what that meant. Unexpected events, such as this pipeline, and new friends, like Sylvia, have been my teachers in learning more about the landscape that is my home.

In 2014, I was in the midst of my dissertation research data collection, interviewing women farmland owners across the state. The focus of my research was conservation, specifically conservation to improve water quality—not about oil pipelines. Of course, oil pipelines are also threats to water, and the women with whom I met had opinions about the pipeline. By fall of 2014, I had connected with two women farmland owners whose land was at risk of condemnation for the proposed pipeline.

On Memorial Day weekend of 2016, Sylvia and I met just north of this point where the pipeline crosses beneath the river and put canoes and kayaks into the water. Sylvia had organized a day of community events with the Bakken Pipeline Resistance Coalition[1] in effort to educate the community about the then-proposed pipeline. We began with a flotilla along the river, over the proposed path of the pipeline, and concluded in town with a reading at the bookstore. Sylvia's extended family joined us, as did Meskwaki tribal members from Tama, and community members from across Iowa. The flotilla was the kick-off to the Coalition's 2016 Summer of Resistance to the Dakota Access Pipeline. We felt, then, that we just might have a good chance to stop the pipeline.

Sylvia calls me back. I leave the stretch of ground referred to a pipeline "easement" in the legal paperwork but which I know to be a trespass. We return through the woods. Sylvia talks about her forest management plan and her hope to maybe try growing mushrooms in these woods someday.

I've been part of the pipeline resistance efforts for nearly three years now, and I've learned a lot from new friends like Sylvia who see both the past and the future of the land. I've lost count of the rallies, petition drops, community meetings, press conferences, and marches I have attended or helped to organize, but I can easily name and share the stories of people now connected forever through their involvement in this grassroots campaign. The pipeline is a toxic trespasser, yet its trespass has united together a motley and beautiful group of resisters, protestors, activists, and protectors. In our work together, we have rediscovered what a powerful thing it is to be a neighbor to one another, and to these rivers.

There has been an ongoing flow of support across state lines from Iowa up to North Dakota over the last three years. Nonviolent direct-action trainings, legal help, financial and material support, allies traveling from one state to another to speak at various rallies and meetings—we have learned from each other and valued the solidarity we've formed through our shared resistance to the pipeline. Similarly, within Iowa, the pipeline has brought together those not often found sharing coffee together these days—farmers and environmentalists, people across the political spectrum, rural and urban residents. One stoic farmer stood at the back of the room as a poet-activist read a poem about fracking in the Bakken region. The farmer admitted to those of us around him, "I've never been to an event like this." Neighboring in this way is new to all of us and there is a lot to learn.

Many are already doing a post-mortem of the local and national organizing against the Dakota Access pipeline—what we learn is important and will continue to inform future resistance to extractive energy projects. What might be easy to miss, though, is the tremendous outpouring of community-building that has grown throughout the past three years: networks forming across historical, ideological, and political divides at a time when the country is increasingly polarized, especially in places like Iowa, a purple state turned red in the 2016 election.

Dakota Access moved in the boring machine to the Des Moines River's eastern bank in Boone County, Iowa in the late summer of 2016. Beginning at the start of 2016, with the flotilla Sylvia helped to organize in Oskaloosa along the South Skunk River and creation of resistance camps along the Mississippi and the Des Moines Rivers, Iowans engaged in many acts of resistance in effort to protect the water. Hundreds were arrested throughout the state. One woman was even arrested attempting to block earth moving equipment on her own farmland. Others were arrested blocking construction equipment, trespassing, and locking down to machines and in the pipeline itself.

In early September, I stood along the Des Moines River with my parents and over a hundred others at another day of action. We started the day with a non-violent direct-action training and I paired up with a friend to provide support, should she be arrested.

Like many people that day and many other days, I stood in front of the equipment attempting to enter and leave the construction zone. Children led chants in the megaphones: "Protect the wildlife, Protect the fish!" People played drums, waved signs, and carried banners while sage burned. After a couple initial warnings, the County Sheriff alerted us to our final warning—letting us know we would be arrested if we did not move. With each final warning, I moved, but some did not, and were arrested. Eventually, the arrestees filled a school bus. Our combined efforts delayed work by a little.

There were final warnings in Boone County, Iowa. Local law enforcement's reactions to efforts there were far different than the violence led by the Morton County Sheriff's office near Standing Rock. Thanks to leaked documents, we now know that Dakota Access hired a private security firm named TigerSwan to infiltrate and surveil resistance efforts, and that TigerSwan colluded with public law enforcement. In one document, TigerSwan staff complains about the Boone County sheriff's office not complying with efforts to squash protest. Still, it was in Boone County that an activist who was locked down to the pipeline was threatened with felony charges and took a plea deal that included 30 days in jail for charges that should have been misdemeanors—trespassing and interference.

Several weeks after our action at the Des Moines River, as the boring machine continued its deep descent below the river, members of the Meskwaki tribe held a water ceremony near the river crossing. Soon after, the drill bit hit sandstone and broke. Finding and transporting the new drill bit delayed construction a little longer.

Energy Transfer Partners—Dakota Access' parent company—first claimed that the pipeline would be operational by the end of 2015, then the target date was pushed to the end of 2016, and then—ironically—Sunday, May 14, 2017, Mother's Day. Finally, after many delays, oil began flowing through the pipeline on June 1, 2017. The Dakota Access Pipeline now crosses Iowa from its NW to SE corners, with a pipe carrying fracked Bakken crude oil flowing beneath the creeks, rivers, farms, pastures, highways, and past towns and cities.

I've driven the stretch of the pipeline's path through central Iowa often over the past three years. The scar of the pipeline's construction might be easy to miss for those who do not know to look for it, but I will never forget it.

First, the stakes with orange flags dotted the route. I have found these stakes in piles along the ditches of gravel roads, pulled by Good Samaritans and left as signs of warning. Then came the heavy machinery, the trucks with license plates from Mississippi, Louisiana, and Texas, and the men. They cleared trees where needed and cut deep trenches across the farm fields and pastures, giant walls of soil lining either side. I lost my breath the first time I saw the deep cut into the earth—I had seen photos of pipeline construction, but did not understand the scale. Dakota Access representatives told the Iowa Utilities Board that they would take good care of the soil horizons in effort to protect the soil's fertility when replaced around the pipeline, but I and many others took pictures of soil piles eroding into flooded areas and construction crews working in wet and raining conditions. Oil companies, of course, know little about environmental care—their expertise and specialties are in extraction and profit. The long blue snake of the pipeline appeared shortly after the trenches, and now hides beneath cornfields and ditches, in the sunken area of a pasture.

The pipeline is 30 inches in diameter and can carry up to 570,000 barrels of crude oil per day, with a potential spillage of roughly one million gallons per hour, flowing past the homes of residents of Sioux Center, Cherokee, Storm Lake, Rockwell City, Boone, Ames, Des Moines, Newton, Pella, Oskaloosa, Ottumwa, Fairfield, and Keokuk. At the larger river crossings, a small yellow sign alerts the public to the hazard beneath the soil at the river crossings—Big Sioux, Rock, Floyd, Little Sioux, Des Moines, South Skunk, and Mississippi.

The names of these towns and rivers may not mean much to most people. Iowa is written off as flyover country, and I've heard some people say Iowa is a good place for a pipeline. They assume that rural spaces are mostly empty, or places that are easy for most to forget—the latter of which may be true.

Many of these towns and rivers, though, are very familiar to me. My dear friend and college roommate's family is from Rockwell City. The state capitol is in Des Moines—I grew up visiting its Adventureland Park and rode my first roller coaster there. In Boone, I learned the story of Kate Shelley's heroism[2] on a Girl Scout trip and was inspired to be brave like she was. Ames is where my parents live and several generations of my paternal family have lived; it is where I graduated high school and also where I completed my doctoral studies. My mom, brother, and I were all born in Newton. Annual school field trips took me to visit Pella's Tulip Time festival each spring. As a child, I often tried on back-to-school shoes at the JC Penney store in the Oskaloosa Mall. The Des Moines River provides drinking water for thousands of central Iowans. My ancestors first settled along the banks of the South Skunk River in central and southeastern Iowa. I have camped and hiked along the bluffs of the Mississippi.

The pipeline crosses my home geographically, but it also has crosses through generational time. In the NW corner of the state, Dakota Access bored the pipeline 85 feet below the indigenous burial mounds at the Big Sioux Wildlife Management Area. Significant indigenous sites line the Des Moines River and South Skunk River corridors, but crews worked through the night and through rain in their haste to get the pipeline in the ground and it is impossible to know what may have been in their path. The risk the pipeline poses to those downstream and to future generations is also largely unknown, though it is well documented that even new pipelines leak and that continuing to extract carbon from the earth to power continued growth is already destabilizing and changing our climate.

Even as the oil flows, so too continues the resistance. Just this morning we've heard the good news of a federal judge's opinion in support of the Standing Rock tribe's claim that the pipeline's permitting violated the law. A legal case still moves forward in Iowa on behalf of the Iowa Sierra Club and some Iowan landowners.

The pipeline is personal. I know that all pipelines and fracking wells are personal to someone—crossing someone's land, polluting someone's water, compromising the health of someone's community, and of course the continued extraction of oil jeopardizes our climate and our collective future. We know, care, and rally around this knowledge. Yet, it's different when it's happening where you grew up, jeopardizing the water you drink and health of your town. I cared deeply about environmental justice before the pipeline, yet my understanding of it was compartmentalized and privileged. The diagonal of this pipeline's path brought the desecration of the fossil fuel industry home; it also inspired me to rethink my relationship with Iowa.

Home is a place, but it is also a verb. *Home*—as in, to return by instinct. How can we best live home as a verb? Like the monarchs, this journey home—however we define it—is one of generations rather than lifetimes.

"There are no unsacred places; / there are only sacred places / and desecrated places," writes Wendell Berry in "How to Be a Poet." The desecrated places are easy to see in Iowa—the soil erosion, the emptied towns, the collapsing barns, and now the scar of this oil pipeline. The sacred places I've found, though, are mobile—they are found in the moments I've shared with others working to protect our shared home. This is revolutionary because it means that sacred places can be everywhere, or anywhere, one continues to care for community despite, or in spite, of destruction.

Home is not an obligation, but an invitation to action. These days especially, home seems to be an invitation to resistance however we can wherever we are rooted—resistance to the ongoing desecration, whatever that looks like where we live. All of our actions are important in different ways, but are not sufficient in and of themselves. What we do must be part of something bigger, a larger shift or turn, as we connect with the many and ever-growing number of people who are similarly re-orienting and returning in resistance: discovering neighbors, protecting the sacred, creating homes.

This weekend I'll return to the Des Moines River where last summer and fall I stood with fellow Water Protectors in effort to stop a pipeline. I expect there will be some grieving for all that is at stake, some thought as to what we should have done differently, but also celebration for all that is sacred in what we continue to share and create together—this community, this home.

NOTES

1. In Iowa, the Dakota Access Pipeline was originally called the Bakken Pipeline.
2. Shelley crawled across the Des Moines River railroad bridge one night to warn an oncoming passenger train about a crash down the line, saving the lives of as many as 200 passengers.

Road Talk

Conversations That Keep Us Going—
An Interview with Danielle Wirth

Betty L. Wells

Danielle Wirth and I have logged many miles as travel companions over the years, supporting each other through trying times and celebrating the good. The 2016 election fed lively road trip talk, pre and post-election. We were devastated, as many others, by the results. For us, practicing ecofeminists, it was a double body blow, an assault on women and on the Earth. Ominous clouds had been gathering. Thunder sounded and lightning struck as the calendar turned from November 8 to November 9. With age-inflected weariness, we concluded: here we go again.

On inauguration day we took a pilgrimage to Springbrook Conservation Education Center where we founded the Women, Food and Agriculture Network (WFAN) in 1997. The trip was less symbolic than practical: to get out of town on inauguration day, to be in a nature setting, to be spared televised images of the new president, and to talk resistance. [PD note: Denise O'Brien is the WFAN founder; www.WFAN.org/founder.]

As a frequent chronicler of Danielle's activism, this essay flowed naturally. She credits me with being partner and co-creator of adventure, but here I celebrate her perseverance. I used the interview format to get Danielle's words on paper, but as this essay has taken shape some of my questions flow into her answers, akin to our frequent conversations.

Betty L. Wells: *Could you say a bit about your roots, as insight into what animates your activism?*

Danielle Wirth: My wellspring is my lifelong love affair for our Planet. My early captivation by Nature deepened into a fascination with ecological processes and the beings that participate in ecological cycles. I was fortunate to be raised by progressive parents in a wild landscape. I wandered aimfully among huge Beech, Oak and Eastern Hemlock trees, protected by faithful canine and equine friends. That early experience imbued me with confidence—not deference to the dominant culture and men in particular. Thanks Mom, Dad, Grandma, Auntie and Uncle! Upon discovering in college that my deepest learning happened beyond four walls, I turned to natural history and ecology. As a naturalist, I shared the stories of the Land. Through work as park ranger and visitor center manager, ecological restoration practitioner and university teacher, I've gathered evidence, like a forest accumulates leaf litter, of how human greed and ignorance ruins the land.

Continued human tenure on Earth requires the biodiversity held by wild places. We need raw, untrammeled, unmanageable, uncontrollable nature for prudential value, for our own good. All life depends on the "collective" of creatures interacting with each other and the elementals of earth, air, fire and water.

BLW: Ecological services is a new name for an old support system.

DW: Deep roots in native savanna and prairie soil now energize my teaching and feeds my soul. I nudge my students to fall in love with their bioregion and its community members. Science points to the grave danger of catastrophic ecological meltdown. My love of other amazing beings meets a bone-chilling fear that we are poised to lose it all. If I can convey the love and excitement for what culture calls "nature," while honestly conveying the possibility of utter catastrophe, my students will come to defend the sacred ground. They deserve hope, too, that Dickinsonian thing with feathers that perches on the edge of the soul.[1]

BLW: Much of your activism centers on water, not surprising since much of recent Iowa environmental politics is about water and agriculture. In the last several years, you've stepped up as a Water Protector in the Bakken[2] Pipeline Resistance. Can you say more about that?

DW: Iowa lost homes for federally protected species when the Bakken pipeline rammed under many large and small rivers, tore through old, diverse forests and uprooted Iowa farmland. Iowa's outgoing governor, Terry Branstad (now Trump-appointed ambassador to China) facilitated the abuse of Eminent Domain for private gain. He received money for his last election from Kelcey Warren, Texas pipeline magnate for filthy Bakken crude. My testimony at hearings about the surety of metallic pipeline failure because of Iowa's complex mesic (damp) soils, and the endangered species harmed by polluted water and buried oil pipelines, falls on ears plugged with dirty dollars. I am pissed. I am furious.

BLW: Your righteous anger reminds me of that old bumper sticker, God is coming and she is pissed!

DW: I am in a rage, but not a blind rage. I am focused. Terry Branstad's legacy is dirty water, depopulated rural communities, a biologically impoverished landscape, and depopulated rural communities. Iowa is a new colony of China. Rural Iowa gets sewage, stench, toxic water, and abused immigrants. China gets pork. This industrial corporate agricultural set up allows rich men to extract profit without making restitution for the land and people they rob and break. Branstad and the Republican-controlled statehouse made compliance with clean water laws voluntary. They gutted the esteemed Leopold Center for Sustainable Agriculture,[3] and even closed the environmental education center we visited on inauguration day

BLW: Much of Iowa is an ecological sacrifice zone.[4] Too many believe that nature doesn't happen here.

DW: We are caught in a culture addicted to the technical fix. The pipeline company is now funding research at ISU to determine the effect of the pipeline on farmland. Care to wager about the results of research? We would be better served by a good dose of precaution, conducting research before the damage is done and with thought to the consequences of our actions.

BLW: The 2015 Des Moines Water Works (DMWW) lawsuit was a bit of a wakeup call about consequences. Can you say a bit about that?

DW: This lawsuit was against drainage districts in three upstream counties in north-central Iowa requiring costly nitrate pollution remediation to make downstream drinking water safe. Although the suit was eventually dismissed, it was a big deal in Iowa as it raised the possibility that big agriculture might be held responsible for cleaning up its own messes. DMWW provides drinking water for ~ 500,000 people in the Des Moines metropolitan area and the first and biggest nitrate removal facility in the world—such is the scale of the problem.

BLW: *Iowa Governor Terry Branstad accused DMWW of declaring war on rural Iowa. His declaration of war claim left me wondering, don't rural Iowans want clean water?*

DW: Of course rural Iowans want clean water! Most of us living in rural Iowa are not among the 25 percent or so who make a living in "agriculture." That bucolic myth of red barns, happy cows in green pastures and a little four-row corn picker is not the reality of mainstream agriculture. The diverse mix of small grains, corn, hay, vegetables, cattle and hogs grazing on crop fields after harvest is all but gone. What's left of the old complex prairie soils now grows a corn and bean monoculture, a system benefitting only a few, while literally mining what is left of the 2-plus feet of rich, dark topsoil, some of the most productive in the world. But it's not Iowa's job to feed the rest of the world. Real food security happens when, worldwide, all farmers are supported so that they can grow healthy food for their family, neighbors and community

BLW: *To my mind, the "feed the world" narrative cloaks questionable agronomic practices with moral certitude. Danielle, you resist publicly—writing letters to the editor, testifying at public hearings and standing at barricades—but also behind-the-scenes, out of the public eye, as when you review applications for confined animal feeding operations (CAFOs). This work is not glamorous, but it is important. Could you explain how it works?*

DW: Construction permits are scored by a bureaucratic compromise called the Master Matrix (MM) developed in 2002. County supervisors use the matrix to score plans to construct factory farms in their communities. MM is a dodge to circumvent true local control. The Iowa Department of Natural Resources (IDNR) has the ultimate say whether or not applications get approved or denied. IDNR approves nearly every application that meets the bare minimum requirements. It is extremely lax regulation—50 percent (which teachers know is an "F" by most standards) is considered a passing grade. Iowa's deregulation of CAFOs caused a $5 billion water and public health crisis.[5] Fixing the details of the MM is not a substitute for true local control over the approval, denial, and siting of factory farms. Local and state politicians need to put people and planet—not corporations—first.

BLW: *In a recent letter to the Des Moines Register, Kamyar Enshayan points to the folly of renaming and reducing the problems of industrial agriculture to simply nutrient management.[6]*

DW: Nutrients are leaking, witness the DMWW law suit. He is pointing out that problems such as pesticides and fertilizer in drinking water, manure spills that kill life in our rivers, multinational meat packing plants and absentee-owned egg factories that evade public health and labor laws, and public health threats from massive hog confinement operations have been incentivized by government programs and shaped by global grain merchants who happen to control all grain markets as well as seeds and inputs.

BLW: *So, the choice is to manage manure and nutrients rather than reducing the leaks and closing loops in the system. You've pointed out, as does Kamyar, that this system is a colo-*

nizing economy that leads to rural decline. Can you say a bit now about when you take direct action and when your resistance takes less overt forms?

DW: I've always been in challenge mode. I generally speak out when something is out of ecological balance, or when civil rights are at risk. For me, it is not an either/or choice, but both. Philosophically, I am a bioregionalist. I am a citizen of my watershed, moving with the seasons, ebbs and flows of the Tallgrass Prairie. I participate in active ecological restoration and witness the local phenology—natural phenomena that recur periodically, such as migrations and flowerings, and their relation to climate and changes in season. When I have the energy, my response—social or ecological—will be direct. When my energy is low or I am recovering from direct action, I respectfully observe, encourage and support those doing the direct action. A younger friend once told me that when I am too sore to move, I need to sit comfortably and become a storyteller. We'll see

BLW: *That seems fitting given your dissertation a few years back on environmental ethics as situated narrative.[7] I remember you saying that people will die for dogma but facts rarely move them. It seems we need better stories to carry our facts and our values. In our recent project with women farmland owners, River Stories: Views from an Iowa Watershed,[8] we used a storytelling approach, PhotoVoice, known for giving voice to oppressed people. I wondered aloud whether our participants, the women landowners, would self-identify as oppressed. Likely not, you said. Their photos and captions told a variety of stories of life in the Raccoon River watershed, but they were not about personal oppression; most were "giving voice" to human and non-human life in the Watershed. Can you say more about your views on speaking for nature?*

DW: At one of my early ecofeminism conferences, philosopher Karen Warren asked: Do trees have standing?[9] What a metaphor! My native friends call trees the Standing People. Standing is also a legal term that determines whether an entity has legal recognition and title to pursue litigation. I live in an Oak Savanna. Trees are neighbors, I respect them. I pay ecological rent by bringing healing "Rx" fire under their boughs so seeds disperse, wildflowers, sedges and grasses are stimulated and alien plants are discouraged from over-powering the natives. I extend reciprocity in my relationships with nature, to plants and animals, to "all of our relations

BLW: *You said something not long ago that I jotted down, about never really winning: "Even though I lobby, I find it is just deflating because the bad guys won it all and they are arrogant and choose not to listen." As seasoned activist, how do you go keep going?*

DW: I will not, as Robin Wall Kimmerer[10] puts it, participate in the destruction of this Earth; I will not be complicit. I cannot say all beings matter and then casually and thoughtlessly buy, drive, eat and seek diversions that prevent me from seeing the reality of my actions. This attunement must be lived. I just entered my sixth decade. I have experience and advanced degrees, and although my scientific testimony at hearings often falls on deaf ears, I can use what's left in my body to cook wholesome food for fellow activists or block access to pipeline construction sites.

There's a shift happening. People are awakening. Iowa "nice" is turning Iowa "angry." Those of us who've resisted, stood up, spoke up and acted up are being joined by more and more people. Things are changing nationally too. Donald Trump presumed he was King. Now, as his unscripted, unhinged behavior and lies made public continue, a special investigation is underway and for once in a very long time, the insulated U.S. Congress is afraid. Will course correction happen soon enough? I do not know, but I am acting as though it will. I can do no less. I also give myself permission to weep, to get angry, to find comfort in friendships, good walks and talks, the sky and knowing that our ancestors struggled and sometimes, it made a difference. I remember that my Great-Grandmother was not allowed to vote until she was older than I am.

BLW: What else makes you angry?

DW: I am put off by willfully benighted people, rich people who never had to learn how to be human because their wealth insulates them from learning compassion, humility, hard work, and seeing the impact of their greed. And recently, the worst of our nature ascended to the most powerful position in the world

BLW: Kathleen Fischer writes that we can overcome the anger that flows from injustice, powerlessness, or the irresponsibility of others by coming together, refusing to be defined by the powerful, and acting to change the system.[11] *You do this all the time.*

DW: This prompted our founding of WFAN [Women Food and Agriculture Network].[12] Our mission and ecofeminist goals[13] were set in positive defiance of our patriarchal rural culture.

BLW: WFAN endures, but so do the challenges: more consolidated land ownership, increased pollution, and a tightening corporate juggernaut. Maybe things would have been worse without our efforts—cold comfort. More encouraging, a new generation of feminist leaders has stepped into our worn shoes.

DW: The 2016 election and aftermath seems the culmination of what has been happening under our noses for some time, and not just in Iowa: an attack on women and the environment, but also on democracy and public institutions. In the last session, the Republican-controlled Iowa statehouse hit the middle class with cuts to public education and broke public unions and collective bargaining. Rampant economic individualism rides roughshod over community and environment, oblivious to the public interest and common good. Public institutions are adrift from their moorings, while corporations have been awarded personhood!

BLW: Deeply interconnected and political challenges call for systemic and strategic responses. It's not easy!

DW: When I wallow in worry about no longer having the solid anchors of predictable seasons to keep me safe in shifting sands, when the ground literally falls out from under me, I remember that I grew up along the ocean. I know how to walk on constantly shifting sand and keep my balance. Sometimes I get knocked down and rise up to meet the next wave. Sometimes I cannot get up until after a second wave breaks over me, burying me with frothy surf. But then, I have always stood up; I pivot sideways, maybe surge forward to find sand that is solid. Sometimes I must step back to find a more solid foothold. We are all scrambling to replace the sand under our feet. Hopefully, we can do it without losing our balance. I have recently learned through a generous Tai Chi teacher how to transfer my weight, and only take the next step when my weight has shifted. It is a slower movement, but more secure. Tai Chi tells me to balance, breath, shift weight.

And, I've been blessed with great friends—like you—who seem to know when to call and check in, drag me out for a walk or a good meal, or a road trip. It's really important that we take care of each other in these crazy times.

BLW: *Yes, we will get through this together. We have covered a lot of ground, Danielle, but have to leave other ground uncovered, as we have now used up our allotted words.*

DW: I am breathing in and slowly breathing out, measured and focused—with gratitude. My prayer is that we all awaken and fully realize that we are in "the Garden" already.

NOTES

1. Emily Dickinson, "'Hope' Is The Thing with Feathers." Digital Public Library of America, http://dp.la/item/8643a746bc8a5c3eed1c0d04e1f85684. ~1861.

2. In Iowa, the Dakota Access Pipeline was originally and is still called the Bakken Pipeline.

3. John Collins. Rethink this Iowa. Do not gut the Leopold Center for Sustainable Agriculture. http://inthesetimes.com/rural-america/entry/20270/iowa-leopold-center-for-sustainable-agriculture-water-soil-cafos-nitrates In these Times. 2007.

4. Dana Jackson. *The Farm as Natural Habitat* (Washington D.C.: Island Press, 2002).

5. http://iowacci.org/in-the-news/too-much-manure-iowa-cci-case-study-exposes-dnr-failure-to-crack-down-on-factory-farm-pollution/; http://iowacci.org/wp-content/uploads/2017/01/Master-Matrix–info-sheet-and-resolution-FINAL.pdf; http://www.sierraclub.org/sites/www.sierraclub.org/files/sce/iowa-chapter/Ag-CAFOs/Matrix.pdf

6. Kamyar Enshayan http://www.desmoinesregister.com/story/opinion/readers/2017/05/23/big-mistake-create-iowa-nutrient-research-center/337599001/

7. Danielle M. Wirth. "Environmental Ethics Made Explicit through Situated Narrative: Implications for Agriculture and Environmental Education." (Ph.D. Dissertation, Iowa State University, 1996).

8. Betty Wells and Angie Carter. "Watershed Stories: Grassroots Efforts in Iowa's Raccoon River Watershed" *Leopold Center for Sustainable Agriculture Grant Report,* Paper 519. 2016. http://lib.dr.iastate.edu/leopold_grantreports/519

9. Karen J. Warren. "Ecofeminism," Environmental Ethics Conference Presentation, Springbrook Conservation Education Center, Guthrie Center, IA, 1992.

10. Robin Wall Kimmerer, *Braiding Sweetgrass: Indigenous Wisdom, Scientific Knowledge, and the Teaching of Plants* (Minneapolis: Milkweed Editions, 2013) p. 2.

11. Kathleen Fischer, *Transforming Fire: Women Using Anger Creatively.* (New York: Paulist Press, 1999).

12. Denise O'Brien is the identified founder of WFAN. www.WFAN.org/founder.

13. Angie Carter, Betty Wells, Jessica Soulis and Ashley Hand, "Building Power through Community: Women Creating and Theorizing Change," in *Women in Agriculture Worldwide: Key Issues and Practical Approaches*, Amber Fletcher and Wendee Kubik, eds. (New York: Routledge, 2016) pp. 225–239.

Section 7. Sick in the USA
When the Personal Becomes Political

Paula vW. Dáil

> This country's morality is best measured by our commitment to our most
> vulnerable citizens: the poor, the disabled, the elderly, and the children.
> —U.S. Senator Hubert Humphrey (D–MN)

On Wednesday, November 5, 2008, the day following Barack Obama's election as president of the United States, then Senate Minority Leader Mitch McConnell (R–KY) convened a closed-door meeting of all Republicans serving in Congress. McConnell wanted the answer to one question: how were Republicans going to prevent a successful Obama presidency? "The single, most important thing we want to achieve is for Obama to be a one-term president," McConnell told The Heritage Foundation a few days later.[1]

The reasons for this singular focus on crashing the Obama presidency, rather than strategizing on how, as the minority party, Republicans could work with the new Democratic president, and a Democratic Congress, to advance the good of the nation, remain murky. McConnell has a known history of racism, and many believe his motivation was simple: he just could not stomach the possibility of a black man being a successful president.[2] Nevertheless, the outcome of this meeting was that Republicans decided to oppose any legislation the incoming president, and the Democratic Congress, brought forth, regardless of its benefit to the American people. Republicans became "the Party of No" and a primary focus for their opposition was healthcare reform legislation, which they knew President Obama was determined to enact—and he did.

In 2010 Congress passed, and President Obama signed, the Affordable Care Act, aka ObamaCare. Although not perfect, the bill meant that for the first time in American history, nearly all Americans finally would be able to access affordable health care. Among other benefits, this government-supported program guaranteed individuals could not be denied health insurance because of a pre-existing condition, and lifetime limits on healthcare costs were lifted.

From that moment forward, Senate Majority Leader McConnell led Republicans in vowing to "repeal and replace ObamaCare" because it was, in their view, "unsustainable." Although it was never clear precisely why Republicans believed this, it became a central theme of the 2017 presidential election campaign and has dominated the opening months of the Trump administration.

ObamaCare is paid for by a combination of new revenues, including tax increases, which Republicans are loath to agree to, and cuts in government spending. Health insurance is purchased through a purchasing pool and government subsidies help pay insurance premium costs. The success of the program depends upon large numbers of healthy individuals purchasing insurance to offset the costs of providing insurance to less healthy individuals.

To date, approximately 20 million more Americans have been able to access health insurance than were able to purchase it before this legislation was enacted. Additionally, because the legislation funds Planned Parenthood, it enables women to receive low-cost pre-natal care, reproductive and other preventive health care. However, because women's reproductive rights are a lightning-rod political issue that conservatives are eager to target, Planned Parenthood is taking the political hit in the repeal and replace agenda, despite its efforts in other areas of women's health care.

The political drama surrounding health care is deeply troubling, particularly for those who believe access to affordable healthcare is the right of every American citizen, no matter their circumstances, and not a privilege reserved just for those who can afford to pay for it. However, the politics of healthcare are particularly upsetting for women who depend upon Planned Parenthood for affordable preventive care, because all proposals to repeal and replace ObamaCare include defunding this critical health care option for women.[3]

Pro-life conservatives believe women's health care is a political issue rather than a private matter between a woman and her health care provider. They want to deny women their legal right to an abortion, if this is their choice. Often, conservatives carry this further and argue for denying women birth control options as part of prescription drug insurance coverage while, at the same time, including coverage for Viagra, a male erectile dysfunction treatment drug. Most women find this unacceptable public policy, for several reasons:

- Women, not men, bear the direct consequences of a pregnancy and believe giving birth to, and raising, children should be their choice, not something that is forced upon them by bad public policy.
- A woman who does not have control over her reproductive life has no control over her life at all. If women are unable to access the birth control or abortion services, they are legally entitled to receive, they become baby machines rather than human beings with hopes, dreams, and the right to a future of their own choosing.
- Denying women abortion and birth control services, while providing men with Viagra to insure their sex lives can continue is not equal treatment under the law; it is male-preference public policy that results in men enslaving women to their own desires and represents a blatant attempt to exert control over women's lives.

McConnell and his fellow Republicans cannot deny any of these allegations because their attempt at reconfiguring ObamaCare was spearheaded by a closed-door committee comprised of 13 male Republican senators, and excluded women and ethnic/racial minority representation. Their proposal defunded Planned Parenthood, which by default eliminated early prenatal care and screening for breast and ovarian cancer for women who rely upon Planned Parenthood's services. Their proposal protected Viagra coverage.

In early 2017, the House of Representatives failed in their first attempt at "repeal and replace." A few weeks later, they narrowly passed a revised version of their bill, the American Health Care Act, which, according to the Congressional Budget Office estimates, would result in 23 million fewer Americans having access to affordable healthcare by 2027.[4]

The Senate version of a repeal and replace bill emerged in July 2017. The Congressional Budget Office projected that, if enacted, this proposal would result in 33 million Americans losing healthcare coverage over the next 10 years.[5] Citing concerns about what they viewed as draconian cuts to Medicaid, the government's indigent healthcare plan, three Republican women Senators, Lisa Murkowski (R–AK), Susan Collins (R–ME) and Shelly Moore Capito (R–WV) said they would not support the bill McConnell brought to the Senate floor for a vote. Because Republicans only have a two-vote senate majority, these three Republican women senators' no votes killed the legislation. "I did not come Washington to hurt people," said Senator Capito, who represents a state battling serious opioid addiction issues as well as other drug and mental health problems, in a statement explaining her decision.[6] She had also repeatedly expressed concerns about the lack of adequate mental health coverage in the new healthcare proposal.

Meanwhile, a frustrated President Trump ordered Interior Secretary Ryan Zinke to express his displeasure over Murkowski's vote directly to her. Zinke told Murkowski that, as a result of her failure to support the Republican repeal and replace effort, pending Department of Interior policy changes could imperil federal funding for her state.[7] "I did have a conversation with the secretary, and he told me what I already knew," Sen. Lisa Murkowski told reporters, "that the president wasn't pleased with the vote I had taken." Trump later tweeted that "Murkowski really let Republicans, and the country down." Not to be bullied by the president, Murkowski stood her ground, and proceeded to vote no on the legislation a second time.

In a sleight of hand maneuver, McConnell invoked the Senate reconciliation rule[8] to allow a simple majority vote to pass the proposed repeal and replace legislation, rather than the 60-vote majority needed to stop a filibuster, which Democrats were sure to attempt, and then regrouped to try again. A few days later, he returned to the Senate floor with another version. Some referred to this as "ObamaCare Lite" while others, including the president, pushed for a repeal bill, with a replacement coming later. The bill failed when Senator John McCain (R–AZ) voted against it, primarily out of procedural concerns. This seemed to be the final deathblow to repeal and replace legislative efforts, for the time being.

However, in a surprise move, in late September 2017, within days of the reconciliation rule expiration date, Senators Lindsey Graham (R–SC) and Bill Cassidy (R–LA) proposed the Graham-Cassidy Healthcare Bill. This legislation decimated Medicaid and, like previous proposals, would cause millions of currently insured Americans to lose their healthcare coverage. McConnell attempted to push the bill to a vote before the reconciliation rule deadline, but was unable to muster the votes for passage. It was now three strikes and you're out for attempts to repeal and replace ObamaCare, which remains the law of the land. McConnell has signaled his intention to move on to other legislative business and not revisit the repeal and replace ObamaCare issue again in the foreseeable future.

However, ObamaCare could still be brought down if President Trump decides, as he has threatened, to terminate the government support that keeps the program afloat. By terminating the required government payments to insurance companies, destabilizing the insurance market and "letting ObamaCare implode," the Trump administration would be taking life-saving health care away from millions of Americans.

Health insurance providers, who have not been part of any repeal and/or replace discussions, insist that the government must continue funding the plan that is currently in place if it is to remain viable. Anticipating a government pullback, several large health insurance providers have pulled out of the market, creating a situation whereby several, particularly rural, areas of the country have no choice of insurance plans. Insurance companies are aware that a Trump administration decision not to fund the government portion of the plan would effectively end the ObamaCare program, cause health insurance costs to skyrocket, and render millions of Americans once again unable to afford health care insurance.

Meanwhile, it has become increasingly apparent that women's health care in particular has become increasingly irrelevant to the conservative agenda driving healthcare reform. Texas has been a leader in this trend, and provides some of the most substantial data to date on the effects of the assault on women's health care, particularly on low income and working poor women.[9] When the ultra-conservative Texas legislature, led by Lt. Governor Dan Patrick, reduced the state's family planning budget from $111.5 million to $37.9 million (a cut of $74 million) it forced closure of 82 family planning clinics and resulted in a disproportionate rise in Medicaid-funded births because women no longer had access to birth control.

Further, between 2010, when the legislation took effect, and 2014, the number of women who died in childbirth doubled from 18.6 per year to 37.2, which is the worst in the nation and higher than the maternal mortality rate in many developing countries. The figure also represents 600 dead women.[10]

Supporters of the policy claim that the increase in maternal mortality can't be blamed on the restrictions the legislation imposed. The American Congress of Obstetrics and Gynecology contends, "In the absence of war, natural disaster, or severe economic upheaval, the doubling of the maternal mortality rate within a two-year period in a state with 400,000 annual births is unlikely."[11] Nevertheless, Texas politicians, apparently having no ability to look beyond their own beliefs, hail their attacks on Planned Parenthood as "victories for women's health." The loved ones of the 600 Texas women who have died in childbirth since this legislation was enacted would strongly disagree.

In Wisconsin, where former 2017 conservative Republican presidential candidate Scott Walker is governor, zealous conservative state representatives Andre Jacque and Jesse Kremer have introduced legislation to prevent the University of Wisconsin Medical School from training resident physicians in abortion procedures. If enacted, the Wisconsin Legislative Audit Bureau predicts the legislation "will likely cause a shortage of OB-GYN physicians in Wisconsin and make life more difficult for low-income women to the point of endangering their health and their lives."[12]

The following essays reflect on several aspects of healthcare.

In "Real People—Real Lives: Conservative Politics Turn Health Care into Hell Care," Alexandria A. Cunningham explains how, for her as a disabled person, politicizing healthcare transformed a moral entitlement into a nightmare. She describes what her medical future holds if repeal and replace legislation is enacted.

Heather K. Sager, Esq., an attorney who has worked in the area of abortion access, takes a broad view of the fight for reproductive justice for women. In "Ten Months Later: A Retrospective from the Front Lines of Reproductive Justice," she explains the threats to women's health care posed by the Trump administration, one of which became reality when he directed that employers could, on religious or moral grounds, refuse to include payment for birth control (including off-label uses) in their employees' health insurance coverage. Most policy analysts believe that by making birth control more difficult to obtain, the abortion rate will significantly increase.

Concerned about the lack of mental health parity in health care coverage, among other things pertaining to mental health care, Dede Ranahan reflects on the need for adequate mental health coverage in healthcare legislation. The most recent healthcare legislation proposals cut mental health services dramatically.

NOTES

1. www.heritagefoundation.org, October 23, 2010.

2. Sam Hall, "Senator Mitch McConnell's Own History of Racism." www.capitalblue.com March 3, 2013.

3. Planned Parenthood also provides abortion services to women; however, the Hyde Amendment prohibits the use of federal funds for abortion except in cases where the mother's life is endangered, even though abortion without restrictions is a legal health care option for American women.

4. www.cbo.gov

5. *Ibid.*

6. www.washingtonpost.com, July 21,2017.

7. Gabrielle Levy. "Trump Team's Troubling Call to Murkowski," *Political Reporter*, July 27, 2017.

8. Reconciliation was designed to bring about discrete budgetary changes at the margins to create changes in revenues and changes in outlays. It was not designed for the major policy changes McConnell was trying to achieve by using this provision of the senate rules of order.

9. Lawrence Wright, "America's Future Is Texas," *The New Yorker Magazine,* July 10, 2017.

10. *Ibid.*

11. www.acog.org.

12. www.legis.wisconsin.gov.

Real People—Real Lives
Conservative Politics Turn
Health Care into Hell Care

Alexandria A. Cunningham

I am a Traumatic Brain Injury (TBI) survivor. Prior to transforming into a pre-existing condition, appointments with my doctor consisted of routine check-ups and sighs of annoyance provoked by being forced to create time in my busy schedule to take a few deep breaths and be sent on my way. Letters indicating a denial of service, care, or treatment never interrupted or interfered with my treatment plan. My doctor ordered medications, tests, or therapies, and my insurance company fulfilled its contractual obligation to cover the services that had been rendered.

Now, my full-time job is managing my health and my health care. I have reached the highest level in an awful game called "Fighting with the Insurance Company: Sobbing Edition." A thick stack of denial letters continues to expand in my filing boxes.

Previously, blissful ignorance shielded me from frustrating realities. Unfortunately, conservative lawmakers and President Trump himself enjoy the protections of that same shield. Trump even stated, "…nobody knew health care could be so complicated." The individuals wielding the power attached to health care reform answer to a man who, in seventy years on this planet, remains entirely unaware of the complexities of our health care system because he can pay for what he needs and has never had to depend upon it. Allow that to sink in for a moment.

The American health care system poses an incredible challenge to individuals attempting to navigate it. An extraordinary amount of my time has been spent on the phone begging for answers concerning my policy and coverage. Between transfers "to someone else" and under-trained staff at the insurance company, more often than not my own policy remained an enigma.

While many of the questions related to my specific condition still present frustrations when I seek answers, the Affordable Care Act (ACA) passed by the Obama administration sought to bring enhanced clarity and protections for consumers in the health care market. Conservative lawmakers are now putting forth an effort to dismantle the ACA at seemingly any cost, disregarding how their proposed changes affect real people's everyday lives. With every Republican "repeal and replace" proposal thus far, the Congressional Budget Office has estimated that over 20 million individuals will suffer the burden of losing their health insurance. For many of these people, a safety net is unavailable.

One of the most crucial components of the ACA involves protections for individuals with pre-existing conditions. Under the rules of the ACA, an insurance company is not permitted to deny me coverage. They are also barred from charging me more for a health care policy than they would charge one of my peers (someone in my demographic range) simply because of my condition. These rules in concert are vital for individuals like me. Current health care revisions proposed by the conservative majority, including the American Health Care Act that passed through the House, allow states to shirk the latter consumer protection so long as they implement underfunded, expensive, and ineffective high-risk pools.

I refuse to entertain the possibility that a state government comfortable with signing a waiver that robs consumers of protections places my interests first when coverage for my condition teeters on the line. Additionally, all states would be afforded the option of applying for a waiver declaring that, if my insurance coverage were to lapse for 63 days, insurance companies could charge me more based on my health history. Timely payment and my health history share no relation, yet law makers intend to allow insurance companies to weaponize a client's health history if that client is unable to pay on time even if a check is simply lost in the mail. The net result is that two built-in rules that could realistically result in my health care costs increasing replace policies that virtually guaranteed me more affordable coverage. Even if the insurance companies are required to cover me, they will gouge their prices and charge me as much as they conceivably can.

"Criminal" most aptly describes the manner in which the insurance enterprise is sure to treat me as a young, disabled, TBI survivor. Providing coverage for pre-existing conditions alone falls short of what disabled people like myself require to thrive. Toting around an insurance card that costs a significant percentage of my total household income fails to ensure that I can access the care that my condition entails.

Don Bacon (R–NE), my congressional representative, offered a resounding and enthusiastic "hell yes" when asked if he supported the American Health Care Act. Rep. Bacon cloaked his approval of this inhumane piece of legislation under the guise of choice. Disgust washes over me when I consider both his response and reasoning. Short of remaining enrolled in Medicaid for the rest of my life, the only health care choice that will be afforded to me if the bill that Rep. Bacon supports becomes law will be just how much I can sacrifice in an effort to provide myself with some semblance of health care in the future. Of course, this assumes that I would be capable of affording health care at all. Scaling back consumer protections including but not limited to those previously mentioned in this essay translates to nothing more than an increase of risk for patients and an influx of cash flow for profit-motivated insurance companies. Once again, the Old White Men in Washington whack us with a sledgehammer and then inform us that their actions are for our own good without even bothering to solicit input from health care consumers.

At this moment, I depend on Medicaid to receive necessary medical treatment. Eventually I hope to transition from Medicaid to private insurance, so the issue of affordability in the future gnaws deeply into my core. "Disturbing" fails to capture the gravity of the effect that preconceived notions about Medicaid recipients has on those who, like myself, are managing chronic conditions. Rep. Jason Chaffetz (R–UT), along with other like-minded conservatives, tends to equate "low income" with laziness, incompetence, and hedonism. Evidently, in their minds, we enjoy living with the constant terror that disconnected politicians and administrators will subject our most valuable resource to arbitrary rules that will compromise our care.

Rep. Chaffetz went so far as to chastise people for owning iPhones, arguing that iPhone funds should have been appropriated to health care. Apparently Chaffetz has never reviewed a monthly explanation of benefits letter. My statement would require a ridiculous number of iPhones to compensate. I would be remiss if I neglected to mention the thinly veiled resentment of low income individuals found in the subtext of his statements on this issue as well.

Malicious roots emerge as the hidden support behind remarks like those Rep. Chaffetz spouted. These roots are saturated in the "boot strap" myth that places blame on individuals for their position on the economic hierarchy without regard for the fact that many factors that lead to economic hardship are equal-opportunity problems that do not discriminate.

In my case, my TBI forced me to cease both academic and work-related endeavors. My TBI remains indifferent to the fact that I graduated college with a 4.0 GPA while juggling numerous extracurriculars and employment. Constantly studying, I turned down invites from friends in favor of polishing papers that were supposed to secure me an opportunity to attend graduate school and earn my PhD in Philosophy. Hours upon hours of researching for and then participating on the debate team, leading conversations about how to advance the success of women in the male-dominated debate community, holding ranking positions in various on-campus clubs, organizing events such as The Vagina Monologues and Take Back the Night, writing and editing for the school newspaper, working 25 to 30 hours per week, and more should not have landed me where I am now.

Rather than drowning in a sea of graduate level texts, each day I struggle with debilitating neurological symptoms while men who revel in their cluelessness regarding economic hardship, and who likely worked half as hard as I did during their academic careers, possess the audacity and arrogance to dehumanize individuals like myself and punish us for being ill and lacking the outrageous resources required to manage a chronic condition. Adding insult to injury, they cannot even be bothered to enact legislation that prevents me from being denied coverage for my pre-existing condition if I decide to pursue private insurance just like they want me to do.

The men who act as the gatekeepers between my healthcare and me lack the experience, knowledge, perspective, bravery, and compassion necessary to be entrusted with decision-making regarding my healthcare needs. Too many times I have seethed with rage while witnessing a group of men decide whether or not I will retain reasonable access to necessary medications. For me, birth control falls into that category. While birth control should be readily available to anyone for any reason, I would wager that the majority of these decision-making men remain unaware of the multitude of conditions that respond to birth control medication. Doctors often prescribe birth control as an off-label therapy to assist in the management of post-traumatic migraines, for example. Birth control also works wonders preventing pregnancy in individuals whose physical, emotional, or financial condition poses risks a person might choose not to take, but what do I know? Luckily, the current regime works fervently to protect me from the horrors of birth control and even plans to allow my tiny woman brain to choose which insurance company I shall permit to accept payments from me in exchange for more denial of treatment letters if any of those companies will cover me to begin with. These men are the true heroes of our time.

To delve further into their humanitarian efforts, the current regime also helps me remember my place in society. I am incapable of imagining the social blunders these men have prevented me from committing. Although my memory issues present with severity, conservative representatives have shown me admirable strength, tenacity, and patience. They generously provide constant reminders about just how little social power disabled individuals should be afforded.

Conservatives cast disabled people as malingerers who wish to lie on the couch all day watching television and dipping their spoons into the Free Health Care Honey Pot. These conservative heroes swoop in, risking the cleanliness of their silk ties and tailored suits, to snatch up essential health benefits, preventive care, cash assistance, and more in an effort to motivate chronically ill people to summon the gumption to shake off the laziness and start contributing to society. Of course, these heroes simultaneously avert their gaze from these disabled individuals, fearing and silencing what they willfully neglect to understand.

Occasionally, the "good disabled people" like myself who defy the stereotype of the welfare queen receive glimmering rewards from these conservative heroes. They love to broadcast that they do not so much mind helping people like us, as if individuals who lack the qualities necessary to deserve excellent care and respect even exist. However, these lawmakers still refuse to guarantee that I will not be turned away or charged copious amounts of cash because of my pre-existing condition. I hope the conclusion of this political saga involves our conservative heroes atoning for perpetuating detrimental myths about Medicaid recipients and realizing that all people, not just the "good ones," deserve dignified health care. Considering that current conservative proposals slash Medicaid funding by as much as $800 billion, I don't feel optimistic about this possibility and realize that I am engaging in some wishful thinking.

As an unexpected twist in this political drama, current conservative proposals that incorporate the issue of pre-existing conditions confine me and virtually guarantee that my dependence upon Social Security and other government programs such as Medicare and Medicaid is maintained. While my circumstances are somewhat unique and include some strange administrative rules, I am not the only Medicaid recipient subject to these rules.

I became disabled prior to the age of twenty-two. Because my taxable income at the time of my application for disability benefits was petite and my injury occurred at such an early age, Social Security calculates my monthly disability payments based upon my father's work history. I receive a small percentage of what his payment would amount to monthly, and because I draw from his earning record, I also qualify for Medicare. Supplemental Security Income bridges the gap between the portion of his payment and the federal minimum amount that disabled people must receive. Receiving Supplemental Security Income benefits automatically qualifies me for Medicaid. Even though I will likely remain disabled for the rest of my life, administrative rules direct that those benefits cease if I marry a non-disabled person because I draw benefits based upon my father's record.

Pretend for a moment that I decide to legally bind myself to another person, and this person is not disabled. Medicare will no longer cover my medical expenses, shifting every penny of my incurred healthcare expenses onto the Medicaid program. I imagine this to be a recurring nightmare for many conservative lawmakers. What if my hypothetical spouse and I possess combined assets that surpass the maximum amount allowed by the Medicaid program? Private insurance then becomes my only alternative, but my inability to perform any employment-related tasks prohibits me from receiving insurance through my own employer, further narrowing my field of prospective insurers. Seeking insurance coverage through my partner's employer or purchasing insurance privately represent the next best options, which are that either these companies outright decline to absorb me into their pool or, if I am unfortunate enough to live in a state where a waiver was granted that would allow them to do so, they inflate my premiums. Even if a company accepted me as a client and charged me an affordable rate, current conservative proposals contain no barriers that would prevent the company from capping my care or my premium costs.

Because medical treatments with the most efficacies often also bear the highest price tag, my insurance coverage could functionally dissipate a few months into the year. Life-time caps would wreck my ability to access care, as well. Being 25 and chronically ill causes lifetime caps to become that much more worrisome. As anxiety-inducing as this is to admit, the people with the most direct power to influence the price of my future health care seem to believe that fairness dictates that I pay substantially more for my care, with little thought to the certain struggle I will face if I am unable to scrounge up the cash to cover my medical expenses—or to the fact that my disability severely limits my earning power and ability to save.

At this moment, seven different medical professionals coordinate my care, and the list of specialists that I must visit continues to swell. A plethora of medications occupy my medicine cabinet. I often muse that my bathroom feels more like an old-timey, small-town pharmacy than a part of my home. Every three months for the past four years, I pay a visit to my neurologist and receive 30 injections. These injections are placed across my forehead, into my scalp, down my neck, and across my shoulders. They form a block-ade that impedes my body's ability to effectively communicate pain signals with the end goal being to decrease the amount of daily pain I experience. Each individual treatment could cost up to $5,000 out-of-pocket for an uninsured individual, and this excludes the amount paid to the doctor for performing the procedure. This procedure alone could cost over $20,000 per year. Nearly inconceivable hardship would follow a lack of quality and affordable health insurance.

Infusions of anesthetic medications comprise another facet of my treatment plan. During my infusions, intravenous medication slowly drips into my system over a period of a few hours. Even though this procedure occurs in my doctor's office rather than in a hospital setting, each daily infusion totals over $300. My last round consisted of three infusions on three different days within the same week. The protocol for this treatment differs depending upon its efficacy and the doctor's preferred methods, ranging anywhere from 30 to 90 days between treatments.

Adequate insurance provides the only power I have over this unrelenting pain, turning it into a serious financial calculation rather than a health-centric decision. No one should ever be forced to live in harrowing pain because they are unable to solve for X in a financial calculation or because their medical bills have surpassed an arbi-trary cap set by their insurance company. Congress has the power to instill regulations upon companies to prevent this from happening, but they refuse to wield their power responsibly.

Chronic pain wedges itself into every aspect of a person's life. Pain is a problem in and of itself, but pain is also like a tree. From its base, many branches grow. These branches lengthen and twist, eventually sprouting leaves and flowers. The roots descend into the soil, ousting everything blocking their path. Suddenly, what was once a twig struggling to survive transmutes into a being of true substance. For me, by the time it flourished into this being, depression had emerged as one of the strongest supporting branches.

With depression comes danger. Grief, frustration, anger, and sadness—all of these emotions influence our worldview and our most introspective moments. The burden placed upon my body, submerged in the tar of chronic pain, reaches beyond the physical into the emotional realm. Combined with the drastic changes after my injury that so severely limited what I am physically capable of doing, my life felt nothing like my own. It felt wrong; it felt simultaneously overwhelming and underwhelming. While lying on the couch I would imagine myself sinking in, melting like butter until the fabric eventually absorbed me and I was no more.

While I stowed this fantasy and most of my feelings about my brain injury away, I am fortunate that a friend and mentor noticed something was amiss. She kind-heartedly paid for one session with a counselor, and this is when I realized that I needed more help than I had been willing to admit. I sought out free counseling through the university I was attending, but traveling to therapy sessions grew too taxing. Not long after terminating my care with the counselor at the university, I relocated hundreds of miles away from my support system. This move also placed me outside of the radius within which my insurance at the time served. Between a lack of transportation and an insurance plan that covered exactly zero therapists in my area, I became responsible for managing my depression, anxiety, panic disorder, and thoughts of self-harm without the guidance of medical professional within over 400 miles of my home.

While I continue to struggle both physically and emotionally, the burden has eased with help from my current team of medical professionals. My neurologist works tirelessly to manage my constant migraine, insomnia, and other devastating neurological symptoms. My therapist conducts appointments at my home, allowing me to analyze and more thoroughly understand my depression and anxiety. When depression screams that the world is bleak and the pain too intense, I have resources that pave the way for the light to return. Rather than grappling with thoughts of self-harm or panic attacks on my own, I have a professional on stand-by. My pain management specialist administers treatments to calm my nervous system, quelling the ferocity and tenacity of my pain.

The status quo of constant pain still reigns, but because I retain access to affordable and quality health insurance, my quality of life has improved dramatically. A strict regimen of medications assists in containing and controlling, as much as is possible, my nausea, vomiting, pain, balance issues, sleep cycles, mood regulation, and more, although these treatments compose only a minute portion of my overall treatment plan.

Without quality health insurance, the cost of my necessary medications alone would send a treasure-hoarding dragon into bankruptcy. My symptoms would pose an even greater threat to my physical and emotional well being and safety than they do now. If my congressional representatives choose their political party's desire to dismantle the ACA over the people they represent and the insurance companies over consumers, my life will fade beyond recognition. All the progress that I have worked diligently to achieve will be ripped right out from under me. My dreams will be lost somewhere out in the void, and my goals will remain unachieved.

Because my representatives conceive of me as nothing more than a freeloader, a population number which they pride themselves on slashing, my loved ones and I will be subjected to unnerving, unrelenting, and agonizing pain. Left without recourse, people like myself living with certainty pre-existing conditions will be left at the mercy of avarice-tainted insurance companies. I state with that should this scenario play out, I will never forget who to hold accountable.

Ten Months Later
A Retrospective from the Front Lines
of Reproductive Justice

HEATHER K. SAGER, ESQ.[1]

No one makes the decision to have an abortion lightly. However, ultimately obtaining an abortion is the legal right of any person who is capable of becoming pregnant,[2] and therefore it must also be accessible. Despite the fact that, during the past half-century, abortion has been treated as a political issue, it is a form of medical care, and decision-making about it should be left between a pregnant person and their doctor.

That is what I believe. And, for the past three years, I have been incredibly proud to serve on the board of directors for the New York Abortion Access Fund (NYAAF). This narrowly focused organization addresses the financial needs of those who are not able to afford reproductive health care. As an abortion access fund, we play a specific role in the movement for reproductive justice: simply put, we help people who cannot afford the cost of an abortion. It's a simple mission with a heavy impact: we ensure that people are able to pay for the procedure that they need and are entitled to receive.

Working with an abortion access fund offers a unique perspective on the ground floor of the reproductive health, rights, and justice movement. Every day we speak with people who are seeking our help and we listen to their stories. And while each client's situation is unique, every person who contacts us has one thing in common: an inability to access and/or afford he reproductive healthcare they need.

Frequently, we serve those living in Pennsylvania, New Jersey, or Connecticut, who must travel to New York because there is no closer clinic available to them. Often, these are people who are just starting new jobs, moving, or who are already mothers and have decided their family is complete. Sometimes, it's families who are facing medical issues with a wanted pregnancy and the legal limitations on reproductive health in their state mean they will be forced to travel to obtain the care their doctor recommends. I have spoken with people who have come from far away, are struggling to find a place to sleep that night and cannot fathom navigating a complicated and alien medical system in an unfamiliar city. "Tye" is one such example:

Tye was a Georgia resident and mother of three. When she contacted NYAAF she said that, as a 40-year-old, menopause came to mind before pregnancy. Her health insurance policy covered the abortion procedure, and so she made an appointment. Everything was going well until the doctors performed the sonogram and told her that she was beyond Georgia's gestational limit—Tye was 21 weeks, and the law banned the procedure past 20 weeks.

The public had only recently been informed of the state's new gestational limit law—which had been prevented from taking effect due to a now-lifted court injunction. She was given a list of states that would permit the procedure and told to find a provider. In the story she shared with us, she explained that it was a very traumatizing experience for her. "You're literally googling things like on how to miscarry on your own—you're just thinking of ways you can correct this. I have no family here and there's no way I'm going to go to New Mexico or Colorado; where would I be going?"

Tye was a New York native, so chose to travel to the state she knew. However, when she informed her insurance company, they told her she was not covered outside of Georgia. The law told her she could not be seen in Georgia and her insurance provider told her she could not be seen anywhere else. She said that she felt like insurance policies and state regulations were forcing her to have a child.

Ultimately, Tye made an appointment in New York. She paid for a hotel, airfare, and paid $800 out-of-pocket. However, having been forced to make arrangements to travel out-of-state, by the time she could be seen, her costs had ballooned up to $6,000. Insurance covered none of this. NYAAF was able to help her.

I, and my organization, operate under the belief that each person is in the best position to make their own reproductive decisions for themselves. But in the hangover of the 2016 election, we have seen a reinvigorated effort to rob people of the legal and financial ability, and cultural support, to exercise the full spectrum of their reproductive healthcare rights. "Sarah" was caught in this trap.

Sarah contacted NYAAF after spending weeks trying to save money to afford an abortion procedure. She had been unemployed for several months and had continually rescheduled her appointments because she could not afford to pay. All the while the costs were increasing because the cost of an abortion increases depending upon gestation.

Sarah found a new job, and would have access to health insurance, so she waited. As soon as her insurance was in effect, she was told she was only covered up to 12 weeks gestation, despite the New York gestational limit being 24 weeks. Fortunately, we were able to help her at NYAAF, but a combination of circumstances beyond her control meant she had to wait months before she could be seen.

Had Sarah lived in a state with more limited legal access to abortion, it would have been worse. She would have potentially had to overcome hurdles such as being forced to make multiple appointments in order to be seen, as many states require a minimum of two appointments before the procedure. The law could have required that she be given medically inaccurate information, been falsely told that a medical abortion is reversible, or that abortion is linked to breast cancer. Or she could have had to meet a 72-hour state-imposed waiting period, which is longer than the waiting period to purchase a gun in many states.

Less than a year ago, immediately following the 2016 election results, I completed an interview on the topic of reproductive rights. Some of the questions I was asked to address included: Post-election, what are those working towards reproductive justice the most afraid of? What can folks do to contribute to reproductive access? What gives you hope in incredibly challenging times? How can supporters help when facing the promise of abortion rights being wiped from our nation? These issues that, in the wake of Donald Trump's win, many were concerned about.

At the time, I wrote about how, for the first time in decades, we were facing the very real possibility of increased, major legal restrictions at the federal level but acknowledged that those in the abortion rights movement faced many more worries. Some of the initial concerns focused on efforts to choke back reproductive rights and on promised new limitations on all healthcare access. We were facing a worsening cultural shift against abortion rights in the political power circles that contrasted sharply to the historic levels of support among the general public. And, the rise of blatantly racist, xenophobic, and classist ideals seeping into public policy and politics meant that many who operated within the arenas where with social justice intersects reproductive health found themselves increasingly concerned.

Currently, federal healthcare programs prohibit abortion coverage. Prior to the election, many in the abortion rights movement had worked to end what is commonly known as the Hyde Amendment, which is the federal legislation that blocks any use of federal funds toward abortion except to save the pregnant person's life or in the case of rape or incest. This means federal Medicaid funds cannot cover the cost of an abortion unless the pregnant person's life is explicitly endangered—even where their health is otherwise at risk or their doctor has recommended the procedure. Only 15 states cover abortion as part of their state-funded Medicaid program.

Not surprisingly, we have not seen much of a political shift in repealing the Hyde Amendment and expect that this battle will continue. Every day the grassroots movement to put an end to this particularly punitive restriction grows and pre-election brought the introduction of legislation to accomplish that goal. But the road to success must be paved with a shift in Congressional and state power. A conservative Congress coupled with a brazenly, if not unpredictably, hateful leader, and supported by extremists at the local levels, are all obstacles to overcome.

In addition to the Hyde Amendment, for years state-level restrictions have crept into the reproductive health care landscape. Although much of this went largely unnoticed by those outside of the reproductive rights movement, hundreds of state-level bills had been introduced across the country, and some were enacted. Not all, but many of these are known as TRAP (Targeted Regulation of Abortion Provider) laws, aimed at forcing clinics and providers to close their doors by suffocating them with bureaucracy and unneeded requirements.

At the time of the election, the expectation was that the landscape would continue to worsen. "Pragmatically, it means that today it's all the more important to provide support in underserved states," I noted.

That statement still holds true and, since making it, more states have enacted new restrictions. These include requirements that clinics meet meaningless standards of which they were not notified prior to closing, such as, for example, the EMW Women's Surgical Center in Louisville, KY. At the time I was interviewed, the was the last clinic operating in Kentucky and was facing a legal battle to keep its doors open after being abruptly shut down by the state's governor. The rationale was, in part that EMW lacked a written transfer agreement with a local hospital, in spite of the fact that a long-standing agreement was already in place and federal law requires that hospitals accept all patients in the case of an emergency.

Indiana, my own state of residence, enacted a law requiring that the court system notify parents in cases where minors seek judicial permission to undergo an abortion procedure. Such a law ignores the need for minors to obtain judicial permission in the first place, and can actively put them in harm's way, because these cases typically arise from the minor's fear of violence or abuse if the parent discovers the pregnancy.

For years, many abortion access-funding organizations have been facing the on-the-ground consequences of state-level actions and, in the wake of the election, we watched as legislatures continued to take aim at clinics across the country. TRAP laws were just one strategy they used. The past year also brought a renewed focus on defunding Planned Parenthood, and setting new limitations on family planning state funding budgets throughout the country.

When those strategies failed, the cultural and financial support for the reignited anti-abortion groups led to new methods of opposition. This past summer saw the closure of one of the three facilities in the country able to perform later term procedures, Germantown Reproductive Health Services. The clinic was closed because the property was sold to an anti-abortion group. The location will now house the Maryland Coalition for Life. The two remaining clinics are in Albuquerque, New Mexico and Boulder, Colorado. Anyone living east of the Mississippi River will be forced to incur expensive and often difficult travel, should they need reproductive health care.

It would be easy, but isolationist in view, to point to these as individual state actions rather than recognize them as a coordinated attack on rights and the result of an emboldened socially conservative political class. State laws aimed at rolling back abortion rights are frequently drafted based on nationally disseminated models, such as those promoted by the American Legislative Exchange Council (ALEC), and the election of Donald Trump has seen a new wave of success in passing these laws and celebrating clinic closures.

In January, shortly after his inauguration, Donald Trump made his first move to limit reproductive rights on a federal level. With the signing of an executive order, we saw the reinstatement and expansion of the Global Gag Rule, also known as the Mexico City Policy. This policy bans nonprofits and non-governmental organizations (NGOs) that receive family planning funding from advocating for abortion, providing abortion services, or educating or informing the public about abortion. This includes international and local organizations, such as health programs working with populations struggling with HIV, maternal and child health issues, malaria, and the Zika virus.

While many in the media, whether through misunderstanding or misrepresentation, presented this only as Trump cutting back reproductive care services, an important point was frequently overlooked: the Global Gag Rule does cut services, to be sure, however, its effects are deeper and more insidious in nature. This particular executive order bans nonprofits that accept U.S. family planning funding from *educating the public or government* or *advocating for* safe abortion services. Forget about providing safe abortion services, this rule bans even referrals to another organization. In other words, the United States government cut funding from any nonprofit that even provides information about reproductive health care. The on-the-ground effects of this are incredibly dangerous and failing to understand this puts people's lives at risk.

In many areas of the world, including parts of the U.S., access to health care is not dependent on a public hospital, which may be located many miles away from the community, but on a small nonprofit or local chapter of an NGO. These groups are often not the well-known names attached to the larger, global organizations that many of us are familiar with, but are service organizations that are embedded within their community. Those who manage and staff these organizations are more than simply meeting an identified need—they are the people that women, families, and those in the community turn to for help. When you place a nearly literal gag on the only reliable and trusted source of information in a community, the result is not less unintended pregnancies and fewer abortions, but a dangerous and potentially deadly promotion of false or total lack of information about a person's own body.

Imagine if your doctor was not allowed to provide accurate information to you about your reproductive care. Thanks to the re-instated Global Gag rule policy, this is the current scenario for many people. This policy forces providers, who are in a position of trust, to withhold information about their care from those who seek it. Thanks to all that preceded, and all that was included in the election of Donald Trump, the landscape of reproductive rights is, not so slowly, devolving to the one that my mother came of age protesting 40 or 50 years ago.

Legal restrictions aside, policy and politics are informed by the stronger themes of our wider culture, and cultural attitudes toward abortion have historically been mixed. Prior to the 2016 election cycle, many in the reproductive rights movement were concerned that a Trump win would normalize anti-abortion attitudes across the country. Those who work within this movement also work towards the acceptance of abortion as part of normal, necessary healthcare. During the campaign cycle, it was heartbreaking to see the president-elect not only validating, but emphatically espousing, the idea that women should be punished for accessing reproductive health care and potentially prosecuted for exercising their Constitutional rights. The aftermath of the election saw no shift in that attitude.

An abortion fund focuses on increasing access to abortion, which is a complex, narrow part of the overall goals of the reproductive justice movement. While abortion funds work to specifically address financial need, an inability to access care does not occur in a vacuum. The reproductive justice framework—a term coined and popularized by women of color—aims to address the multi-layered and interlocking ways in which race, class, gender identity, orientation, religion, and more, impact individual, familial, and community experiences. This framework recognizes prominent reproductive health issues, such as abortion rights or access to birth control, not as singular end-goals for reproductive health, but as part of a larger picture of the health, happiness, and overall well-being for all individuals, their families, and their communities. Those who utilize abortion funds do not share just one narrative; many struggle with the myriad of issues that the reproductive justice movement aims to address.

The result is that as we see racism, xenophobia, homophobia, transphobia, anti-semitism, and Islamophobia increase and be supported by our country's leader, we also see people's ability to access their reproductive rights impacted. We know that women and all people of color are disproportionately affected by an inability to access care, and as we face the threatened end of programs such as Deferred Action for Childhood Arrivals (DACA), or the attempted exclusion of trans healthcare in federal programs, our country would have to be blind to fail to realize that these interconnected actions will simultaneously create deeper reproductive health disparities.

Immediately after the election, the abortion access fund I work with was fortunate to be on the receiving end of what I later came to think of as the early resistance reaction. We were incredibly lucky that in their anger and fear for the future, many chose to use that energy to contribute to something positive, and sought us out as their channel. Post-election, NYAAF saw an incredible increase in people contacting us to volunteer and in those wanting to financially support our organization. We experienced a historically sharp rise in donations. In difficult times, seeing people rally together is lifesaving power.

At the time, I reflected on the importance of supporting local aborting access funds in areas with significantly restricted access to abortion care, such as in states with few clinics or strong TRAP laws. Donations and funding have always been an important way to offer support, but post–2016, I have come to believe that the best way to fight is with your voice. In the immediate aftermath of the election and beyond we need people to speak up and speak out. This is truer today than it was ten months ago.

Abortion access and reproductive justice does not happen by itself. The people most affected by the shifting reproductive justice landscape—those who contact us—are afraid. They are afraid and continue to feel ashamed and alone. Often, the best thing we have to offer them is a friendly voice this is without judgment and that understands. Many people do not realize that in their everyday life, they can be that source of understanding.

With all the articles written about how those of us in the abortion rights movement, and those of us supporting the movement, need to show up for each other, it is important to note that the best thing supporters can do is show up in the public sphere and speak openly and kindly about abortion. Something as simple as talking helps because it brings us one step forward in normalizing a medical procedure that has become so stigmatized. Not everyone can safely speak, but for those of us who can, it is important to have the uncomfortable conversation and say the word "abortion."

There are many great organizations out there fighting the social justice fight day in and day out. Show up to their events, be there with them at the protests and rallies, and if you can, donate and urge others to donate. Remember that large protests and rallies are valuable, but so are letter writing campaigns, small fundraising events, and all the less fun, less glamorous work, like stuffing envelopes.

Most of the above was written 10 months ago, when my heart was heavy and I needed to speak from a place of hope. Sadly, none of the observations I made then have stopped being true. While the legal and cultural landscape is worsening, I believe there is hope. Now, more than ever, we have an opportunity to give more of ourselves, to speak loudly and with love, and to help our country move beyond the point where we find ourselves just 10 months after Donald Trump was elected president.

NOTES

1. I am a member of the New York Abortion Access Fund board of directors; however, this essay was not written on behalf of the organization.

2. This essay references any person capable of becoming pregnant, including individuals in the transgender or gender non-conforming communities who may not identify as women, but who are still able to conceive.

A Canary in the Coal Mine

Dede Ranahan

I'm the 73-year-old mother of a son who died in July 2014. He was a patient in a hospital psych ward where I thought he'd be safe. Here's my story.

Patrick was born on August 26, 1968. He arrived two weeks early, weighing in at only five pounds, nine ounces. From the start, Pat's life was difficult. He had severe jaundice as a newborn, painful colic for four months, and on his first birthday weighed not quite fifteen pounds.

Nevertheless, I was a happy mother. I didn't think my child, with his particular issues, was that different from any other child and, besides, Pat was adorable with blonde hair and big blue eyes. He was precocious and interested in everything he could climb into, onto or around. He called trucks "fucks," hated to go to bed, and captivated adults because this tiny little person was so loquacious and inquisitive. When Pat was born, I quit my job with Pan Am so I could be a stay-at-home mom. Quitting my job didn't really make sense. Pat's dad was a third-year student in medical school and money was scarce. (Recently I found a copy of our monthly budget that I'd written down on a scrap of paper. We were living on $400 a month.) But, more than anything, I wanted to be with my little boy, so I took a job caring for an 85-year-old woman and brought Pat with me to her apartment. The poor woman lived with a foul-smelling colostomy that it was my privilege to change each day while her daughter was at work. But I could be with my son and that's all that mattered because he was, in short, the world's greatest child.

Fast forward to March 16, 1993, at 9:15 in the morning. I was rummaging through a kitchen cupboard looking for St. Patrick's Day decorations. In the back of the cupboard, I found a statue of Merlin the Magician. With four children in my household, I discovered things all the time with no clue as to their origin. So too with Merlin.

As I studied this funny little man, Patrick, now 24, five feet and eleven inches tall, and living at home after graduating from college, walked into the kitchen. I turned to him and asked if he'd like to have the statue. He answered, "Yes," and as the statue slipped from my hand to his, the last conversation I ever had with my son, as I'd known him, ended. With his next breath he said, "Mom, I smell gas."

By midnight, my son saw FBI men lurking in the shadows. He bolted out the front door and ran up the freeway toward Berkeley because "the revolution is starting." In the early hours of the morning, the California Highway patrol picked him up and 5150'd (involuntary commitment) him to a psych ward. He was experiencing a psychotic, bipolar episode.

146

As other families like mine know, our family history came to include hundreds of dramatic stories in our efforts to cope with Pat's mental illness. Not only were we dealing with the fragmentation of my son's health, we were also dealing with the fragmentation of our family (my marriage would not survive) as parents and siblings struggled to deal with mental illness and how it affected each of us as family members.

For us, support systems failed. Health insurance remained unavailable. Professional guidance proved to be non-existent to ineffective to incorrect. Medication would remain a guessing game. Social Security created a bureaucratic nightmare that only made things worse.

Disagreements about proper courses of action arose between husband and wife, parents and offspring, and between brothers and sisters. Each member of our household experienced disequilibrium at some point.

Over the years, I turned into a mother bear fighting for her cub. I read everything I could get my hands on about bipolar disorder. I wrote letters to legislators and others asking for assistance. I trekked to Washington, D.C., and handed my son's file to President Clinton. In this process, I learned about the frustration and suffering that so many families endure in their efforts to find help for their loved ones who live with severe mental illness. I decided I had two choices. I could either curl up in a fetal ball and die (as I sometimes wished to do) or try to effect some change about a terrible problem that affects so many.

Not sure how or where to begin, at 52 I went back to school and got a Master's degree in non-profit administration. My first job was as a development director at a nearby university. There I established an Institute for Mental Illness Education, which, among other things, produced symposiums for teachers—first grade through university level. The goal was to bring discussion about mental illness into the public arena and to provide programs that would be helpful to teachers in the classroom. The symposiums included workshops divided by student age groups. Plenary sessions covered topics such as developmental and cultural perspectives, mental health resources available to students, and discussions about hope and recovery and what is possible. The symposiums sold out.

When an advisory group and I first named the institute, it was our belief that the time had come to use the terminology mental illness without embarrassment or self-consciousness; that semantic dancing about how to talk about mental illness contributed to its stigma. Unfortunately, some in the community held that we shouldn't use the words mental illness. After a year of arguing back and forth, political correctness won out. The institute was renamed The Institute for Mental Health and Wellness Education.

I wasn't a good bureaucrat. I became frustrated with what I perceived as lack of vision and moved on. In 2004 and 2005, as Walk Director, I launched the first two NAMI-Walks in San Francisco. From 2007 to 2010 I served as the Mental Health Services Act (MHSA) Policy Director for NAMI California. In that latter capacity I interfaced with multiple bureaucracies—state and local governments, non-profit groups, and mental health organizations. Once more I became disenchanted. I saw what we call our mental health system at close range. Departments were siloed with little coordination between them, communication between agencies was fraught with in-fighting and competition for limited resources, mental health professionals of all types were in a supply and demand crisis, and public awareness and education cried out for substantial increase.

In January 2010, I retired. I was burned out. All my passion, energy, and effort seemed, in my eyes at least, not very productive. And Pat was now 17 or 18 years into his journey with mental illness. He was living with me, then not living with me, then living with me again. Both of us were exhausted and always waiting for the next crisis. I posed questions like the following at crisis intervention trainings I gave to county sheriff department personnel. These questions underscored some of the chaos in our lives:

- How much do you panic the first time your twenty-five-year-old son is 5150d (involuntarily committed) to a psych ward, you know nothing about the mental health system, and you aren't told for 24 hours where your son is or what is happening to him?
- Do you feel kicked in the gut when you finally get through to the social worker in charge of your son's care and he says, "I'm not surprised your son is here given what's going on in your household"? Reeling but still standing, you ask, "What is going on in my household?" And this trained professional tells you, "You're making pornographic movies and forcing your son to act in them."
- How do you deal with your frustration when you call the county mental health access line and the recording refers you to a different number? Eleven phone calls later, the recordings and occasional live voices have referred you back to the original access line.
- Do you believe the doctor or your own parental instincts when a $300-an-hour psychiatrist tells you, "Your son is just refusing to grow up. Cover his living expenses for a month and then, if he doesn't shape up, he's out on the street"?
- Do you give up, after a week trying to keep your son, who's on Haldol and still psychotic, at home while waiting for a doctor's appointment, when the doctor refuses to renew the prescription? Your son yells, "Fuck," bolts out the door, and disappears down the street. You collapse on the front porch of the medical office building and the staff locks you out, leaving you in a crumpled heap, because it's their lunch hour.
- How do you maintain your composure when your son, psychotic and without medication, takes off on his motorcycle for a solo cross-country trip?
- How do you convince a police officer, when your son smashes the windows of a car parked on the street because "My sister is in there and I have to save her," that he needs medical help, not arrest?
- How do you find your son and bring him back from South Korea where he's been hired by the government to teach English in a jungle school somewhere?
- How do you live with yourself when you realize you don't have the emotional stamina to let your son stay in your house, and if you don't let him stay, he'll be homeless?
- How do you not smile when, some days, your "crazy" son makes more sense than his doctors? And a lot of other people.

Now here I am, looking on the upcoming three-year anniversary of Patrick's passing. I'll never, ever get over this. My grief will evolve but I'll never get over losing my son. So why am I still at it—writing this essay and engaging in other advocacy efforts? Why don't I just call it a day? My son, after all, is dead after a shitty life suffering from a cruel, unrelenting mental illness after trying so hard for so long with so little help. Here's the thing. Thousands of individuals and families are still out there, living shitty lives and suffering from cruel, unrelenting mental illnesses; after trying so hard for so long with so little help. I can't quit advocating while concern for the mentally ill and their families is still at the bottom of the proverbial heap.

Our mental health system is fraught with needs that must be addressed. Here's a partial list:

- Mental illnesses exist on a continuum of severity and some such as schizophrenia, bipolar disorder, extreme depression and obsessive-compulsive disorder are more debilitating than others. Roughly 4 percent of mental illness sufferers (or 11 million) fall into the seriously mentally ill category. Some argue—and I agree—that, at present, too much funding goes to the less severely affected.
- Serious mental illnesses need to be reclassified as brain diseases—which they are—so the affected can receive treatment and coverage in the physical health system.
- Differences in approach, or the "medical model" versus the "recovery model," need to be reconciled. In simple terms, the former argues for more meds and more beds. The latter argues for more peer support and social services. Both approaches are necessary at different times for different patients.
- HIPAA (Health Insurance Privacy and Portability Act) is often misinterpreted. It precludes family caregivers from getting timely, life-saving information. This law needs to be rewritten.
- Tensions arise between family advocacy groups and consumer advocacy groups. They need to work together.
- The Affordable Care Act (ACA) requires mental health services and treatment for substance abuse to be benefits of health plans. The 21st Century Cures Act of 2016 mandates tough enforcement of parity regulations for mental health and physical health. Medicaid expansion, passed under Obama, is currently the single largest payer of services for the mentally ill. While the ACA needs improvement, the repeal and replace law–Patient Freedom Act—passed by the House of Representatives in 2017, jeopardizes all of these coverages.
- The mental health system dumps the mentally ill into the prison system. This must stop.
- The list of needs goes on and on. We need better training and better pay for mental health care providers; we need repeal of the IMD (Institutes of Mental Disease) exclusion which limits the number of hospital beds available to mentally ill people; we need expanded AOT (assisted outpatient treatment) programs that are delivered with care and compassion; we need housing, supported employment, and supported education.

When I worked as the MHSA Policy Director for NAMI California, as other mental health actors were citing glowing statistics about MHSA implementation, I was collecting on-the-ground stories from families in California. I'd catalogue their statements and pass them out at MHSA meetings. These stories contradicted the other reports. Some of my colleagues began to call me "the canary in the coal mine."

Today my advocacy efforts are focused on my blog, Sooner Than Tomorrow—A Safe Place to Talk About Mental Illness in Our Families. As I collect stories from families of the 4 percent who suffer from serious mental illnesses, I'm experiencing déjà vu. The stories I post speak of failures, not successes, in our mental health system. Together, the other writers on my blog and I are "canaries in many coals mines." What does this mean? The "canary" is someone who acts as an early reporter of disturbing conditions.

It's distressing. As "canaries" our early admonitions are not early at all. Back in the 1830s Dorothea Dix campaigned to remove people with mental illnesses from jails and prisons. She said, "I come to place before the Legislature of Massachusetts the condition of the miserable, the desolate, the outcast. I come as the advocate of helpless, forgotten, insane men and women; of beings sunk to a condition from which the unconcerned world would start with real sorrow."

I won't reflect on the lack of progress in mental health care–I'm calling it mental illness care–187 years after Dorothea's efforts. If I do, I'll become discouraged—again. I'll be tempted to believe the Office of Human Priorities will never include a Department of Serious Mental Illness or a Secretary of Treatment and Care for the 4 percent.

I'm the 73-year-old mother of a son who died in July 2014. He was a patient in a hospital psych ward where I thought he'd be safe. To honor my son, I'll continue to be a "canary in the coal mine." I'll keep collecting and sharing stories. Stories about tragedies that could have been prevented. Stories about the need for beds and housing. Stories about outrageous HIPAA requirements that prevent us from helping those we love. Stories about our missing and homeless children and mothers and fathers. Stories about our sons and daughters languishing in jails and prisons and solitary confinement without treatment. Stories that don't mesh with bureaucratic reports.

We mustn't wait another 187 years to end the suffering. We need change. Sooner than tomorrow.

SECTION 8. THE LAMP BESIDE THE GOLDEN DOOR GROWS DIM
Immigration in 2017 America

PAULA vW. DÁIL

> The bosom of America is open to receive not only the Opulent and respected Stranger, but the oppressed and persecuted of all Nations and Religions; whom we shall welcome to a participation of all our rights and privileges....—President George Washington

America has a long, proud history of welcoming immigrants. Unless you are of Native American heritage, your ancestors came to America from somewhere else. They probably didn't speak English and had no employment skills other than nimble hands, strong backs and a willingness to work hard. They left their families and their homelands seeking a better life, and America welcomed them and gave them a chance. They build the America we know today and without them, we would not be the nation we have become.

Nevertheless, the issue of immigration policy and reform has been part of the political discourse for several years and was front and center in the 2017 presidential campaign rhetoric. "When Mexico sends its people, they're not sending their best. They're sending people that have lots of problems, and they're bringing those problems with them. They're bringing drugs. They're bringing crime. They're rapists. And some, I assume, are good people," Donald Trump said in a speech on June 16, 2015, when announcing his candidacy for president of the United States at Trump Tower in New York City. These 40 words put America on notice that, under a Trump administration, immigration policy was going to change dramatically.

Trump continued his immigration reform theme throughout his campaign, focusing primarily on Hispanics, who enter the United States from Mexico across the Arizona, California, New Mexico and Texas borders. He proposed building a border wall that, he insisted, Mexico would fund. "We're going to secure the border ... we have some bad hombres here and we're going to get them out. Right now, we're getting the drugs, they're getting the cash," Trump said during the October 16, 2016, presidential candidates' debate.[1] He added that he would not grant amnesty to illegal immigrants.

Meanwhile, Mexico made it very clear that it did not support building a wall between the U.S. and Mexico. Former Mexican president Vincente Fox told Trump, "Donald, under no circumstances will we pay for this stupid, useless, racist monument."[2] In a more direct comment, Fox reiterated that "Mexico isn't paying for any fucking border wall."[3]

It is true that, historically, 52 percent of all unauthorized immigrants entering the U.S. came from Mexico.[4] However, in recent years, unauthorized immigration from Mexico has decreased while illegal migration from Asia, Central America, and sub-Saharan Africa has increased.[5] What has been ignored in the discussion about undocumented immigration, and with regard to enforcement actions, is that, according to existing law, being in or remaining in the U.S. unlawfully is not a crime.[6]

Currently, two-thirds of America's undocumented immigrants have lived in the U.S. for at least 10 years, a number that has increased significantly since 2005.[7] Further complicating the issue is that most immigrant families have mixed legal status, with one parent having legal immigration status and the other being undocumented.[8]

With regard to the crime rate issue, several well-documented studies have found that immigrants are less likely than native-born Americans to engage in antisocial behavior or to commit unlawful acts.[9] In 2009, 68 percent of incarcerated immigrants were imprisoned for immigration related offenses, not for a crime that threatened public safety.[10]

Nevertheless, the number of Border Patrol officers nearly doubled between 2004 and 2010, increasing from 10,819 to 20,558. Apprehending unauthorized immigrants by Border Patrol officers in the El Paso federal judicial district, which is one of five federal judicial districts along the El Paso border sector, accounted for 93 percent of all federal immigration arrests. It is widely believed that concentrating federal law enforcement efforts on immigration violations diverts resources from other types of public safety enforcement, including drug, property and gun crimes.[11]

Offenses attributed to immigrants, especially those who are undocumented, are usually specific to non-citizens, for example those just having entered the U.S.[12] About half of the 675 immigrants picked up in roundups across the United States in the days soon after President Trump took office either had no criminal convictions or had committed only traffic offenses.[13] Sociologist R.J. Sampson contends that "…cities of concentrated immigration are some of the safest places around," yet U.S. immigration-enforcement apparatus is being wielded against a widening swath of the immigrant community, regardless of their ties to this country, regardless of whether or not they are actually criminals.[14][15]

As regards employment and paying taxes, evidence is that, over the long term, immigration has had no negative effect on local wages and employment.[16] Immigration, especially in high-tech employment areas, has had a very positive effect on economic growth in the U.S. and many undocumented immigrants fill positions that the U.S. workforce is unable, or unwilling, to fill.[17]

Immigrants' contribution to the U.S. tax base is substantial. Using an Individual Tax Identification Number, undocumented immigrants pay an estimated $11.74 billion a year in federal, state and local taxes. On average, 8 percent of their total income goes toward paying taxes, whereas the top one percent of U.S taxpayers pay an average of 5.4 percent in state and local taxes.[18] If all undocumented persons were given a path to citizenship, state and local tax contributions would increase by an estimated $2.18 billion per year.[19]

Additionally, undocumented people also pay sales tax, tax on utilities, and property taxes on their own homes or property taxes that are built into their rental costs.[20] Using New Mexico as an example, undocumented persons currently pay over $67 million in state and local taxes. This figure would increase to over $75 million if these persons were granted citizenship.[21]

Deferred Action for Childhood Arrivals (DACA), instituted by the Obama administration, and largely affecting Hispanics, is also under siege. Trump has rescinded the policy, which protects nearly 800,000 immigrants who entered the country illegally as children, commonly referred to as Dreamers, from deportation. It's not clear whether he plans to let the Dreamers stay until their work permits expire, or begin deporting them immediately.[22]

Attorney General Jeff Sessions said that former president Barack Obama, who started the program in 2012 through executive action, "sought to achieve specifically what the legislative branch refused to do." He called it an "open-ended circumvention of immigration law through unconstitutional authority by the executive branch," and said the program was unlikely to withstand court scrutiny. In response, Obama called the threatened action against Dreamers "cruel and self-defeating...."[23]

Business leaders say the Dreamers make important economic contributions and that ending the program will negatively impact economic growth and tax revenue. This will be acutely felt in the wake of Hurricane Harvey, for example, which caused massive damage to Houston, TX, and the surrounding gulf coast region in late August 2017, followed shortly thereafter by Hurricane Irma, which leveled large areas of Florida. These areas will require years of a sustained rebuilding effort at a time when there is already a construction worker shortage. Because construction is a common employment opportunity among Dreamers and other immigrants, particularly Hispanics and Latinos, ending the program will have a direct, negative effect on the U.S. economy.

Matters became significantly worse for immigrants in early August 2017, when the U.S. Justice Department announced that it will be withholding federal crime-fighting funds from cities that do not actively work to cut illegal immigration, namely "sanctuary cities" that try to shield illegal immigrants. "The Department of Justice is committed to supporting our law enforcement at every level, and that's why we're asking 'sanctuary' jurisdictions to stop making this job harder. By taking simple, common-sense considerations into account, we are encouraging every jurisdiction in this country to cooperate with federal law enforcement," Attorney General Jeff Sessions said in announcing the crackdown.[24]

Albuquerque, New Mexico; Baltimore, Maryland; San Bernardino, and Stockton California; have all been told that they must comply with specific federal immigration policy enforcement guidelines in order to qualify for the federal funds they have requested. While Chicago was not included on this list, Mayor Rahm Emanuel said that Chicago "won't be blackmailed into changing its values as a city welcoming of immigrants" and filed suit in federal court against Sessions and the Trump administration over this directive.

Sessions immediately hit back: "The Trump administration will not simply give away grant money to city governments that proudly violate the rule of law and protect criminal aliens at the expense of public safety. So, it's this simple: Comply with the law or forego taxpayer dollars."[25]

Notably, Hispanics are not the only immigrants targeted by the Trump administration. On January 27, 2017, one week after assuming the presidency, Trump issued Executive Order 13769, titled Protecting the Nation from Foreign Terrorist Entry into the United States. The order was immediately labeled a "Muslim ban" because the order targeted Muslim-majority countries that the Trump administration argued "pose a threat to national security." Several organizations, including the American Civil Liberties Union, went to court to stop the order from taking effect. The courts ruled against the Trump administration, prohibiting its enforcement, and forcing a modification of the order.

On June 26, 2017, the United States Supreme Court breathed new life into the travel ban. Justices modified the scope of lower court rulings that had completely blocked key parts of the modified executive order that Trump had said was needed to prevent terrorism attacks. The court allowed the temporary ban to be put into effect for people with no strong familial, employment or other ties to the United States.[26]

Meanwhile, based upon the Trump administration's belief that rapid growth of immigration over the past half century has harmed job opportunities for American workers and threatened national security, in the spring of 2017 Senators Tom Cotton (R–AR) and David Perdue (R–GA) introduced the Reforming American Immigration for Strong Employment (RAISE) Act. An attempt at comprehensive immigration reform, the legislation specifically targets green card holders.[27] The bill stalled until August 2, 2017, when it was resurrected in a White House ceremony.

This revised immigration proposal would award points to green card applicants based on such factors as English-speaking ability, educational levels and employment skills. Cotton said that while immigrant rights groups might view the current system as a "symbol of America virtue and generosity," he sees it "as a symbol we're not committed to working-class Americans and we need to change that."[28]

Overall, the proposed RAISE legislation represents a profound shift in immigration policy that has been in place for more than 50 years, and, over a ten-year period, cuts immigration by half, from one million to 500,000 per year. The proposed bill, which President Trump "strongly endorses" also ends a visa diversity lottery that has awarded 50,000 green cards a year to areas in the world that traditionally do not have as many immigrants to the United States and to cap refugee levels at 50,000 per year.

President Trump claims the bill is "the most significant reform to our immigration system in half a century" and would "reduce poverty, increase wages and save taxpayers billions and billions of dollars.... The bill would favor applicants "who can speak English, financially support themselves and their families, and demonstrate skills that will contribute to our economy." Trump also contends the current green card system provides a "fast-track to citizenship." In truth, having a green card has historically been the standard path to citizenship, and most green card applicants are individuals who enter the United States to work or to join relatives who live here legally.

Political observers suggest that RAISE is unlikely to succeed, for several reasons: First, Republicans hold a narrow senate majority and would have difficulty getting the 60 votes needed to prevent a Democrat-led filibuster. Second, in addition to fierce resistance from Democrats, the bill also faces pushback from immigrant rights groups, as well as opposition from business leaders and some moderate Republicans representing states with large immigrant populations. Regardless, it is unlikely the immigration issue, which is a core piece of the overall Trump agenda, will go away, and future policy efforts are likely to mirror RAISE in significant ways.

This is the political environment in which Rabah Omer, a Muslim-American citizen who immigrated to the U.S. from Sudan, presents a compelling case for recognizing the inherent strength in American diversity. Her essay, "This Land Is Our Land: Embracing the Strength in Our Diversity," offers an explanation for why immigrants make America a better country.

It is also the environment Tayler Bowser returned to in early 2017 after volunteering in a Syrian refugee camp in Greece. Her essay, "Stories from Inside a Refugee Camp," paints a portrait of the refugees she met, and argues for a U.S. refugee and immigration policy that offers prompt, ongoing assistance to these individuals and families, which is in direct opposition to the RAISE proposal.

And, this is the environment Ari Belathar, who is living in exile in the U.S. finds herself in as she looks toward an uncertain future. The newly proposed U.S. immigration policy is sure to strike fear in the hearts of immigrants in this country, and among those around the world who see America as their last, best hope for a better future, but Belathar explains that they should not be afraid because "If You Push Us to the End of the World, We Will Spread Our Wings and Fly."

NOTES

1. www.cnn.com.
2. www.AzCentral.com, June 17, 2017.
3. www.theguardian.com, January 25, 2017.
4. J.M. Krogstad, J.S. Passel, and D. Cohn, "Five Facts about Illegal Immigration in the U.S.," Pew Research Center, www.pewresearch.org, November 3, 2016.
5. *Ibid.*
6. Arizona v. U.S., 567 U.S. 387 (2012), 132 S.Ct. 2492, 2505 states that "As a general rule, it is not a crime for a removable alien to remain present in the United States" and distinguishes between an administrative warrant such as those served by Immigration and Customs Enforcement (ICE) agents and a judicial warrant that is issued upon a finding of probable cause that a person has committed a crime. The law states that, "When an alien is suspected of being removable, a federal official issues an administrative document called a "Notice to Appear," which does not authorize an arrest."
7. *Ibid.*
8. *Ibid.*
9. W. Ewing Martinez and R.G. Rumbaut, American Immigration Council Special Report, www.americanimmigrationcouncil.org.
10. *Ibid.*
11. J. Gramlich and K. Bialik, "Immigration Offenses Make Up a Growing Share of Federal Arrests," Pew Research Center, www.pewresearch.org, April 10, 2017.
12. *Ibid.*
13. Martinez, *Ibid.*
14. *Ibid.*
15. The American Immigration Council, www.immigrationcouncil.org, April 5, 2016.
16. J. Preston, "Immigrants Aren't Taking Americans' Jobs, New Study Finds," www.thenewyorktimes.com, September 21, 2016; www.washingtonpost.com, April 12, 2017.
17. *Ibid.*
18. L.C. Gee, M. Gardner, M.E. Hill, and M. Wiehe, "Undocumented Immigrants' State & Local Tax Contributions," www.immigrationresearch.org, 2016.
19. *Ibid.*
20. *Ibid.*
21. *Ibid.*
22. www.reuters.com, September 1, 2017.
23. www.washingtonpost.com, September 5, 2017.
24. www.cnn.com, August 4, 2017.
25. Michale Tarm and Sophia Tareen, "Chicago Sues Over Sanctuary City Threat" www.ap.com, August 8, 2017.
26. U.S. Supreme Court, www.supremecourt.gov.
27. Currently, most green card applicants are individuals who enter the United States to work or to join relatives who live here legally. Immigrants whose green card applications are successful are allowed to lawfully remain in the U.S. Green cards are valid for 10 years for permanent residents, and 2 years for conditional permanent residents.
28. www.ap.com, August 3, 2017; John Wagner, www.cnbc.com. August 3, 2017.

This Land Is Our Land
Embracing the Strength in Our Diversity

Rabah Omer

Political questions are far too serious to be left to the politicians.—Hannah
Arendt

The day following the Trump election victory, I was walking, as usual, in my neighborhood. It was a windy day and I had wrapped a winter scarf around my head. A neighbor yelled, "go home!" I ended my phone conversation to make sure I had heard the right sentence. I stopped and looked around to see the neighbor waving his hands in a despicable manner. "I am talking to my dog," he said.

This neighbor has seen me previously, many times, walking in the mornings. Sometimes we exchanged greetings, but this time it was different. I was speaking a foreign language on my phone; I had a winter headscarf wrapped around my head, which could be mistaken for a hijab, and Donald Trump had just been elected president of the United States.

I am an observant Muslim woman living in the U.S. I belong to an extended family that includes physicians, engineers, and business managers. I have been in the U.S. for 12 years and am a naturalized American citizen who took the following oath of allegiance to the country I have chosen to live in, be part of, and contribute to:

> I hereby declare, on oath, that I absolutely and entirely renounce and abjure all allegiance and fidelity to any foreign prince, potentate, state, or sovereignty, of whom or which I have heretofore been a subject or citizen; that I will support and defend the Constitution and laws of the United States of America against all enemies, foreign and domestic; that I will bear true faith and allegiance to the same; that I will bear arms on behalf of the United States when required by the law; that I will perform noncombatant service in the Armed Forces of the United States when required by the law; that I will perform work of national importance under civilian direction when required by the law; and that I take this obligation freely, without any mental reservation or purpose of evasion; so help me God.

I cherished the opportunity I had to take this oath. I am proud to be an American citizen, and I love this country. And for me, unlike native-born Americans, citizenship is a conscious choice I willingly and thoughtfully made, and there is nothing about being an American citizen that I take for granted. As a citizen of a participatory democracy, I understand my responsibilities to do my part to sustain that democracy. This is why I have written this essay; writing is a form of speaking up to critique and reveal the underlying elements giving rise to the current political climate.

The incident with my neighbor was my first brush with the new reality inspired by Donald Trump's victory. In the following days, I observed and experienced a few more similar incidents. But most alarming of all was when I heard from friends and acquaintances that, after finding graffiti that included Nazi symbols on the school's sign, they pulled their children out of a community Sunday school that teaches Arabic language. Some of the people were actually contemplating leaving the country, just to make sure their children would have a safe, non-traumatizing environment in which to live and grow to adulthood.

As the month of fasting and spirituality for Muslims, Ramadan, approached, many families decided to not have the Ramadan meal in the Social Hall of the community mosque as they had done every previous Ramadan. Usually, breaking the Ramadan fast with families and friends together in the hall is the favored tradition. It is also a good opportunity for everyone, including the children, to socialize and feel a sense of community. But with the threats, and a looming sense of intimidation and danger, they decided to withdraw from these dearly treasured traditional activities of the Muslim community.

Later, as friends and acquaintances shared their personal experiences with the "new reality," I tried to make sure that the children did not listen to the stories, fears and worries of their mothers.

The children, like most of their mothers, are American citizens and they must, and need to, form a positive sense of belonging to the place where they are being raised, educated and socialized. It is not healthy for them as individuals, and not conducive to the ideals of the nation and its future, as well as the future of all humanity, to instill in them that differences ought to be fought and that their value as humans is degraded because of these differences.

Neither should they, or any other children, be exposed to notions of violence and threats. Deciding to actively shield the children in our Muslim community from stories of hatred and threats and intimidation was my first conscious act of resistance to the new Trump Administration. It sends the message that we will not give into, or partake in a reality of hatred and divisions. It assures that we are protecting the future of the nation by sanitizing children's imagination from hatred and racism. Yet, I know this is not enough.

As I had followed the unsettling rhetoric of Trump's campaign it seemed as unreal as the "reality" TV shows in which Trump starred. Now, on the day after his successful election campaign, I began to sense the implications of Trump's victory.

It is profoundly important to recognize the urgency of resisting the new reality stemming from this victory (and from my experiences that arose as a result) and the ideas, questions, worries and fears this new reality ignites. Marching in the streets, telephoning political representatives, donating to various organizations, and participating in advocacy groups and campaigns are crucial. Attending town-hall meetings and contributing to the community groups are equally essential acts of resistance. Also, following the news diligently and being more politically aware are all critical to developing a meaningful resistance.

Yet, my understanding of American politics generally, and the current political climate particularly, is that nothing mushrooms into a big cloud of smoke overnight. Most political and social events have deep-rooted causes and contributing factors that smolder for a long time before exploding. Then, when they do explode, a reactive, firefighting type of resistance, results.

This temporarily stops some decisions, like banning entire nations from entering the country, and they slow—or are slowing—the enactment of other decisions. However, to prevent reaching this phase in the future, we need to look deeper. We need to ask: what does it mean to have a community? Who and what decide your value as a citizen? What and who are our definers? To what extent are we free to choose homes? Who is "we" and who is "I"? What are the boundaries between "us" and "them?" To what degree do we have the freedom to choose language, religion, gods, cultures, names and other human conditions? Who holds the measure of people's worth? What should we value more, or less?

These are the general questions the current political atmosphere brings forth, which makes this a valuable opportunity to reflect and evaluate. The present political climate can be a turning point pregnant with evolution and positive change into the future, if we take advantage of it and move it in the right direction. This can happen only by looking into the underlying social and cultural elements giving rise to the current political climate.

To be able to resist, it is critical to answer the questions that explain what carried Trump to the highest office in the country. The overwhelming evidence points to cultural and social resentment as a major thread shared by the socially and economically diverse groups that voted for Donald Trump. His message of hatred and racism appealed to them.

The most pressing concerns are the ones that highlight the discrepancy between the nation's highly valued ideals of compassion, reason, and respect and its decision to elect a president who stands for the opposites of those ideals. Also, the contradiction between the nation's self-image as *the* melting pot of the world and the cultural and social resentment expressed in voting that negates America's cherished principles of protecting and advocating for freedom. Also, we need to ponder what we mean by "civilization"; what it means to be civilized and who decides it? As an act of fundamental resistance, rather than accept them, we need to unpack and address the underlying elements of these discrepancies. This is a complicated task that would take a very long time to complete, and that we must begin now.

I propose that the American educational system has a profound role to play in shaping public opinion, and is the best place to start addressing these questions. Considering that migration from one nation to another is as old as humanity itself and a migration story exists somewhere in the family history of every American, this is an issue that we must fully understand.

Migration is more natural than borders. This does not mean it should occur without rules and regulations. But being fearful of and hateful toward immigrants in a nation of immigrants is incomprehensible, and we must reflect on how our educational system addresses migration. What ideas about foreigners are conveyed in our taxpayer-supported public-school classrooms?

We need an educational curriculum that debunks the myths associated with migration that, unfortunately, inform the policies of immigration. For example, despite the expansive studies and figures presented by researchers that crimes are not associated with immigration these myths seem to shape the attitudes of the public and of policy makers. Additionally, immigration invigorates the economy by enhancing purchasing power and adding to the labor force. It also enriches the culture and nourishes the nation with new young ideas and inspirations. These are the findings of frequent studies by researchers.[1] Yet, myths and stereotypes supersede scientific findings in the issue of immigration.

I don't understand why our nation, which holds reason as one of its highly regarded principles, allows myth and stereotypes to reign over its attitudes. Addressing this issue in a profound manner, through the education system is critical to resisting hatred and racism.

What seems to be absent from the public's consciousness is that, as a natural human activity, migration is not always a convenient or voluntary endeavor. Immigrants are not irrational creatures or casual reckless predators hunting for a chance to demolish Western civilization and hijack its values. Instead, most of the time people are forced to migrate, leaving behind loved ones, homes, personal and family histories, cherished memories and connections.

We should examine, with compassion and within the controlled setting of a classroom, what forces cause people to choose turbulence over stability, discrimination and hatred over love and understanding of their original communities, humiliation and persecution over security and warm sense of belonging. And here I do not call on sympathy but reason. Why reason? Because it reveals the root causes of immigration of a majority of people in our present reality. These people are uprooted from their original home communities as a result of the politics espoused by countries more powerful than their own including the U.S.

For instance, the wars in Iraq, Palestine, Afghanistan, Libya and Syria drove thousands of Muslims from their homes and forced them into displacement. Also, the Cold War that was fought by proxy armies on behalf of the two powerful camps at the time (the U.S. and the Soviet Union) drove thousands of people around the world from their homes and into exile. Moreover, in the past as well as the present, powerful countries support(ed) dictatorships around the world causing many of their citizens to escape political oppression and seek dignified living in other places around the world.

Additionally, economic policies espoused by powerful countries and imposed on other nations through the International Monetary Fund and the World Bank have forced migration. These two, very powerful, economic forces launched a series of economic policies around the globe that caused thousands of people to lose jobs, along with any sense of security, and forcing them to seek better lives in the uncertain world of a foreign country. Most of these wars and policies claimed to be in the "best interests" of these people: either to free them from a dictator, to "modernize" them, or to protect their human rights.

Until Donald Trump entered the political arena, America had, generally speaking, recognized the issues underlying involuntary migration and welcomed immigrants. The nation had honored the promise on the Statue of Liberty, standing in New York harbor to symbolize the dreams an immigrant coming to America hopes to achieve:

> Give me your tired, your poor,
> Your huddled masses yearning to breathe free,
> The wretched refuse of your teeming shore.
> Send these, the homeless, tempest-tossed to me,
> I lift my lamp beside the golden door![2]

Now, as a direct result of Donald Trump's political promises, when these people arrive on our shores because of the misery we, along with other powerful countries, created in their homelands (assuming they are able to come to America at all) we fight their presence.

It falls to the educational system to connect these dots and foster a broader perspective on immigration. If this does not occur, we cannot resist hatred racism and fear of others.

I believe that, as an act of profound resistance as well as a step toward a brighter future, we need to publicly debate these issues and push for an educational system that addresses immigration from its different, and complex, aspects. This includes teaching the right histories that reveal the root- causes of the current waves of migration around the world.

If we are to raise future generations to have a global consciousness and respect for other nations, it is critical to adopt an inclusive world history in our school curricula. We need to write, publicly debate, and advocate for such curricula by becoming actively involved in our children's schools as members of parent-teacher organizations, faithfully attending school board meetings, and running for election to the school board itself.

Additionally, educational curricula must debunk the myths associated with migration which, unfortunately, are currently informing American immigration policies. Despite the expansive studies and figures presented by researchers that crimes are not associated with immigration these myths seem to shape the attitudes of the public and of policy makers.

Immigration invigorates the economy, empowers purchasing power and supplies labor. It also enriches the culture and nourishes the nation with new ideas and inspirations. These are the findings of frequent studies by researchers. Yet, myths and stereotypes supersede scientific findings in the issue of immigration. Why a nation that holds reason as one of its highly regarded principles allows myth and stereotypes to reign over its attitudes and policy-making? Addressing this issue through the educational system is critical to resisting hatred and racism, and goes deeper than merely donating to a foreign cause, which the American public is often the most generous among nations in supporting. Yet if these same people Americans donate to support abroad became a neighbor living next door they, risk being met with a new hostility emboldened by the contentious leadership style of the Trump administration.

And here lies the significance of leadership, even in a nation with a profound democratic tradition like the U.S. has. The implication of Trump's leadership is not only in the decisions and policies he makes but also in the hatred and racism he inspires and emboldens in others, and fails to recognize that we are a diverse nation and that there is profound strength in that diversity. Our Education system should address these issues of diversity and immigration comprehensively.

Democracy and freedom are not about institutional procedures and voting. It was not a coincidence that Thomas Jefferson, the author of America's Declaration of Independence from England, and a drafter of the U.S. Constitution, established an educational institution (the University of Virginia) at the same time he conceived and developed the principles upon which our democracy is based. Jefferson understood that without informed, critically thinking citizens we cannot maintain our democracy and its ideals, and this can only happen through an active, organic educational system that fosters critical thinking, embraces diversity and fosters global awareness.

I often ask myself why it so often seems to fall to women to lead resistance movements seeking social change. Women are better suited to form a powerful movement for profound resistance because of their peculiar position as a disenfranchised social group that encompasses other forms of oppression and discrimination. In other words, women experience gender discrimination in society on an ongoing basis, with the possibility of other form(s) of subjugation adding additional layers of complication onto their lives, depending upon their class, race, profession and immigration status. Representing and experiencing this multilayered repression automatically equips women with the energy and wisdom necessary to resist injustice in its varied forms.

For example, women can relate to the phenomenon some researchers call "feminization of migration" or "global chains of mothering" where women are forced to leave their children behind with other women at their home countries and seek jobs in rich countries, legally or illegally, in domestic care profession or in other types of cheap labor. These female migrants are forced into such ample sacrifices as a result of the international system of political economy where economic liberalization policies imposed by powerful nations on their countries caused them to lose jobs. Also, economic expansion in rich countries places much of the responsibility of care-giving for seniors and children on women, thus creating the demand for cheap domestic labor.[3]

Additionally, powerful countries have supported, and continue to support, many of the world's tyrannies and dictatorships, resulting in women becoming the sole providers for their families after the state has prosecuted or imprisoned their male partners. Conflicts and civil wars are also main that uproot women and places upon them the responsibility of being the family bread-winner, which often necessitates their migration away from extended family.

In many cases, female migrants are physicians, lawyers, engineers and teachers in their home countries, but choose care-giving or domestic labor in rich countries to afford better lives for their families. This female migration phenomenon uncovers an interesting truth: contrary to what people in the rich countries believe, the global north actually relies on the global south for cheap labor. This reliance enables women in the global north to fulfill their gender-based aspirations and empowerment. That is, women in rich countries are able to achieve their independence because they rely on the cheap labor migrating from disenfranchised nations. This fact debunks the common belief that the global south depends on the North economically. It also reveals that the global north, the receiving nations of labor, causes the "brain drain" of sending countries.[4]

Understanding the root-causes behind such phenomenon, as an example, and our complicity in some of its causes empowers our resistance to racism and other forms of discrimination. Also, realizing that many women in rich countries actually fulfill their aspirations and empowerment through the hard work of migrant women in care-giving profession and domestic labor also broadens our perspective on the issue.

As disenfranchised groups, women in the U.S share a deep common interest with immigrants, workers, women of color and women in general. Hence, women can forge bonds of solidarity and effectively argue for the rights of immigrants, people of color, workers, and other women by revealing the root-causes and the truth behind a variety of phenomena.

Also, women are, most often both the primary teacher and primary parent for children, thus exerting great influence over them as they grow up. Mothers attend parent-teacher conferences, supervise homework, and carry on the conversations about how their child's school day went. This places them front and center as partners in their children's educational experiences, and in a uniquely powerful position to influence how the school that is educating their children operates, including how it deals with bullies and what it teaches about civility and appropriate social behavior. Being aware of their power within the educational system that is instructing their children is a crucial first step women must adopt as they resist the Trump administration policies and rhetoric.

A second step is to encourage school systems to hire qualified immigrant women as teachers, teacher aides and school support staff. This allows the children to experience one-on-one interactions with the immigrant populations in their communities and come to know them as individuals. This helps immigrants successfully integrate into their new communities and helps debunk the myths surrounding them. Knowledge is always a powerful form of resistance.

Further, women's capability to relate to various forms of injustice places on them both the responsibility and the effective ability to develop a more farsighted approach to resistance. That is why the 2017 Women's March to Washington was bigger and more powerful than a mere response to Trump's misogynistic commentaries and vulgarism.

A march that began as an expression of the wrath and rejection of multiple manifestations of injustice represented by Trump's rhetoric and decisions has evolved into a movement aiming to accomplish the more farsighted goals of resistance. Women have formed a women's movement with an expansive agenda. If this agenda is to be realized, the deeper issues that gave rise to the current political reality must be identified, called out, and targeted for demolition. This is how the 2017 women's movement will transform the currently abrasive culture into a foundation for a better future in the America we all love.

NOTES

1. www.adl.org/education/resources/fact-sheets/myths-and-facts-about-immigrants-and-immigration.
2. Emma Lazarus, "The New Colossus," www.poetryfoundation.org.
3. See Zuhal Yesilyurt Gunduz at: www.monthlyreview.org/2013/12/01/the-feminization-of-migration.
4. *Ibid.*

Stories from Inside
a Refugee Camp

Tayler Bowser

In snowy Belgrade, Serbia, an hour before my midnight departure and just days after the New Year, I called my mom. She answered 5,500 miles away on our Wisconsin farm. I informed her I was bound for Greece, not to island hop, but to volunteer at a refugee camp.

After studying in Spain for a semester, I wanted to travel to Greece to witness the realities of the European refugee crisis and determine what I could do about it. I hoped to meet the refugees, to better understand their situations, and to get to know them as people. In doing so, I came away with a passion to do more, especially given the building tension with U.S. refugee policies and the lack of action to help those in need.

A few hours after my arrival, I ventured from my hostel near one of Athens' bustling tourist squares and the looming Acropolis Hill. After a short metro ride to the outskirts of the capital city, I walked past a recycling center and watchful stray dogs. Proceeding through the main gate of Camp Eleonas, I discovered the camp has three sections: two operated by the Greek Ministry of Migration and one under the jurisdiction of the Greek military.

Project Elea,[1] the NGO with which I volunteered, helps in sections one and two, which together house 1,500 refugees. The section operated by the military does not permit NGOs to assist. Refugees are free to come and go from the camp, but there are always guards ensuring safety and order.

Upon my arrival, volunteers from the United States, Europe, Australia, Africa and the Middle East greeted me. Some of the refugees came from Syria, Iraq, Iran, Afghanistan, Pakistan, Cameroon and Somalia. A few refugees even helped the Project Elea team. Some volunteers confessed their surprise to see Americans helping. One volunteer from Spain pointed out, "There are more of you than I thought I'd meet," and admitted, "I did not think Americans cared about the refugees. But it's good. I am happy to see you here."

Experiences like this one helped me realize I can change others' perceptions of Americans. My presence let refugees and volunteers know that some Americans do care, want to help, and do not fit the American stereotype associated with our federal government's negative political views on refugees. Just ask the children.

I befriended a boy named Samir from Aleppo, Syria. Not more than ten or twelve years old, he was outgoing and constantly full of energy, as were most of the children at the camp. A couple of days after I started helping, I heard whoops as he and two other boys, Yad and Omid, ran up to me from their lookout post at the edge of the camp and hugged me endlessly. The children always ask volunteers their names and where they come from. While they did not understand "the United States," they did understand "America," and repeated it after I said it, eyes lighting up with big smiles. To them, being from America is a good thing.

I mentioned this interaction to an Afghani refugee and volunteer while discussing my desire to someday visit his country. He responded, "The people will love you. The people will take you in and accept you. When you go, you can stay with my family. It is the government that would not want you there. But the people, they love America."

While some embrace differences, others stand firm in their views of *us* versus *them*. Around the world, individuals find comfort in what they know and understand. However, culture, language, religion, and traditions separate many and can create division and stereotyping between people.

Project Elea helps break down this rigidity. Through activities among adults and children of different nations, communication and interaction allows people to realize we are more alike than different. We are all human, and even though we come from different places, the politics and hatred of a few do not define everyone.

I helped with activities including Zumba for the girls, rap music time for the boys, arts and crafts, woodworking, henna, chess, women's self-expression, bicycle workshop sessions, movie nights, English conversation for adults and children, and play time with small children. Games of soccer, volleyball and basketball also kindled excitement and camaraderie among refugees. Sometimes those with specific skills set up activities. Different volunteers give yoga lessons. A refugee, who had been a tailor back in Afghanistan, now teaches women in the camp how to sew.

The children living in the camp do not receive a formal education. They have been through so much psychologically that they need structure to learn and express themselves and time to act like children. While these activities are not enough to replace formal education, they provide something, especially on the days when extra hugs are needed.

Project Elea volunteers also sort and distribute donated clothing. In January, winter clothes were in high demand. With heartbreak, I watched children play outside in the bitter cold in sandals and without gloves because we could not supply them with proper clothing. Yet I felt joy when a young mother, grateful for the winter jacket I gave her, whispered over and over in broken English, "thank you, beautiful, thank you," while clutching it against her chest.

We handed out meals twice a day, with the following day's breakfast given at dinner. The hot food comes in little plastic dishes, provided by the Greek government. Usually consisting of some type of rice or pasta with a little sauce and small pieces of meat or beans, these bland, repetitive meals provide more calories than nutrition. We always handed out bags of pita bread and oranges and tomatoes when we had them. Once a week, families with young children receive a liter of milk. For some residents, the food handed out supplements their own cooking, using hot plates in their homes.

The Greek government provides a small monthly stipend that makes it possible for refugees at Camp Eleonas to have this freedom to obtain additional living supplies. A few times I noticed other NGOs handing out food outside the gates of camp. Refugees also venture further into the city to get what they need or even just to spend an afternoon exploring.

One older gentleman remained silent each time he came to the dinner window. He carried two crates, getting food for both families living in his container. Asked what he needed, he only showed me the number with his fingers. His silence and sad, dull eyes stayed with me. After a few days, I remembered his numbers, confirmed them with him, and told the other volunteers what he needed. Soon, he started to say "hello" or "good evening" when he picked up his meals. The simple reminder that someone cares goes a long way.

Some refugees shared stories of their families that involved heartbreaking realities of persecution, separation and death. Many families are split up, with some members still in their home country, while others are spread across Europe. One boy, around ten years old, explained he looks forward to the day he can leave the camp because it might mean he will join his brother and father in Germany, whom he has not seen in a year. One mother spoke of her thirteen-year-old daughter, killed by an ISIS fighter, and the strength it took to flee on foot, leaving everything she knew behind, to save her other child. Another refugee, Kambiz, shared that he fled Iran because of the oppressive government. He escaped first to Turkey with a few of his family members and then by a crowded boat to Greece. He recounted the terrifying journey, describing alarmingly high waves slamming into the boat and spraying the passengers. They believed all were going to die, and people cried and shouted out. Kambiz did not know what to do, so he started to pray. Somehow, their boat made it to one of the Greek islands, where a ferry later brought them to Athens. And now, like many, Kambiz has been waiting in limbo at Camp Eleonas for more than a year.

Before fleeing Iran, Kambiz studied politics at a university and wants to continue his education. One of the universities in Athens started free English lessons for adult refugees a few days a week. While not a perfect replacement, this program gives the refugees a sense of purpose and empowerment in a situation where they are not self-sufficient. In learning English, refugees can more easily immerse themselves in Western culture, take university courses, or get jobs following resettlement—moving on with their lives after months in limbo.

In the meantime, refugees find difficulty in obtaining employment while still in Athens. To work legally, refugees must be fully registered with the Greek government and have their full registration card, which takes time. In addition, the Greek unemployment rate is 23 percent,[2] so jobs for both Greeks and refugees are scarce. And without a known departure date, finding employers willing to employee refugees for what may be a short amount of time can be difficult.

Kambiz admitted his time in the camp has been tough mentally, but he knows his perilous journey out of Iran was worth it. By chance, at Camp Eleonas he has been reunited with one of his good friends from home. Neither knew the other fled, and both are grateful for their friendship while they wait.

These camps are not meant to be permanent homes; they are supposed to serve as temporary space until refugees move onto the next leg of their journey. The problem comes when countries refuse to accept these people and processing paperwork takes numerous months.

The world knows of the refugees and crowded camps, but well-off countries like the U.S. would rather let these people wait than accept them. I have researched our refugee admissions program in the U.S. and discovered it is designed to stretch the waiting time out by creating a long and difficult immigration process that deters refugees from entering our country.

The recent attempts to create a U.S. travel ban encourage stereotyping that fuels fear, and some of those in politics and mass media wield their power to fuel this fear and separation. Instead of acceptance, it seems many are punished for the actions of the governments they left behind.

The fear surrounding refugee resettlement causes many Americans to cling to whatever idea surfaces next: create an extreme vetting process; close our borders; deny asylum to specific citizens, including Syrians who have lived under dictators for decades and who have suffered for the last six years as their bombed, bullet-filled nation remains a civil war zone. The lucky flee, but many others remain in their homeland, now a carcass fought over by groups of rebel fighters, the Syrian government, and global powers.

Grateful to be away from such violence, refugees' dangerous and now impoverished circumstances do not end when they enter a refugee camp. Life consists of handouts, continued worries, and little control over their lives. Volunteers who have helped at other camps describe situations where families are piled into tents without heat or running water, serving as their only form of year-round shelter. During one of my first days, a fellow volunteer referred to Camp Eleonas as "a five-star hotel compared to the other camps in Greece" because refugees are housed in metal containers consisting of two living areas, roughly 10' × 12' each, with a sink for cooking and washing. Each side generally shelters four to seven people; all share one bathroom. Though small and cramped, Eleonas' refugees are better off than many waiting for resettlement.

A few refugees spoke perfect English, and in another setting, I would have no reason to believe they were not fellow Wisconsinites. One had worked for a large airline company, and speaking English was a necessity. Imagine the great change that comes from working in a modern airport to living in a 10' × 12' space in a metal box on the outskirts of Athens.

On one of my last days, a boy came to get the dinner for his family, excited and chatting to those around him. He proclaimed it was his last day at camp, as his family was going to Frankfurt, Germany. I told him I had been there, offering that Frankfurt is a lovely city. He grinned, nodding, and said he was happy, though I sensed a little anxiety as well.

These children have lost the luxury of innocence. Forced to grow up fast, they bear witness to the harshness of our world. This boy had to rip out the roots he planted at camp and again leave behind what he came to know and understand. Yet again, he must start over in a new country, with new people and a new culture, trying to pick up the pieces of his lost childhood.

Even with this loss of innocence, for the children who will go to school once they are placed in a different country, integration may be easier than for adults. During English conversation, children make connections and remember words more quickly than adults. While they do not receive a formal education, a program in the public schools allows the children to attend Greek language classes for a few hours after normal school hours have ended. The Greek teachers stay late to take on this task. Combined with volunteers speaking English and Spanish, some are little sponges, and readily soak up this mixture of languages.

Assisting with adult English conversation led me to eager students and new insights. I remember sitting with one woman who spoke Farsi (Persian) and another who spoke

Arabic. At different levels in their English proficiency, I tried to determine a middle ground. I realized one woman did not have translations in her notebook—a volunteer wrote the sentences and vocabulary, but the woman did not understand them. I tried to explain their meanings so she could include her translation but soon realized she did not know how to write in her own language. This woman turned to her son, also learning English, and he copied down the translations for her. We also drew pictures of what the words described. Her determination shows the commitment many refugees put forward to immerse themselves in, and become part of, the new cultures in which they will be placed.

I was not prepared for the way in which this woman's reality, which exposed my privileged upbringing, shook me. Never in my life have I been so grateful to come from a society encouraging women's education and literacy.

The sharing of cultures goes both ways at Camp Eleonas. Sometimes families invite volunteers into their small homes for dinner or tea. The abundant food these new friends shared, insisting we take more when they had so little, revealed their hospitable, warm nature. I sipped tea long into the night as we laughed and shared stories. I was filled with wonder as we listened to Afghani music strummed from a homemade guitar, pieced together using string, a board, nails and recycled plastic.

To say this volunteer opportunity provided an enriching personal experience under-states how moved I feel reflecting on my short time there. I bore witness to the results of slow-acting governments, yet unwavering humanity at its finest. I participated in a safe and dynamic society for everyone, created from different cultures living and working together.

In addition to new friends, I now have experience to support my beliefs regarding the urgency to intensify aid for the refugees. My time in Athens exposed me to the power of education and the importance in an informed public to create change in government. As informed citizens, we must speak out against the flawed U.S. refugee policies.

For this reason, since returning home, I have spent additional time researching U.S. policy and the European refugee crisis. I spoke about the reality in one of my university classes and wrote an article for my local newspaper about my experiences. The oppor-tunity to write this essay continues to allow my voice to reach greater audiences. I want all Americans to understand the persecution and danger these refugees have faced and continue to face; they wait in limbo for resettlement, putting their lives on hold, and remain targets for discrimination even after resettlement because of a lack of knowledge and acceptance.

More Americans must follow global issues and create opinions based on facts rather than listen to hollow accusations and fear promoted by those holding political power. The public influences decisions of government policy, so the public must speak out about the lack of action the U.S. government allows to continue. Politicians must also educate themselves on the reality of this crisis and see the refugees for what they are—people. It is a matter of humanity.

I came to know the refugees the U.S. is so reluctant to assist. They are children pulled from collapsed buildings, mothers leaving behind their cultures, fathers piling their families on rubber dinghies, and brothers and sisters separated by miles and borders. They are normal people, like anyone living in the U.S., and they were living normal lives with homes and jobs and families, until forces beyond their control changed their lives forever.

Refugees have different cultures, just like many of us in this melting pot we all call home. But more similarities than differences exist among us. Refugees must flee because there is no other option. It's get out or die trying. These people want to stay alive and keep their families alive. They want a chance to live in safety and peace; it does not get more human than that. As fellow humans, we must help. As citizens of the wealthiest nation on earth, we must force our government to intensify its response.

NOTES

1. www.projectelea.org.
2. Angeliki, Koutantou, "Greek Unemployment Eases to 23 Percent in October, Eurozone's Highest." www.reuters.com, January 21, 2017.

If They Push Us to the End of the World, We Will Fly

Ari Belathar

Last January I was invited to take part in Together We Rise, a Counter-Inaugural Celebration of Resistance in Boston, Massachusetts. As an artist who has been subjected to persecution, illegal imprisonment, torture and exile, I was asked to talk about the role of the artist in times of oppression. The following is the testimony I gave at the Strand Theatre on the evening of January 19, 2017, surrounded by a community of dreamers and fighters— all worried about our rainbow world that was suddenly turning upside down.

Buenas noches. Good evening, ladies, gentlemen and gender dissidents!

I am here today because when I was 19 years old, I was persecuted and subjected to illegal imprisonment, torture, and exile, due to my work as an artist, student activist, and independent journalist.

I am also here because the first phone call I got after Trump's victory, was my sister calling from Chicago asking if I would adopt her kids in case she is deported. Our voices were shaking as we made plans for the unthinkable.

When I was invited to participate in tonight's event, I was asked to talk about "The Role of the Artist in Times of Oppression." The role of the artist in times of oppression…. The notion was utterly confusing to me because the role of the artist in times of oppression is to be an artist. Because the role of art is not to open doors that are already unlocked. The role of art is to open doors that are locked, that are sealed. The role of art is to tear down walls, open windows and let the sun shine through to illuminate the life that is inside us all.

Tomorrow, in the United States of America, a man takes power. A small man whose biggest dream is to build walls, big, solid, impenetrable walls, and I am not only talking about the border wall between Mexico and the United States. I am talking about invisible walls that have separated us for centuries. He and his cabinet will work tirelessly to reinforce those walls. It is our job as artists to tear them down. It is our job as members of our community to tear them down, to let the light of solidarity and being stronger together shine through!

Art cannot exist in isolation; the artist exists so long as he or she is part of a community, and a community exists so long as it creates art that reaches fourth to everyone and speaks out loud to them.

True art should be made by all and not by one ... to benefit all, not just the 1 percent.

We have serious reasons to be concerned, afraid even, about the days to come. But we also have serious reasons to remain hopeful. As long as we keep tearing down the walls that separate us, we will be fine.

This is your time Usonians—is it ok if I call you Usonians? I do not like the term Americans because it erases the rest of the continent. This is your time my dear Usonians to tear down the walls that you have been made to believe are the foundation of your entire existence. This is not the time to challenge white supremacy; this is the time to destroy it ... to tear it down.

To be an artist is to imagine what does not exist so that it will come into existence ... and if we imagine it together everything will change.

And while we are tearing down white supremacy, let us tear down all walls, all prisons ... and capitalism, which is the largest prison of all.

> The morning is an illegal child
> > innocent
>
> who runs seduced
> by the cold air
> that pierces
> through the bones
> and quietly
>
> with the fallen night
> makes a star

Trump and his henchmen are merchants of darkness, but we are the makers of the stars ... artisans of light!

And if they push us to the edge of the world ... we will open our wings, and fly!

SECTION 9. SOMEWHERE OVER THE RAINBOW

America's Gender Anxiety

PAULA vW. DÁIL

> Every single American—gay, straight, lesbian, bisexual, transgender—every single American deserves to be treated equally in the eyes of the law and in the eyes of society.—President Barack Obama

For the LGBTQIA community Donald Trump's election turned the yellow brick road leading to the land Judy Garland sang so wistfully about in *The Wizard of Oz* into a long and winding trail littered with potholes.[1] "It's sad to see racism win, it's sad to see homophobia win, it's just terrifying," said 14 year-old Maddie Harris. "I'm terrified, sometimes, to be out ... but honestly, I can't let fear rule my life."[2]

Candidate Trump, holding a rainbow flag, the symbol of the LGBTQIA movement, pledged support for the LGBTQIA community. "Ask yourself who is really the friend of women and the L.G.B.T. community, Donald Trump with actions or Hillary Clinton with her words?" he said in a speech on June 13, 2016, following the Pulse Nightclub shooting in Orlando, Florida.[3] "I will tell you who the better friend is, and someday I believe that will be proven out, big-league." He went on to support transgender woman Caitlyn Jenner's right to use the bathroom that matches her gender identity.

However, a clue to Trump's sincerity regarding his promises to LGBTQIA voters was clearly evident in his selection of Indiana governor Mike Pence as his vice presidential running mate. Pence, an evangelical Christian who believes marriage is between one man and one woman, brought a long political history of not supporting the LGBTQIA community with him when he joined the Republican presidential ticket.

Since winning the presidency, Trump's actions have not been, as he promised, friendly toward the LGBTQIA community. To the contrary, he has been disposed toward actions that are distinctly anti–LGBTQIA.

Within a month of taking office, the president, by Executive Order, withdrew federal guidelines specifying that transgender students have the right to use public school restrooms that match their gender identity. By taking a stand on a contentious issue that existed prior to his presidency, and has become one of the central battles over transgender rights, Trump sent a clear signal that he was not necessarily the "friend" to the LGBTQIA community that he claims to be.

The Trump administration went on to order the nation's schools to disregard the memos the Obama administration issued during the previous two years indicating that prohibiting transgender students from using facilities that align with their gender identity violates federal anti-discrimination laws. In its letter to the nation's public schools, the Trump administration does not offer guidance in this issue; it merely states that the president was withdrawing the Obama directive because it lacked extensive legal analysis, did not go through a public vetting process, sowed confusion and drew legal challenges.[4]

Another move viewed by many in the LGBTQIA community as a blatant attack on their rights occurred when, on the National Day of Prayer, the president signed an executive order relative to religious liberty that many believe will open the doors for further discrimination against gay Americans on religious grounds. Initially the American Civil Liberties Union signaled that they would take the administration to court over this order, but later backed down, saying the order has no teeth. "It turned out the order signing was an elaborate photo-op with no discernible policy outcome," the organization tweeted. "Trump's assertion that he wished to 'totally destroy' the Johnson amendment [a provision of the U.S. tax code that regulates the relationship churches and religious organizations have with political issues] with this order has proven to be a textbook case of 'fake news.'"[5]

Perhaps it wasn't. In July, Trump appointed Kansas Governor Sam Brownback, a vocal opponent of gay rights as the nation's "Ambassador-at-Large for International Religious Freedom." It is unclear what this position entails.

Trump had already broken with tradition at the start of Pride Month by not issuing a proclamation which many in the LGBTQIA community viewed as deeply disappointing. However, according to Ken Kidd, an organizer for the New York–based direct-action group Rise and Resist, things could be worse—and they just might be heading in that direction. "The only reason things aren't worse now is because of the resistance," he said, praising the push back against the Trump administration through protests and social media. "Our community is under siege."[6]

Kidd has a valid point. In addition to Pence, the Trump administration has another traditionalist in Attorney General Jeff Sessions. Both men have major roles in shaping the administration's policy agenda, and bring a long history of opposing civil rights for LGBTQIA individuals, including failure to enforce workplace protections and hate-crime laws.

In early August 2017 Sessions filed an amicus brief with the federal court concerning a major case, *Zarda v. Altitude Express*, arguing that it's not illegal under federal law to fire an employee based on his or her sexual orientation. This runs contrary to most interpretations of federal civil rights laws, which is that they are intended to prohibit all forms of discrimination against all minority groups, including the LGBTQIA community, based upon sexual orientation.

A few days previously, Trump himself, without consulting his military advisers, tweeted a proclamation that, going forward, transgender individuals would be barred from military service. Secretary of Defense General James Mattis, furious that the president was using Twitter to make military policy, made no promises about actually implementing the directive.

Trump argued that the ban was necessary because "[o]ur military must be focused on decisive and overwhelming ... victory and cannot be burdened with the tremendous medical costs and disruption that transgender in the military would entail." In reality, there is no basis for Trump's claim. Data from countries, including Israel and Canada, that allow trans military service, show that allowing trans people to serve openly has little to no effect on military readiness or costs. In an angry rebuke of the president's directive, House Minority Leader Nancy Pelosi (D–CA) pointed out that the military "spends more money on Viagra than it does on medical care for transgender soldiers."[7]

On August 25, 2017, Trump pushed the transgender issue further by formally directing the military not to recruit transgender individuals and banning the military from using its resources to provide medical treatment regimens for transgender individuals currently serving. Trump also directed the departments of Defense and Homeland Security "to determine how to address transgender individuals currently serving based on military effectiveness and lethality, unitary cohesion, budgetary constraints, applicable law, and all factors that may be relevant."[8]

Defense Secretary James Maddis responded that he will not move forward with implementing this policy until it has been further reviewed, and ordered a study of the actual medical costs associated with transgender individuals on active military duty. At month's end, several former military chiefs of staff and human rights groups joined in a lawsuit to block the ban, arguing that it harms readiness, staffing, recruitment and morale.

Indications are that Trump will continue pushing these issues. He has said he will support the First Amendment Defense Act (FADA) sponsored by Senators Ted Cruz (R–TX) and Mike Lee (R–UT), which uses a religious argument to prohibit the federal government from taking "discriminatory action" against any business or person that discriminates against LGBTQIA people. The act clearly aims to protect the right of all entities to refuse service to LGBTQIA people based upon the belief that marriage is or should be recognized as the union of one man and one woman, and that sexual relations are properly reserved to such a marriage. This legislation makes no accommodations for alternative, non-mainstream lifestyles, thereby marginalizing the 10 million Americans who do not identify as heterosexual.[9]

Meanwhile, the LGBTQIA community carries on, living their lives as best they can, just as every other human being, and American citizen, tries to do. This is echoed by transgender woman Rachel Eliason, whose essay "Feeling Like Sisyphus: Transgender in the Trump Era" illustrates the struggle when trying to move forward in an environment that, in 2017, not only wants to hold you back, doesn't want you to move at all.

And, as mother (Michelle Bowdler) and daughter (Rebecca Gorman) explain in their essay, "Families Resist: LGBTQ Rights in the Trump Era," dealing with the issues that are thrown their way as a lesbian family as effectively as they can while living responsible lives, successfully raising children, and contributing to the wider society in countless, very important ways is their life.

What sets Rachel, Michelle and Rebecca apart from the average American citizen is that theirs is a life of continual political struggle and resistance to policies that make their lives harder. What is notable about their situation is that, rather than wearing them down, the struggle makes them all stronger.

Notes

1. (LGBTQIA) refers to lesbian, gay, bisexual, transgender, queer, and by implication, intersex and asexual sexual orientation or identification.
2. www.cnn.com, Nov. 30, 2017.
3. www.cnn.com, June 14, 2016.

4. www.washingtonpost.com, February 22, 2017.
5. www.cnn.com, May 4, 2017.
6. www.riseandresist.org.
7. www.cnn.com, August 2, 2017.
8. www.cnn.com, August 25, 2017.
9. www.galllup.com, January 11, 2017.

Families Resist

LGBTQ Rights in the Trump Era

Rebecca Gorman *and* Michelle Bowdler

A story of resistance by a lesbian mother and her teenage daughter. Together, Michelle and Rebecca describe their experience as an LGBTQ family; and how their rights are being threatened by the Trump-Pence Administration.

Michelle: The last several months have been extremely challenging for millions of Americans as we wait and watch to see if the new administration will enact promised legislation based on the hateful rhetoric of their campaign. The promise to "make American great again" is a promise to return to a time when discrimination was commonplace. For those who are not white, straight, physically healthy, able-bodied, Christian and economically secure, returning to the past is terrifying. For some, it is life threatening. Understanding the risks to our precious freedoms motivate us with urgency and resolve to mobilize and resist. Our essay concerns the future for LGBTQ people and their families living under the Trump/Pence administration.

What do we know so far? When pressed on specific LGBTQ issues, including marriage equality, Donald Trump has equivocated. He has stated repeatedly that he is a "traditional guy" who does not favor marriage equality, while also saying that it is "settled law"—hardly a ringing endorsement. He articulates that he is a strong proponent of states' rights, a concept with an ugly history. This term was used as a rallying cry for the likes of George Wallace in the 1960s to ignore federal civil rights legislation. One of Trump's first executive orders was to rescind President Obama's directive that public schools allow transgender students to use a bathroom of their chosen gender identity. Why he thought this was a national priority is stunning.

Mike Pence, as Governor of Indiana, signed a "religious freedom" law that, for all intents and purposes, legalized discrimination of LGBTQ people if someone claimed they were doing so based on religious beliefs. He changed the wording of the law only after resounding backlash. In 2006, he said gay couples signaled "societal collapse," and opposed repeal of "don't ask don't tell" as a congressman.

Mary and I became a couple about 25 years ago. At the time, I did not care much about marriage or think of it as a right that LGBTQ activists should prioritize. After many years together, we had two children. We lived in Massachusetts and thought it was a progressive environment in which we hoped they could thrive. Unlike racial or religious

175

bias, kids of LGBTQ parents most often do not share the part of their parent's identity that is questioned or diminished by the majority, yet still are affected by how society views their parents. While we believed we could help our children handle whatever came their way, we hoped to inure them from the pain of intolerance.

Becca: Do you know that feeling when you get hit in the stomach really hard? Like the-wind-gets-knocked-right-out-of-you-forcing-you-to-crumble-onto-the-ground-all-you-can-do-is-look-up-at-the-spinning-world-stars-and-water-clouding-your-eyes-and-wonder-if-you'll-ever-breath-again, kind of hard? Well, I do. The immediate shock of the pain is hard to forget, and every time it happens it is still just as surprising.

It all began when the boy leaned over during assembly to whisper in my ear; it was as if the words that came from his mouth were a sixteen-wheeler careening full speed into my lower abdomen: "Did you hear that the new kid has two dads?" The laugh that followed was almost as deep as the shade of red that blossomed on my cheeks as I tried to hold back my tears and remember how to breathe again. My gasping lungs left me speechless as I wrestled to keep the river of confusion, anger, and sadness inside me from flowing down my face and onto my favorite shirt—the faded blue t-shirt that one of my two moms had just cleaned for me the night before because she knew I wanted to wear it to the school-wide assembly.

The boy turned back towards the stage to watch the new student speak. The noise of my laughing classmates washed over me like massive waves daring me to drown in their contempt. The collection of robust, mocking snickers found its epicenter inside of me and stuck, leaving ripples of insecurity that would last for years.

Every sequential "faggot" and "that's so gay" I overheard in hallways, locker rooms, and buses faded into the chorus of laughter—cementing a belief, somehow, that I should be ashamed of my family. My fear of homophobic teasing haunted me from traveling to away basketball games to the parent pick-up-lines to my eighth-grade graduation ceremony. I spent years trying to hide the truth about my family from classmates like him.

Michelle: Mary and I did not know Becca endured bullying at school. Maybe she thought it would hurt us to know she was being teased because of her parents. Our children were wanted, provided for, and cherished in every possible way. And yet the world we brought them into—even in Massachusetts—still had those who believed having two moms or two dads was weird, abnormal, a joke.

Becca: Seven years later, as a 14-year-old teenager, I remembered myself back in that auditorium gasping for air as I read the definition of "gay" in Apple's MacBook dictionary application while doing homework. One of the definitions stated: "Stupid, foolish—'Making students wait for the light is kind of a gay rule.'" As I read the definition over and over again, the rush of shame I was so used to feeling when confronted with homophobia transformed into anger.

I wrote a letter to the CEO of Apple sharing my disappointment with the company for condoning the use of "gay" in a manner that marginalized and made fun of LGBTQ people. The letter would go viral. In a matter of days, I went from someone who was haunted and immobilized by homophobia to an internationally publicized advocate fighting against it.

I remembered the ripples of laughter as I heard the words: "Did you hear that the new kid has two dads?" I saw my petite, third-grade frame sit up a little on the cold auditorium bench as the tears that had been clouding my eyes dissipated. That laughter sent one final shiver down my spine as I sat up proudly, the auditorium bench from seven years ago transformed into the couch in my living room. I turned to the news camera and said words I had hidden my entire childhood: "My name is Becca Gorman, and I am the proud daughter of two moms."

I was given a unique opportunity at a young age: the chance to speak truth to power and be heard. I cannot help but feel proud of the impact I made. I stood up and advocated for the millions of people affected by homophobia, using my own story as an example of the need for change. Following a childhood where I had felt so vulnerable, I became a leader in my community and helped with many LGBTQ projects after being asked to join Family Equality Council's Outspoken Generation. Most importantly, I actively chose to fight a battle I hadn't expected to win, and came away with a strengthened sense of understanding that I value dearly to this day: my family is something that I feel proud of. I only wish I could have reached out to that scared little girl in the assembly who felt so ashamed, not understanding why her family was a source of laughter to her classmates. I want to make sure that type of pain and embarrassment is not a reality in the childhoods of hundreds of thousands of children of gay men and lesbians in the future. Making sure LGBTQ rights are not stripped away is an important part of that effort.

My two kind, thoughtful, wise mothers are the reason that I am the person I am today. They taught me how to ride a bike, do laundry, throw a baseball, and say please and thank you. They taught me how to stand up when I fall, to never give up, to follow my heart, and to carry my head high. They taught me how to be a listener, an advocate, to fight injustice—to never be afraid to stand up for what I believe. I don't see anything "stupid" or "foolish" about that.

Michelle: Seeing the joy in our children's eyes on the day of our marriage is something I will never forget. It was one of the first times in my life as an LGBTQ member of society that I truly felt like I was not on the outside looking in.

Why did my views on the importance of marriage equality change? For one, the reality of economic insecurity finally hit me. If a married heterosexual person dies, his or her surviving spouse receives their Social Security benefits to help them survive financially. Their assets are not subject to estate taxes. If something were to happen to Mary or me, there would have been no federal support regardless of the length and strength of our commitment to one another and the needs of our family. We had to file as single on our federal taxes, and we were not confident when traveling to other states that we would be allowed to make decisions about one another should a catastrophic event occur. Our relationship was not protected and we were not equal under the law. Equal protection doesn't have qualifiers—equal if you look like the people in power; equal if those writing laws decide what you are doing is acceptable to them. Marriage rights legitimize relationships that should not need legitimization, but do. It has felt amazing to have our relationship acknowledged *by law* and to come closer to having the rights and protections of other citizens. It is unnerving to wonder if and when these protections might be rescinded.

Becca: June 26, 2015, was a momentous day for our country and my family. My parents and I were headed to New York City when the decision was announced. "Hey moms," I yelled when I got the news alert. "You aren't just gay married anymore, you are just plain married." When we arrived in New York City, we immediately headed for the Stonewall Inn where we were joined by thousands at the birthplace of the gay rights movement. Rainbow flags in both hands, I stood in a sea of pure joy, relieved and ecstatic that the fight to eliminate discrimination for LGBTQ citizens had taken such a monumental step forward. Later in the day, I read Supreme Court Justice Anthony Kennedy's statement arguing specifically for the rights of children of LGBTQ couples to be considered. He voiced:

> This provides powerful confirmation from the law itself that gays and lesbians can create loving, supportive families. Excluding same-sex couples from marriage thus conflicts with a central premise of the right to marry. Without the recognition, stability, and predictability marriage offers, their children suffer the stigma of knowing their families are somehow lesser.... The marriage laws at issue here thus harm and humiliate the children of same-sex couples.[1]

Many of my own personal struggles with homophobia were reflected in his comments and my childhood experiences were validated by a man of great power. Although homophobia would not end solely by the recognition of gay families by law, I considered this a huge accomplishment. I felt as though our country's leaders were finally treating my family with the respect we deserved. It was a great and unforgettable moment.

Less than two years later, on November 8, 2016, I sat in front of my computer screen having forgotten how to breathe. I watched state after state turn red, the predicted winner dial turning further and further towards a Trump victory. I don't think I have ever felt my existence more threatened listening to Donald Trump's victory speech. My mothers, brother and I were in constant communication as the election results rolled in. The mood of our normally upbeat, funny group chat had turned to one flooding with existential concerns about the security of our family. I sat on the hallway floor in my freshmen dorm sobbing uncontrollably. America (including the majority of my extended family) had just elected a president and vice president that amplified and gave a platform to homophobic voices—the voices I thought had been silenced by the June 26 Supreme Court decision.

The day after the election, a photo went viral on Facebook. It displayed a note that was left on the car of a gay couple in North Carolina. It read: "Can't wait until your 'marriage' is overturned by a real president. Gay Families=Burn in Hell. #Trump2016 #REPENT #GODBLESS." Reading these words, I was filled with sadness and fear as I questioned my family's security. What if they do overturn the Supreme Court ruling? What if the new administration takes steps to restrict the rights of my family? What if violent acts of homophobia like this one become acceptable and widespread?

Over the past few months, I have had a difficult time turning my anger into action. I took steps to become more involved with the Family Equality Council's Outspoken Generation, and am currently working on two projects aimed at sharing the experiences of the kids of gay couples after the election. I have done my best to call my elected officials in response to bills and nominations I disagree with. I have participated in many organized protests in response to the current administration's actions. I think that the Trump/Pence Presidency has proven how important and influential speaking truth to power can be.

Michelle: I met my future wife in 1988 at a time when homophobia had a huge impact on national policy and on many individuals' lives. We had many gay male friends with HIV/AIDS, and saw firsthand how little their lives meant to the rest of the country and to President Ronald Reagan. We carried signs in marches that read Silence = Death and waited 5 years for the president to say the word AIDS publicly after over 20,000 people had already died, most of them gay men. That experience is seared in my memory. It cannot and should not be forgotten. There is no doubt in my mind that if AIDS had been an epidemic that affected everyone equally, it would have been a national emergency.

A president sets the national agenda in more ways than one. He or she makes recommendations on funding, moves a nation with his or her priorities, and speaks volumes with his or her silence. We have already seen this pattern emerge with our new president, who comments selectively on international events he labels as terrorism, but is often silent on situations where religious minorities and people of color are targeted. He expresses outrage about slights against himself or his administration, but is quiet about an alarming increase in targeted violence. His silence is not benign and it is not accidental. It gives permission. It emboldens and gives rise to the kind of behavior my daughter described above: "Gay Families=Burn in Hell. #Trump2016 #REPENT #GODBLESS." It is deeply concerning that so many now feel bolstered to hate and discriminate openly.

Michelle and Becca: Plain and simple, we are a family. We were a real, true family before the Supreme Court decision, and we will always be a real and true family—full of love and respect and hope in the future. We want to have a government we can feel proud of, that reflects decency and compassion and equality, not one that diminishes "the other" and invalidates their experiences. So far, resistance has been effective.

During the campaign, Trump had promised to undo all of President Obama's executive orders. In the first few days of the Trump/Pence administration, there were stories that there was an executive order drafted that would overturn enforcement of LGBTQ rights in the workplace. After strong pressure from the LGBTQ community and allies, that draft order was not signed. We plan to continue to march, make phone calls, write letters, submit essays for publication and use social media to speak out. We are holding our collective breath, while also taking steps to speak up and fight for the basic rights and dignity of all of our citizens. Becca turned 18 in the fall of 2016 and voted in the November elections, as did her brother, who is 2 years older. One of the additional steps we plan to take is to encourage young people, in particular, to use this important tool of democracy to make themselves heard and to work on voter registration in our community.

The fear we feel and see in others only strengthens our resolve to speak out and use our voices. Our new shared activity seems to be attending rallies and protest marches. We are grabbing one another's hand, picking up signs and looking to the future knowing that our rights are fragile and in jeopardy. Our family, our country and the future are all worth fighting for.

NOTE

1. Anthony Kennedy, "Read the Supreme Court Ruling that Recognized Gay Marriage Nationwide," *Time*, June 26, 2015.

Feeling Like Sisyphus
Transgender in the Trump Era

R ACHEL E LIASON

The question I've often been asked is "what is like being a transgender in the time of Trump?" My only answer is that I feel like Sisyphus, the mythical Greek ruler condemned to push a boulder up a hill, only to have it roll back down again, and again and again for all eternity.

What does this have to do with being transgender? There have been transgender people for as long as there has been recorded history. In the ancient Middle East, they had names like assini, galatura or kurrgaru. They played an important role in the goddess religions of Inanna and Ishtar. In Roman times, they were called galli. On the subcontinent of India, they were hijra. The hijra still exist there today.

They weren't fully accepted. The Greeks and Romans considered it a form of divine madness. Some Mesopotamia tribes revered transpeople; others, like the early Hebrew tribes, condemned them. In a book on the hijras of India, a middle class Indian woman summed it up the best: "Of course, we accept them. But it's not like we invite them to tea."

Sometimes I think about this long history and I am so happy and proud. We have a long rich history. From the earliest times, transgender people have been carving out a space to exist. To realize that there was a time that transpeople were holy and sacred makes it easier to bear the current state of things.

Other times it makes me sad. We had a place, no matter how precarious. We had a community, a mythos and a culture of our own. Where did it all go?

It's been mostly lost to history. The city-states of Mesopotamia fell to patriarchal Assyrian tribes. Priestesses, whether transgender or cisgender, were relegated to history. Rome fell and the galli disappeared. For a time, the haters won.

Flash forward a thousand plus years to 1924–1933, considered the golden age of the Weimar Republic in Germany and, for the modern LGBTQIA community, a tentative new beginning. A progressive culture meant growing acceptance for gay and lesbian people. Magnus Hirschfield, a gay man and a doctor became the first to take the stories and identity of transpeople seriously. He developed medical procedures to help them become what they knew they already were on the inside. First there was Lily Elbe, in Dresden in 1930, then Dora Ricther, in Berlin, in 1931. Then, in 1933, Adolf Hitler.

Hitler brought an abrupt end to the social liberalism of the Weimar era, which ground to dust under the heels of the Nazis. Hirschfield's books were burned and his research destroyed. Weimar Germany has become a foot note in history, no more. Any openly LGBTQIA people went to the concentration camps along with the Jews, the Gypsies, and any other "undesirables" Nazi Germany declared "unfit."

And so it goes. We push the boulder up the hill. And it rolls back over us.

We didn't give up so easily, however. Williem Arondeus fought for the Dutch resistance. His last words echo through time, "Let it be known that homosexuals are not cowards!" No matter how far down the boulder rolls, there are always a few left to push it back up.

In the fifties, we were called transsexuals. Under men like Harry Benjamin protocols were created to help people transition. Private George Jorgensen fought against the Nazi's from inside an American Army foxhole. In 1952, he would push the boulder in another way, returning to Europe to become Christine Jorgensen, America's first transsexual. She hated the publicity around her transition, but she bore it with a grace few could have mustered.

There were good things and bad. The good: there were treatments to help those that needed to transition. Transgender people of that generation carried their "papers," letters from their doctors and therapists. We didn't have civil rights but respect for the medical community gave a modicum of protection.

The bad outweighed this. There was no space for non-binary people, no place for those that didn't want to, or couldn't, do medical transition. Such treatments were rare and hard to obtain. Trans men were almost completely ignored. Social acceptance was a long way off.

But we pushed the boulder. We persisted.

In the late sixties, new coalitions emerged, transgender people and gay and lesbian people. It came to a head at the Stonewall Inn in the summer of 1969. It started as a police raid on a gay bar. Young LGBTQIA people, tired of being harassed by authorities, rioted. The riots lasted three days and by the end became a political movement.

The pride movement was born. With the help of our gay brothers and lesbian sisters we pushed the boulder higher and farther than anyone would have thought possible.

As the 80s dawned, new threats emerged. AIDS. A conservative backlash led by Reagan and the religious right. An easy roll to the top became a literal fight for our lives. Thousands of gay men and transwomen died as the boulder that was AIDS rolled over us. Thousands more marched in the streets. The slogan "Silence Is Death" still reverberates with those that lived through those times.

I was a kid living in a very conservative part of the country at that time, and mostly I remember the backlash coming from preachers saying it was god's punishment for sin. I remember students in my high school who believed, with no trace of irony, that AIDS was something that only happened to gay men and simultaneously, something you could catch from just touching them. It was a scary time and I stayed in the closet.

Eventually pressure from activist groups resulted in money being assigned to research. Eventually drugs were developed that, while they don't cure AIDS, can control it.

Those who made it through alive kept pushing. In the 90s and the first decade of this century there was marriage equality, Don't Ask, Don't Tell and many other legal battles. Slowly we began to gain momentum again. The top of the hill was in sight.

I was there for much of that. I came out, first as bisexual in the 90s and later as transgender. I marched with my LGBT brother and sisters. Together we pushed the boulder. We saw a huge groundswell of support, more and more people pushing at our side.

The Iowa Supreme court ruled in favor of marriage equality in 2009 and I can still recall the sense of triumph as we all gathered in outside the Ritual Café in downtown Des Moines to hear the news and toast a new era. In 2015 the nation as a whole followed suit, the Supreme Court affirming the rights of all couples to legally wed.

In the meantime, the policy of Don't Ask, Don't Tell was removed and the military became open to those in the LGBT community that wished to serve their country. There were even those who mistakenly believed we were at the top of the hill, that we had achieved full equality. It wasn't true, not by a long shot, but I understand how it felt. We had achieved so much. We felt unstoppable.

Then came the 2016 election. There was Donald Trump. There was Mike Pence. There were numerous attempts to pass restrictive "bathroom bills." Too many of our youths are still subject to conversion therapy. There was, and still is, a growing wave of violence against transgender people.

Now I know how Sisyphus felt watching the boulder roll back down the hill.

You want to give up. You've fought so many battles already. But you know you won't give up. You can't give up, because this is what we do. We push the boulder.

Our opponents call it a culture war. They speak of winning and losing. In the end, they are going to lose, because they don't understand the nature of the task. There is no winning for you in this fight because I am not pushing against you. I am pushing for my life, for the rights of people like me to live our lives in peace. I am pushing for a better future.

There is you and there is the boulder. If you chose the right boulder, the right task, one that will make the world a better place, then all you must do is to keep pushing. Sometimes it will roll a long way. Most times it will only move a fraction of an inch. Occasionally it will roll back over you. It doesn't matter.

What matters is that every day you set your intentions to make the world better and you push. Endlessly. No great push is going to make the world a perfect place. No backslide is going to crush us all.

The Trump administration feels like a big back slide. It feels like our rights could go up in a single puff, in precisely the same way Weimar Germany vanished.

There are also, suddenly, a lot more people pushing this boulder. Activist, new and old are coming out of the woodwork everywhere. The women's march attracted over five hundred thousand women to Washington, D.C. Mirror protests held worldwide involved as many as five million protesters.

The most hopeful sign for this new movement is how broad it is. A willingness to be inclusive of a range of people and issues from Black Lives Matter to transgender people gives me hope that old divisions on the left will be set aside for good.

Since then, groups like Indivisible have only grown. Protesters are showing up to town hall meetings in such numbers that many conservatives are refusing to hold them. From protests to phone calls to senators, the people are awake, and they are pissed.

How far will we push this time? That remains to be seen. This might be a temporary flash in the pan, but it doesn't feel that way on the ground. It feels like a groundswell. It feels like a lot of people are deciding it's up to them to make politics work again. We are showing up to town halls, calling our senators and showing up to protest. We know what we want. Now all we have to do is keep pushing until we get it.

SECTION 10. WHEN BLIND JUSTICE ISN'T BLIND
Women Face the Criminal Justice System

PAULA vW. DÁIL

An awful lot of the trouble women in prison have gotten into is a direct result of associating with bad men.—Stan Stojkovic

"Women in prison spend a lot of time wondering about their relationships with men, and whether they are attractive enough to grab onto one," explains University of Wisconsin–Milwaukee Criminology Professor Stan Stojkovic.[1] "They don't seem to have much sense of themselves as worthwhile human beings regardless of whether they have a man in their life." Sociologist and Edgewood College Professor Sister Esther Heffernan, who has studied women and the prison system for more than 50 years, agrees, adding that, when looking at the relationship between women and the criminal justice system, it is important to recognize that most women encounter the criminal justice system first as a victim: "Frequently, they have past experiences with sexual abuse or incest at the hands of a man, usually their father, brother, or other male relative they know and trust. This always, always negatively impacts their self-esteem and sense of self-worth. These women have never had appropriate male role models, and become extremely vulnerable to the emotional pull of any man who shows an interest in them—and make bad relationship decisions as a result."

Self-esteem is a very deep problem, Heffernan stresses: "Every woman needs a critical mass of self-esteem to operate effectively in the world, and if she lacks this, for whatever reason, she is at an acute disadvantage … she'll fall for anything, and follow any man. She won't even plea-bargain to get a shorter sentence if doing this puts her relationship with the man, who is usually her partner in crime, in jeopardy, but more often than not, when a woman commits a crime, a man is involved…. and if she is sentenced to jail or prison, he leaves her and goes searching for another woman. Why some women make these bad decisions defies reason."[2]

Nichole, a 23-year-old single mother currently living in a homeless shelter, explains it this way: "I'm way too nice where men are concerned. I've done a lot of things I know I shouldn't because some guy asked me to, and am just lucky I haven't gotten caught … so far," she says.[3] The majority of women who go afoul of the law have become involved in drug and alcohol-related crimes, or committed welfare fraud (a felony) or crimes of opportunity such as shoplifting or petty theft. Sometimes they engage in property crimes, weapons violations, drunk and disorderly conduct, prostitution, illegal gambling, curfew violations, and loitering.

Homeless shelters are heavily populated by women fleeing domestic violence, which is strongly related to drug and alcohol abuse, and teenage runaways who commit petty crimes and are often motivated by deep anger and an inability to trust anyone. Regardless, their lives are such that most are destined, sooner or later, to become involved with the criminal justice system, if they haven't already, and that system isn't necessarily going to serve them well.

Donald Trump began his presidency by promising to address what he termed the "rising specter of American carnage—the crime and gangs and drugs that have stolen too many lives and robbed our country of so much unrealized potential."[4] Trump's America is a dark place, despite the reality that the overall national crime rate is 42 percent below what it was 20 years ago.[5]

"So far, many of the administration's actions are symbolic. But they evidence a clear return to the discredited 'tough on crime' rhetoric of the 1990s, that suggests a significant departure from the Obama administration's approach to criminal justice," write Ames Gravert and Natasha Cambi of the Brennen Center for Justice at New York University School of Law.[6] "Trump's turn also directly contradicts the emerging consensus among conservatives, progressives, law enforcement, and researchers that the country's incarceration rate is too high, and that our over-reliance on prison is not the best way to address crime. As crime remains near historic lows—despite local, isolated increases—these proposed changes are, ultimately, solutions in search of a problem. Taken to an extreme, they would set back the national trans-partisan movement to end mass incarceration."

Gravert and Cambi offer the following policy analysis regarding the potential for criminal justice reform under a Trump Administration.[7]

Misguided Fears of a New Crime Wave

President Trump has repeatedly cited misleading statistics to push a false narrative about rising crime and calls for urgent, drastic action. This focus on fear over fact, unprecedented for a modern president, helps justify the administration's most controversial policies.

Trump and his new attorney general, Jeff Sessions, insist that they must "make America safe again," citing outside forces that have brought in drugs and violence, and using this to justify a Muslim travel ban, a border wall with Mexico, and mass deportations. The administration has also issued several executive orders focused on combatting this phantom crime wave, without offering solutions to solve the real and serious localized problems of violence in cities like Chicago and Baltimore. The taskforces created by these orders may recommend new federal criminal laws or new mandatory minimums, especially for crimes against police officers and drug offenses.

This new tone from Washington also risks derailing a decade-long bipartisan effort to reduce prison populations in states. If the public incorrectly believes that crime is rising, there may be less support for state and local reform.

A New War on Drugs?

President Obama and his Attorney General, Eric Holder, took several steps to reduce the federal imprisonment rate, which has dropped by 9.5 percent since 2007. In 2013, the Justice Department deprioritized prosecuting nonviolent marijuana cases, providing more latitude to states, and issued a directive to federal prosecutors to reduce charges in lower-level nonviolent drug cases.

Attorney General Sessions is poised to reverse those reforms. He has been a vocal opponent of bipartisan criminal justice reform, derailed a Republican-led, modest sentencing reform bill last year, and opposed many of Holder's initiatives. Since taking office, Sessions has given several speeches calling for a return to harsher federal charging policies, and issued memoranda directing U.S. Attorneys to stand by for such major policy shifts. Sessions could revoke key Holder-era initiatives and direct federal prosecutors to pursue maximum penalties in drug cases even in states where marijuana is legal. Notably, the administration has shown interest in expanding treatment options for opioid addiction, which disproportionately affects white, rural communities, while increased marijuana prosecutions would affect minorities and communities of color more.

Increased Immigration Enforcement and Detention

Shortly after the election, Trump pledged to deport as many as 3 million undocumented immigrants, including mothers whose children were born in the U.S. and are American citizens. He has since issued several executive orders directing the Justice Department to more vigorously enforce immigration law. Sessions responded by fast-tracking the hiring of new immigration agents, ordering all U.S. Attorneys to prioritize immigration cases, and threatening to strip funding from cities that do not cooperate with federal immigration authorities (i.e., "sanctuary cities"). The Department of Homeland Security is also expanding its detention capacity.

In July 2017, Maricopa County, Arizona, Sheriff Joe Arpaio was found guilty of criminal contempt for defying a court order to stop detaining some undocumented immigrants, including women. President Trump, calling Arpaio "a great patriot," issued an executive pardon the following month, before Arpaio was sentenced for his crime. Senator John McCain (R–AZ) responded that the pardon represented "blatant disregard for the rule of law and woeful ignorance of the separation of powers" on the part of the president. Speaker of the House of Representatives Paul Ryan (R–WI) concurred.[8]

McCain and Ryan were correct. Contempt of Court is a violation of a court order, issued by a judge, and regards the ability of a judge to enforce its orders. It is not a crime against society or the government, thus does not fall within the purview of a presidential pardon. The case is a separation of powers issue and remains to be seen whether the pardon will hold up to a legal challenge by the judge who issued the contempt order and can claim Trump exceeded his presidential power to issue an unconstitutional pardon.

In practical terms, Trump's action was a blanket endorsement of racial profiling and empowered neo–Nazi and white nationalist groups to target various immigrant and other minority groups. It also encouraged wider opportunities for bigotry and hatred to flourish.

Decreased Oversight of Local Police

Historically, the Justice Department has played a key role overseeing and regulating civil rights violations committed by local police departments. Under Obama, the Justice Department opened more than 20 investigations into police misconduct and enforced more than a dozen "consent decrees" with local police departments. These settlements, overseen by a federal court, require officers to work with communities and improve policing practices.

Sessions outright rejects this role for the federal government, labeling it as part of a broader "war on police." He has directed a review of all existing consent decrees and attempted to stall pending agreements. This trend will likely continue, potentially emboldening police departments to become more aggressive.

Increased Use of Private Prisons

Sessions recently revoked an Obama-era memorandum that directed a wind-down of federal use of "private prisons"—correctional facilities operated by private corporations on behalf of the Bureau of Prisons. Now, the BOP is free to continue and expand the use of private prisons, a signal that Sessions expects the federal prison population to grow.

Possible Federal Sentencing or Reentry
Legislation

Last year, Republicans, including Sens. Chuck Grassley (R–IA) and John Cornyn (R–TX), and House Speaker Paul Ryan (R–WI) led a bipartisan effort to pass the Sentencing Reform and Corrections Act (SRCA). The bill would have reduced mandatory minimums for some nonviolent and drug crimes. Then-Senator Sessions led an effort to defeat the bill, labeling it a "criminal leniency bill." In response, Senate Majority Leader Mitch McConnell, fearing a split within his own party, declined to bring the bill to a floor vote, despite overwhelming support for the initiative.

In January 2017, Grassley and Ryan committed to reintroducing some version of the law, yet are rumored to be waiting for the administration to announce its position before moving forward. In March, Trump dispatched senior advisor and son-in-law Jared Kushner to meet with Grassley and Sen. Dick Durbin (D–IL) to discuss sentencing and reentry legislation. Kushner, whose father spent two years in prison for white-collar offenses, supports criminal justice reform. Trump's personal positions on reform are unclear.

It remains to be seen whether advice from Kushner and backing by conservative reform advocates will influence the president. Some conservatives support expanding reentry services, and modest sentencing reductions, for low-level offenders, which is the category most women offenders fall into. The Trump Administration could take a similar stance by backing modest prison reform in Congress while continuing to pursue aggressive new prosecution strategies. Sessions is a hard-liner on sentencing and does not favor sentencing reform.

In a glimpse into Sessions' view of women, he directed the Justice Department to prosecute liberal activist Desiree Fairooz for a second time, because she laughed at him during his confirmation hearing. Initially she was found guilty of disorderly conduct, but the verdict was vacated by a judge who disagreed with the prosecutors' argument that laughter was disorderly.[9] Sessions' decision to pursue this is directing resources better spent on prosecuting serious crimes toward a misdemeanor conviction punishable by up to 300 days in prison for first-time offenders

From a different direction, U.S. Secretary of Education Betsy DeVos has indicated that she plans to change the way colleges and university handle allegations of sexual violence on campus. Her comments signal the possibility of a major shift in the way colleges enforce Title IX, the federal law that prohibits discrimination based on gender in education.[10] DeVos has not indicated what these changes will be, but as a crime that uniformly affects women, this does not bode well for women victims, and may impinge upon their due process rights.

None of this is positive news for women who encounter the criminal justice system. However, there is another concern: Donald Trump has a tendency to blame the victim when a crime occurs, as evidenced by his response to the Charlottesville. Trump claimed that Charlottesville citizens who resisted the neo–Nazis and other hate groups who came to Charlottesville were as much to blame for the violence as the hate group instigators.[11] This suggests he won't be sympathetic to adjusting sentencing criteria to reflect women's unique circumstances, or get tougher on crimes such as rape or sexual harassment, which he has been personally accused of, doesn't seem to understand and apparently sees nothing wrong with.[12]

With this in mind, retired Wisconsin Supreme Court Justice and worldwide advocate for restorative justice practices, Janine Geske discusses her views regarding what women are up against in the criminal justice system. "Is There Justice for Women in America?" offers insights into several issues women face when they encounter legal difficulties, and what needs to change to make the law fairer for women offenders.

Rape victim Michelle Bowdler expresses her concerns about the massive nationwide backlog in rape kit testing and explains what this failure means to women victims. In her essay "I Am Not Resigned and I Do Not Approve," she stresses the importance of women staying engaged in the fight for justice for themselves.

Taking on an entirely different problem, Mariya Taher, who works with victims of female genital cutting practices, which she believes must be stopped, explains the conflict that arises when cultural practices run afoul of the law, and what this means for U.S. immigrant communities. "When Culture and Gender Violence Clash with the Law" describes the personal and community conflicts that arise when accepted cultural practices among some religious and ethnic groups are harmful for female children, and often illegal, yet women from these backgrounds often wish to honor.

Notes

1. For a full discussion women's relationship with the criminal justice system, see "A Man Is Not the Answer" in Paula vW. Dáil, *Women and Poverty in 21st Century America, Ibid.*, pp. 84–116. *Ibid.*, p. 86.

2. *Ibid.*

3. *Ibid.*

4. Donald Trump Inaugural Address, January 21, 2017.

5. Ames Gravert and Natasha Cambi, *Criminal Justice in Trump's 100 Days,* Brennan Center for Justice, New York University School of Law, April 20, 2017.

6. *Ibid.*

7. *Ibid.*

8. www.washingtonpost.com, August 27, 2017.

9. Dana Milbank, "Apparently, It's Illegal to Laugh at the Attorney General," www.washingtonpost.com, September 7, 2017.

10. "DeVos Plans to Scrap Obama Rules on Campus Sexual Assault," www.ap.com, September 8, 2017.

11. For more on the Charlottesville protests, see the section titled "Not My President: America Goes Dark."

12. Trump admitted to sexual misconduct with women on a 2005 Access Hollywood recording.

Is There Justice for
Women in America?

An Interview with Wisconsin Supreme
Court Justice Janine P. Geske (ret.)

Paula vW. Dáil

According to 2015 ACLU data,[1] the U.S. has the highest prison population in the free world and, between 1980 and 2014, the number of women in prison grew by an alarming 700 percent—increasing at a rate 50 percent higher than that of men. Over the same period, the number of women in local jails increased 14-fold. These increases reflect the unequal, biased relationship African American women, whose rate of imprisonment is double that of white women, have with the law and with the criminal justice system.

Today, there are more than 200,000 women behind bars, and more than 1 million women are on probation and parole. Most have never committed a violent crime.[2] Additionally:

- Approximately 60 percent of imprisoned women are mothers;
- Women in the federal system are more likely to be incarcerated for a nonviolent offense. Some 94 percent of women in federal prison, and 63 percent of women in state prisons, are serving a sentence for nonviolent drug, property or public-order offenses;
- Incarcerated women often struggle with drug abuse, mental illness, and ongoing relationships with bad men, further complicating their ability to return to life outside;
- With limited resources, prisons and jails are often poorly equipped to address the challenges women face when they enter the justice system;
- Women often leave prison having little hope of long-term success, facing great parental stress, having few options for financial independence or the ability to find employment and affordable housing;
- There are also costs—both emotional and financial—for women whose spouses or significant others are incarcerated. Family members are primarily responsible for court-related costs associated with conviction, and 83 percent of those family members are women.

These data beg several questions pertinent to women and their relationship with the criminal justice system:

Paula vW. Dáil: *Why is the criminal justice system (CJS) so willing to imprison women for non-violent offenses?*

Janine P. Geske: Women often are charged with multiple offenses because of the nature of the crimes they commit. Women frequently are charged with multiple counts of fraud, embezzlement, shoplifting, theft, or welfare fraud. These offenses, individually, are often pretty minor crimes involving small amounts of money. Women are often not caught until they have committed multiple counts, which exposes them to felony convictions. Women frequently steal money to support a man in their lives, to feed a drug problem or to have more money to spend on their children. Women are also prone to gambling addictions.

Because of the myriad of challenges in the lives of the women who get caught up in the criminal justice system—drug/alcohol addiction, domestic violence, single parents of multiple children, poverty—they are often not successful at community supervision. There are insufficient resources to help a woman turn around the trajectory of her life despite a frequent desire to do so. Women's terms of probation and parole are frequently revoked which results in a prison sentence.

PD: *Similarly, why is the CJS willing to arrest, and deport, immigrant women who have lived in this country for years, never committed a crime, and have children they will be separated from if they are deported. From the legal perspective, why pursue this particular issue when it consumes scarce law-enforcement resources better applied to more serious crimes, harms so many people, and benefits no one?*

JPG: Immigrant women with children are easily found by those trying to deport people. Women tend to be "sitting ducks" for government officials because their children are enrolled in schools and the women tend to stay in one place in order to provide a stable home. It appears to me that there is a bias in deportation approaches focusing on women who are either bringing children into our country or having children here and thereby giving them citizenship.

Some believe that the problem with our undocumented females is that they are having children who ultimately grow up and commit crimes. There appears to be very little understanding of the dangerous challenges that women and children have frequently faced in their native countries.

PD: *One of the most complex relationships women have with the law concerns their reproductive rights, which are under assault in state legislatures across the nation. It is also in this domain where the law manipulates women's lives the most. Despite* Roe v. Wade, *in May 2016, an Indiana woman was successfully prosecuted for feticide resulting from an abortion and faces 20 years in prison. What is your take on this?*

JPG: Even though women leaders have made progress in our political institutions, most legislatures, governors' offices and courts still remain dominated by men. It is my experience that most women, regardless of where they stand on the issue of abortion, understand that the decision to end a pregnancy is a psychologically very tough choice. These are not simple decisions and yet many in positions of power have concluded that the issues involving reproductive rights can be addressed with bright line laws.[3]

Because abortion is such an emotional issue, the immediate reaction of those who are opposed to women having that choice is to punish "the violators." We are lacking in leaders who understand the personal complexities of these public policy debates and resist having serious discussions about how these issues should be addressed.

PD: *Jails and prisons often end up being mental health facilities for alcoholics and drug abusers, which are equal opportunity gender issues, but in terms of prison populations, tend to affect more women than men. The proposed new health care reform legislation is going to decimate funds for mental health and addiction treatment. Describe the negative impact this will have on sentencing options for women, particularly first- time offenders?*

JPG: Mental health needs in our correctional institutions is a critical problem. Many poor women, who have suffered from sexual abuse, domestic violence and other traumas, numb themselves with drug and alcohol at an early age. When many of them commit criminal offenses, they desperately need drug and alcohol treatment.

Currently there are very few treatment centers that will take a woman along with her children. Most jails and prisons do not have substantial treatment options for women. The proposed new health care bill will only exacerbate the problem. If the women do not receive treatment, they will continue to get into legal trouble as well as negatively impact the lives of their children

PD: *The relationship between poverty and crime is proven beyond doubt. However, for the same criminal behavior, the poor, and poor women in particular, are much more likely to be arrested, charged, convicted, sent to prison, and to serve longer sentences than non-poor.[4] Can you comment on this inequality?*

JPG: Poor women suffer a great deal in the criminal justice system. In some states, they do not receive very good legal representation. But an even bigger problem is that a defendant, who has access to financial assistance, can come into a sentencing court and be in a treatment program, have had family members help them find a job, and be able to present a more promising future with a stronger likelihood that they will not reoffend.

Poor women rarely have succeeded at finding any of those options available to them so they come into court with their addictions and problems with no proposal on how they could address those issues in the community. They then present themselves as a big risk of reoffending if they are not incarcerated.

PD: *Similarly, as regards, for example, prostitution, which is always a two-person crime and a significant income source for poor women. Yet, women are far more likely to be arrested and charged than are the men involved. Is this because law enforcement remains mostly male, and they are willing to look the other way as when a soft crime such as prostitution involves a man? Aside from human trafficking, which we all agree is a heinous crime, should simple prostitution by a consenting adult female, be a criminal offense?*

JPG: I have no problem with prostitution being decriminalized as long as there are plenty of safeguards for the women built into the law. However, the great majority of the prostitution charges we see in the criminal justice system are against poor young women who have not freely chosen prostitution as a job but instead are often being trafficked (or managed) by a dominant, violent male. Most of these women have been abused and are turning what monies they make over to the men who traffic them. These women cannot see a realistic path out of their lives on the streets.

PD: Most women who enter the CJS do so first as a domestic or sexual abuse victim, and only later engaged with the system as an offender. Yet the CJS has been historically slow to prosecute domestic violence and sex abuse cases. Why is this?

JPG: This is a complicated problem. Many women have been sexually abused as children by family members or others who are close to their families. Those crimes are usually not reported until many years later, when it is much harder to successfully prosecute the offender. Historically many domestic violence cases were not prosecuted because there was a sense by many in positions of authority that this violence was an internal family problem and should be handled in that context. That approach has substantially changed over the last 20 years. There are specialized courts, trained police officers, domestic violence advocates and strong domestic violence networks to support survivors of familial violence. Even with all that support, close to 50 percent of women who have called the police decide, for a variety of reasons, not to proceed with a criminal charge.

Finding better ways to help support and protect these women and their children remains a critical challenge. Sexual assault generally can be a very difficult case for a prosecutor to bring. Jurors can be very harsh in judging the victim's credibility. It is incredibly traumatic for a victim to have taken a case to jury and have the jury return with a not guilty verdict.

PD: Can you speak to the issue of how difficult it is to successfully prosecute sexual assault crimes, which uniformly affect women more than men?

JPG: There are three categories of sexual assault cases we see in the courts: interfamily assaults, acquaintance assaults and stranger assaults. The interfamily cases (sometimes incest) are often reported months or even years later. The victim will frequently be vague on the details of the crime (date, hour, other facts) which can lead a jury to having reasonable doubt of a defendant's guilt. Additionally, other family members often will put pressure on the victim not to proceed (sometimes because of a belief that the victim is lying).

The acquaintance assaults are also very difficult for jurors because they often cannot understand a couple who know each other (and care for each other) getting to a place where one person is forcing himself on the partner and the partner is clearly not consenting. Many of those cases also involve the offender and the survivor having consumed alcohol or drugs which again makes the evidence for conviction tougher to show.

Finally, the stranger assault usually involves an issue of identification. The victim is often the only one who can identify the offender and without other corroboration (like DNA), juries will often acquit the defendant.

PD: Please comment on the rape kit backlog problem and whether it is, at its core, a low-priority issue the backlog of the DNA testing of rape kits is a very serious problem.

JPG: I have a difficult time understanding why crime labs and prosecutors have not made the testing of DNA samples a high priority. There are many reasons why these backlogs should be quickly cleared.

First of all, if the prosecutor can charge a specific offender because of a positive DNA match, the victims on those cases might not have to continue to live in fear that the rapist will return to attack them and could find some peace from a successful prosecution.

Second, sexual assault is such a serious offense with a high level of recidivism. If the responsible offenders are not prosecuted, they are likely assaulting new victims in our community.

PD: *In addition to prostitution, which crimes that uniquely affect women do you feel should be de-criminalized?*

JPG: Many of the crimes women commit are economic. During the time I was a trial judge from 1981 through 1998, I saw many women who were charged with welfare fraud. Those cases bothered me a great deal. Most of the cases involved women who were both collecting welfare while working part-time and not reporting the additional income. The women would often explain that their jobs were sporadic and not regularly scheduled. They often worked as aides in nursing homes. They would describe the problem of trying to report their income from a few days and then being cut off of welfare. It would often take a month or more to go back on the benefits even though they could easily go the month without being called in to work. So often the women were using this "extra" income to pay for school needs of their children.

I frequently thought how crazy this all was. We were turning the women who were trying to work their way off of welfare into felons. I do not know if there are as many of these charges since welfare reform but many of the crimes committed by women/mothers are economic. More effort ought to be made to encourage and assist them to make restitution to the victim and become full time employees somewhere.

PD: *We have a "groper-in-chief" president who has dramatically lowered the bar as concerns appropriate behavior toward women. Under these circumstances, what can the average woman domestic violence or sexual assault victim do to influence the justice system to act in her best interests?*

JPG: I would encourage women to seek out resources in their communities to assist them and support them while they go through the criminal justice system. There are many agencies and people who are very willing and capable of supporting survivors as they proceed through the criminal justice system.

Female survivors of crime also can have significant impact on legislatures. It is no longer politically okay to ignore a crime victim talk about how terribly she was treated by people in the criminal justice system.

PD: *The recent assault on free speech on college campuses are part of wider efforts to curtail the right to protest, which is so vital to women resisting the ever-present efforts to take away/manipulate their rights. It looks like Wisconsin is going to pass a law to this effect. Do you think violations will be successfully prosecuted or is this just legislative hot air?*

JPG: The challenge for people is that the assaults on free speech often becomes partisan and aimed at a particular part of our population. This needs to be a nonpartisan issue, allowing everyone, particularly on our campuses, to have their first amendment rights protected. I believe our governmental units are not currently working well so I worry that people's rights can easily be infringed upon with carelessly drafted legislation.

When legislatures enact unconstitutional statutes, people must turn to our appellate courts to protect those rights. Unfortunately, some of our judges are becoming politicalized rather than remaining impartial and without bias. It is critical that all of us stay vigilant on what our democratic institutions are doing and to work against corruption of our constitutional rights.

PD: Women respond well to talk therapy and opportunities to tell their stories as a means to "sort themselves out" and change their behaviors. Does this make them more likely to benefit from alternative sentencing opportunities and restorative justice efforts long-term?

JPG: Absolutely! Women generally respond very favorably to restorative justice approaches both in terms of sharing their own personal stories as well as empathizing with victims who describe the harm they have suffered. Women also tend to be more creative in finding ways that they can "help restore the harm" by either doing things for the victim and/or giving back to the community.

PD: Finally, Donald Trump has invited you to meet with him, and with Attorney General Jeff Sessions, in the Oval Office to discuss issues particular to women and the criminal justice system. What would you say to President Trump? To Attorney General Sessions?

JPG: If I had the opportunity to talk to the President I would bring a few mothers with me who could tell him their personal stories, which are typical of many women in poverty both from large cities as well as from farm country. They could share the trauma they have experienced, the hardships they have faced, their experiences in the criminal justice system and their hopes and dreams for their children. It is very difficult for anyone to hear a person describe her own personal journey and discount it. This would be much more effective than having me describe what women face.

I would have the Attorney General also sit in on this meeting but then I would have victims of crime also describe their satisfaction with restorative justice approaches (as opposed to the court system).

Finally, I would present the many studies that exist to show that restorative processes (over courtroom approaches) generally reduce recidivism, increase victim satisfaction and increase the amount of restitution that is paid by defendants. The Attorney General is taking a "tough on crime" approach. He needs to hear what it is that victims and the community really want to have happen after someone is convicted.

PD: Is there anything else you'd like to say about women's relationship with the CJS?

JPG: I am always struck by the statistics showing that about 75 percent of the children of parents who have been incarcerated will be jailed sometime during their lifetimes. We are spending way too much money on locking up women and thereby harming the community and their children. Instead we should be offering creative and rehabilitative services thereby benefiting the victim, the community and the offender and her children. Our current system is not only not working, but is creating future offenders of their children. It makes no sense.

NOTES

1. www.aclu.org.
2. Dáil, *ibid.*
3. Bright-line laws impose a clearly defined rule or standard, composed of objective factors, which leaves little or no room for varying interpretation. The purpose of a *bright-line* rule or law is to produce predictable and consistent results whenever it is applied.
4. Dáil, *ibid.*

I Am Not Resigned
and I Do Not Approve

Michelle Bowdler

> Our task, of course, is to transmute the anger that is affliction into the anger that is determination to bring about change. I think, in fact, that one could give that as a definition of revolution.—Barbara Deming

Every day since Election Day I wake up and wonder how it is that over 60 million people living in this country could have voted for a candidate who admits to sexually assaulting women as the next president of the United States. As a sexual assault survivor, I just can't understand how his victory was possible, and I struggle with what his ascendency says about the soul of our country. What does his triumph say to our young girls about their safety, self-regard and value? And what does it say to young boys about how criminal behavior toward women can be minimized, overlooked and ultimately rewarded?

On January 20, 2017, this man swore to uphold, protect and defend our Constitution and our country's laws as its leader. As a nation, we must reckon with the fact that Donald Trump, now the 45th president of the United States, while describing his own illegal behavior, has spoken some of the ugliest words many of us have ever heard spoken aloud. Both Trump and American voters know that sexual assault, at least in theory, is a punishable felony which, if successfully prosecuted, can include prison time, a permanent criminal record, and lifetime registration in the national sex offender data base. Why voters chose to ignore this simple fact of law is deeply disturbing.

For those of you who may have tried to block that searing quote from your memory, please forgive, but it needs to be stated and seen. I recommend reading it aloud to see what it feels like to hear these words come out of your own body. It is difficult to get through it:

> I moved on her, and I failed. I'll admit it … I did try and fuck her. She was married … I moved on her very heavily … I moved on her like a bitch. But I couldn't get there…. You know, I'm automatically attracted to beautiful—I just start kissing them. It's like a magnet. Just kiss. I don't even wait. And when you're a star, they let you do it. You can do anything…. Grab 'em by the pussy. You can do anything.[1]

It was not only what Trump said, which was horrific enough, but the manner in which he said it. He bragged, with no sense of contrition that he could do what he wanted, whenever he wanted, no matter the experience of the other. Trump asserted that he could behave aggressively and grope women without any need for permission because of his power and privilege: "When you are a star, they let you do it." What's more, he was darn sure they liked it!

A live microphone captured him speaking these words a little more than a decade ago while Trump was filming a TV segment for *Access Hollywood*. He never thought it would be released to the public; he was caught in a private moment, unrehearsed and unconcerned about how he might be viewed in a larger arena. He was just being himself, saying how he feels and what he believes. And as Maya Angelou once said, "When a person shows you who they are believe them, the first time."

Once his words became public during the campaign, Trump issued several weak excuses. It was "locker room talk" he said. This explanation was denounced by several professional athletes, who said they knew of no locker room where sexual assault was commonly bragged about, and that they would not be silent if it were.

Trump explained the tape was a decade old, meaning he should not be held accountable because time had passed—as though time is a giant eraser for words and deeds. His long track record of saying demeaning and degrading comments about women seemed of little concern to him. He wanted us to believe that there was no connection to the way he spoke about women for years that would make us think he was someone who also, by his own admission, "grabbed them by the pussy" if he felt like it.

Trump has called women fat pigs, rated them on a 1–10 "hotness" scale on the Howard Stern Show, and said he would improve the Miss Universe Pageant by making the bathing suits smaller and the heels higher.[2] I could go on. There are literally 50 million hits when one types into a search bar: *Donald Trump and the worst things he's said about women*. Welcome to the world under our new Groper-in-Chief.

Trump polls initially declined following the tape's release, so he continued to issue excuses. He took to attacking his opponent, Hillary Clinton, with a common sexist notion—that a woman's *response* to a wrong done to her by a man is somehow always worse than anything a man could ever do. He denied responsibility for his own actions and implied that when a man makes unwanted overtures toward women, it's somehow *their* fault for encouraging him. He excused his terrible comment about grabbing women by their genitals by pointing out that Hillary Clinton stayed with her husband after he had an affair, labeling her an "enabler," and, therefore, supremely flawed. Huh? The moral equivalency between one candidate admitting sexual assault and another working through a crisis in her marriage escapes me.

Trump's response was classic of abusers—justifying their own behavior by describing someone else's, hoping you just might think it's worse. It's called changing the subject and it is one of the oldest tricks in the book. America shouldn't have fallen for it.

Somehow, Trump managed to eke out a victory, winning by a narrow margin in states that gave him an Electoral College win. Nevertheless, he lost the popular vote by over three million votes. He defeated the only woman to ever be nominated to represent a major party as a presidential candidate. Remarkably, this "grab them by the pussy" remark, and dozens of other remarks, over a period of years, demeaning women and defending men accused of sexual harassment were not sufficiently outrageous or unacceptable to disqualify him as a candidate.

We really must ask ourselves why he did not go down in flames after his comments became public. I find myself wondering if perhaps it is because Donald Trump knows something the rest of us are reticent to admit—rape and sexual assault really do not seem all that important to our country.

Rape is the least reported, and least successfully prosecuted, felony. Only 3 percent of rapists ever spend a day in jail.[3] Almost daily, there are news stories about rape and sexual assault that illustrate the problem—perpetrators given light sentences, a rapist having his character praised by the judge passing sentence, politicians having trouble passing legislative reforms for issues important to the safety of women soldiers, like sexual assault in the military.

Sexual assault and sexual harassment are minimized and excused all too easily, and victims are commonly disbelieved. Trump bragged about sexually assaulting women and then several women said that they were, in fact, grabbed by this self-acknowledged groper. Still, all he had to do was call them liars and threaten to sue them, and it worked.

Where does this leave rape survivors who already live daily with both the pain and trauma of their assault as well as society's minimization? And where does it leave any citizen who cares about social justice and basic decency, whether a rape survivor or not? The standards for president have never been lower, and as a sexual assault survivor, my heart is broken. What's more, the fact of Trump's abuse of women seems to have been put to the side as the nation's collective psyche has now been diverted away from this issue and toward worries over nuclear war, the destruction of our planet, or the very real possibility of millions of people losing their health insurance.

But what Trump said must not be put aside; it must not be forgotten.

So much about this election surprised me, but this specific aspect of Trump's victory has stung me in a way that is both deep and familiar. My experience as rape survivor has given me a lens with which to view policy and social justice concerns that has informed my thinking over the years. It is the thousand hurts inflicted by failed prosecutions, and failed public policy that, over time, can leave rape survivors feeling like what happened to them really matters to no one.

I was raped three decades ago. It was a brutal attack by two men during a home invasion. I did not expect to survive. But I did and eventually picked up the pieces of my life, and thought I had moved past it all. Eventually I learned that trauma doesn't work this way. You don't just move on with the passage of time and leave your trauma behind because it changes you forever. You wind up with it sitting next to you for the rest of your life, sometimes companionably, helping to remind you not fight for justice for others, and sometimes, not so companionably, leaving you feeling more scared and scarred than you ever thought possible.

Almost a decade ago, I read that my home state of Massachusetts had almost 16,000 DNA samples sitting untested in our state Crime Lab, going as far back as the mid–80s.[4] I began to wonder if my rape kit had been gathering dust for decades, untested and uninvestigated. Was that why I never heard from anyone about my case? As I tip-toed into the possibility of trying to go back and find out more about my own unsolved case, I began reading estimates that there were perhaps as many as 400,000 untested rape kits sitting neglected in warehouses and police departments around the country. When these kits began to be tested, some cold cases were solved; serial rapists identified, and women who waited years for information and peace of mind finally had a modicum of closure.

There is no other equivalent major felony where evidence as compelling as DNA sits is collectively ignored. If rape victims are generally considered not credible, evidence is untested, and cases that are brought to court rarely result in conviction, one has to wonder if rape and sexual assault are really considered to be crimes in our nation. Not only did this not disqualify a presidential candidate, he actually won the election!

Until the 2016 election, the only time in my entire life I ever heard the word "pussy" actually spoken aloud in my presence was during my own rape. I was not human to my assailants. I was an object to be entered. They wanted "some pussy." As I endured a violent assault that lasted for hours, it was the utterance of that very word that made me feel like my life was in jeopardy. I was not a human being who longed for a future, who was loved and precious to my friends and family. I was a pussy, an object, nothing more. When I heard that same word come out of the mouth of a man who wanted to lead our nation, I was beside myself—scared, saddened and horrified.

There has been no shortage of stupid comments about rape during election cycles. In 2012, Todd Akin, a senate candidate from Missouri said, while trying to defend his anti-abortion stance, that a women couldn't get pregnant from rape because if it's a "real rape" the body has a way of shutting that whole thing down. He lost his election. Senate candidate Richard Mourdock, from Indiana, said that a pregnancy that resulted from rape was a gift from God. He lost too. Four years later, though, the U.S. electorate did not reject a man who showed similar disregard for women, describing them as objects for him to grab at will, at his pleasure, with complete disregard for her feelings or rights.

The first major march of the resistance after Trump's election showed hundreds of thousands of women marching in pink knitted "pussy" hats and that word has been spoken more in the last few months than any other time I can recall. I can't say I am enjoying it much. I understand it's a way of trying to take back power, to name the absurdity of Trump's election, but I don't wish to be lighthearted about his appalling words. To me, that word will always be a word that signifies objectification, erasure, and a threat to my existence.

I am watching and waiting to see what Trump will do about sexual assault in the military, Title IX protections on college campuses, and support for the Violence Against Women Act. Will a man with his history of bad behavior toward women use his bully pulpit to ask police officers to investigate rape? Will he do as Joe Biden did and go to campuses around the nation talking about consent? Will he say that a woman whose pregnancy is a result of rape has the right to terminate that pregnancy?

People's beliefs inform their actions and their actions reflect their beliefs. The man now running our country is an acknowledged sexual predator. I am dismayed and terrified. I will not forget his words and I suggest you ignore them at your own peril.

The last line of my favorite Edna St. Vincent Millay poem, "Dirge without Music," is most apt here. Now, in this moment in history, as someone who understands all too well that objectification of women is dehumanizing and dangerous: "I am not resigned and I do not approve."

Notes

1. Transcript, Donald Trump's Taped Comments about Women. www.newyorktimes.com, Oct 8, 2016.
2. "Donald Trump Said a lot of Gross Things About Women on the Howard Stern Show," www.buzzfeed.com, February 24, 2016.
3. Rape Abuse & Incest National Network Statistics.
4. Estes, "Crime Lab Neglected 16,000 Cases," *Boston Globe,* July 15, 2007.

When Culture and Gender Violence Clash with the Law

Mariya Taher

From a young age, we are taught lessons about the moralities of life. Right versus wrong. Good versus bad. White versus Black. Only after we reach adulthood, do we also learn that moralities can be ambiguous. That a practice, tradition, or custom thought for centuries to be correct, could in fact be incorrect. This is how the story of female genital mutilation or cutting (FGM/C) unfolds.

FGM/C is a practice that involves the ritual removal of some or all the external female genitalia, and is a practice that is now known to occur in the United States.[1] In April 2017 the first of its kind federal prosecution of a FGM/C case occurred in Michigan, when federal authorities charged six people: including two doctors, a physician's wife, two mothers and a sixth woman for participating in various degrees of subjecting young girls to the practice of Female Genital Cutting. Additionally, in 2016, the Centers for Disease Control and Prevention estimated that more than 500,000 women in the U.S. are at risk for FGM/C.[2]

To an outsider, on first appearance, the words female genital cutting (FGC—as I prefer to call it) can make a person cringe. The words appear vile. Inhumane. Not a combination of words that should ever be strung together to indicate something that happens to girls from around the globe. 200 million girls, if we go by UNICEF's official statistics.[3]

For me, female genital cutting is tradition, and one that I was raised with. One that I celebrated. One that I underwent myself at 7 years old when I visited relatives in India. You see, I was born into the same religious minority sect as the people charged in the April 2017 federal prosecution. At the time it occurred to me, though, the United States had no laws banning it. That law didn't come into effect until 1996. It was not until 2013 that a law explicitly stating that girls could not be taken out of the country to have FGC performed on them was passed. When it happened to me, it was perfectly legal. It would not be until high school, around the time when the U.S. would pass 18 U.S. Code § 116, the act banning FGC, that I began to question FGC and contemplated the moralities attached to this inhumane practice.

On one hand, my mother ensured I underwent FGC because her mother ensured she undergo it because, well, we all loved each other, and it was what was done to ensure that each generation of girls in my family grew up to be the best possible version of themselves. This could only happen if we each underwent FGC when we turned seven years old. On the other hand, FGC is performed to control a woman's sexuality. It is steeped in the idea that FGC makes a woman pure, which implies that women are born full of sin and that an action must be taken to rid them of their sinful behaviors. Never mind the human rights implications associated with carrying it out.

In time, I came to understand that FGC is a form of violence that is a social norm for the community, one that had been justified over the centuries through religion, culture, and tradition. This makes it an altogether controversial form of violence that is difficult to end. Only when the traditional, cultural, and religious reasons were stripped away did it become easier to see that what remained was a form of patriarchal oppression silently handed down by generations of women to maintain control of our gender. Female genital cutting is a silent oppression taught to us by our ancestors. It is a morality that should be put into the "wrong" category, but had somehow been misconstrued to fit into the "right" category.

Various human rights doctrines implied it was wrong to carry out FGC. The Convention of Elimination of All Forms of Discrimination Against Women, the Convention on the Rights of the Child, the International Covenant on Economic, Social and Cultural Rights, and the mother load of all human rights doctrines, the Universal Declaration of Human Rights, are just a few of the pieces of paper that stated FGC should not have happened to me, to the little girls in Michigan, or to any little girl, anywhere in the world.

The practice had to be undone. Depending on the country one lived in, laws began to back up the human rights conventions. Calling it child abuse. Calling it inhumane or barbaric.

In the decades since the passage of these human rights conventions and these laws, we have learned that it is not enough to stop the practice. Activists like me, who have years of experience engaging with communities in which it occurs, understand this simple truth.

So, we have given up our rights to privacy, and shared our stories of undergoing FGC publicly in an effort to turn the tides on the continuation of FGC. We do so in the hope that if we start the discussion, our communities will engage with us and our social ills will come to the surface. It is through this means that we know we can persuade our communities to end FGC. Our awareness and advocacy campaigns are designed to break the silence associated with this form of violence. We provide forums for discussion and dialogue that help reframe and reshape the way communities view FGC. We look to take away the notion that FGC is a needed social norm, and to instead show that FGC is a violation of our inherent human rights as women and as children.

For my part, to speak on this topic, to share my own story of undergoing FGC, has meant that I have had to learn how to become comfortable with speaking about something so private in a public way, with the knowledge that when I did it, I would thereafter be labeled a victim—a term I do not associate with myself. Through first-hand experience working in anti-domestic violence nonprofits, I have learned that the term "victim" can be incredibly debilitating. No one wants to be thrust into the role of a victim. We want control over our lives. The label "victim" highlights to others that our control was taken from us.

There are other matters I, and others, have contemplated before making a decision to publicly speak on this issue. What would happen to my parents, whom I love dearly, if I choose to speak publicly about what happened to me? The law had given us the legs to stand on to undo such an atrocity, and technically, at the time my FGC occurred, there was no law in place at the federal or state level to ban it, but still, I did not want the hand of law to impose itself on my parents whose only fault was having faith in their religion. Even if no legal action occurred against those I loved, how would they be viewed by friends who were from outside their religious community? I could never think of parents as child abusers. Nor would I ever want others to view them in that way.

I also wondered how would they be viewed by those within their religious community? Would their fellow community members become upset with them for the actions of their daughter who shed light on a practice that, for their religion, was deemed essential, but by doing so had cast the community in a negative light? Would my family be ostracized or shamed internally by their community members?

The law could not protect my family from excommunication from their community and, as immigrants who transplanted to the United States in the 1970s, their ethnic and religious community made them feel at home. They felt a little less like they were foreigners who came from thousands of miles away. They needed to belong. Continuing traditions, even harmful ones, ensured that they did. These fears and concerns are the same ones every person affected by FGC must contemplate before making their own decision on how public they will become with what has happened to them. For my part, it took me seven years to become as comfortable as I am today in speaking on this matter.

Equally, it took seven years to have my family confidently support me in publicly discussing this topic. In fact, decades after many activists started this work, today, I now hear from dozens of men and women who are in support of ending it. But when I made that fateful decision, to speak publicly myself, I was terrified at the thought of losing my family, losing my privacy, losing my ability to define myself as someone who was not a victim as labeled by outsiders.

I had no idea that there were other matters, other oppressions, other moralities I should have contemplated as well. Other moralities I am sure the families of those affected by the recent arrests in Michigan contemplated before making the fateful decision to have their daughters undergo FGC. Moralities, that I am sure still more families contemplate as they decide whether or not to come forward with their own story of undergoing FGC or the story of their loved ones undergoing FGC. But before we speak of their moralities, let me speak of my own.

On June 22, 2016, ABC news released a short segment called "Underground: American Woman Who Underwent Female Genital Mutilation Comes Forward to Help Others,"[4] highlighting my story and the work I do to advocate for the end of female genital cutting. Overnight, my personal life became public. Dozens of additional media sources picked up the news story and spread it further, ensuring that the story reached all sectors and all corners of the globe. I should have been proud. My voice, my tale, was being heard.

Instead, the next day, as I Googled my story, waves of anxiety passed through my system. Conservative news sources had appropriated my story and twisted it to serve their own agendas; they attacked Islam; they attacked immigrants. One tag line I came across in an article read, "The gruesome practice of female genital mutilation is at record highs in America due to the influx of Muslim immigrants." These conservative news sources ignored the part in my story where I stated I was a U.S. born citizen, and somehow, even though I never once referred to the religion I was raised in, they assumed it was Islam, when, in fact, Christianity practices FGM too.[5] I was a survivor of violence. I was speaking up about what happened to me in hopes of preventing others from having to undergo it, but after reading that tag line, I wished I had never spoken up.

By sharing my story, I had contributed to the spread of false truths or, as we call it in this political climate, "alternative facts" being shared globally about Muslim groups and immigrant groups. More fuel was added to the fire to justify actions that would prevent Muslim immigrants from being let into the United States. Had I inadvertently contributed to justifications that would be helpful in upholding Trump's rhetoric that Muslim were dangerous? That these people should not be let into the United States? I learned that by speaking up about one form of oppression—a form of gender violence, I had unintentionally spread misconceptions about groups of people that had increased xenophobic and Islamophobic attitudes and behaviors.

The same is happening now, today, with the news that as many as 100 girls may have had their genitals cut during a twelve-year conspiracy involving the health professionals charged for performing FGC in Michigan. The media has jumped on this controversial and unfolding drama, and has come to highlight FGC in the news in the U.S., as never has happened before, but with this increased attention, one image falsely dominates the airwaves: FGC has only ever happened to immigrant, Muslim girls or FGC only occurs to "others" or to people of color. As before, during my ABC News interview, I feel devastated.

This falsehood has led to unintended consequences in which immigrant and refugee populations are misleadingly targeted for the practice. The image does not pay heed to the fact that, until the 1950's, FGC was performed by doctors in the United States and Europe on white women to treat conditions such as "hysteria" or "lesbianism."[6] Nor does this image demonstrate that today, labia plasticity (essentially a form of FGC since any alteration of female genitalia not done for health or therapeutic reasons is defined by the World Health Organization as FGC)[7] is one of the fastest growing cosmetic surgeries, with ads for the procedure targeted at teens. In fact, just recently the American College of Obstetricians and Gynecologists updated its guidelines on labial surgery in adolescents to include the fact that performing unnecessary labial alterations in girls' younger than 18 violates U.S. federal law.[8] Yet this lack of awareness, this belief that FGC occurs to "others" demonstrates that there is a racial element connected to the continuation of FGC as well.

Though it felt unfair and morally unjust, my personal experience and the Michigan experiences has taught me that to address one form of violence, it is necessary to learn how to address multiple oppressions simultaneously. This is very difficult in today's political climate.

For those of us who choose to advocate against practices deemed "culturally acceptable" for so long, but which, in the purview of human rights, is never to be performed, we have had to learn how to navigate a dichotomy between coming forward to elevate a really serious issue—a human rights violation—when the consequences of doing so in a right-wing political climate can lead directly to xenophobia and islamophobia.

Today, I am more cautious about how I share my story. I do not want to ignore that FGC is promoted by some as a religious requirement, yet, I equally do not want to contribute to the defense's argument that FGC is a religious requirement that must be protected by the First Amendment, as is being argued in the Michigan case. And so, I make certain to mention that female genital cutting happens to people of all different ethnic, racial, and religious backgrounds, even to U.S. born, white women (in Dec 2016, the

Guardian published a story about Renee Bergstrom, a white, midwestern, woman who underwent FGC because her Christian denomination practiced it).[9] And I emphasize that regardless of who it happens to, FGC still violates the right to health; rights of the child; rights to sexual and physical integrity; rights to be free from discrimination; and rights to be free from torture; and cruel, inhuman and degrading treatment.[10]

On paper, the law is clear: cutting any part of a young girl's genitalia is illegal and no custom or ritual can be used to justify it. In simplest terms, FGC is child abuse and gender violence (though we may love the ones who were instrumental in our FGC being carried out). It shouldn't matter what background a person comes from, a violation is a violation, and FGC should never occur in the United States or to U.S. residents. Yet, still, people seem afraid to touch the issue and I must admit that the defense's argument of religious freedom is not that far-fetched when I take into consideration some of the challenges in my advocacy work in the last few years. The dominant image that FGC occurs to "other" communities and that perhaps we in the U.S. do not understand the custom or ritual endures and seeps through in the most unexpected of places.

Currently, in Massachusetts, where I live, there is pending state legislation to protect girls from this harmful practice. Yet, advocates pushing for the legislation have had a challenging time passing it because of the belief that female genital cutting does not occur to U.S. women in this state. Liberal legislators whisper caution when it comes to enacting laws condemning the practice, themselves fearful that a law would only target the "others," the people of color, the Muslims who take part in this practice (though they might not say it in those exact words). There is even reluctance on the media's part to publish news articles on FGC at the state level because they claim there is a lack of evidence that girls are cut in this state.

Of course, it is challenging to have girls come forward to admit they underwent FGC! It doesn't matter what background you come from. It's a topic that no one wants to be named a "victim" of. Nor does anyone want to have their parents labeled as child abusers. When we look at other forms of gender violence, for instance domestic violence, we can acknowledge that no one in that type of situation would immediately be comfortable coming out and stating they were a victim of physical or mental abuse by their significant partner or parent, so why would it be any less challenging for a girl who had undergone FGC to come out and say that a loved one, perhaps her mother, took her to have it done. Very few do speak on the topic as openly as I do, and I only did so after years of weighing my moralities and struggling to make the decision.

The legislators' and media's responses in Massachusetts frustrate me. It makes me wonder why women like me, who are U.S. born but who were cut elsewhere are not evidence enough that FGC is an issue affecting this state's residents that needs to be addressed. I wonder why the Centers for Disease Control and Prevention coming out with a study in 2016 indicating that half a million women and girls were at risk of it in the United States or that Massachusetts ranking 12th in terms of states with the highest risk populations, isn't enough evidence to suggest FGC is a problem here.[11]

Gender violence is not an easy topic to discuss, particularly when the form of violence being discussed is still addressed as an "other" world issue. Yet, through all these experiences, I have learned that to best speak on the topic of female genital cutting, I must find a way to balance a desire to protect my community, my parents, my friends, with a desire to be real about the health, violence, and safety concerns that the practice of FGC carries for girls who undergo it. I must learn how to balance the elements, scale my moralities, and determine what weighs more right than wrong when deciding if I should speak out about this issue and determining in what manner to speak out about the issue.

When I shared my story, all I wanted to do was be a voice for women and girls who for many valid reasons could not be a voice in speaking up against this form of gender violence. I didn't know that speaking up to stop one form of suffering could cause suffering in other ways, that it could further stigmatize immigrants and increase xenophobia.

It is unfortunate that the same forms of suffering are also occurring in response to the aftermath of the FGC case occurring in Michigan. It is unfortunate that as this investigation in Michigan continues, I am now hearing stories of families from the affected community being pulled apart, loving parents, ones like my own, being called child abusers and worse. Yet, we want FGC to end.

This is the complication and the irony of the work that I do today just so that future girls won't have to undergo the cut. The practice is illegal and reflects a morality that should always be put in the "wrong" category. But because of our current political climate, I often wonder if speaking up causes more harm than good. What will it really take, I wonder, to keep girls safe from this practice? How can one speak up and still keep others safe from the backlash that occurs at the highest levels of our government, where immigrants are already being vilified and are facing legal jeopardy?

NOTES

1. A. Renee Bergstrom, "FGM happened to me in white, Midwest America," *Guardian*, Dec. 3, 2016, https://www.theguardian.com/us-news/2016/dec/02/fgm-happened-to-me-in-white-midwest-america.

2. Howard Goldberg, Ph.D., Paul Stupp, Ph.D., Ekwutosi Okoroh, MD, Ghenet Besera, MPH, David Goodman, Ph.D., Isabella Danel, MD. "Female Genital Mutilation/Cutting in the United States: Updated Estimates of Women and Girls at Risk, 2012," Center for Disease Control and Prevention, National Center for Chronic Disease Prevention and Health Promotion, Division of Reproductive Health, Atlanta, GA, Jan. 14, 2016, https://www.uscis.gov/sites/default/files/USCIS/Humanitarian/Special%20Situations/fgmutilation.pdf.

3. Radina Gigova. "200 Million Women and Girls Live with Female Genital Mutilation, says U.N.," CNN, Feb. 6, 2016, http://www.cnn.com/2016/02/06/health/200-million-with-fgm/.

4. Olivia Smith. "Underground: Risk of FGM Increasing for Women in the U.S., says CDC," ABC News, Jun. 22, 2016, http://abcnews.go.com/U.S./underground-american-woman-underwent-female-genital-mutilation-forward/story?id=39728421.

5. Bergstrom, *Ibid.*

6. Helen King, "The Rise and Fall of FGM in Victorian London," *Conversation* (Cambridge, MA), March 12, 2015, http://theconversation.com/the-rise-and-fall-of-fgm-in-victorian-london-38327.

7. Roni Caryn Rabin, "More Teenage Girls Seeking Genital Cosmetic Surgery," *The New York Times*, Apr. 25, 2016.

8. "Breast and Labial Surgery in Adolescents," American College of Obstetricians and Gynecologists. Obstet Gynecol, January. 2017, http://www.acog.org/Resources-And-Publications/Committee-Opinions/Committee-on-Adolescent-Health-Care/Breast-and-Labial-Surgery-in-Adolescents.

9. Bergstrom, *Ibid.*

10. K.G. Fisaha, "Female Genital Mutilation: A Violation of Human Rights," *Journal of Political Science and Public Affairs*, 4:198, 2016.

11. Goldberg et.al., *Ibid.*

Section 11. Saving Public Education One Teacher and One School at a Time

Paula vW. Dáil

> The new movement for privatization has enabled school choice to transcend its tarnished history as an escape route for southern whites who sought to avoid court-ordered segregation in the 1950's and 60's.—Diane Ravitch

It was not coincidental that, at the same time they were conceiving the participatory democracy that frames the U.S. Constitution, the founders recognized the need for a system of public education to uphold it. "Education was deemed a public responsibility of the federal government, a bulwark of freedom and security," explains University of Vermont Emeritus Professor S. Alexander Rippa.[1] "President Washington, in his Farewell Address published in 1796, urged the advancement of education for the national welfare. Of all these eighteenth-century statesman, no one, perhaps, displayed more interest in the subject and certainly no one had more confidence in education as an instrument for the preservation of freedom than Thomas Jefferson."

With this auspicious history, the majority of Americans believe publicly funded education is the fundamental backbone of the nation. With this in mind, it is fair to ask: why is public education so controversial? Why is education so politicized? Is the battle about funding education that erupts year after year in the 13,506 school districts and 178 state-dependent school systems in the country really just about money?

There are no easy or obvious answers to these questions, and the critical insights needed to understand them are embedded in the realization that, above everything else, education offers the most direct path to personal power. This places education front and center in the quest to fulfill the American dream. Simply speaking, individuals who become educated have a greater breadth of knowledge and are able to earn more money than those with lesser educations, and the more money an individual has, the more powerful that person is. Additionally, increasing educational opportunities produces a better-trained workforce, which increases a nation's gross national product, leading to greater national wealth. As a result, education is the primary engine driving economic development.

Conversely, the surest way to keep a population oppressed and unable to compete for the social and financial resources that guarantee personal freedom and independence is to suppress their educational opportunities. Never has this been truer than in the cultural history of the Old South.

Despite the preponderance of "plain folk," economic power and political leadership were still vested in approximately four thousand families holding the most tillable land. The fact that a large middle class was so completely obscured by the wealthy and politically dominant planters was "the great tragedy of the ante-bellum South," Rippa says when explaining America's educational history. "By 1850 about a thousand southern families at the top of the social structure received an income of over $50 million annually, which was almost as much as the combined income of all the other families in the Old South. It was this relatively small upper-class who held the reins of political power and represented the South in federal councils for the next several generations."[2]

Bearing this history in mind, perhaps the greatest and still ongoing challenge public education in America has ever faced is racially motivated school segregation. "The most important decision the U.S. Supreme Court ever handed down was *Brown vs. The Board of Education*," claimed Iowa State University Constitutional Law Professor Alston Shakeshaft.

The 1954 *Brown vs. Board of Education of Topeka, Kansas* case led to a landmark decision in which the Court declared state laws establishing separate public schools for black and white students to be unconstitutional because, justices declared, separate education could not be guaranteed to be equal education. This decision forced public schools to racially integrate, allowing African American students to attend predominantly white schools, thereby enabling an historically enslaved race to begin the long journey toward independence from white rule. Equally important, the decision also opened a national conversation on school choice that remains ongoing.

The other area in which education is all-powerful is in framing social values through curriculum choices. This is most recently evident in the backlash response to the 1960s peace and love social protests, when conservatives began running for positions on local school boards where they had decision-making power over textbook choices and curriculum content. This increased the impact of the evangelical right's conservative social influences on, for example, health education where students learn about evolutionary human development and reproductive and sexual health. The conservative view is that imparting this information is a parental responsibility and does not belong in a school curriculum at all. One result has been that students from families who believe in creationism will not be taught about evolution, which is the scientifically accepted theory of human development.

While curriculum decisions are the purview of local school boards, establishing academic standards are state-level decisions and are not handed down by the federal government. The new federal education law, signed into law in 2016, is very explicit in prohibiting the education secretary from forcing states to adopt certain academic standards. Some states favor a statewide core curriculum, and a national-level recommendation on this exists, but it remains controversial.

School boards are also policy makers. Decisions about, for example, whether students can use the bathroom of their gender preference, or must use the bathroom assigned to their gender at birth, for example, are made in the board rooms of governing school district boards comprised citizens elected to the position by their surrounding communities. However, as elected public officials, school board members must comply with certain laws regarding how they make their decisions, and are required to hold meetings open to the public.

The realities surrounding today's K–12 public education system are that, although all public schools are supposed to be equal, they are not. The quality of facilities, teachers, textbooks, extra-curricular offerings, educational enhancement opportunities, equipment, special and remedial education, and administrative abilities all impact educational quality, and vary dramatically, based primarily upon available funding.

There is no single formula that governs school funding, but all schools receive some revenue from the federal government, usually about nine percent of their total budget. Individual states and local school districts make up the remainder, which varies by state. Most of the federal dollars flow through programs such as Title I (No Child Left Behind), which provides money to high poverty rate schools. The Individuals with Disabilities Education Act (IDEA) assists states and local schools in educating children with disabilities. Other federal programs include, for example, Head-Start Pre-K programs, basic skills enhancement and improving teacher quality. However, much of a school's budget is a result of the state and community in which the school resides:

> States and local communities provide the majority of K–12 education revenue. Each state determines how much if its schools' budget it will contribute. A handful of states provide at least 50 percent of their schools' total budget.... Hawaii and Vermont each supply close to 90 percent of their schools' revenue. More than half of the 50 states provide less than 50 percent of their schools' budgets, with Illinois, South Dakota, and Texas providing the least amount, at around 32 percent.[3]

Federal funding also comes to schools through the U.S. Department of Agriculture, which administers the National School Lunch Program that provides low-cost or free lunches to more than thirty million children each school day.[4] This school-based child nutrition program also includes reimbursement for snacks served to children in after-school educational and enrichment programs.

Most state support for schools is generated through property taxes, although other tax dollars from, for example, lottery sales, sales tax, vehicle taxes, etc., can also be earmarked for education. Other revenue sources include state and federal grants, private foundation grants, local fundraising, and special referenda, when voters in a school district agree to a time-limited additional school tax, usually to pay for infrastructure improvements, including equipment. Some states prohibit school districts from going to referendum to obtain additional operating dollars, and/or limit how often a district can go to referendum for additional money. While all public education is supported through taxes, in states where school funding heavily depends upon property tax revenue, school quality rises and falls based directly upon geography, and wealthier communities have better schools.

Post-secondary education funding works differently. Two-year technical and community colleges and state universities receive state funding as well as federal dollars, which come with strings attached in terms of admission and faculty hiring standards. Private universities that accept federal dollars are held to the same criteria, whereas those that don't accept federal money have much more flexibility in terms of students they admit and teachers they hire.

Federal dollars in the form of student loans and grants are available to students in both two and four-year post-secondary colleges. Another important source of federal revenue for universities is through federally funded research grants, which will pay both the direct and indirect costs associated with the research project. The federal government assigns an indirect cost rate to individual universities that conduct government research, based upon several criteria. Large research universities may have an indirect rate that exceeds 100 percent, whereas smaller ones may have a rate of less than 50 percent. For example, when a research grant having a direct cost budget of $150,000 is awarded by the federal government to a university with a 90 percent indirect cost rate, the actual amount of money that university receives is $235,000. Indirect cost reimbursements and student loans and grants are both areas where federal policy can directly and significantly impact education.

As president, Donald Trump is all over the map in terms of federal spending for education. Just weeks after proposing a $9 billion cut in federal education program dollars, he said he plans to "spend a lot of money" on education in order to increase the graduation rates in skill areas needed to fill current employment gaps. "We're going to spend a lot of money ... and we're going to get some great talent having to do with education because there is nothing more important than education," he said in a speech to business CEOs.[5]

He went on to decry the Common Core State Standards, extol the benefits of charter schools, and promised to return the decision-making power regarding education policy over to state and local school leaders. "I like the fact we're getting rid of Common Core," Trump said.[6] "We have to end it. We have to bring education local…. We can't be managing education from Washington."

"Charter schools are another thing people are talking about a lot," Trump said. "The charter schools of New York have been amazing. They're doing incredibly well. People can't even get in. I don't call it an experiment anymore. It's far beyond an experiment." Notably, his frame of reference for discussing charter schools is the New York City public school system, which is notoriously underfunded, lacks minimally adequate infrastructure, and struggles with both student and teacher retention. Trump has had no personal experience with this, or any, public school system.

Charter schools are unique, and controversial public schools that are publicly funded, often privately operated, and are not necessarily held to the same achievement standards as traditional public schools. Generally speaking, they tend to gain a foothold in large cities with high rates of urban poverty. Because they are public schools, they are open to all children, are taxpayer supported and do not charge tuition or have special entrance requirements. However, because they are frequently independently operated, using taxpayer dollars, charter schools are controversial.

"The transfer of public funds to private management and the creation of thousands of deregulated, unsupervised, and unaccountable schools have opened the public coffers to profiteering, fraud, and exploitation by large and small entrepreneurs," Says former assistant Secretary of Education Diane Ravitch.[7] "The public is only dimly aware of the reform movement's privatization agenda. The deceptive rhetoric of the privatization movement masks its underlying goal to replace public education with a system in which public funds are withdrawn from public oversight to subsidize privately managed charter schools, voucher schools, online academies, for-profit schools, and other private venders."

Trump has proposed an additional $168 million for charter schools in his fiscal 2018 budget request—part of a $1.4 billion increase for a large umbrella of school choice proposals. This is in keeping with the philosophy of Trump's appointee as Secretary of Education, Betsy DeVos, a billionaire school choice advocate who has spent significant political capital promoting private school vouchers and tax credit scholarship programs. This is her only qualification for the position Trump appointed her to.

DeVos' tenure as Secretary of Education got off to a rocky start and she has not been well received by either parents or teachers. She came to the position after having spent two decades promoting for-profit charter schools in Michigan and, for her, the evidence of accountability for these publicly funded schools is whether they remain open. "I think the first line of accountability is frankly with the parents," she said in her gaffe-filled Senate confirmation hearings. In order to secure the position for her, Vice President Pence had to cast the tie-breaking senate vote.

Meanwhile, DeVos continues to encounter protesters at most of her public appearances. As a result, her security detail has had to be increased, costing taxpayers nearly 8 million dollars during the first 5 months of her tenure.

Another aspect of school choice DeVos supports is the school voucher program, which assists families with tuition costs incurred in sending their children to private, frequently religious-based, schools. Since taxpayer dollars are being used to educate children about particular religious values, critics claim the practice violates the separation of church and state provision of the U.S. Constitution. Voucher school programs are also criticized for their lack of transparency and research on their effectiveness has had very mixed results, with most well-designed, carefully-executed studies indicating no improvement in student performance.[8]

Critics see DeVos as hostile to public education and indifferent to civil rights. They feel she is heavily biased toward school choice and should not have signed off on repealing some protections for LGBTQIA students. Six months into her tenure, no definitive school choice plan has been forthcoming, although a federal tax-credit voucher program has been part of the tax overhaul discussions. "She [DeVos] has made things much harder for herself by acting as the secretary for school choice instead of the Secretary of Education," says Mike Petrilli, president of the Thomas B. Fordham Institute.[9] "She has missed the opportunity to make it clear that she wants to see all schools succeed."

As details of the DeVos-Trump education budget continue to emerge, the proposed 9 billion dollar (13 percent) educational funding cut threatens to dismantle public schools through massive cuts to teacher training, after-school programs in public schools, and transfers of public funds to private school vouchers. The budget also calls for investing 1.4 billion dollars in new money into school choice, including private school vouchers.

"Every budget is a statement of values and this one could not be more clear in the vision it presents: starve the public school system and privatize education," writes Stephanie Johnson, Neil Campbell, Kami Spicklemire, and Lisette Partelow of the Center for American Progress.[10] "Dismantling our nation's public education system while investing in unproven schemes to incentivize private school vouchers that have no evidence of improving student achievement could have devastating consequences for students that could take decades to fix."

There is also the issue of teachers' unions. The National Education Association (NEA) is America's largest labor union and strongly opposed DeVos' appointment. Arguing that she is an ideological extremist with a record of undermining the public schools her department would oversee, the NEA mounted an aggressive, albeit unsuccessful campaign against her confirmation.

Meanwhile, teachers unions across the country have been facing difficulties at the state level. In 2011, in one of his first acts as governor of Wisconsin, Republican Scott Walker and his Republican legislature passed Act 10, which dramatically curtailed collective bargaining for most public employees, including teachers' unions. Public-sector unions now have to win support from a majority of employees in the bargaining unit, not just a majority of those voting in the certification election every year. That status allows them to negotiate only a sliver of what they could before and pay raises are capped by inflation. Walker faced massive public outrage, which led to a recall election. However, in what had been widely regarded as a politically progressive state, he prevailed. It is too soon to know how devastating this will be to the Wisconsin public schools.

"Disabling or eliminating teacher unions removes the strongest voice in each state to advocate for public education and to fight crippling budget cuts. Stripping teachers of their job protections limits academic freedom," Ravitch says.[11] The move also makes the teaching profession less attractive to capable individuals who make the best teachers.

Ultimately, public education is about the future, and the extent to which Pre-K–12 public schools are funded and otherwise supported is a measure of the extent to which a country is willing to invest in its children and its future. "The school eliminates prejudice and fuses diverse nationalities into a new society.... The social factor in school is the greatest factor of all; it stands higher than subjects of learning, than methods of teaching, than the teacher himself," pioneer progressive educator Frances Wayland Parker decreed. "Children in a public school, before prejudice has entered their childish souls, before hate has become fixed, before mistrust has become a habit, learn to live and work together. This mingling, fusing and blending gives personal power, and makes the public school a tremendous force for the upbuilding of democracy."[12] This remains the ideal for public education; however, the reality is far afield of Parker's progressive ideals.

Speaking wistfully of the bygone era when there was bipartisan support for the goals of advancing public education, University of Wisconsin retiring Alumni Director Paula Bonner observes that, today, "Education is a political football instead of being a place of common ground … the rise of divisive, partisan politics is really challenging … now we're trying to hold up the dam."[13]

Denver, Colorado, public school parent Cassi Clark describes the fight against charter schools she faced in "Goodnight Public Education: The Fight to Save Neighborhood Schools." Cassi offers a snapshot of the politics behind the charter school movement in her community and how difficult going up against this shift is.

Taking a different approach, Madison, Wisconsin, public school teacher Abigail Swetz confronts the issue of how disturbing Donald Trump's behavior as a national role model has been and her concerns about the messages, particularly concerning bullying, that his example is sending to young people. In her essay "Stand Up. Speak Out. Be Kind," which she read at the 2017 Madison Women's March, she explains how she decided to bring Donald Trump into her classroom and confront his behavior head-on, and what happened when she did.

NOTES

1. S. Alexander Rippa, *Education in a Free Society: An American History*, 8th ed. (New York: Pearson, 1996).

2. *Ibid.*

3. www.censusbureau.gov, 2015.

4. www.usda.gov.

5. Laura Camara, "Trump Proposes Spending Big on Education Weeks After Proposing Billions in Cuts," *USA Today*, April 4, 2017.

6. Common Core is the set of academic benchmarks regarding student achievement by the time they finish each grade. They were develop by the National Governors Association and business groups in direct response to business leaders complaining that students were not graduating high school with the skills and knowledge needed for college and career.

7. Diane Ravitch, *Reign of Error: The Hoax of the American Privatization Movement and the Danger to American Public Schools* (New York: Vintage Books, 2014).

8. Joshua Angrist, Parag Pathak, Christopher Walters, "Explaining Charter School Effectiveness," Working Paper # 17332. National Bureau of Economic Research, www.nber.org.

9. www.edexcellence.net.

10. Stephanie Johnson, Neil Campbell, Kami Spicklemire, and Lisette Partelow, "The Trump-DeVos Budget Would Dismantle Public Education, Hurting Vulnerable Kids, Working Families and Teachers," Center for American Progress, March 17, 2017.

11. Ravitch, *Ibid.*

12. Quoted in Rippa, *Ibid.*

13. John Allen, "The Boss Signs Off," *Badger Insider,* Fall 2017.

Goodnight Public Education
The Fight to Save Neighborhood Schools

Cassi Clark

> Since its inception in the United States, the public school system has been seen as a method of disciplining children in the interest of producing a properly subordinate adult population. Sometimes conscious of explicit, and at other times a natural emanation from the conditions of dominance and subordinacy prevalent in the economic sphere, the theme of social control pervades Education thought and policy.
> —S. Bowles and H. Gintis, Schooling in Capitalist America

We live in an America on the precipice of a values decision. Do we believe money, business, and the economy should drive our government? Or do we think people, community and equality should drive the government?

Those of us in the resistance likely fall in the latter category; I definitely do. But I am not so enlightened as to have understood the extent of this values brawl on November 9, 2016, the day after Donald Trump was elected president of the United States. It took Denver Public Schools (DPS) closing our son's public pre-school—6th grade Montessori to wake me up. It turns out public education today exemplifies the values struggle going on nationwide, and I had to resist.

About 20 years ago, several communities and education experts decided they wanted control over the schools in their neighborhoods and the freedom to introduce new education models. They brought forth a massive lobbying effort to start the charter school system. The idea was that parents should get to choose the schools their kids go to and that there should be choices in each neighborhood. For example, if your kid is particularly artistic, perhaps he or she would do better at an art oriented school.

However, because we live in a profit-motive, capitalism-rules culture, this idea was quickly corrupted in two directions. First, under the George W. Bush administration, Congress passed the No Child Left Behind (NCLB) bill that created our oppressive testing system and penalized the schools and teachers serving the most vulnerable students by withholding funds and linking teacher performance evaluations to test scores.

Second, seeing that there were problems with our educational system, billionaires like Bill Gates and the Koch brothers decided an economic approach to education would be worthwhile and threw money at the issue. This was the beginning of the contemporary educational reform movement.

Antonia Darder, quoting Alex Molnar in *Giving Kids the Business: The Commercialization of America's Schools*,[1] said that "simultaneously with a depressed economy and worsening condition for workers, we find 'the rhetoric about the catastrophic failure of the American public schools [has] become even more feverish.'" She added that Reformers "offer a public-spirited justification for introducing education to the profit motive and giving educators a healthy dose of the 'real world' in the form of competition. Most important, they keep the focus on schools and off the failure of business to promote the well-being of most of the countries citizens."[2]

Thus, education reform was born, or begat. In order to make room for charter schools operated by corporations, education Reformers believe in closing public schools. Every year, many school districts target the bottom 5 percent of their schools for closure. For Reformers, business is everything, and so they run schools like businesses, and apply business language accordingly. DPS Superintendent Tom Boasberg actually brags about his "Portfolio Management" system, like a CEO bragging about his franchises.

Autonomy is a key component of the Reform ideology, making each school its own competitive product. Under this model, schools must lobby for building space, air conditioners, new books, etc. In order to maintain enrollments and resources they have to develop their own partnerships with outside organizations to meet the needs of their communities, and then market themselves.

Autonomy does give principals the leeway to lead as they see fit, and schools with well-connected principals who network well and have a strong supporting parent organization do thrive. But, schools with new principals who've come from outside the school's community, who are not adept at networking, and/or are not connected to a city's nonprofit world are left floundering with no support from the district. For example, Gilpin Montessori Pre-school was in a prime location, on a beautiful historic campus and in gentrifying neighborhood. The school had been targeted for closure for about 6 years, but it wasn't until the district was able to bring in a new inexperienced principal with no connections to the city and little ability to network that they were able to justify closing the school.

In Denver, as in many districts, autonomous principals are also allowed to conduct Reduction in Building Staff (RIBS).[3] In Denver, this policy is frequently invoked to fire a teacher without cause, i.e., to eliminate a teacher a principal doesn't like.

As reported in a research paper by the Grattan Institute 2013, autonomy grants school leaders the authority to decide how their schools operate. But they are no better at implementing high-quality systems of teacher development, appraisal and feedback, and other policies than are centralized schools. "School leaders should be empowered to run their schools well. But empowerment means much more than autonomy."[4]

Reformers also value accountability and, in order to simplify education success, they pray at the altar of standardized tests. Parents, students and teachers have been decrying testing pretty much since NCLB passed. Its negative effects include teaching to the test, as opposed to teaching students to think; penalizing teachers in high-needs schools by linking their performance reviews to the test scores; and using erroneous, lacking and often lagging data to close schools.

William J. Mathis, managing director of the National Education Policy Center at the University of Colorado Boulder, puts it this way:

> Measuremyopia is characterized by a fixation on indicators that are easily quantifiable and reliable. For traditional economics, that indicator is money. For schools, this leads researchers (of many

persuasions) to standardized test scores.… Fundamentally, the problem is that none of the variables are particularly good indicators of what they are supposed to measure. For example, test scores are only a small part of schools and seniority [are] not a good measure of teacher quality. Further, the basic model assumes that the world is linear, relationships remain static, and that groups and individuals behave in predictable ways.… Cohesiveness, cooperation, altruism, caring and the common good are vital to a democratic society. But these are alien concepts to economists' visions of school reforms.[5]

Darder adds, "The singular indicator of test scores has achieved an overarching prominence, seriously limiting education debates.… Rather than entertaining questions regarding student abilities and overall performance, the current questions that dominate educational debates all loop back to the issue of testing and the improvement of test scores."[6]

In Denver, students can opt out of the standardized tests. However, if enough students choose this option, a school will drop lower on the district's School Performance Framework (SPF) and could be in danger of being closed. The SPF ratings are supposed to be based on the three previous years scores however, in Gilpin's case, one year's scores had been invalidated by the state due to a new (PARCC) test, but in order to push the process along the district counted that year as a 0 and failed the school. Consequently, Gilpin was slated for closure because of low test scores.

To "legitimize" a school closure, the district also requires a School Quality Review (SQR) conducted by a third-party contractor. The SQR was supposed to reflect the positive culture and otherwise immeasurable aspects of education. After the school board voted to close our school, we discovered through a Colorado Open Records Act (CORA) request of district emails that Gilpin passed the SQR, but the company that performed the review was asked to change the score so we would fail. At Gilpin, kids self-integrated. They took responsibly for their actions. They showed great character—and they were failed.

The reform values of autonomy and accountability are also used to justify the fundamental-ideology of Reformers: the closure of public schools to open corporate charter schools. This is the philosophy of Trump appointee Betsy DeVos, the new U.S. Secretary of Education. If schools fail standardized tests, principals and teachers can be blamed, since they were "autonomous," and public neighborhood schools can be closed and replaced with charter schools, DeVos believes. This is not a move to give local expert educators more room to experiment with new education models, as was the original intent of charter schools. Instead, it is a policy used to allow corporate charter companies to open more schools nationwide. DeVos and the Reformers are using charters to privatize education. This does not create the diversity of educational opportunities the district claims.

In Denver, there are four types of charters that serve specific demographics, or public schools, which have limited funds and must compete for building space and students. With limited funds, public schools are now forced to market themselves against charter schools that have separate corporate budgets for air conditioners, marketing and lobbying.

So, why do we care if schools are public or charter?

In an ideal world where teachers and students of all backgrounds are treated equitably and fairly, and community is sacred, we wouldn't. But the reality is that charter schools take public funds, but are not required to follow the regulations that public schools do. All four of the corporate charters that have been approved to open more schools in Denver next year opted out of numerous district regulations without being required to, or providing a rationale. These "onerous" regulations include the Procedures for the Investigation of Public Complaints of Discrimination or Harassment, Procedures for the Investigation of Employee Complaints of Discrimination or Harassment, Regulation regarding the Public's Right to Know—Freedom of Information, and school safety, to name just a few.[7]

The effect of freedom from accountability is that charter schools do not have to hire educated or licensed teachers, pay them even the low going rate, or serve all student types. And if the total number of licensed teachers falls below 50 percent, the district administration doesn't have to negotiate with the teacher's union. Thus, a charter school–first district is union busting one of the few, and biggest unions, for women. Let's be clear: women are expected to take nurturing jobs, accept being underpaid, and roll over when we are undercut by profiteering. The net effect of these regulations is to institutionalize racism and sexism, while the charter school's corporate owners make a profit off the public funds.

Building on the idea that charter schools offer parents a choice of quality schools—the free-market applied to education—Secretary DeVos, along with Reformers all around the country, have been talking about school choice as the cure to all of our education woes. However, the Civil Rights Project analyzed 40 states, the District of Columbia, and several dozen metropolitan areas with large enrollments of charter school students and found that, "charter schools are more racially isolated than traditional public schools in virtually every state and large metropolitan area in the nation."[8]

This matters in terms of policy and rhetoric because, according to DeVos, who was backed by Republicans and Democrats on this, *school choice* was one of the solutions to the school segregation problem. However, in a collaborative study between Penn State University and University of Texas at El Paso, Stephen Kotok, Erica Frankenberg, Kai A. Schafft, Bryan A. Mann, Edward J. Fuller found that "on average, the transfers of African American and Latino students from traditional public schools to charter schools were segregationist. White students transferring within urban areas transferred to more racially segregated schools. Students from all three racial groups attended urban charters with lower poverty concentration."[9] In another study, published in Education Finance and Policy by Richard O. Welsh from the University of Georgia, Matthew Duque from the Center for Education Policy Research at Harvard University, and Andrew McEachin from the Rand Institute found that "high-achieving students switch to high-quality schools whereas low-achieving students transfer to low-quality schools."[10]

Here's what *school choice* looks like in our historically black Denver neighborhood somewhat divided regarding gentrification. There are four elementary school choices open to everyone:

1. A highly reputable exemplary charter school housed in a downtown building with no outdoor playground and a waiting list. This school primarily attracts educated, middle+ class white families.

2. A school that has been targeted by DPS for closure for about six years now. It is mid-level on the SPF and is co-located with a corporate charter focusing on STEM (Science, Engineering, Science and Math).

3. A corporate charter that targets black families and whose approach is strict

discipline, including lines on the hallway floors that students must follow with their hands stuck tightly to their bodies. It is nicknamed "Jail Prep."

4. A public neighborhood elementary that still uses a zero-tolerance approach to discipline, despite the fact that the policy has been proven to disproportionately penalize black male students; and where the kids in the Federal Head Start program are separated out. The net effect is that middle class white students are, from a young age, taught that they are better than their counterparts, and no one is taught conflict resolution. This is the only public pre-school in the neighborhood.

Reformers would argue that we could go anywhere in the city. But, as stated above, it doesn't happen. Many parents in our neighborhood cannot get their kids to a school across town, and the rest of us have the apparently erroneous belief that our kids ought to be able to go to school in the neighborhood we choose to live in.

Students that ride Denver's so called innovative "Success Express" (I suspect called innovative because it makes business sense, not because it's effective at getting kids to schools) often have to ride for an hour or longer to go even a few miles to a school outside their neighborhoods. This might make sense for a high schooler, but it is too much to ask of students in the lower elementary grades. Preschoolers are not offered transportation at all. Then, of course, there is the issue of the "good schools" having wait lists, which is why many more affluent families chose to buy homes in the "good neighborhoods," further segregating and disempowering low-income communities.

Elaine Simon, co-director of the urban studies program at the University of Pennsylvania, points out that closing neighborhood schools harms neighborhoods. She wrote, "Schools are often the one institution still surviving in low-income neighborhoods, and they serve as a point of pride and community for families. Nonetheless, the new 'education Reformers' prioritize closing schools over improving them, using the argument that we are in a time of public sector austerity, which means a need to orient to market forces."[11]In other words, Reformers believe we should be orienting to money rather than communities. This is how racism continues to be institutionalized.

School choice is not about parents having a plethora of good schools to choose from that meet their needs. It's about a school district deciding what companies it wants to run its schools, and keeping disenfranchised people from having a strong community center to hold them together and build power around.

When it came to closing Gilpin Montessori, DPS claims to have included the community in the discussion. However, the meetings were held at the school where only a few parents came and no one from the outside neighborhood was invited. None of the community leaders or registered neighborhood organizations were informed of the situation or the meetings. And the meetings themselves consisted of power point presentations of what the district was going to do. There was no discussion, no listening to the community, and no real community involvement in the decision.

Those of us who resisted brought the issue to our neighbors, we informed the Registered Neighborhood Organizations, the NAACP, local neighborhood leaders, and the media. We even walked around the neighborhood handing out fliers and talking to people whose families had gone to the school for generations. And, when we discovered the changes SQR score, we brought to it the school board; they didn't bat an eye. The unfortunate reality is that the Reform ideology that Denver public schools, and other districts nationwide, have adopted has failed women, people of color and low-income families.

The public good, by definition, needs to exist separate from the free-market. If we value the education of all people, the strengthening and integration of communities, and leveling of the playing field, we cannot let the Reformer's free-market approach to education stand. If we value democracy, the voices of all the people, then we must educate and empower all the children equally. Here in Denver we have a vision of community schools, supported by a district that shares our values of equality, empowerment, community, and quality education for all. We embrace restorative justice polices, social justice curriculums, diverse and integrated schools.

We are fighting back by organizing our communities in a grassroots, boots on the ground, door-to-door effort to run pro-community school candidates in this November's school board election. The core value driving this campaign is that every neighborhood deserves a great public school and a place for communities to come together.

DPS is fighting back by denying 18-year-old school board candidate Auontai (Tay) Anderson access to the facilities his competitor has been allowed to use. His competitors attack his age and background, but he grew up in the schools they want to close, the community they are disempowering. His competitors are funded by the Gates Foundation and the Koch Brothers. The fight is not easy, but we persist.

In Michigan, the Detroit Public Schools Community District filed a lawsuit against the Michigan School Reform Office over their decision to close 16 schools.[12] The district has been told they are not allowed to use school funds in the lawsuit.[13] The fight is not easy, but we persist.

If we want a society that values women and people of color, we must teach these values to our children. We must take control of our public education system away from the capitalists who use it to control us and keep us down. We must have a vision of what good government looks like, what good public education based on elevating rather than controlling and subordinating looks like. Then we must oust the politicians who have been or are being paid for by mil/billionaires. And we must not let them represent us in D.C. The fight is not easy, but we persist.

We must show up at school district meetings, even if it's not about our kids' school, even if we don't have kids. We must get our neighbors to vote in school board elections. We must educate our networks on the issues with Reform and the risks of privatizing this imperative public good. We must remember, and then remind, our communities that our power comes from our schools, that having a working democratic government requires a well-educated populous, and that we cannot have this if mil/billionaires continue to deprive women, low-income families, and people of color their rights to quality and equal education. The fight is not easy, but we persist.

Notes

1. Gustavo E. Fischman (Editor, Contributor), Peter McLaren (Editor), Heinz Sünker (Editor), Colin Lankshear (Editor, Contributor), Mike Cole (Contributor), Antonia Darder (Contributor), Ramin Farahmandpur(Contributor), Robert Fitzsimmons (Contributor), Bernardo Gallegos (Contributor), Henry Giroux (Contributor), David Theo Goldberg (Contributor), Rhonda Hammer (Contributor), Dave Hill (Contributor), Donna Houston (Contributor), Douglas Kellner (Contributor), Michele J. Knobel (Contributor), Peter Mayo (Contributor), Michael A. Peters (Contributor), Ludwig Pongratz (Contributor), Laura Pulido (Contributor), Erika Richter (Contributor), Albert Scherr (Contributor), Juha Suoranta (Contributor), Tuukka Tomperi (Contributor) et al., *Critical Theories, Radical Pedagogies, and Global Conflicts* (Lanham, Md. : Rowman & Littlefield Publishers, 2005).

2. *Ibid.*

3. www.westword.com.

4. www.grattan.edu.

5. Beware Economists Bearing Education Reforms, www.nepc.colorado.edu.

6. Fischman et. al., *Ibid*.

7. These Twenty-two Schools Just Won Approval from the Denver School Board, www.chalkbeat.org May 19, 2017.

8. www.civilrightsproject.ucla.edu.

9. www.journals.sagepub.com/doi/full/10.1177/0895904815604112.

10. www.rand.org/pubs/research_briefs/RB9966.html.

11. www.washingtonpost.com, June 3, 2013.

12. www.freep.com, March 20, 2017.

13. www.freep.com, June 22, 2017.

Stand Up. Speak Out.
Be Kind

Abigail Swetz

My name is Abigail Swetz, and I am a proud public-school teacher. There is a lot that is wrong with the American education system, but none of these things involve students. The students are amazing—they are kind; they are passionate; they are committed to social justice; they are going to change the world someday. And someday, we will all look back and realize that one day was November 9, 2016.

I love teaching in an election year. As a U.S. history teacher, my ultimate goal is to create active citizens out of my students, and in this country, that means I want them to grow up to be informed voters. So, we start young. I know I did. I was raised to know that voting is a civic duty of democracy, and I work to impart that sense of duty to my students. This year above all, they got it. Let me tell you how I know that.

While I do love teaching in an election year, this year made me nervous. I teach young women. I teach queer students. I teach students of color. I teach Muslim students. I teach the diverse future of this great country.

Teachers are expected to remain politically neutral in the classroom, and I struggled with that idea when presented with the two candidates in the 2016 presidential election, and the threat to the emotional safety of my students one of them posed. There is nothing more important to me than to keep my students safe, to provide a safe space for them to be who they really are, to explore what that means, and to examine their own and each other's beliefs. That doesn't mean discussions don't get contentious sometimes, but those conversations happen in an environment where students feel safe to express their opinions and even to change their mind when presented with compelling evidence.

That is why we created an election social contract as a class—a set of rules we would follow when discussing the election. It was a collaborative effort, and this is what the students came up with:

Seven Rules to Live by in Our Classroom

1. Be curious and open-minded.
2. Speak your mind truthfully.
3. Think critically and explain your opinions with facts and reasoning.
4. Listen to each other.

219

5. Respect each other—disagree with each other's ideas NOT with each other as people.

6. Be kind.

7. Get involved—decisions are made by those who show up.

Next, we started studying the election. First, we examined the issues by diving into the party platforms. We investigated the ideological and policy differences between the parties. The discussions were emotional and passionate but also curious and open-minded and respectful—all in keeping with our social contract. I did my best to ask questions without inserting my opinion. But the day came when we had to move from policies to people and take a look at the candidates not just the parties. I was about to bring Donald Trump into this safe space.

I made a decision. I decided to follow my conscience as an active and informed citizen and my duty as a teacher entrusted with her students' safety and decided to not remain neutral. I told my students that I respected people's right to hold opinions different than my own. I told my students I respected many politicians from both sides of the aisle and that their ideas deserved our curiosity, our open minds, and our healthy debate. And I followed our social contract and spoke my truth. I told them I was their teacher and that my number one job was to keep them safe. And I told them that in all the anti-bullying training I had ever been taught, the most important of the lessons was to never be a bystander to bullying. And so, I refused to be one. I told my students that Donald Trump's behavior during this campaign was wrong, that it was bullying behavior, and that it would not be tolerated in my classroom, and I encouraged them to start looking at the election itself through the lens of our classroom's social contract.

And they did. Then November 8 came. And then November 9. And I didn't know how to keep them safe anymore. I didn't know how to teach this.

Finally, I turned the class over to my students. We talked. They felt bewildered; they felt sad and lost; they felt more than a little betrayed. And then something really special happened. We cried together.

I had agonized over what to do that day all the previous night and early in the morning. All I had written in my lesson plan book was "process the election," but I wasn't sure how to do that in the face of their raw emotion. As we talked, and as students cried together, I started crafting a writing activity.

I told them a wise president once said, "We must find time to stop and thank the people who make a difference in our lives." I told them President John F. Kennedy would want them to reach out and thank people. I told them that a lot of people were going to be hurting today. I told them it was a good day to think about expressing kindness. To think about gratitude. Who are you thankful for today? Who in your life could use a word of kindness? I told them, "Write them a letter, a letter telling them why you are grateful for them and thanking them for being in your life."

And this is when the magic truly happened. You could have heard a pin drop.

I had asked them to be kind, to reach out, and they were, and they did. They wrote to their parents, to neighbors, to teachers, to friends, to mentors in the community, to family. But most touching of all, they wrote to each other. They reached out to classmates they saw hurting, classmates having an especially hard time, and they said, "I'm here for you." And they were.

The next four years are going to be tough. And we are going to have to make them full of speaking out and standing up and very strong activism. But first, we will need to make them full of kindness. That is how I am going to be an active citizen. I will speak out. I will stand up. And I will be kind.

So, let's all take inspiration from some of the wisest people I know, the 14-year-olds in my classroom, and reach out to someone in kindness. Let's start today. Let's start now.

There is so much to be done. And we are the ones to do it.

Section 12. When They Go Low, We Go High

Swimming in the Deep Rivers of Racism

Paula vW. Dáil

> The racism I endured as First Lady of the United States was extremely painful. It cut deep. And as women, we are living with small tiny cuts, and we are bleeding every single day. And we're still getting up.—Michelle Obama

Many people truly believed that Barack Obama's successful campaign for president of the United States signaled the dawn of a new America. They thought the nation had finally moved past its embedded racism and was about to become a post-racist country, that the Civil War had finally ended, and that the racist Old South had been laid to rest in the archives of history.

Sadly, they could not have been more wrong. Many Americans still can't resist an opportunity for a racist jab and the Obamas stepping onto a national stage just opened that door wider. Ugly racism, in the form of radio and television comments, magazine covers, and other public media outlets walked right through. This climate endured throughout the Obama presidency.[1]

Toward the end of his term in office President Obama summed up racist America: "The legacy of slavery and Jim Crow continues," he said. "Discrimination exists in almost every institution of our lives. You know, that casts a long shadow and that's still part of our DNA that's passed on. We're not cured of it. Racism we are not cured of, clearly."[2]

Unfortunately, Obama was correct, particularly when considering that the man Americans elected as his successor has an alarming history of racist behavior so significant that David Duke, former Imperial Wizard of the Klu Klux Klan (KKK), endorsed his candidacy. It took Donald Trump a long time to disavow Duke's endorsement, and he only did so under pressure.[3]

Duke's endorsement should not have been too surprising to anyone who has paid any attention whatsoever to Donald Trump over the years. In his business dealings Trump ran afoul of the laws regarding housing discrimination so many times the cases came to the attention of the U.S. Justice Department. He went more public in his racist beliefs when Barack Obama declared his candidacy for president of the United States. Shortly afterwards Trump started the birther conspiracy rumor, falsely claiming that Obama, who was born in Hawaii, was born in Kenya, not in the United States, thus not entitled to assume the presidency. Despite clear evidence that he was wrong, Trump perpetuated this falsehood for nearly ten years, apparently motivated by his inability to accept that an African American was a "real American" and had been elected to the presidency by a significant majority of American voters.

Trump has been heavily critical of the Black Lives Matter movement, taking a "what, my life doesn't matter?" attitude. He invited African American County Sheriff David Clarke of Milwaukee, Wisconsin, to speak at the Republican National Convention, because Clarke had gone on record calling out the Black Lives Matter movement as "part of the problem in America."

However, the extent of Trump's racism isn't confined to African Americans. He heavily criticized the family of a Muslim-American U.S. soldier killed in Iraq in 2004 when Khiz Kahn, Capt. Kahn's father spoke at the Democratic National Convention, and criticized Trump's intention to ban Muslims from entering the country. "I'm sure Capt. Kahn is a hero," Trump said, "but a lot of Muslims are terrorists."[4] Trump went on to suggest that her husband had "muzzled Mrs. Kahn" so she could not speak for herself.

Ibrahim Hooper, the spokesman for the Council on American-Islamic Relations, responded that, "It's really despicable that anyone, let alone a presidential candidate, would choose to dishonor the service of an American who gave his life for this nation." Ms. Khan, he said, "was obviously there to support her husband, who was offering what many people believe was the most impactful speech of the entire convention."[5]

Peter Wehner, a speechwriter for President George W. Bush wrote on Twitter: "Memo to Trump supporters: He's a man of sadistic cruelty. With him there's no bottom. Now go ahead & defend him."

Earlier in his campaign Trump denounced U.S. District Judge Gonzalo Curiel, who was presiding over two cases in which the plaintiffs alleged that Trump University duped them out of tens of thousands of dollars by leading them to believe they would be educated in Trump's real estate strategies. Trump accused Curiel, who did not dismiss the charges against Trump University, of being unfairly biased against him because Curiel is Hispanic. "He has an absolute conflict presiding over the litigation given that he is of Mexican heritage and I'm building a [Mexican border] wall. It's an inherent conflict of interest," Trump said, referring to his campaign pledge to seal off the U.S.-Mexican border.[6]

In another racist move, Trump commissioned a study group to explore voter fraud upon becoming president, even though such fraud has never been documented to exist in the U.S. and many believe is a veiled effort to suppress voting among African Americans and other ethnic minorities, who traditionally vote democratic. He also gave an inflammatory, combative speech to police officers in Suffolk County, New York, advocating for rough physical treatment toward immigrants and other criminals. Calling gang members "animals," he praised heavy-handed, aggressive law enforcement: "When you see these thugs being thrown into the back of a paddy wagon. You see them thrown in rough.... Please don't be too nice. Like, don't hit their head and they've just killed somebody. You can take the hand away, OK?" he said.[7]

Trump used his executive power to pardon Sheriff Joe Arpaio, the bombastic sheriff of Maricopa County, Arizona, who was been found guild of criminal contempt of court for willfully violating a court order to stop racial profiling. "He has done a lot in the fight against illegal immigration. He's a great American patriot and I hate to see what has happened to him," Trump said.[8]

Even though Trump has a strong history of high profile racial battles and enjoys Duke's continuing support, he denies that he's racist or sympathetic to white nationalist groups who promote racism or anti–Semitism (see more on this in the essay "Dancing with The Devil: Donald Trump's Moral Failure"). That Trump's son-in-law Jared Kushner, the grandson of Holocaust survivors, and Trump's daughter Ivanka, who converted to Judaism, have defended the president against those charges doesn't really matter because Trump is boastful, proudly disruptive, and often rewarded for saying outrageous, politically incorrect things. Undoubtedly some supporters cheer him on because he is willing to say things they cannot, or are unwilling, to say, and enthusiastically encourage him to go up against the liberal's penchant for political correctness.

Donald Trump's successful campaign for president thrilled domestic hate groups. They cheered when Trump mocked the Black Lives Matter movement by countering, "all lives matter." Hate groups are all for building a border wall and anything else that would keep foreigners out because, they believe, everyone in the U.S. should speak fluent English, say "Merry Christmas" and celebrate Easter.

Hate groups got even more excited when former right-wing Breitbart News media mogul Steve Bannon, CEO of the Trump election campaign who supports the "alt-right" movement, was appointed Trump's chief strategist. These folks are among the 45 percent of President Trump's loyal political base who are not college educated, have annual incomes below $50,000 and an "America: love it or leave it" mentality, and are a major factor in his political success.

Under these circumstances, it was not surprising that the normally loquacious, verbally excessive Trump, who has never been known to lack an opinion on anything, was suddenly silent the morning of August 12, 2017, when Charlottesville, Virginia, erupted in racial violence. Hours went by without so much as a single presidential tweet. His first statement on the event was a tepid one. His second response claimed that even though a hate group-fueled militia had invaded Charlottesville, both sides were responsible for the violence.

Charlottesville's mayor, Democrat Mike Signer, said Trump made a choice during his campaign to "go right to the gutter, to play on our worst prejudices…. I think you are seeing a direct line from what happened here this weekend to those choices," Signer said.[9]

In *Devil's Bargain: Steve Bannon, Donald Trump and the Storming of the Presidency*, Bannon claims that attempts by Democratic presidential nominee Hillary Clinton to tie Trump to the alt-right and nationalists did not move voters. "We polled the race stuff and it doesn't matter," Bannon said.[10] Perhaps it doesn't matter to Donald Trump, but it matters a great deal to a lot of other people, every single day of their lives, in the thousands of ways race intersects with education, economic opportunity, health, social connections, and all the other variables that combine to comprise the American dream. Clearly, Trump has no comprehension of this issue whatsoever.

In the wake of Charlottesville, civil rights leaders called for action. Leaders from several religious and secular groups representing organizations such as the National Council of Churches, the Anti-Defamation League and the NAACP Legal Defense and Educational Fund, called on Trump to more strongly condemn the Charlottesville incident and disavow the support he has received from white supremacists and hate groups. Mary E. Hunt, executive director of the Women's Alliance for Theology, Ethics and Ritual (WATER) said, "The events in Charlottesville make clear that our work to bring about justice and peace has only just begun. We pledge the resources of WATER to this task and add our voices to those who denounce white supremacy and racism. Watching this unfold only adds urgency to the moment."

Several groups also called for bipartisan congressional oversight hearings of the departments of Justice and Homeland Security. They are requesting that both departments report regularly on their efforts to stamp out hate crimes, dismantle violent white supremacist groups, and deal with the threats posed by violent white nationalists. However, many believe that under Attorney General and former conservative Republican Alabama Senator Jeffrey Beauregard Sessions' leadership this is unlikely to occur.

Meanwhile, it emerged that Trump's two staunchest supporters were Vice President Mike Pence, who stressed that he "stands by the president," and KKK leader David Duke. Following Trump's restatement of his "both sides are to blame" position, Duke tweeted, "Thank you President Trump, for your honesty and courage to tell the truth about #Charlottesville and condemn leftist terrorism in BLM [Black Lives Matter] and Antifa [antifascists]."

This is the unfortunate racial climate in Donald Trump's America in 2017 that Georgia essayist and poet Erica Gerald Mason reflects upon going forward. "The Resistance Will Be Beautiful" describes what it was like to wake up in a "new America" on November 9 and offers a firm, unwavering resolve to stand up and resist any efforts to take back the gains made in the years since the 1960s Civil Rights Movement, when Rosa Parks refused to move to the back of the bus.

In "Our Country 'Tis of Thee" Darlynne L. Campbell, who teaches in an urban, inner-city public school, reflects on present-day racial America reminds readers that this is every American's country, and that an unwavering attitude of peace and love is the only way forward.

NOTES

1. Early in the Obama presidential campaign Fox news anchor Megyn Kelly and news contributor Michelle Malkin referred to Mrs. Obama as "Obama's baby mama." Not likely any news anchor would refer to Melania Trump, Laura Bush, or any other First Lady in such insulting and disparaging terms. A few days earlier, the May 29, 2008, issue of *The New Yorker* magazine featured a cartoon depiction of Mr. Obama dressed as a Muslim, standing next to a portrait of Osama bin Laden, fist-bumping his gun-slinging wife while an American flag burns in the fireplace. The implication was that the Obamas were somehow insufficiently patriotic or soft on terrorism, or that black people winning the White House was somehow more horrifying than a terrorist attack. The magazine claimed it was satire—a humorous attempt to take aim at the racist stereotyping of the Obamas. Black people, and other minorities didn't think it was funny.

2. Andrew Malcom, "Obama Declares Racism Inhabits American DNA," *Investor Business Daily*, June 23, 2015.

3. www.cnn.com, March 3, 2016.

4. Maggie Haberman and Richard A. Oppel, Jr., "Donald Trump Criticizes Family of Slain U.S. Soldier, Drawing Ire," www.newyorktimes.com, July 30, 2106.

5. *Ibid.*

6. www.wsj.com, June 2, 2016.

7. www.cnn.com, July 29, 2017.

8. www.foxnews.com August 17, 2017.

9. *Face the Nation*, www.cbs.com, August 13, 2017.

10. Joshua Green, *Devil's Bargain: Steve Bannon, Donald Trump and the Storming of the Presidency* (New York: Penguin, 2017).

The Resistance Will Be Beautiful

Erica Gerald Mason

I had lunch plans for the afternoon of November 9. A noon-ish gathering with my besties to mingle over a meal at our favorite hibachi place four towns over. I didn't go to lunch that day.

Here are some things I knew before November 8, 2016: I knew my neighbors in an Atlanta suburb to hold conservative Christian values. I knew they despised vulgarity, praised acts of charity and kindness, and were doing their best to raise thoughtful children. I knew they would most definitely reject an ideology of division and fear.

I was wrong.

I thought I knew the woman with whom I spent many Tuesday mornings volunteering at a local charity. The same woman who herself was an immigrant. The woman with a love of wine and a deliciously dirty joke, I knew she would be alarmed at the strong anti-illegal immigration rhetoric coming from the Grand Old Party.

She was not.

I knew my high school bestie, the smartest girl I knew—the girl who was a whiz at accounting, the girl who was an excellent mimic, the girl who would roll down the windows to her car and sing along to Madonna songs on the radio–I knew she, a lifelong conservative, would rise above the "they're both bad candidates" conversation and voice her concern for her party's endorsement of a candidate so seemingly antithetical to their core beliefs.

She did not.

I was sure the women I knew—the women I surrounded myself with and called friends, the women who would take the clothes off their backs and give it to a person in need, the women whose hearts were made of gold and platinum, who worked from home and had slightly more free time now that their children were older—I knew with every fiber of my being that we would show the world what kind of America we wanted to live in. I knew these women would resist and rally. Not just for themselves, but for hundreds of thousands of people in danger of such drastic policy change.

They did not.

I knew with 100 percent certainty that my family members, the ones who were centrist voters—the one's who were not really Democrats or Republicans, the ones who were the moderates, the middle of the road population, the people who, just like me, started from nothing and remember those early days, the people who remember the overall civility and statesmanship of their elected officials, the one's whose children, cousins, nieces, were members of the very minority group the incoming administration either ignored, belittled, or showed no willingness to condemn acts of hate against those same people— I was positive they would express frustration at the inherent sideline of our most marginalized populace.

They did not.

I was sure my acquaintances, the ones who voted third party, even after I (and every other forecaster in the world) pleaded with them that a vote for a third party was a vote for the worst presidential option—I was sure that same conscience that would not let them vote for either candidate would be the same conscience would compel them to become more active citizens, to speak out against inhumane policies and dogma.

It did not.

After everything I thought I knew, more than anything I thought my country thought of me, and others like me, made America great. I thought the social progress our country had made would move forward. I thought the Affordable Healthcare Act needed drastic revisions; I thought jobs needed to return to the Heartland. I thought school kids deserved the same nutrition standards we hold for ourselves. I thought our country didn't tolerate racism, sexism, homophobia, xenophobia, nationalism, willful ignorance, and deliberate meanness.

I was wrong.

So yes, the election results were stunning. It shook my belief system to its core. I went to sleep on the night of November 8, worried about America and my place in it.

I woke up in a new America on November 9. And I'm not ashamed to admit I spent most of that morning in tears. My husband left for work at 8 a.m. and returned at 6 p.m., and I was still in the same place on the sofa, my head in my hands, sobbing. I didn't cry for Hillary. I cried for America. What was our country becoming? What will my children inherit? What can I do to make them feel safe, when I felt as if the country delivered a giant "FUCK OFF" message to a large segment of the population? And as if my friends, neighbors, and family members were fine with that message?

And so on November 9, 2016, I did what I had done every day for the previous 470 days. I wrote a poem before breakfast:

> and I didn't think
> the sun would rise today
> but it did; like it always does.
> and the warmth on my skin
> of something bigger than myself
> (bigger than all of us)
> made me glad.

And I felt a little better. Not good, but better. My friend, a lifelong Republican, called me in tears: "I didn't think he would win, Erica. I never thought he would." My mother, who marched during the Civil Rights Movement, was equally numb. But she called me and made sure I was ok. "We'll cry today," she said. "And tomorrow we'll get up and fight." My youngest daughter, my baby, my most empathic kid, hugged me more in a 24 hour period than I think she's ever hugged me. My beloved dog Piper, always perceptive, always understanding, laid across my feet as I sat on the sofa—her warm body rooting me to my home, as if to say you belong here, you belong to me, and that will never change.

I questioned my writing a poem before breakfast. What did it mean in this new

America? Did the world need love poems, such the type I write? Or did it need poems of ferocity and resistance. I wasn't sure.

And in the days that followed, desperate for laughs and a minor distraction, I scrolled through dozens of Twitter memes with President Obama and Vice President Joe Biden. Planted squarely in the middle of the photos was a post about how the author was excited to get a "real" First Lady and not an ape, like the soon-to-be former First Lady.

"No, no, no, no," I said and kept scrolling. I didn't need to read more of the post itself or its responses—I already had a good idea of what it said. I went to high school in Evansville, Indiana (population ~130,000); I lived in Springville, Indiana (population ~1300). I only lasted a year in that city. I lived in the city limits of Kennesaw, GA (population ~21,000), home of the beloved Dent Meyers, infamous for his love of the Confederacy and the KKK, the many loaded weapons he carries, and for the "If It's Brown, Flush It" bumper sticker.

I don't need to know what these people think. I've been told what they think of me my entire life.

By the people shouting the n-word at me from passing cars. By the boys who told me they could bring home any girl they wanted, but never, EVER a Black girl. By the well-meaning teachers who were impressed by how articulate and respectful I was. By the colleagues who were surprised that I was familiar with the works of Jane Austen and Emily Dickinson. And recently, by the local Republican party, who had a singular message in the election to fill the congressional seat left by the newly appointed Secretary of Health and Human Services Tom Price: the Democrat's candidate is Not One of Us.

Not One of Us is an awful place to be. Like Rudolph the Red Nosed Reindeer's Island of the Misfit Toys, the label Not One of Us means there is something broken and irreparable about a segment of our society.

We aren't broken. We are mended. Sometimes in the only way we know how: by walking towards togetherness and away from separation.

I remember what it was like to leave Evansville for Indiana University: from the place where I knew every corner to a place where no one knew I existed. When I arrived at the Indiana University campus, for the first time I felt like anything was possible. And for a long time it was. I met my now-husband. We became parents. After we became parents the cracks began to show. Back then, if you drove 15 miles in any direction, the progressive bubble burst into a more conservative landscape. A lovely place to live if you are white, Protestant, straight and held what locals considered to be traditional values. My husband and I quickly learned you could only cross off one of those attributes and still be accepted. Two was too much. And so we moved to Atlanta. A diverse city, in certain parts. But diverse nonetheless. Where we knew our kids would be surrounded by a community where people from all walks of life co-mingled.

And still.

Georgia is still segregated. By choice and by zoning, if not by specific laws. Buford Highway in Atlanta is a United Nations of international cuisine and overlapping cultures. And yet many of my neighbors in the predominately white areas of Cobb County are too scared to visit. Most people in my area rarely make the 45 minute car ride to Atlanta to visit let alone eat at an ethnic restaurant. I remember feeling so happy to explore the area, excited to learn about cultures other than our own. And I remember feeling mortified when my family and I stumbled upon a Chinese New Year celebration at a local business. And believe me when I say we did our best to melt into the background like wallpaper, so we wouldn't disturb the party. I was humbled by just how nice people were to my family and me—a gathering of strangers huddled against a wall. Outsiders in every sense of the word. The feeling of acceptance and love as one of the organizers came over and invited us to stay was, to use a cliché, beautiful.

More of that kind of kinship, please.

There's an old saying that's been attributed to everyone from Anthony Hopkins to Eleanor Roosevelt: what other people think of me is none of my business. And now more than ever, it's true. And yet, now more than ever, it's dangerous if we believe it to be true. Because really, when it comes to the superficial trifles of life, it doesn't matter what you think about me. I'll wear my hair how I like. I'll dress how I choose. I may or may not wear makeup. But somewhere out there, an invisible jagged line appeared. Where the superficial becomes the subterranean: poor people shouldn't have affordable health care, immigrants don't have rights, women have no authority over their bodies. The former is forgivable; ignorable, even. The latter requires vigilance. And conversation. We're all just people, after all.

I've decided to set up camp on that jagged line. A homestead of one, with plenty of room for others, should you care to join me.

I peel off little pieces of my heart and pin them to the page every day. I hope that my poems give readers an opportunity to see a little bit of themselves in my words and maybe see the world as a smaller, friendlier place. One where you can have a conversation about the person you are, how you got to where you are, what informs your opinions. To be open to reading a news article you disagree with and have a conversation with someone who thinks differently than you. To listen with an open heart and no other agenda than to learn. To stop saying, "You're wrong," and start saying, "I don't understand."

To make those who wish I would disappear realize that I'm not going anywhere and that I don't want them to go anywhere either. To see me. To see the world. To unzip their old ideas. To challenge what we've been told. The freedom to admit we're wrong without fear of rejection. To challenge what we've been told. To talk to each other. To love each other. To respect each other.

To talk to each other like old friends, instead of sworn enemies.

Because now more than ever, we need to understand something fundamental and timeless:

It is possible to live a life of beauty and bravery. Never let anyone tell you can't do both.

Because the bravest act of revolution is to see the hate thrown at you and let it land at your feet. Refuse to pick it up. Refuse to do anything other than step over it and let it dry out in the sun. You will go to the town hall meetings. You will make the phone calls. You will look those who try to intimidate you in the eye and hold their gaze. And when they see you, they will see what I see:

Ferocious beauty.

Because you know what I hold in my hand, with the tightest of grips?

The idea that life can be ugly, but we are beautiful.

We are. Always.

Our Country 'Tis of Thee

DARLYNNE L. CAMPBELL

Peace is a five-letter word that modern society seems to consider trite. However, this simple word is the foundational principle of the world's most compassionate activists. Consider Mother Teresa, now a saint, Mohandas Gandhi, and Martin Luther King. The words of each of these people of wisdom are fraught with references to peace. Living in tranquility among the beauty of heaven and earth is surely the stuff of our most innocent dreams.

Pageant darlings have proclaimed world peace their dearest wish. In truth, America prides herself on being a peaceful land. One where camaraderie is common. A place where a person can become whatever they dare dream, and work hard enough, to become. America is the land of the free and the home of the brave. We hold massive destructive weaponry, but only to keep the peace. Our days of conquest and manifest destiny have ended. We seek only to live and enjoy the fruits of our labor.

The one thing that destroys the tapestry of peace is our refusal to trust one another. Our Achilles heel is our inability to trust that the fellow person who lives, works, and plays as we do, wants that same peace that we want.

Americans can be grouped into stripes and stars. The stripes are not all exactly the same but, for the most part, they are structurally the same and stem from one general location. Though some are one way, and others are a different way, they are all still stripes. The same with the stars who all are stars though some have a higher placement while others are of a lower standing. The stars and the stripes have others like them in other places but the group of stars and stripes that comprise the American flag set the standard for all the other stars and stripes in the world. One thing that constitutes beauty is contrast. Therefore, the stars and the stripes, though different, are spectacular together.

The problem is not their differences. The problem is they don't trust each other. The stars are in a place with a dark background. Though the background of the stars is dark, none of them would ever wish to purge it because the stars' brilliance shines brighter for it. The darkness wraps them as they stand in an upraised albeit secluded place. The stripes have a more prominent bearing which unfortunately lends itself to an illusion of sameness. This sameness illusion causes most stripes to perpetuate a false dominance over the stars.

In case you are unclear, the explanation of the previous analogy is as follows: The stars are meant to represent Americans who are descendants of enslaved Africans. The dark background, which illuminates their brilliance, is the stars, or Blacks; ancestral history of enslavement. The stripes are the various groups descended from Europeans who, by coincidence of color, benefit as part of the dominant class in America. The broad swath of stripes represents the strong lineage of white immigrants.

Now consider the American Flag in its current machination. Wouldn't the tapestry of stars and stripes be more impressive if the stars, dark past included, and the stripes, variances now discernible, were not segregated? Imagine a flag that weaves the stars and stripes together to truly represent America and its people.

How does a fragmented blocked flag represent a land of free and brave people who are encouraged to roam its lands and become whatever they dream to be? Do we really believe this land is your land and this land is my land? Yours and mine, by definition, means ours. If it is ours then we are all responsible for fixing it.

I found out the hard way how broken America really is.

Yesterday, this guy called me a nigger. Outright to my face! His voice was loud, clear, and unashamed. We were in an affluent neighborhood at an intersection to a busy biking and walking trail. Surely this should be a safe place, right? I mean energy drink swigging, methamphetamine-riddled racists do not jog or cycle. My attacker was not a skinhead or a toothless deplorable. He was cycling in what I assume was a pretty expensive biking pants outfit. Based on the clarity of his remark, and the fact that he was with others, I know he was not ashamed. He was not alone and spewing his private thoughts in anonymity. He was with two other cyclists when he yelled the "n-word."

Sadly, neither was I alone. According to my 14-year-old son, the guy yelled these exact words: "The light was red you fucking nigger." I only clearly heard the word "NIG-GER." I had just made a right turn on a green light while he and the other bikers waited to cross. Because his exact words were, "The light is red you fucking nigger." I assumed I must be mistaken on the green light. Truthfully, he may have been right, about the light, since I am not the world's most alert driver.

But America isn't like this anymore, right? So, he must have been extremely angry. He may have been having a terrible day; perhaps he was only out cycling because his friends convinced him to go on a bike ride to clear his mind.

Let's postulate, shall we? Let's say he was recently fired from a dream job for flirting with a minority woman. Only let's say the woman lied, she just wanted his job. Doesn't that explain how he could get so angry that he would fearlessly utter something so wretched? No. I'm sure you will agree there is no reason why someone should be allowed to cut into another person's soul in that manner.

Because this is post post-racial America (don't laugh) I have to believe this guy is an anomaly. In my life, it certainly is not common for me to hear whites use the "n-word." I believe Americans have learned the lessons taught during the Civil Rights Movement and will never allow themselves to return to a water hose society. As surely as Germany will never stand for another Adolf Hitler, the United States of America will never allow another Bull Connor.

So, this anomaly has to have happened because I provoked this otherwise good guy. I think most educated people believe that the lower rungs of society, Black and White alike, invite the negativity they encounter. That was my surely subconscious conviction. Yet, I have a graduate degree, I am married, and I am law abiding. I am a professional, which means I am separated from the masses of people who work for hourly pay. I'm a Christian—I mean really Christian. I don't even drink alcohol! Surely, my life keeps me safe from the types of people who still espouse racist beliefs, right? Perhaps it was karma returning to me from a time I played the Black card inauthentically, or inadvertently taught my children that the white man is the enemy?

My husband and I have worked hard to insulate our family. My children have only known segregation and blatant racism in family night movies. We have made sure they were aware, but unharmed, by images of American slavery. In fact, I make it a point to pause and discuss particularly strong images. As an educator, I know it is critical that adults uncover the layers of emotions such images of savagery, degradation, and servility evoke. As for the "n-word," our home has a contradictory relationship with its usage. As a rule, I don't curse so in our home the "n-word" is akin to "f-bombs." If my kids hear me speak the words "nigger" or "nigga" they get a shocked look on their faces.

When do I use the word you ask? I use it when expressing endearment, or wrath. I will often speak it to bring home a punch line. For example, one night we discovered one single roach in our apartment kitchen. I scoured everything, I put chemicals all the crevices, but I was still a nervous wreck for two days thinking we were dealing with an infestation. My husband, in an attempt to calm me, suggested perhaps I had been mistaken about the bug's true genealogy. My wide-eyed reply was, "No, that was a Nigga!" He understood exactly what I meant and we laughed uncontrollably. Notice the ending is "a" rather than "er"—a suffix difference that is like a gulf stream leading to a dangerous semantic whirlpool. Why I consider it my prerogative to use the word in any form is another subject for another day.

On the day when the cyclist called me a nigger he destroyed the carefully crafted anti-racism cocoon that held my children. Why did I build this cocoon? I had to know it was futile to try and keep racism away from two dark skinned boys. If I had been sensible I would have known the cocoon's futility. Perhaps I had been lulled to sleep, like countless people on the planet had been, in the wake of the "Yes We Can" euphoria that overtook us with Barack Obama's successful 2008 presidential campaign. Even though my kids' schools are bastions of diversity, I should have known the cocoon's mission was futile.

Perhaps it was my own upbringing that did it, made me think my kids would go untouched by racism in America. I grew up in a town with almost no diversity. All of the cultural events were geared towards one group, all the restaurants flavored their foods to fit one group, the clothing stores, the schools were 99.5 percent racially homogenous-student body and faculty. That city was home of the Gary National Black Political Convention held in 1972 and the Jackson Five. Nearly every school in the city was named after a prominent figure in Black history. The few not named for Blacks were named or those revered by them, such as Franklin D. Roosevelt. Obviously, I grew up insulated from traditional white racism. It is plausible that I thought I could do the same for my kids. Plausible but stupid, on many different levels.

Just like any other deadly epidemic, the only real protection from racism is exposure. One must be exposed to it in order to build a natural resistance. Routine immunizations prove this over and with terrors such as polio and rubella. Why wouldn't racist hatred be the same? Racism, like rubella and polio, infects us in our youth at our most vulnerable. After running its course, it either kills, or severely cripples our sense of equality. To rid ourselves of this scourge, all of America must stand in line and receive our preventive medicine in the form of exposure.

So often we hear the rhetoric of a "conversation" about this or that. Like every other cliché, it's cliché because it is true. The first place we start this conversation on racism is with our children. We must tell them, "Yes, I am racist. No, I do not want to be. I learned these things from my parents. I am telling you this because we are going to reverse what you have learned starting now."

Why start with the most innocent of us when discussing something so putrid? Because they are the ones who will hold us most accountable when we retreat into anger, jargon, political apathy, and stereotyping. Furthermore, it is their childlike innocence that we must draw upon. It will take childlike belief in the power of peace to strengthen the fiber of America.

We stand at the beginning of what could be the greatest coup of the racialized era. Remember of course race has not always been an entity, yes differences always existed, but race is a figment of a commerce-centered scheme. This admission is the first vital step in our coup.

Why call a peace movement a coup? The word "coup" means to overthrow an existing system of governance and to replace it with another. That is absolutely what I seek to do. I readily admit to wanting to depose the political schemes of wealth-mongers and overthrow those whose political schemers who force feed Blacks a steady diet of anger and stoke the fury of angry whites who long for "better days." Both groups believe in the American promise wholeheartedly, thereby in the fight to protect their piece of the pie. The hardest part of this coup is getting both sides to consciously agree when, in fact, they agree on more things than they disagree.

We all intrinsically want the same things. "Life, liberty, and the pursuit of happiness." That founding principle supersedes every other personal designation including gender, sexual orientation, and physical ability, even religion. The idea of a coup does not evoke an image of a peaceful transition of power and, indeed, may not be for every dissenter.

Nevertheless, tactics and motive are to be 100 percent peaceful. The seductive revenge politics of today have no place here. This means there is no room for a competitive argument over whose life matters more when it is clear that America's life is at stake. There is no place for bickering about who is more terrible.

Revenge politics must go. Only forgiveness politics will prevail in this most important mission of the common era. Consider again the peaceful predecessors who have led us in human centered movements. Mahatma Gandhi, Dr. Martin Luther King, and Mother Teresa never wavered from a peaceful outlook. Gandhi believed wholeheartedly in humanity, exemplified with his preemptive peaceful plea to Lord Irwin. Gandhi's letter to the Viceroy was an effort to prevent even a peaceful protest. He believed it imperative to appeal to the mind and heart of the man. Of course, the Salt Protest went forward, however Gandhi's peaceful non-violent approach eventually won out.

Likewise, Dr. King's commitment to peaceful non-violence in the face of an all-out assault made America look herself in the mirror. Eventually, King's peace also led to national freedom. Our nation was able to say we have had it all wrong and admit that it is time to change. Dr. King's work exposed the ugliness, and the ugliness fought bitterly against him. The ugliness killed President Kennedy when he showed he would side with peace over power.

The ugliness eventually receded, but not before 1965, when America looked in the mirror, saw her own ugliness and admitted she needed work, and then passed Civil Rights legislation to begin the process. Today, she must again face that mirror. Those who seek to help America must denounce their anger, because anger and hatred killed Dr. King. Instead, America must employ the tenets of love he espoused.

Mother Teresa achieved sainthood in our hearts long before she did in reality. As a child, when anyone I knew thought of a living person who was doing the most to make the world a better place it was always Mother Teresa. Not a rich woman with great branding and a foundation, Mother Teresa was a poor widow's daughter who was taught that everyone is "your people."

I steadfastly believe that love is revolutionary force that has carried African Americans from slavery to the presidency. No other plan has ever truly worked for us so much as peaceful intervention and compromise. No this is not weak negro politics as some of my sisters and brothers may be thinking. We are Black but our brothers and sisters in this movement have to be of every shade or it does not prevail. As Mother Teresa's mother said, "Some of them are our relations, but all of them are our people."[1]

America, the world really, stands at a crossroads. Can we be the world leader moving forward in love that is now so desperately needed? If so, as Blacks, the foremost factor we need to include is forgiveness. In America this will be desperately hard for the Black person, but the key to forgiving is that you can and must forgive whether or not the person requests or even deserves it. This is true now and will always be true.

Radical resistance is love and forgiveness in the face of hate, love in the face of insult, degradation, meanness, unfairness, and power. Love for the people who are wronged and love for those who hold power over them. Radical resistance is speaking up in love, not in arguing and fighting back. This is true now, and will always be true.

NOTE

1. https://www.biography.com/people/mother-teresa-9504160.

SECTION 13. WHEN WE FIGHT, WE WIN

United, We Move Forward

PAULA vW. DÁIL

Never underestimate the power of a woman to define her own destiny.—
Emmeline Pankhurst

"What happens when the people of a great nation gradually realize that their leader may not be, er, quite right in the head?" Nicholas Kristof recently asked, in an opinion editorial in *The New York Times*.[1] He went on to suggest the answer could be found in the story of Caligula, who became the Emperor of Rome in AD 37. According to Kristof, the story goes something like this:

Caligula was a colorful, flamboyant character who had led a life rich with gossip potential prior to becoming emperor. Despite having no prior political experience, he sailed into the position on his energy, charm, spontaneity, and unusual ability to connect with the common people, with whom he communicated constantly.

Initially, Caligula spent a lot of time criticizing his predecessor and reversing everything that the prior emperor had accomplished. He promised a massive tax overhaul and made grandiose pledges of infrastructure projects, including a scheme to cut through the Isthmus of Corinth. However, due to his lack of political leadership skills and mistaken belief that people should do what he told them to do, just because he said so, he proved completely incompetent and totally ineffective when it came to actually accomplishing something.

An additional problem was that Caligula's personal extravagances were costing Roman taxpayers a lot of money. This eventually lead to a budget crisis that threatened to shut down the Roman government and bring the empire to a halt because it was out of money.

Caligula began to panic. In a desperate move, he reportedly opened a brothel in the imperial palace to generate additional revenue. He also introduced new taxes. When this wasn't enough, he began to confiscate estates, antagonizing his wealthy supporters among the Roman elites, and sometimes killing them.

A narcissist and megalomaniac, the more trapped Caligula felt, the more unhinged he became. He supposedly rolled around on a huge pile of gold coins, engaged in conversations with the moon, which he would invite into his bed and replaced the heads of some statues of gods with likenesses of himself. Occasionally, he appeared in public dressed as a god and he set up a temple where the faithful could come to worship him.

The Roman Senate became increasingly alarmed. Caligula ignored them and aggravated tensions by scathingly denouncing the Senators, relying on sarcasm and insult, and showing complete and utter contempt for the legislative body. He came to believe that his only ally was his horse, Incitatus, upon whom Caligula bestowed a collar of precious stones. Caligula also built Incitatus a marble stall and frequently invited the horse to eat dinner with him.

Princeton University Roman historian Edward Champlin says that Caligula had a penchant for "blurting out whatever is on his mind"—such as suggesting that Incitatus could become "Special Councilor to the Emperor." Because leaders of great powers are often taken not just seriously but also literally, these rash statements caused great upset in Rome.

Eventually Caligula offended nearly everyone. He created continual political chaos and couldn't deliver on his promises. His mental instability became more and more obvious and evidence that he simply had no idea how to govern increased as time passed. Within a few years, he had lost all support. Yet even as Caligula wreaked political havoc, Rome's values, institutions and mores remained steady and inspired resistance.

Caligula was an abominable ruler of a great nation. Yet Rome proved so resilient that it survived not only Caligula, but also Emperor Nero's equally bad leadership a generation later. Nero's frustrations over not getting his own way led him to torch Rome, slaughter Christians, commit heinous acts against his mother, his wife, and his male lover, and badly mismanage the empire. Yet Rome remained standing.

"If there's a hero in the story of first-century Rome, it's Roman institutions and traditional expectations," says Emma Dench, a Harvard scholar of the period. "However battered or modified, they kept the empire alive for future greatness."

The lesson in this ancient history, Kristof suggests, is that Rome was somehow able to inoculate itself against unstable rulers so that it could recover and rise to new glories. "Even the greatest of nations may suffer a catastrophic leader, but the nation can survive the test and protect its resilience—if the public stays true to its values, institutions and traditions," he writes.

Kristof is correct, as far as he goes. What he fails to recognize is that the Roman Empire eventually did fall, and that staying true to a nation's social and political mores, values and traditions requires strong, effective, and ongoing leadership from somewhere within the existing political structure.

Nearly two thousand years after Caligula, millions of American women suffered a stinging political blow when Donald Trump prevailed over Hillary Clinton in the 2016 presidential election. It wasn't that a woman had finally made it into the presidential race and then lost that was so upsetting; it was the kind of man who had won that had turned America and the world upside down.

Women know that there will be a woman president of the United States sooner rather than later and don't spend much time questioning this assumption. The larger issue is whether that woman will succeed as president, and this depends entirely upon how much political support she has and how powerful her enemies are. Both questions will be answered in large part by the women who are willing to step up and fight protracted battles on the front lines and in the trenches of American politics.

Hillary Clinton had to claw her way through the heavily male-dominated American political environment to get to the top of the Democratic presidential ticket. This took her a long time, and she made a lot of enemies along the way but, to her everlasting credit, she stuck with it, because that's how much she cared about America. Her resolve to stay with the fight, even when it got ugly and bitter, and when most people would've quit, guarantees that history will treat her well.

And, it must never be forgotten that, by the numbers, Hillary Clinton defeated Donald Trump by three million votes. She lost the presidency only because of a unique provision in our electoral system that allows a candidate to win the popular vote and still lose the presidency. Nevertheless, Hillary Clinton, not Donald Trump, was the candidate the voting majority chose to lead them, and the fact that she is not our leader is the clear and simple reason why so many people, particularly women, believe that Donald Trump is not their president.

Eight months into what has been an off-the rails political roller coaster ride, a new political movement, based upon progressive political ideas and a solid sense of who America is and what the nation really stands for, is emerging from the ashes of the Trump victory. This effort began to take shape the day after he was elected president, went public the day after his inauguration, is being led by women, and being upheld by the men who love them and care just as much about the country as women do.

It's too soon to know exactly how this will play out, so it is not possible to write a conclusion to this book of essays. However, one thing is very clear: the emerging women's movement has staying power, energy, determination and an iron will to succeed in stopping Donald Trump's misogynistic anti–American agenda. Women will not allow Trump, and the 25 percent who are his hard-core base supporters, to pussy-whip the country into becoming the land of the rich and the home of the white.

It's not yet evident how this resistance will evolve. It may occur within the existing political party structure consisting primarily republicans and democrats, or 2017 may signal the beginning of a multi-party system that allows for more nuanced political philosophies and more choices for voters. Regardless, women, who are 52 percent of the American population, will be the major players in the political future going forward, and the wisest political initiatives will embrace this fact and run with it.

Democracies are fragile governing systems and across history none have lasted more than 300 years. American democracy is 241 years old, and if it is to endure, it only has 59 years remaining to right itself. This is not a very long time in the history of a great nation. The hope for the future is in the women who have never been politically active before who are ready to step up and work hard to Make America Great Again. This will occur on their terms, and in ways that are remain true to America's deepest and dearest values, because, like every essayist and interviewee in this book, women across the nation truly believe that ours is a democracy worth saving.

In her essay, "The Birth of an Activist," Kathy Steffen describes her evolution into becoming politically active, and the fear she overcame to step forward from the rural upper Midwest to join the movement.

Attorney Heather Sager explains why she left her native home in New York City for the Indiana flatlands. In "Being the Change: A New York Liberal Takes On Indiana Politics," she explains how she came to realize that if she really wanted political change, she had to be that change.

Scott Thompson offers a male perspective on the current political environment and a statement on why he was compelled to join the women's movement in "How Can I Not Resist?"

Finally, Unitarian minister the Rev. Sandra Ingham's essay, "You've Come a Long Way, Baby, but Not Far Enough," points out how far women have come and then issues the clarion call going forward by challenging readers to answer the question "What will you do to resist?"

NOTE

1. Nicholas Kristof, "There Once Was a Great Nation with an Unstable Leader," *The New York Times Sunday Review*, August 26, 2017.

The Birth of an Activist

Kathy Steffen

It's 2 a.m. and my cell phone dings. I'd gone to bed because I couldn't stand to watch anymore. I roll over and pick up my phone to see a message from my sister (who had bought a red, white and blue jacket to wear to the inauguration of the first female president).

A sad, crying face on the screen.

A flash of him mocking a disabled reporter. His dismissal of the grief of a Muslim mother of a fallen U.S. Army officer ("She had nothing to say. She probably, maybe she wasn't allowed to have anything to say. You tell me."). His claim that a judge was biased because he's Mexican (the judge was born in Indiana). The now famous words his supporters excuse and sweep under the rug: "I just start kissing them. It's like a magnet. Just kiss. I don't even wait. And when you're a star, they let you do it. You can do anything.... Grab 'em by the pussy. You can do anything."

I do not sleep that night. A chasm opens wide ... wider as I toss and turn, sure I'll fall in forever. Sure that we all will and will be lost forever. Although the knot in my stomach radiates waves of panic through me, even as I struggle to catch my breath, I know I'm one of the lucky ones. I wonder about other, more vulnerable women—the ones who are raising children on their own, who depend on food stamps for their family's survival, who need Planned Parenthood for cancer screenings, women who rely on Affordable Care or Medicaid for their own and their children's healthcare. What about women who are disabled or mothers of disabled children? What must this night be like for them? How huge does their fear grow? Does it take them over? Does it engulf them?

How can it not?

In the days to come, amidst shock, disbelief, and tears, one word keeps bobbing to the surface. *RESIST*. I hold to it like the lifeline it is. It's present in conversation, Facebook posts, tweets and e-mails. But how, I wonder. I am helpless. There is nothing I can do, not me, one insignificant gnat, facing Goliath. What difference can I possibly make? I'm sick at heart and scared to death. How can someone like me resist?

Discovering My Courage

I am terrified of crowds and more than a little claustrophobic. But, after a week of anger, shock and frustration balled in my gut, friends offered a road trip to the Women's

March on Washington the day after the inauguration. Crowds? A potentially volatile situation? Unknown experience in an unknown place? My first instinct: nope. Not a chance.

These friends are a couple who lead by example and planned to include their teenage daughter so she could experience a first-hand civics lesson and moment in history. I didn't want my example to be cowardice. So, on January 21, 2017, after driving 14 hours to get close to D.C., and surrounded by five friends and my husband, we boarded an overcrowded train to the Capital and joined an estimated 500,000 (and over 2 million people worldwide) for the march on Washington.

The train kept stopping and finally, sat for an eternity (which, of course it wasn't, but in that dark tunnel it sure felt like hours). Unknown to us, the platform at the downtown station had become a slow-moving mass of humanity, so the Transit Authority was keeping the crowd manageable by backing up trains. Over 250,000 people rode the transit system that day.

Not knowing why we stopped, standing in a jammed train in a dark tunnel, I put my hand on my abdomen and breathed deep, hoping my panic wasn't showing. And hoping I wouldn't go into a full-fledged panic attack, something I had experienced several times in my life. I reached up and touched the pink pussycat hat a dear friend had knitted for me and looked at the face of our friends' teenage daughter. She smiled at me. *Don't let your fraidy-cat show* flashed through my mind. My mantra! *Don't let your fraidy-cat show*. I managed a smile back.

I met wonderful people from all over the country. I laughed at the cleverness of protest signs and cheered at truths shouted over loudspeakers. I met teachers from Minnesota and thanked them. A disabled young man, boy really, limping along with twisted limbs and carrying the sign: "My President Can't Laugh At Me" brought a hot sting of tears. Such courage. My heart raced as a group of men in "Make America Great" hats goaded protestors around me. The responses "We love you!" and "We hear you!" and "You matter!" were delivered with big smiles.

I knew I was experiencing a part of history that I would have missed without my friends and husband. I kept in the moment, hyper-aware of all going on around me. The awe of the day edged out the panicked voice in my head telling me one small thing could send the crowd into a trampling stampede of death.

Don't let your fraidy-cat show.

I'm forever grateful to my friends and husband for making it possible for me to experience the march. I didn't overcome my fear, but engaged actively in democracy despite real and imagined terrors. Fear is responsible for what is going wrong in this country and when we act based on fear, trouble follows. The man who grabbed power used fear to win the election: fear of "the other" or people who are not like the majority, who don't believe what we do, fear of terrorism, economic ruin, of gangs and criminals taking over, of drugs and terrorists pouring into the country over borders.

Don't let your fraidy-cat show.

Discover Yours

I'm at least ten times more courageous with friends. Okay, maybe 100 times. Enlist the support of yours. If there is a march, team up with others making the trip. You'll share stories, jokes, smiles, and become closer as you stretch your own courage muscles.

I found a local group on Facebook who meets in the flesh once a month. I read about issues in my area and now go to township meetings, realizing democracy truly begins at home and then keeps going. Find your friends and engage with them. Get involved with local issues. Create your personal community of democracy in action.

There are many ways to show support. My pussycat hat was my Icon of Bravery (and sits now on a bust of Beethoven, reminding me I can overcome fear, and what I do does matter). The woman who knit it for me couldn't go to a protest, but wow, can she knit! That hat is my armor, made lovingly by a friend. Every time I touch it I feel brave. Every time I see it I am reminded to engage in democracy, not just hide and hope for the best.

It's perfectly fine to be afraid of iffy situations. Fear is a survival instinct that, if kept under control, serves us well. There are some situations that should be avoided. You feel true danger in your gut, and your best choices are to remain quiet or go the other way. If that is the case, listen to your instinct. But if you are reacting to imagined fear of terrible things to come (anxiety) find a way to go through it and act.

During the march we suddenly found ourselves hemmed in with more people pressing from the trains and side streets. Panic began to rise in me as a wall of people pressed from all sides. We decided to head to the edge of the crowd, and it took awhile, but holding on to each other, we made it. More and more people poured in and where we had been standing became not just crowded, but a sea of humanity that allowed for no movement and would take hours to escape. We were still there, still part of everything, saw and heard the speakers thanks to enormous screens and an excellent sound system. Still in the midst of protesters, but not the crush, and my heightened sense of danger evened out to emotions that were manageable.

Survival instinct is one thing, but if it seems like anxiety (listen to yourself, you can tell the difference) then go ahead and be afraid, surround yourself with friends, breathe deep, jump in, and don't let your fraidy-cat show.

Discovering My Voice

I avoid confrontation. My think-on-my-feet muscle is weak. I am a deliberate (translation: slow) thinker and don't do well with snappy comebacks. I have memories of stuttering as a child, not being able to find the right word. The thoughts in my head moved faster than what I was able to express. I grew out of stuttering, but even as an adult it comes back under stressful situations. I forget words. Talk in circles. For me, getting into a heated debate is a terrifying prospect.

Yet debate and opposing viewpoints are at the heart of democracy. Different ideas from different walks of life. Diversity is the key, and honestly, no one is going to align 100 percent with what anyone else believes. Conversations, the cornerstone of democracy, are everywhere. It was time to join them.

Prior to the March I joined the Facebook group Pantsuit Nation (over 110,000 members strong), and in addition to the support and camaraderie, I read personal stories, each one making me realize I wasn't alone in my frustration and fears. I read of women terrified at the cuts that are coming, of what such cuts mean to them and their families: loss of basic healthcare, cancer screenings, disability aid and medication, even loss of food. Government workers who have lost free speech. My original gut reaction of fear and frustration was an honest, shared one. Through the group, I learned about and joined the Forward Action Wisconsin Network. From there I discovered *5 Calls*, a website and app that sends e-mails prompting me to make five calls to representatives and senators. The link provides phone numbers for my local representatives (or federal offices, state politicians, etc., depending on the issue) and scripts based on what I indicate are the important issues for me.

I prepared for my first call by reading articles and making notes on my chosen issue so I wouldn't be stumped for words or an answer if someone asked. I could barely make the call—my palms were sweating so much. After several attempts, I got through to an answering machine. I stumbled through the script and a funny thing happened. On the next call I didn't stumble quite as much. The script helped me focus my speaking points and I used them other times when expressing my views. I find it much easier to speak out when I've had practice and have a full understanding of an issue.

I think best on paper so I write out my beliefs in a journal, and that has become a guiding force for discovering and developing my voice. I also list facts, because writing something down has always made it easier for me to remember. Once written, facts become part of my ability to express myself. And, I am recording history, for better or worse. Right now, history is definitely tipped to the worse side, but I am actively adding my voice to hundreds of thousands of others.

RESIST.

Discover Yours

Pantsuit Nation, Forward Action Wisconsin Network and *5 Calls* are my secret weapons. They are places where I read, get information, facts (not alternative) and find support. Safe places where I can articulate my feelings. I have several trusted news sources where I read about issues. There is help and information everywhere.

Find out what works for you and take baby steps. Start your journal and begin a conversation with yourself. Don't want to make calls? Have a postcard party and enjoy the support of friendship while talking about issues. Your voice will emerge.

Begin your discussions by holding them in a safe place with people who you know will be kind. A group with similar viewpoints is a good place to begin, and you will be surprised at how "similar" viewpoints can be different in subtle ways. You will learn by listening. Among friends is the best way to practice. Nurture your voice. Let it out. It will develop and grow stronger as you use it.

Discovering How to Speak Up

I do "likes" on Facebook when I agree with something my liberal friends post. Armed with my newfound voice, I began to make comments, thinking I was in a safe Facebook bubble. Imagine my surprise when opposing viewpoints appeared, some of them quite nasty. People I didn't know. Now what was I going to do? My blood pressure rises when a thoughtless Facebook meme (akin to shouting insults over a fence) is posted as a response, or when I am called a "libtard."

I recalled the group at the Women's March. They didn't allow "haters" to get under their skin. I was raised to be polite, kind, compassionate and respectful, and I employ such when voicing my beliefs. I focus on what comes from my heart, and a lover of lists, wrote out my "Rules of Engagement" or guidelines. My rules also give me the confidence I need. At least, some of it. I still get a gut-clench when in a discussion with someone who doesn't agree with me. But my list helps and reminds me to keep to conversation (not name calling) even if the other side doesn't.

I take a deep breath and ask questions: why do you believe that? Have you had that experience? Tell me about it. What do you think is a better solution? Why? Then, I truly listen. Questions (as long as they are true questions and not sarcastic) are a doorway to conversation. Questions begin a conversation; judgment and name-calling serve no purpose.

The Rules of Engagement

Choose your battles. Only comment when it's important to you and on what is important to you. In this political climate it's easy to get overwhelmed; there are so many issues and the list is growing. As I learned from *5 Calls*, focus on your top few. I recheck every week, but keep three at the forefront of my efforts.

Take a breath. Before your brain can work and you are able to articulate, your emotion has to come under control. Deep breathing works wonders and a breath will give you a few needed seconds to gather your thoughts. The more you practice calming yourself, the sooner you can begin an honest conversation.

Know what you are talking about. Read about your chosen issues from reputable sources and check facts. Practice if that gives you confidence as it does me.

You are beginning a conversation, so treat it as such. Remember: polite, kind, compassionate and respectful. Do not approach a discussion as a confrontation, or it will quickly escalate. Ask questions. Listen. Don't make your comments personal or derogatory (even if the other party does) or you will soon be having an argument that will serve no purpose other than leaving everyone involved frustrated.

Don't worry about "winning" or getting the person to change his or her point of view. When you have an exchange where you present facts, ask questions, and listen, you are making a positive contribution to the democratic discussion. That in itself, is a win. People may not seem to listen or change at first, but words do matter and change doesn't happen in an instant.

Practice "active listening" and rephrase what the person has said and ask additional open-ended questions. This proves you are listening and contemplating someone else's viewpoint, and often times all he or she wants is to be heard.

Of course there are those whose only goal is to fling names and get into a heated argument. Both sides have to be open to listening to make a conversation and sometimes, try as you might, that doesn't happen. Listen to your gut and smile and back away (remembering to be polite, kind, compassionate and respectful) if needed.

Discovering Power

My fear early on was, am I an insignificant helpless peon? What if my efforts won't make a difference? There has yet (as of this writing) to be one piece of successful legislation—never mind the dictator sport of executive orders; don't let those deflect and discourage you. Politicians have faced a deluge of phone calls and accountability at town hall meetings, some to the point of disconnecting their phones and not showing up. They screen attendees, but there are protests outside. People have found their voice and power. Including me.

My early belief that others would speak more eloquently was fear keeping me quiet. I needed to add my voice. We all, no matter our education or debate expertise, need to speak out. Each unique voice strengthens the conversations on democracy. Every one of us needs to be heard. There are times when conversations on democracy are vital—and this is one of those times. Our democracy is being dismantled piece by piece, and I will not stand by in silence.

I have gone from watching democracy happen to becoming a part of it. No matter how nervous or anxious it makes me, I will continue to use my voice for myself and others. It's not always comfortable, and sometimes I have to take a deep breath and enter into uncomfortable discussions or situations I'd rather ignore. The issues facing us are too huge to resolve themselves or to hope ethics will trump money in Washington. Start small and build. Become an active participant in democracy.

RESIST.

Do so with compassion and respect, with listening, with having conversations.

RESIST.

Make a difference.

RESIST.

Being the Change

A New York Liberal
Takes On Indiana Politics

HEATHER K. SAGER, ESQ.

The morning of the U.S. presidential election, I donned a black and white patterned suit coat over a pair of slacks and a blouse. I headed to check-in to serve in an election protection role, and eagerly awaited the day.

In August of 2016, I had quit my job in New York City and moved to Indianapolis. I had upended my career in state politics and the legislature to relocate to Mike Pence's state. Friends and colleagues were aghast. How would I live in Idaho, or Iowa, or wherever it was I was going—without sensible mass transit, pizza by the slice, or things to do on a Thursday night? The phrase "career suicide" was bandied about. But my reason was simple: I needed to invest in, and build up, my life outside of work.

Weeks earlier, I had serendipitously attended a talk featuring feminist icon Roxane Gay. One curious Brooklynite asked why she remains in her current role, in a small town, in Indiana. Professor Gay responded that sometimes you need to be the change you want to see in the world. For Gay, that change is existing in a space where a visible, successful black professor is considered extraordinary, and where her presence means she can help black students see themselves in their school's faculty.

Professor Gay's words impacted me throughout my transition to the Midwest. If everyone with my values flees to coastal citadels, I reasoned, then we cannot hope to influence the rest of the country. For now, I could be a left-leaning vote in a right-leaning state, and that would be a good change.

Excited to be in a place where I could put my skill set to good work, I tried to jump in with both feet. The first challenge was early voting. Although Indiana law provided that I did not need an Indiana-issued identification to vote, a trip to the Bureau of Motor Vehicles (BMV) found me arguing loudly with a clerk who insisted that I did. The conversation ended with him telling me to submit an absentee vote in New York.

Refusing to accept his answer, I pored over whatever information I could find to help me avoid another BMV showdown. My frustration grew: if a vote is the cornerstone of democracy, then why were these clerks trying to stop me from casting mine? I read statutes. I visited the library. I called state employees. Eventually I discovered I could sidestep this particular BMV policy by sending my vote through the mail (along with some evidence of my new address).

Finally, with my ballot cast, my indignation subsided into a lingering headache. Indiana, a state whose culture of "election integrity" was strengthened by a victory in the Supreme Court of the United States in 2005, was an early adopter of voter ID laws. I considered that I am peculiarly and particularly equipped to sort out the needed paperwork: I am an attorney. I have experience in politics. And, I am personally invested in ensuring that I vote. But the process was still very worrisome. What about all the folks who were given an incorrect version of the law but did not know to challenge it? Or know how to challenge it? Or who didn't have the extra time I had to invest in figuring this out and making it possible to actually cast a ballot? The barrier felt simultaneously real and invisible.

I moved forward. I joined local organizations. I attended as many events as I could fit into my schedule. I made phone calls. I had some hard conversations with my people. I campaigned.

Back home in New York, I had spent years watching the rise of Donald Trump's brand and, simultaneously, the destruction his purported Midas touch brought to New Jersey and New York. Now, in the Hoosier state, I often found myself acting as a translator between my new social circles and my friends and family back home. *No*, I would tell new friends at happy hours, *Trump actually hasn't been a successful businessman. I've watched him reduce successful businesses to rubble, and then watch others use the Trump name to build them back up.*

I would tell my new contacts about the friend I had who lived in one of Trump's buildings and who found himself with regular construction projects in his shoddily made home. *No*, I would tell old friends as we Skyped and G-chatted our evenings away, *not everyone in the middle of the country thinks that everything is okay. Many people here are scared and worried and fighting their hardest.*

And I began to realize that one of the biggest mistakes that east-coast progressives make is assuming they understand parts of the country into which they've never stepped foot. We are aware that our collective smugness loses conversational value outside of the city, but it also stops us from connecting with people. And please don't misunderstand: I know east-coast pride. But while I regard my own snobbery as a birthright, it was a hard-earned lesson for me to understand that you can't unite people under shared values when you automatically reject a person's values based on what you've assumed them to be.

The morning of the presidential election, and four months into my new life in Indiana, I donned that white and black patterned suit coat in solidarity. (The only pantsuit I owned was intended for a wedding that I would be officiating later that month, and I doubted that the grooms would appreciate my breaking it out early, especially for political reasons.) I dropped my partner off at work, and I made my way to the local union hall to start my election protection shift.

My mother had called me that morning to mark the day that we would see a first woman president. She told me how proud she was of me and how excited that she would get to see this day come with her daughter. The memory of that phone call, and the excitement of her voice, still warms me. The idea of being a part of this Election Day was thrilling, despite a long morning walk, anxiety over potential protests at the polls, and a breakfast of stale donut halves.

The day was uneventful, but the evening saw an excited rush to one poll location to ensure that everyone in line would be allowed to vote prior to closing. Afterwards I went home, changed, and headed to a friend's home to have a ladies' Election night. You all know the rest of that night's tale.

I woke up the next morning in a haze. I cried with my partner. We lay together and comforted each other. I wept knowing that the people of my country could be outright accepting of the idea that my gender, many others' races, colors, cultures, religions, and communities, all could be treated as not fully human. I now realize this part wasn't news to many, and that the fact that I found it shocking is, in and of itself, a privilege I enjoyed. I despaired at the very few down-ticket seats that my new state had elected blue. I felt isolated in a state that had turned so deeply red and missed the comfortable cultural buffer of my big blue city.

In the days following, I grieved. I argued and fought with people. I listened to Kate McKinnon's rendition of "Hallelujah" on *Saturday Night Live* repeatedly. I cried more. I attended every protest I could find. I refused to take down my campaign lawn signs. I searched within myself for the next steps in the work I knew needed doing.

Ultimately, I refocused my energy on the reproductive justice movement that I was still involved with in New York, and care deeply about, in the hope that my ongoing work in New York with the New York Abortion Access Fund would resonate with those resisting the new administration. New York is an abortion-tourism state, and as state restrictions on abortion get tighter, New York sees more and more people travel in to seek the care that they need. That travel, the waiting, and the process of it all ultimately makes treatment significantly more expensive for each patient than it needs to be. I am proud that I can help them maintain access to reproductive care.

I also reached out in my new home. I was invited to speak at a rally in support of Planned Parenthood on the steps of Indiana's state capitol. Excited to be another of the voices that had been speaking loudly, and for a long time, in a state that often refuses to listen, I accepted. I spoke about my work in New York, my own experience with abortion, and the need for accessible care in every state. I spoke about seeing people travel from my new state of Indiana, to my home state of New York, seeking the health care that I had been able to take for granted.

As I told my story, for the first time in my life, I was loudly protested by men with gruesome signs and a powerful loudspeaker. Young people from across the state of Indiana formed ranks in front of the protestors and chanted. They competed for space, attention, and ideology, and they raised their signs of hope higher. Grateful, I continued speaking to them.

Months after the election, local news broke that Indiana's voter registration rolls were purged of nearly 500,000 names. Understanding the need for updated rolls, I read the news and hoped that these updates might be accompanied by some kind of regulatory voter registration reform. No luck yet.

During this year's legislative session, the Indiana state legislature passed a new parental notification of abortion law. Facing yet another state restriction on abortion, in a state that is already one of the most restrictive in the nation, one reporter noted that opponents of the bill asked, "for a year off from passing contentious abortion laws."[1] No luck there, either.

There are still many days where I play that translator here. When Trump's travel ban was first implemented, my sense of anger and helplessness led me to spend one eventful evening, and several subsequent days, cultivating a crowd sourcing web page to send food to protesters at John F. Kennedy airport. I felt a particular sense of solidarity with the many Hoosiers who jumped at the opportunity to contribute.

The weather is too warm for that black and white suit coat now. But we are moving forward. Here, resisting permeates everyday activities in both subtle and conspicuous ways. At times, we softly float progressive lingo at cocktail parties in the hope that those in conversation with us will pick up the cue. At times, we take any opportunity to correct the false and dangerous myths that encompass the man our country elected. And still at other times, we form ranks and raise our signs and our voices higher to make room for a grateful speaker to tell their story.

NOTE

1. Darcey Costello, "Indiana House Approves Abortion Parental Notification Bill," www.ap.com, June 5, 2017.

How Can I Not Resist?

Scott Thompson

I've never thought of myself as a feminist. As a middle-aged, straight, white male, I've never felt the indignity of racism, misogyny, or bigotry. I was raised in a rural Illinois town. My parents grew up during the Great Depression. My dad left high school in the eleventh grade to pick coal. Albert was a World War II veteran and an active Republican who was elected to the office of County Sheriff. He admired Richard Nixon and worked hard for his party. He raised me to do the same.

My mom was one of eleven children. Mary was raised in a house filled with FDR and Kennedy Democrats. She worked her way through nurse's training, and for 38 years worked in a small town hospital caring for others. Together, my parents raised me to be respectful, work hard, and act like I knew something.

Because of my upbringing I have empathy. I'm a guy who believes in fair play and in the Constitution. I've seen the real document, first hand. I've read its faint, hand-written script. I believe in the words written in the Constitution and the spirit in which they were written. I believe in the liberal interpretation of those words. I believe the Constitution applies to all Americans, and to all women and men who are on our soil.

Over the years I mindlessly volunteered for countless Republican candidates. It was mindless in the sense that I didn't appreciate the true impact of the Conservative movement until the middle of George W. Bush's time in the White House. I was just a predisposed Republican who failed to think critically.

In 2006 I married a mouthy, tough-as-hell West Virginian woman. Ruth worked her butt off while raising her daughter and finishing her Bachelor's and Master's degrees. She takes nothing for granted, yet has faith in positive outcomes. She's comfortable taking chances, because she's had to take chances to survive. Ruth helped me to see the world through a different lens. Her experiences and interests complement my empathy for others. We make a pretty good team.

Ruth and I supported Hillary Clinton in the 2016 election. We each felt she was not only the best Democrat for the job, but she was better prepared, more experienced, and a professional. Despite what her detractors might have said, she was exactly what this country needed in leadership.

For myself, Hillary represented the extension of what Barack Obama had started. Hillary was value added; she could speak to the struggles of women in a first-person voice. Hillary was the pragmatic candidate. Hillary was the tough candidate. Hillary was going to be the first woman president of the United States. Hillary was vulnerable, but damn it, she was going to win.

In 2008, I cast my ballot for Barack Obama. He was the first Democrat presidential candidate for whom I voted. We had been in what seemed to be an endless war, and after a 25-year sales career, I was unemployed. We didn't need more killing; we needed a change. The country needed empathy from a president who acted like he gave a damn, and I needed a job.

The 2016 election cycle was different from what either Ruth or I had ever experienced. Living in Iowa, and seeing the candidates up close gives you the opportunity to experience each of them, regardless of party. That experience reinforced what we already felt; Hillary was by far the best candidate.

I knocked on thousands of doors for Hillary. And I mean thousands of doors. I made thousands of phone calls for her too. In my eyes, Hillary represented the promise that had eluded women. Hillary's candidacy was representative of the struggle for voting rights, equal pay, and the right to choose. Finally, women were going to matter in a presidential election. The more I pondered her candidacy, the more I believed. I was all in for HRC! Women were going to be the difference makers in this election.

In 2016, I witnessed my friends and complete strangers express their optimism. I saw hope and joy in their faces at rallies and events, at phone banks, and at their doors. My LBGTQ friends had an ally on the presidential campaign trail. I began to see and feel, if only tangentially, their optimism in the promise of what the future held for them. Especially for them.

Opposing Hillary, we had Donald Trump, the pussy grabbing, misogynistic leader of the Republican Party who became the eventually successful candidate for the next president of the United States.

Damn, how I hate saying those words! This is only the second time I can remember saying his name and the office in the same sentence. Trump, the guy who said women should be punished for having abortions. The guy who bragged about grabbing women by the pussy. Eyes rolled at the mere mention of his name.

Then, November 8 hit like a bag of fucking bricks.

The bad news began coming in early. Exit polls in Florida and North Carolina weren't coming around as we had expected. It was going to be a bad night, I could feel it.

Ruth and I attended what had been planned as a victory party for Democrats. It wasn't a victory party, but I still can't describe what it was. Before midnight we knew our fate. We were stunned, shocked, and in disbelief. Not only did we lose the White House, but in Iowa the GOP took both the House and the Senate. Funding for Planned Parenthood will be gone (and it is). Access to abortion will tighten (and it has). The fight to maintain marriage equality may enter a new phase, the fight for dignity and respect, and the same equal rights as any other American would start over yet again.

Ruth is a strong, tough woman, and she was in tears. She wasn't only scared for herself, but for future of our daughter, our transgender and gay friends, our African American friends, and those with disabilities. Suddenly, the America that had seen continuous struggles for equality and damn few but important victories had become white, straight, male, intolerant, and uncivil once again. Only this time, it was staring us in our faces. We knew this was bad. Really, really bad.

On the afternoon after the election, Ruth and I stopped at our favorite restaurant for dinner. Working behind the cash register was a young lady. She was visibly shaken and she was crying. The election of Trump had scared her to the point of tears. Ruth hugged her and did what she could to reassure her that things would turn out all right.

As we sat down at our table, another young woman sat down beside us, flipping off the television and saying: "FUCK YOU ... FUCK YOU ... FUCKER ... FUCK YOU!"

For a moment, I thought she was suffering from a mental health issue. I looked at the woman, and for a moment I wasn't sure what to do. She apologized and began crying. "I'm scared," she said. Ruth looked up at the television and there was an image of Trump on CNN. The election of Donald Trump had scared an adult to the point of tears and anger. That's where we have found ourselves; the newly elected president evokes fear and anger from people. Worse yet, those who are the most scared and those who feel they are the most vulnerable are reduced to apologizing for their fears. And for a moment all we could do was console her and tell her we need to fight back. It was at that moment I began to appreciate the full gravity of what women were experiencing. The fight, in which I thought I was a fully engaged participant, was much more than what I had perceived. I was only a participant on the periphery. What I didn't realize at the time? I was about to become more involved than I ever anticipated.

As news of the Women's March on Washington spread, Ruth committed to attend. As much as I wanted to attend it with her, the 18-hour bus ride to D.C. was not an appealing idea. Plus, the expense of attending seemed out of the reach of someone like me, on a graduate student salary. However, it was important to my wife that I attend with her. It was important to me, also. In a way, it would serve as the cathartic button that healed November's bruising losses. Yep, in part I was doing this for myself.

The ride to D.C. reminded me of the optimism I experienced during the campaign season. Women, some strong, some quiet, some loud, all on buses headed for Washington. It was their event and I was attending as a witness, so I thought.

Women, men, and children of all ages, all colors, all religions were on the National Mall. There was singing, chanting, and laughter. Certainly, there were signs of protest and defiance, but it was peaceful. The only angry person I recall was the anti-march protester standing atop a pop machine outside the Smithsonian. The day was about shaking fear and anger, and taking action. For myself, January 21, 2017, was my birth into the resistance movement.

I'm part of the resistance but I don't really identify as being inside the movement. Because I have enjoyed a life of relative privilege, I've not felt the pain of segregation. I've not been targeted by politicians or religious leaders for my lifestyle, color, gender, or sexual orientation. However, I've seen members of my family, my friends, and strangers victimized by hate and ignorance. I won't bear witness to another person crying because they fear their president. This is my county, so this is my fight too. I can't stand idly by and let this nation burn to the ground.

On November 8, 2016, we experienced the open acceptance of politically institutionalized hate and misogyny. In my opinion, this is one fight that if you're not fighting against the problem, you are part of the problem.

Nothing, absolutely nothing, short of invoking violence can be left unsaid. There are no words that are too profane. But demonstrations and words are not enough. Ruth and I have started a Political Action Committee, CaucusCouplePAC. We spend time organizing our neighbors and recruiting new voters, in our precinct and on the south side of Des Moines. Candidates call us for our support, because they know we're serious.

We attend town halls and hold our state and federal legislators accountable for the votes they cast. We've set standards for the candidates we choose to support. Our support goes to candidates who are willing to raise the money necessary to fund a serious campaign. Protest candidates and those who seek to "raise the level of the discussion" need not ask us for our help. We need candidates with a plan to lead, women and men with moxie who know how to get legislation passed. There is far too much at stake now.

On August 19, 2016, Donald Trump asked: "What the hell do you have to lose?" My answer is: "A lot. We have a hell of a lot to lose."

You've Come a Long Way, Baby, but Not Far Enough

The Rev. Sandra L. Ingham

"Stupid bitch," the young man called me when I insisted that he and his three companions move from their precarious perch off the trail on the South Rim of the Grand Canyon. To reach that spot, they had to walk around a clearly worded sign telling hikers that the area was off-limits and dangerous.

No one had ever called me a stupid bitch before, at least not within my hearing. I was somewhat amused, but mostly puzzled and annoyed. The words seemed like an overreaction to someone who was trying to help these Canyon novices be safe. I wondered if the stupid bitch utterance was a result of his cultural conditioning. Had he ever thought about what those words meant?

This unaware young person inadvertently did me a favor, though—make that two favors. After six months of being in what I can only describe as a "wakeful coma" and wallowing in a depression created in the wake of the November 2016 election, I tried to convince myself that I no longer cared about the larger world. But, here I was being passionate about something again—the environment. Stepping off trail in the fragile desert environment of northern Arizona is dangerous for living things other than humans. That was the first favor.

The second favor I received from that young man was a better understanding of what the word intersectionality means. To use an expression that I am hearing a lot lately, especially from people of color, I was woke a little. I began to have a more accurate grasp of the complexity of speaking truth to power, of what resistance really entails. We can't continue to pick and choose which oppression we are going to concentrate on; we have to resist on all fronts falsely constructed by the dominant culture.

I had actually emerged from my wakeful coma enough in March to be aware that it was Women's History Month. Being a minister gives me many opportunities to try to speak truth to power. Which is what I attempted to do that month in a sermon titled "You've Come a Long Way Baby?!," a title that I used sarcastically. Because although women have come a ways, to say we have come a long way seems to be overstating where we are. Here are some of the questions I asked in that sermon.

Do we still need shelters for battered and abused women? Yes, we do. Do women make the same amount of money as men do in comparable positions? No, they do not. Has the United States ever had a female president? Close doesn't count. Even though 52 percent of the American population is comprised of women, are there equal numbers of men and women in Congress? Not even close. Do men do 50 percent of household chores? Rarely…. I could go on!

Initially this essay was titled, "Responding to Misogyny: What's a Woman to Do?" Now I think that title is too limiting. What I want to address in this essay is the entirety of the dominant culture. What I want us as women in 2017 to resist is *all* of the evils perpetrated and perpetuated by the straight white male dominant culture: misogyny, racism, war, homophobia, destruction of the environment, classism, ableism, militarism—the list seems endless.

I realize now that for a large part of my adult life, I wasn't consciously responding to misogyny because it was so insidious that I was unaware it was even there. (This admission is embarrassing, though I don't think that it should be!) However, from my early teens on, I was very much aware of militarism and the stupidity of war. When I was a senior in high school, my best friend and I were quite certain that, after our college years, we would do work that would be instrumental in ending war on the planet. What I didn't understand and what it has taken me decades to be more fully aware of is the fact that underlying the oppression of war is misogyny! I didn't connect the dots.

I came into the world, a world of war, in December of 1944. I was lucky in my "choice" of families because I was surrounded by kind, nice, caring people throughout my childhood. It would be many years before I realized that I had entered a culture that at its very core did not value women—a misogynist mess of a world. It would be a long time before I realized that my entire life has been a mostly quiet, somewhat confused resistance to misogyny. How could anyone hate women?

One of my earliest memories of what it means to become a person is this: I wanted to be a boy. Not literally a boy. I have never had a feeling of being in the wrong physical body. No, I wanted to be a boy because even to my "child eyes," it was clear to me that boys got to do what they wanted to do—not just as children, but, more importantly, as adults. On some deep, intuitive level, I knew that the male species had an infinite number of options that I would never have.

Growing up in the late 1940s, through the 1950s and into the early 1960s, I thought that I only had one option: wife and mother. Now I realize that one of the subtexts in that cultural atmosphere—one that I inhaled deeply—was that girls aren't quite good enough to do the important work of the world. This can also be translated to mean that women are not the equals of men; they are just a little bit, just slightly, inferior. What a subtle, effective way to erode a person's self-esteem!

Oh there were plenty of clues in my growing-up years that all was not right with the world as far as women were concerned. I knew women were treated differently than men. But, why? I didn't get it. For example, there was Ethel Wood, the daughter of friends of my grandparents. My grandparents only spoke of Ethel in hushed tones and when they thought I wouldn't overhear them. They spoke of her in a dismissive, even derisive, tone, implying that she was a little crazy. What had she done? Graduated at the top of both her high school and college classes, for one thing—this was in the early 1920s. Very few women went to college in that time period.

Then she had the audacity to go into business—clearly a man's world—and worked her way up to an important managerial position at a large company in Cleveland, Ohio. I know this because I have the newspaper article from my hometown newspaper that chronicles this remarkable story, the gist of which is that women don't belong in business.

What is most telling about the story of Ethel Wood for me is the way my mother talked about Ethel. There was nothing dismissive or derisive in my mother's tone; I detected envy and admiration in my mother's voice when she talked about Ethel Wood. I was no more than 10 or 11 years old during this time. Years later, when I dropped out of college in 1964 (I would return, thanks to my mother's urgings) because I was pregnant (though married!), Ethel Wood let me know, in no uncertain terms, that I was making a huge mistake. For the rest of her life, she would refer to me as "the dropout"!

As I grew into young adulthood, there were more and more incidents that pricked my bubble of naiveté about the dominant culture. There was the mixed volleyball team—that is, men and women on each team—my then-husband and I joined. There were different rules for men and women. Men got one serve only; women got to take two serves. I refused to take two (it didn't hurt that I was a better server than most of the men) unless everyone got to take two.

What I couldn't believe was not how I was treated when I announced this. What was unbelievable to me was the bullying my husband endured from the other men: "Guess we know who wears the pants in your family." It went downhill from there. And what was with the sexual harassment I experienced from a boss, an unattractive old man, at least to my 19-year-old self? Creepy! Yet he clearly thought his behavior was normal.

Trivial stories, perhaps, in the overall scheme of things … and yet predictable stories about accepted behavior so illustrative of women's position as second-class citizens in the early and mid–1900s. I completely bought into the culture's narrative about the roles of men and women—the "proper" roles, I mean. It didn't occur to me to question that my purpose in life—as defined by the dominant male culture—was to get married, have children and live happily ever after. I understood that my career choices were limited to secretary, nurse, and teacher (I was too short to be a stewardess). Nevertheless, I managed to end up as a freshman at American University in Washington, D.C., in the School of International Service, with the intention of becoming a diplomat.

What was I thinking? I didn't even finish the first semester. There was that high school sweetheart back in Pennsylvania. Was wanting to be with him and get married the result of cultural conditioning or just teenage lust? Maybe both.

Fast forward to the present. Since the November 2016 election and entering my semi-awake comatose state, I have found myself slipping into uncharacteristic cynicism and despair, into a dark place that I don't like. Since Trump began his presidency (I refuse to say since Trump was elected), I have felt that so much of what I have worked for throughout my lifetime is being destroyed or soon will be: peace among nations, stewardship of the earth, equality for all people, health care for everyone. The list goes on and on.

We are back to my childhood in so many ways. Women might have thought that we were getting close to having the proverbial "level playing field," but we aren't even *on* the field as full, complete humans most of the time. We are still stuck in our second-class citizenship role. Last month, the Unitarian Universalist Association, which has been in existence for over 55 years and brags about being one of the most progressive religious organizations in the world, elected its first-ever female president! A year or two ago, on one of my hikes to the bottom of Grand Canyon, two men my age (late 60s) stopped me with horrified looks on their faces. "Where is your group? Did you lose your way?" (We were on a main trail, hard to lose your way if you stick to those.) Exasperated, I asked them if they would have reacted the same way had I been male. They admitted they would not have thought to treat a man the way they had treated me. It should be noted that I was not exhibiting any distress, clearly had enough water, and was wearing exceptionally good hiking shoes. In other words, I knew what I was doing.

I recently read William Barber's remarkable book, *The Third Reconstruction*, an important book about many different oppressions. In the book, Barber recalls a speech that Martin Luther King, Jr., gave in 1965 calling for labor and civil rights activists to "join forces." King goes on to say, "The two most dynamic Movements that reshaped the Nation the past three decades are the labor and civil rights Movements." And I think, reading these words, "Wait, the *two* most dynamic Movements? Weren't there *three* dynamic movements? What about the Women's Movement?"

Listening to National Public Radio a few weeks ago, I heard a sports announcer talking about the French Open. He talked about who would be in the men's semifinals that day, but made *no mention* of who had won the women's finals the day before. This pattern of keeping us "in our place" is subtle, insidious, frightening, and intimidating, even now, well into the twenty-first century.

There were the two conversations that I had this month, in June of 2017… One was with a woman who said that she thought Trump had a valid point when he said that what Bill Clinton did in terms of sexual harassment was worse than what he, Trump, had ever done. Excuse me?! Bill was not running for office—his wife was. Reverse the genders of the people in this anecdote, I suggested, and consider the situation if a woman was harassing a man. It won't work, I said, because of our cultural conditioning. It won't have the same shock effect.

And that same week, I had a conversation with the property manager of my apartment complex who admitted he had voted for Trump. Up until then, this man and I were usually on the same page politically. I must have looked dumbfounded because property manager tried to explain his vote. He thought Trump as a businessperson could make the workings of government more efficient. Excuse me?! Did property manager not hear Trump's pussy comment? That should have been the end of a Trump campaign right then and there.

Whoa! This state of being awake is mind-boggling and exhausting. As I have more and more "woke" moments, I become more and more incredulous and somewhere beyond angry.

There is more awakening to come…. I have just returned from the Unitarian Universalist Association's annual General Assembly, held this year in New Orleans. We have grappled with racism for years at these gatherings. Ours is a denomination that prides itself on being acutely aware of injustice and oppression in the world and in the forefront of actions and efforts to do something about them. Yet we never seem to make significant progress in the area of racism.

This General Assembly was transformative for me personally. Layers of denial about swimming in the waters of white supremacy within the larger ocean of the dominant straight white male culture began to lift. I began to feel lighter in a way, less encumbered by veils of naiveté and fogginess. I had a huge "light-bulb moment" there in New Orleans last week. I could see more clearly what is real and what we women have to do—we white women, that is. We will not be successful in our resistance to the dominant male culture unless and until we work with our sisters of color.

How can I find the time, the energy, the resources to fight this anti-racism battle at the same time as I am hoping to be a part of the 2017 women's movement and the "birthing of this new political movement," words taken from the "Resist: Women's Voices Speak Truth to Power" call for essays.

Is there a 2017 women's movement? Is there a birthing of a new political movement?

Are these movements limited to women? What about all the other oppressions? If we are going to speak truth to power, shouldn't we be speaking that truth to all forms of power that are complicit in maintaining the dominant culture? Do we have to limit our resistance to only one area? Or can we tackle them all at once? Is that impossible? If so, why is it impossible? Are there not enough resources? Is there not enough time?

Over the past few years, I have been concerned about the inability of the left, of progressives, to speak as a united front, to harness our energies so that we might be less scattered and more effective. There are so many legitimate causes begging for our attention. How do we respond to all injustices? How do we resist all oppression—not only misogyny, but also racism, environmental degradation, poverty and elitism? How do we carry on our resistance in an effective, tough, organized way?

Is this where intersectionality comes into play? Or is intersectionality just a complicated word "to confuse those of us who truly understand feminism," asks Dani McClain, in her article in *Yes! Magazine's* Summer 2016 issue. Simplifying greatly, intersectionality means inviting all the people from the margins of life—aka oppressed peoples—to come into the center to resist with us so we can work together to dislodge the dominant culture.

And what, then, does it mean to resist? It means to challenge the dominant culture by paying attention. Paying attention to language, what words we use and how we choose our words. Paying attention to what is actually happening to women, yes, but also to people of color, to all marginalized people. Paying attention to the stories, the stories about those who have gone before us, but also to our current stories of what is happening in our lives.

What does it mean to resist? It means building relationships—even if these relationships last for only for a few minutes. Recently, in New Orleans, I met an amazing young couple. They had been on a bus when their suitcase was stolen, leaving them homeless and very hungry. I was going to ignore his request for money—I can't give money to all the street people asking for it—when he almost started to cry because the last person he asked for money cursed him. This he could not believe. I stood there in the drizzling rain and talked to him about how fragile and precarious life is, how easily many of us could end up on the streets were it not for having jobs and/or strong support networks.

Then, his wife joined us; she had gone to get some coffee. They were cold because they were wet. I gave them a whopping amount of cash—ten whole dollars. We talked some more about what they would do next, about the human condition, about kindness, about greed. They hugged and kissed me and thanked me over and over for spending time with them, although it couldn't have been more than 15 or 20 minutes. They went one way and I, well, I went back to my nice, dry hotel room to get ready for dinner at a very good restaurant.

I believe that all politics is personal and that the personal is political. I could have gone the easy route and ignored this couple, which I almost did. Why is it so difficult for many conservatives to understand the concept of "There, but for the grace of god or the universe, go I?" Can the right wing not grasp the fact that many of us live paycheck to paycheck and many are just a major medical emergency away from or, as in this case, a robbery removed from, being on the streets? We don't all have strong, deep-rooted support systems.

What does it mean to resist? It means constantly standing up to the bullies who keep coming out of the woodwork in this particular political climate because they have been given license to do so by the current administration. Resisting means constantly being on guard for backlash; backlash is everywhere. Recall what happened in Austin, Texas, this spring when a theater held a for-women-only screening of the movie "Wonder Woman." The backlash began immediately after the announcement of this special screening when a man sent an email to Austin Mayor Steve Adler demanding that men boycott Austin because the city was "kissing up to women." This letter writer went on to say, "The notion of a woman hero is a fine example of women's eagerness to accept the appearance of achievement without actual achievement." Fortunately for us feminists, Mayor Adler appears to be a feminist himself. His response was to label the email's views as "uninformed and sexist rantings," an "embarrassment to modernity, decency, and common sense." How refreshing—an elected male official standing up against backlash.

Standing up to bullies and resisting the kind of backlash that happened in Austin demands that we have the courage, however fearful we may be, however weary we may be, to speak truth to power. After the white supremacist marches in Charlottesville, Virginia, in August of 2017, many people were too shocked and shattered, scared and sad to find any words of protest, let alone to take any actions. I found it difficult to get out of bed for several days, not a constructive reaction and not a space that I want to occupy for long. We have to get out of bed (metaphorically and literally) and say what has to be said—say it over and over again.

Backlash that occurs over a women-only screening of a movie is one thing. What happened in Charlottesville is another thing entirely, on a different, more frightening, level. Young, white males carrying torches, chanting Nazi Germany–like slogans, not even bothering to wear hoods is an event that cannot be ignored. It is not about Confederate statues. it is about preserving the deeply embedded culture of male white supremacy. Though they weren't chanting specifically anti-women slogans, those men may as well have been. I take every oppression personally and seriously. When the dominant culture goes after one marginalized group, then my marginalized group is also threatened.

Unfortunately, the first response from the president of this country was a non-response. Mr. Trump, the so-called leader of our country and therefore one of the most powerful people in the world, told us that "many sides" were responsible for stirring up the violence in Charlottesville. Unbelievable! There are no sides here, except the sides of love and hate. By choosing not to make a strong statement accusing the Nazi-mimickers of acting like, well, Nazis, Trump, once again, demonstrated that he is incapable of basic human empathy. Worse, he made it clear that, in this country, you have permission to dismiss and/or diminish others with impunity.

This forces ordinary people of good will to ask the following: where were the voices of those currently in power in our government when Trump gave this "all clear," go-ahead signal to the bullies and the backlashers? Where were the voices speaking truth to power when the word pussy was used by Trump when he was a presidential candidate in 2016? Where were they when this candidate bragged about his sexual conquests? Where were the voices speaking truth to power when the same kind of march happened in Charlottesville in May of 2017, just three months earlier? And, where are they now? There have to be more voices or Charlottesville 2017 will fade into the background in the coming weeks and months. We cannot let that happen.

What is that truth we should all be speaking to power? The truth is that there are no sides here, despite Trump's declaration that many sides are responsible. There is only one side that is viable in the twenty-first century if the human race is going to survive. We are all in this journey of life together—interconnected, whether we like it or not. We survive together as humans by recognizing our interdependence or we perish together by not acknowledging it and acting accordingly. There is only one side.

What does it mean to resist? It means to keep organizing rallies and attending them. It means remembering how powerful and awesome those January 21, 2017, rallies were— 100,000 people in Madison, Wisconsin! That was a momentous moment of awakening and awareness. Resistance means being aware of our anger and reminding ourselves that anger—and even rage—have their place in our resistance. It means that we prepare to speak truth to power by reading, studying, confronting our personal prejudices.

What does it mean to resist? It means understanding what beloved community is all about. If we don't know what that term means, then how can we work towards building it? Resistance involves vision and imaging—imagining a future without oppression. If we can imagine it, we can create it.

What does it mean to resist? It means keeping on keeping on no matter how discouraged, cynical, frustrated, scared, and hopeless we become. It means refusing to let the moment pass without doing something.

What does it mean to speak truth to power? It means speaking truth to power about *all* oppression and injustice. It means, of course, speaking this truth out of our own power and perspective—the feminist perspective, while always being aware of the other voices coming out of their own histories of oppression, telling their own stories of injustice— stories that are every bit as valid as our feminist ones. I have an opportunity to do this each time I present a homily during a Sunday morning service. I have always used stories in my reflections. Now I am trying to use more stories that are not from the white, patriarchal culture. Whenever I am asked to speak about inequality and oppression, I attempt to do so keeping that mantra going in my head: Speak Truth to Power. And, every day, I try to commit at least one random act of resistance to the dominant culture.

What will you do?

References

Bergstrom, A. Renee. "FGM Happened to Me in White, Midwest America." *The Guardian*, Dec. 3, 2016.

Carson, Rachel. *Silent Spring*. Boston: Houghton Mifflin, 1962.

Carter, Angie, Betty Wells, Jessica Soulis, and Ashley Hand. "Building Power Through Community: Women Creating and Theorizing Change." In *Women in Agriculture Worldwide: Key Issues and Practical Approaches*. Amber Fletcher and Wendee Kubik, eds. New York: Routledge, 2016.

Clinton, Hillary Rodham. *What Happened?* New York: Simon & Schuster, 2017.

Cramer, Katherine. *The Politics of Resentment: Rural Consciousness and the Rise of Scott Walker*. Chicago: University of Chicago Press, 2016.

Dáil, Paula vW. *Women and Poverty in 21st Century America*. Jefferson. NC: McFarland, 2012.

Dean, Michelle. "Making the Man: To Understand Trump, Look at His Relationship with His Dad." *The Guardian,* March, 2016.

Diagnostic and Statistical Manual of Mental Disorders, 5th Edition. Philadelphia: American Psychiatric Association, 2013.

DuBois, W.E.B. *The Souls of Black Folk*. New Haven, CT: Yale University Press, 2015.

Dunlap, Riley E., and Aaron M. McCright. "Organized Climate Change Denial." *The Oxford Handbook of Climate Change and Society*. New York: Oxford University Press, 2007.

Ehrlich, Paul. *Population Bomb*. New York: Ballantine Books, 1968.

Fisaha, K.G. "Female Genital Mutilation: A Violation of Human Rights." *Journal of Political Science and Public Affairs,* 4:198, 2016.

Fischman, Gustavo E., et al. *Critical Theories, Radical Pedagogies, and Global Conflicts*. Lanham, MD: Rowman & Littlefield, 2005.

Gajanan, Mahita. "Psychiatrists Disagree Over Whether They Should Discuss Trump's Mental Health." *Time*, July 25, 2017.

Goldberg, Howard, Paul Stupp, Ekwutosi Okoroh, Ghenet Besera, David Goodman, and Isabella Danel. "Female Genital Mutilation/Cutting in the United States: Updated Estimates of Women and Girls at Risk, 2012." Atlanta: Center for Disease Control and Prevention, National Center for Chronic Disease Prevention and Health Promotion, Division of Reproductive Health, 2016.

Gravert, Ames, and Natasha Cambi. *Criminal Justice in Trump's 100 Days*. New York University School of Law: Brennan Center for Justice, 2017.

Green, Joshua G. *Devil's Bargain: Steve Bannon, Donald Trump and the Storming of the Presidency*. New York: Penguin Books, 2017.

Hanson, James. *The Storms of My Grandchildren: The Truth About the Coming Climate Catastrophe and Our Last Chance to Save Humanity*. New York: Bloomsbury USA, 2009.

Hochschild, Arlie Russell. *Strangers in Their Own Land: Anger and Mourning on the American Right*. New York: The New Press, 2016.

Holmes, Jack. "Stephen Miller Is Ready for His Authoritarian Close-Up." *Esquire*, February 2017.

Jackson, Dana. *The Farm as Natural Habitat*. Washington, D.C.: Island Press, 2002.

Kathleen Fischer. *Transforming Fire: Women Using Anger Creatively*. New York: Paulist Press, 1999.

Kennedy, Anthony. "Read the Supreme Court Ruling That Recognized Gay Marriage Nationwide." *Time*, June 26, 2015.

Kimmerer, Robin Wall. *Braiding Sweetgrass: Indigenous Wisdom, Scientific Knowledge, and the Teaching of Plants*. Minneapolis: Milkweed Editions, 2013.

King, Helen. "The Rise and Fall of FGM in Victorian London." *The Conversation*. Cambridge, MA: 2015.

Kirk, Russell. *The Conservative Mind*. Washington, D.C.: Regnery Publishing, 1953, 2001.

Klein, Naomi. *This Changes Everything: Capitalism vs. the Climate*. New York: Simon & Schuster, 2015.

Levy, Gabrielle. "Trump Team's Troubling Call to Murkowski." *Political Reporter*, July 2017.

Lubchenco, Jane. "Environmental Science in a Post-Truth World." *Frontiers in Ecology and the Environment*, 2017.

Macilwain, Colin. "The Elephant in the Room We Can't Ignore." *Nature*, March 2016.

Maso, Carole. "Break Every Rule." In *Break Every Rule: Essays on Language, Longing, and Moments of Desire*. Berkeley, CA: Counterpoint Press, 2000.

McAdams, Dan. "The Mind of Donald Trump." *The Atlantic*, June 2017.

McKibben, Bill. *Eaarth: Making a Life on a Tough New Planet*. New York: Times Books, 2010.

Muir, John. *My First Summer in the Sierra*. Boston: Houghton Mifflin, 1911.

Orbe, Mark P., and Tina M. Orbe. *Interracial Communication: Theory into Practice*. Thousand Oaks, CA: SAGE, 2013.

Ravitch, Diane. *Reign of Error: The Hoax of the American Privatization Movement and the Danger to American Public Schools*. New York: Vintage Books, 2014.

Rippa, S. Alexander. *Education in a Free Society: An American History*, 8th ed. New York: Pearson, 1996.

Smith, Allan. "$52 Million to $0: That's How Much Hillary Clinton's Campaign Is Outspending Donald Trump's on TV Ads." *Business Insider*, August 26, 2016.

Tocqueville, Alexis de. *Democracy in America, Volumes I and II: 1835*. Translation by Henry Reeve (Kindle Edition).

Wangari, Maathai. *Unbowed: A Memoir*. New York: Anchor Books, 2008.

Williams, Terry Tempest. *When Women Were Birds: Fifty-Four Variations on Voice*. Basingstoke, UK: Macmillan Publishers, 2013.

Wirth, Danielle M. "Environmental Ethics Made Explicit Through Situated Narrative: Implications for Agriculture and Environmental Education." Ph.D. dissertation, Iowa State University, 1996.

Wood, Julia T. *Gendered Lives: Communication, Gender, and Culture*. Belmont, CA: Wadsworth Publishing, 2012.

Wright, Lawrence. "America's Future Is Texas." *The New Yorker*, July 10, 2017.

Yousafzai, Malala (with Christina Lamb). *I Am Malala: The Girl Who Stood Up for Education and Was Shot by the Taliban*. New York: Little, Brown, 2013.

About the Contributors

Ari **Belathar** is a gender-queer Mexican poet and playwright living in exile. After illegal imprisonment and torture by the Mexican National Army because of her work as an activist and independent journalist, she escaped to Canada. She has been a writer-in-residence at several universities, participated in various international residency programs, and been published in literary journals. She now lives in the United States.

Michelle **Bowdler** is the executive director of health and wellness at Tufts University in Boston, MA. She has published articles and blogged about social justice, particularly sexual violence. She has been addressing the hundreds of thousands of untested rape kits in police departments and crime labs nationwide. She received a Barbara Deming Memorial Fund Award in 2017.

Tayler **Bowser** is a biology and professional writing graduate of Carroll University in Wisconsin. She is passionate about human rights and the environment. She is presently serving with Ameri-Corps in Sitka, Alaska. Her home base remains in Wisconsin.

Sandra J. **Callaghan** received an MS in Urban Affairs from the University of Wisconsin–Milwaukee. During her 45-year working career she was a union steward and unit vice-chairperson. She also served as president of her local school board for three years. She lives in Wisconsin.

Darlynne L. **Campbell** teaches high school English in an urban, inner-city school. She read Black history extensively as a child and this guided her thinking as she grew into adulthood. She lives in Indiana.

Angie **Carter**, Ph.D., is a sociologist, scholar and activist. She studies grassroots and community-based responses to extractive energy and agricultural production. She co-created the Bakken Pipeline Resistance Coalition against the Dakota Access Pipeline in Iowa. She is an assistant professor of environmental and energy justice at Michigan Technological University.

Cassi **Clark** has a background in public administration and writes about outdoor adventuring, educational programming, and motherhood allegories that "support all mommas." She is a mother, community member, and an Indie BRAG (Book Readers Appreciation Group) Medallion Award winner. She lives in Colorado.

Alexandria A. **Cunningham** is a traumatic brain injury survivor. She graduated from McKendree University in Illinois with a degree in philosophy. She lives in Omaha, Nebraska, where she engages in disability advocacy.

Paula vW. **Dáil**, Ph.D., is an emerita research professor of social welfare and public policy. She was founding director of the Center for the Study of Poverty at Virginia Tech University and director of the Child Welfare Research Project at Iowa State University. She has written more than ninety research papers, six books, and has guest edited several academic journals. She is the recipient of multiple awards for her research, graduate teaching, and non-fiction writing.

Rachel **Eliason** is a transgender woman whose writing explores diverse social topics and characters. She addresses LGBT issues and coming of age in her young adult novels. She also writes science fiction and fantasy under the pen name R.J. Eliason. She has spoken at schools, colleges and LGBT centers on a wide range of issues. She lives in Iowa.

Janine P. **Geske**, J.D., is a retired Wisconsin Supreme Court Justice. She was a Marquette University Distinguished Professor and served as the Association of Marquette University Women's chair in humanistic studies, interim dean of Marquette law school and head of Marquette's restorative justice program. She was chair and a faculty member at the National Judicial College in Nevada and has earned numerous awards. She remains active as a legal conflicts mediator.

Ashley **Goff** is a preschool teacher finishing her undergraduate degree in early elementary education at the University of Maine–Augusta. She was inspired to join the 2017 Women's March in Washington, D.C., after taking a women's studies class that changed her perception of the world. The march solidified her commitment to the contemporary women's movement. She lives in Maine.

Rebecca **Gorman** is a member of the class of 2020 at Middlebury College in Vermont. She believes that speaking truth to power has never been more necessary and has developed an interest in advocacy work on domestic violence, rape prevention, and LGBTQ rights during the past four years. She lives in Massachusetts.

Patti **Herman**, Ph.D., is recently retired from a career focused on the well-being of children and families, both within and outside of this country. She lives in rural Wisconsin.

Mary E. **Hunt**, Ph.D., is a feminist theologian and a co-founder and co-director of WATER (Women's Alliance for Theology, Ethics, and Ritual) based in Washington, D.C. She is widely published in the areas of theology, ethics, and social justice. She is a recipient of the Rabbi Martin Katzenstein Award and the Peter J. Gomes Memorial Harvard Alumni Award. She holds degrees from Harvard and Marquette universities and the University of California–Berkeley.

The Rev. Sandra L. **Ingham**, M.Div., is a Unitarian minister and a graduate of the Starr King School for the Ministry, the University of California–Berkeley Graduate Theological Union and Thiel College in Pennsylvania. She staffed the Unitarian Universalist Association Midwest Leadership School in Wisconsin where she lectured. She is active in MOSES (Madison Organizing in Strength, Equality, and Solidarity), a grassroots organization focused on prison reform. She lives in Wisconsin.

Pam **Kidd** organizes a monthly group of local political progressives who oversee the charity Children of Zimbabwe. She is a writer for Guidepost's Book Division and was the recipient of the 2016 Nashville Democratic Woman of the Year award. She lives in Tennessee.

Danielle **James** is an author and a #Blogher17 Voices of the Year honoree for short fiction. She received the 2017 Diversity in Tech Award for creating technology opportunities for underrepresented groups. She won the Harman Writer-in-Residence contest and was a semi-finalist for the Brooklyn Nonfiction Prize at the Brooklyn Film and Arts Festival. She lives in New York.

Miriam R. **Kashia** is retired from a private psychotherapy practice. Following service in the Peace Corps in Africa, she walked across America with the Great March for Climate Action. She made three trips to the Standing Rock Sioux Reservation between North and South Dakota, and was arrested twice while peacefully protesting the Dakota Access Pipeline. She is active in several environmental groups. She lives in Iowa.

Ahna **Kruzic** is a community organizer turned activist. She has worked as a researcher, digital strategist, designer and works at nonprofit Food First. She helped build the Bakken Pipeline Resistance Coalition, an Iowa-based initiative that has worked to stop the Dakota Access Pipeline. Her career focuses on building a socially, environmentally, and economically just future. She lives in California.

Jennie **Lusk** is a lawyer and an assistant attorney general and director of the Consumer and Family Advocacy Division under New Mexico Attorney General Hector Balderas. She drafted parts of the brief challenging Deferred Action for Childhood Arrivals (DACA) and organizes the New Mexico Coordinating Council on Immigration. She was executive director of the New Mexico American Civil Liberties Union and raised funds for the United Nations Children's Fund and for the repeal of the death penalty. She lives in New Mexico.

Erica Gerald **Mason** is a writer and poet who writes about creativity, happiness, love, feminism, pop culture, and current events. She is the author of *I Am a Telescope* and her work appears in literary journals and other publications. She was a featured poet in the 2016 and 2017 Sundance Film Festival Indie Lounge. She lives in Georgia.

Rabah **Omer** earned a degree in veterinary medicine and has gone on to study politics and anthropology, tackling research questions that affirm her belief that social affairs should focus on the ideal that people are valuable for their intrinsic worth as human beings. She aims to earn a Ph.D. in the social sciences. Originally from Sudan, she is a naturalized American citizen living in the Midwest.

Dede **Ranahan** is an advocate for mental health care. She established the Institute for Mental Illness Education at the University of California Cal State–Hayward campus. She was walk director for the first National Alliance for Mental Illness (NAMI) Walk in San Francisco and worked as NAMI's policy director for the Mental Health Services Act. She created a website where families can talk about mental illness in their loved ones. She lives in California.

Gabrielle E. **Roesch-McNally** received a Ph.D. in sustainable agriculture and sociology from Iowa State University. She studies resilience and climate change adaptation in diverse ecosystems. She has been fighting for social and environmental issues since she was in fourth grade doing presentations on an early guide to environmentalism. She lives in Oregon.

Rebecca **Roth** is a life-long activist. She entered college as an adult returning student, earning two degrees in special education. After teaching for 23 years, she retired to do volunteer work. She lives in New Mexico.

Heather K. **Sager**, Esq. is an attorney working in politics, government, and reproductive health. She worked in Southeast Asia on maternal mortality and human rights access, and later on domestic violence and reproductive justice issues. She joined the New York Abortion Access Fund board of directors and now works in public health. She lives in Indiana.

Kathy **Steffen** is an award-winning novelist and author of the *Spirit of the River* series: *First, There is a River, Jasper Mountain,* and *Theatre of Illusion.* She has published articles and essays on the writing process and her fiction has appeared in anthologies and online. She speaks at writing programs and teaches fiction writing at the University of Wisconsin. She lives in Wisconsin.

Nikki **Stern** is the former New Jersey governor's 9/11 Families Advocate and former executive director of Families of September 11th. The group was recognized by conflict transformation NGO Search for Common Ground for organizing community forums between Muslims and non-Muslims after 9/11. Her book *Hope in Small Doses* was an Eric Hoffer Montaigne Medal finalist. Her essays have appeared in multiple publications. She lives in New Jersey.

Abigail **Swetz** is pursuing an MA at the University of Wisconsin-Madison. She was previously a public school teacher and her students inspired her to write the solo performance work "An UnCommon Core," which she performed at the Kansas City Fringe Festival and the empowHER Reading Series. She was the GSAFE Educator of the Year and a University of Wisconsin Rockwell Cooperating Teacher. She lives in Wisconsin.

Mariya **Taher**, M.S.W. and M.F.A., focuses on research, policy, program development and direct service. She worked at W.O.M.A.N. (Women Organized to Make Abuse Nonexistent), Inc., Asian

Women's Shelter, and Saheli. She was a 2014 Woman's Policy Fellow for the Women's Foundation of California and lecturer at San Francisco State University. Manhattan Young Democrats named her an Engendering Progress honoree. She lives in Massachusetts.

Alice A. **Thieman**, Ph.D., is a retired cognitive psychologist and professor at Iowa State University. She is active in volunteer work and an Indivisible group committed to resisting Trump administration policies. She lives in New Mexico.

Ruth Burgess **Thompson** is an Iowa state employee and AFSCME (American Federation of State, County and Municipal Employees) member. She volunteers with Planned Parenthood and the Iowa Democratic Party and is a disability rights advocate. She lives in Iowa.

Scott **Thompson** is pursuing a Ph.D. in rural sociology at Iowa State University. He teaches sociology at Des Moines Area Community College and Grandview University. He volunteers at Planned Parenthood and the Polk County and Iowa Democratic Party organizations. He lives in Iowa.

Betty L. **Wells**, Ph.D., is a professor of sociology and extension sociologist at Iowa State University. She facilitates self-organizing to meet the challenges of sustainability with natural resources, food and agriculture. She teaches courses in community engagement, diversity, and sustainable agriculture. Her research is community-based and uses critical systems theory and feminist perspectives. She is a founding member of the Women Food and Agriculture Network.

Danielle **Wirth**, Ph.D., is a former park ranger and naturalist. She teaches ecofeminism at Iowa State University and environmental science and policy at Drake University. She focuses on organic food standards, local food security, the impact of pesticides on human health and environmental quality, the restoration of native plant communities, and environmental ethics. She lives in Iowa.

Index